THE STONES

Philip Norman was born in London and brought up on the Isle of Wight. He joined the *Sunday Times* at the age of twenty-two, soon gaining a reputation as Atticus columnist and for his profiles of figures as diverse as Elizabeth Taylor, P. G. Wodehouse, Little Richard and Libya's President Gaddafi. In 1981 he published *Shout!*, a ground-breaking biography of the Beatles that was a bestseller in both Britain and America. He has also written definitive lives of Elton John and Buddy Holly.

Although he resists classification as a 'rock biographer', a musical theme pervades almost all of Philip Norman's work. In 1983 he was named one of the twenty Best of Young British Novelists for his autobiographical novel, *The Skaters' Waltz*. His shorter fiction includes *Spring Sonata*, a novella set in an Edwardian music hall, and *Words of Love*, about Buddy Holly's last hours, which later became a successful television play. His journalism has been published in three collections, *The Road Goes on For Ever*, *Tilt the Hourglass and Begin Again* and *The Age of Parody*.

He is married, with a daughter, and lives in London.

THE STONES

PHILIP NORMAN

PAN BOOKS

First published in 1984 by Elm Tree Books/Hamish Hamilton

First published in paperback 1993 by Penguin Books

First published by Pan Macmillan in an updated edition 2001 by Sidgwick & Jackson

This edition published 2002 by Pan Books
an imprint of Pan Macmillan Ltd
Pan Macmillan, 20 New Wharf Road, London N1 9RR
Basingstoke and Oxford
Associated companies throughout the world
www.panmacmillan.com

ISBN 978-0-330-51154-4

1 3 5 7 9 8 6 4 2

A CIP catalogue record for this book is available from
the British Library.

Typeset by SX Composing DTP, Rayleigh, Essex
Printed and bound in the UK by
CPI Mackays, Chatham ME5 8TD

To Angela Miller

Contents

PROLOGUE

Prologue

'Some girls give me children . . .'

The Rolling Stones at Wembley Stadium, June, 1999. A fitting encounter, you might think, between two of the most notorious old hags in British popular culture.

Wembley from a distance may still look a proud enough place with its triumphal avenue for Cup Final heroes, its towering fortress walls and wedding-ice art deco domes. But venture nearer and you discover the reality – the rusting turnstiles, the grim stone stairways, the concourses reeking of stale beer and onions. On the terraces, the incalculable human traffic of seventy-six years has left the floor coated in a kind of primordial black slime. It sucks at your heels as you sit there on your demeaningly small metal seat, inhaling the vast outdoor fug of nicotine and Carlsberg Special Brew. If ever a great British institution cried out for the wrecker's ball, this is it.

The same might be said of tonight's headline attraction, a supergroup just as huge and history-packed and decrepit. Once, undisputedly, the world's greatest rock 'n' roll band, kings of Wembley or any stadium you cared to name; now, a quartet of old reprobates, staggering on too-high heels, back to draw yet again on what someone aptly called 'the biggest cashpoint in the universe'. And at their head, a man who now knows how horrifically sudden can be the descent from idol to Aunt Sally.

Few modern reputations have seemed to crumble so disastrously as that of the artist once known as Michael Philip Jagger. As recently as a decade ago, Jagger was still adulated as a twentieth-century sexual icon with the combined allure of Valentino and Nijinsky, respected as the dynamo who kept the Stones rolling from age to age with his phenomenal physical fitness, admired for having risen from proto-punk callowness in the 1960s to become – in the words of his most incendiary song lyric – 'a man of wealth and taste'.

Then, in the early and mid-Nineties, all that carefully crafted image and autodidactism and social climbing suddenly went to hell. Jagger's repeated undignified flings with women in their twenties finally goaded Jerry Hall, his helpmeet of twenty years, to petition for divorce on the grounds of 'multiple infidelity'. His response was to counterclaim that their wedding, nine years previously in a Balinese woodcarver's hut, had no legal validity. To the press and public, the Nijinsky of the rock stage metamorphosed into a randy old skinflint vainly seeking to renew his youth with girls young enough to be his daughter; pathetically unable to commit himself even to a woman who had borne him four children, and willing to resort to any strategem that might stop her getting her hands on his money.

Contempt for women might not be anything new with Jagger, but his perceived contempt for his public had never reached such a pitch before. The Stones' summer 1999 return to Britain had actually been scheduled as part of their Bridges to Babylon world tour a year earlier. It was called off after tax changes in Gordon Brown's 1998 Budget threatened to erode a tour gross conservatively estimated at $300 million. The 300,000 fans who had already bought tickets learned that they would not see their idols until sometime in the next and more favourable tax year.

Although the decision was presented as a collective one by the band, everyone knew, or thought they did, who wielded supreme executive power within it. The nation that had first raised Jagger to superstardom (as well as handcuffing him and flinging him into prison) bridled under the outrageous snub. Not since the late 1960s had there been as many negative Jagger headlines, and even then they did not so insistently rhyme Jumpin' Jack Flash with 'cash cash cash'.

This Stones Wembley Stadium concert on a muggy, overcast June evening is thus an almost visible mountain for Jagger to climb. The audience who have waited almost a year for their tickets to be honoured seem in anything but a party mood. A good third are female, today's genuine Honky-Tonk Women who drink beer from the bottle, smoke and swear as lustily as any man. Short shrift here, you'd think, for the Stones' extensive male-chauvinist back catalogue, Under my Thumb, Brown Sugar, 19th Nervous Breakdown, Stupid Girl and all the rest. Their $4 million stage set, flanked by gold Hindu goddesses and giant braziers, arouses puzzlement rather than awe. Wasn't punk rock meant to have blown away all such pomp and hubris more than twenty years ago? Even the ubiquitous Jagger logo – the tongue sagging lasciviously from overstuffed, ungracious lips, reproduced on tickets, programmes, posters, T-shirts, red fabric waving-mitts – seems to have lost its old power to tickle and titillate. This is a night, you feel, when Mick really had better watch his mouth.

Then comes the big surprise. Almost since Rolling Stones concerts began, audiences have been resigned to waiting two or even three hours before the band can be bothered to play. But this evening, we are barely thirty-five minutes past the scheduled show time. The giant Hindu goddesses suddenly take on an eerie golden glow, like ropey special effects in a Ray Harryhausen film. White neon light frames the oval video screen suspended above the stage. There on film are the four Stones, clad in maxicoats, with every facial line airbrushed out, loping along in a formation that might have been choreographed by Quentin Tarantino – Reservoir Dogs with the faces of Marcel Marceau mimes.

And here they are in the etched and weathered flesh: Charlie Watts, at fifty-eight paradoxically the youngest looking of the four, wearing the same glum look he's had since the year of the Profumo Scandal; Ronnie Wood, at fifty-two the 'baby' of the group, with the elfin frame, silver bangles and ink-black pompadour that, you feel, the Arts Council could usefully fund as a perfectly preserved specimen of 1970s rock stardom; Keith Richards, at fifty-six no longer the Human Riff so much as the Walking Cough, his white shirt split all down a skeletal ribcage, his scanty hair dyed blue and hung with what seem to be old-fashioned women's suspenders and metal mousetraps. And, in the eye of the human storm, where he has lived for almost forty years, he-e-ere's Mick.

Even for one more than usually well versed in all Jagger's multifarious schticks and posturings, it is an impressive moment. At this distance you cannot see the granite-grooved face, the sunken-in eyes, the lips no longer full and saggy but pinched and bloodless. You can see only the undiminished hair in its endlessly modish cut; the taut frame and knock-kneed, flat-footed walk, more like that of a gawky schoolgirl than a fifty-six-year-old grandfather. You can see only the sparkly jade-green frock coat and, underneath, the turquoise croptop showing the same strip of bare flat stomach that all the young kids do.

This is a new Jagger – one that generations of Stones fans who have wriggled deliciously under the whips of his scorn or apathy would scarcely recognize. His first spoken words into the microphone are not the time-honoured raucous 'A-a-awright!' or sardonic 'Good evening, Wembley!' but a heartfelt apology for arriving almost a year late. 'I'm sorry it's taken so long,' he says in his plain-spoken middle-class English voice (one of the wide choice of accents he has available), 'but we really appreciate your waiting.'

It is no mirage. Mick Jagger has turned into Mr Nice.

Ronnie Wood's mock-Tudor hunting lodge is just a mile or so across Richmond Park from Downe House, the twenty-six-room mansion Jagger ceded to Jerry Hall when their marriage was annulled. Before the annulment, Ronnie and his wife Jo would regularly visit Jagger and Jerry. Since the annulment, they still regularly visit Jagger and Jerry. 'We were over there for a meal the other night,' says Jo Wood, a pouty-pretty blonde like a younger Barbara Windsor. 'It cracked me up so much, I started to laugh. Mick says, "Wossamatter with you?" I said "You two! You get on far better now than you ever did when you were married."'

When the doughty Texan supermodel finally dragged her rock star consort into Britain's High Court, in July 1998, two experts in Indonesian matrimonial law were co-opted to help a High Court judge rule on the Balinese marriage that never was. But far more intriguing, and typical of the real as opposed to the mythic and self-mythologizing Mick Jagger, is the split-up that never was.

Anyone who was ever on a Rolling Stones tour can attest to the scale of Jagger's libido. The question 'Does Mick play around?' draws an unfailingly strong response from those whom fate, kindly or otherwise, has brought into his orbit. 'Huh? What? Are you kidding?' almost splutters his first wife, the much maligned Bianca. A one-time Stones PR man replies with an epigram honed during long hours of resentful discretion. 'Does Mick play around? Does Dolly Parton sleep on her back?'

The relationship with Jerry Hall, whom he wooed away from rival singer Bryan Ferry in 1977, brought nothing even remotely resembling monogamy, according to insiders. Jerry would be around for the major Stones concerts, but out on the road Mick carried on as before. Indeed, it was an area in which his usual scrupulous regard for appearances deserted him. One Stones aide remembers him giving a string of important press interviews in his hotel suite while in the adjacent bathroom a female companion crouched behind the shower curtain.

Times had changed, however, from the groupie scene of the 1960s when girls who slept with rock stars talked about it only with hushed gratitude to their best friends. The era of the paparazzi and kiss-and-tell memoir brought Jagger a notoriety he had scarcely known three decades before, even when he stood in the dock at Chichester Assizes in one of the most notorious drugs trials of the 1960s.

His alleged romantic dalliances became the leitmotif of his life with Jerry, attracting increasing amounts of publicity that seemed to bother him proportionately less and less. He was variously said to be involved with American actress Uma Thurman, supermodel Elle McPherson, American sex-therapist Natasha Terry, Hungarian porn star Orsolya Dessy, Italian model Carla Bruni, Czech model Jana Rajlich and British model Nicole Kruk. All were enviably youthful and beautiful, although the pillow talk, in some cases, must have been fairly dire.

Jerry, friends say, had acquiesced to an open marriage that allowed both Jagger and herself, if she chose, to have affairs on the side. But the deal was that there must be no children on the side. This broke down in 1998 when Luciana Morad, a twenty-nine-year-old Brazilian lingerie model, announced that Jagger had made her pregnant in the course of an eight-month clandestine affair. The baby was born in May, 1998 – a boy, significantly possessed of full and pliant lips. Jagger initially denied paternity but changed his tune after being compelled to take a DNA test. Morad's laywers were initially said to be claiming £6 million for the child's upkeep, though they would ultimately settle for $6,000 per month. His mother named him Lucas, expressing the (perhaps over-optimistic) hope that his father would also put his name down for Eton.

Jerry, throughout the whole saga, seemed to preserve her Texan charm and poise, referring to her errant mate as to a slightly ludicrous child – 'Oh, that danged Mick! Ain't he jest *too* much!' But in private there were heavy scenes, for example when Jagger was found to have revisited his old Italian flame, Carla Bruni, a few days before an assignation with Morad. 'I saw Jerry and Mick together at one of Elton John's dinner parties,' a friend recalls. 'Jerry just sat there glaring at him all evening. He responded by getting drunker and drunker. He ended up doing backing vocals while Elton sang.'

To understand Jagger, as the wisest of his women, Marianne Faithfull, once said, it is no good looking for comparisons in the modern world. You must look back to Louis XIV, the Sun King, or to the gilded boy despots of ancient Rome and Egypt. Jagger created the concept of the rock singer as a twentieth-century god, and none has received more idolatry. Unlike almost all other of his kind, he has experienced no sudden fall from fashion, no painful process of self-reinvention and clawing back to the top. For almost four decades, his life kept on the same unreal plane of mass-worship, flattery deference and illimitable free will. The result is bound to be a vanity that no earthly instrument can measure. Jagger's stage performance, at its best as well as most embarrassing, is always essentially a process of making love to himself. The main attraction of his first wife, Bianca, seemed to be that she looked uncannily like him; each morning when they awoke together, Narcissus could gaze into the pool.

The real Jagger is hidden deep away, like the living organism inside a Dalek, behind riveted sheets of light-reflecting image. In 1962, when a teenage hustler named Andrew Loog Oldham became the Stones' first serious manager, he noticed one priceless attribute in the shy LSE student vocalist still then known as 'Mike' Jagger. It was a talent for mimicry, both vocal and physical, that picked up and retained other personalities like Velcro. You can still see them all there in Jagger's stage act – the walk from James Brown, the wiggle from Tina Turner. He can change personalities between press interviews, being thoughtful and serious for the *Guardian*, crude and blokeish for the *Mirror*, camply outrageous for *Time Out*.

The real Jagger is utterly unlike the prancing, androgynous fawn that, to his inner dismay, became the emblem of insurrection and anarchy in the 1960s. The real Jagger is a slender figure, slipping unobtrusively into the back of a box at Lord's to watch the cricket. The real Jagger is not reckless and defiant like the song lyrics he writes but incurably cautious, never quite liking to venture outside the Stones despite the varied solo careers – actor, writer, even politician – he might have had. The real Jagger is so nervous of his own extraordinary past that he affects to remember almost nothing that ever happened to him. The real Jagger is addicted to mingling with bluebloods but never quite able to repress a pinchbeck gleam of commonness, the old-fashioned word for naff. (Remember the photograph of him shaking hands with Prince Charles, his left hand still oafishly thrust into his trouser pocket?)

Jagger's love of top people is surpassed only by his devotion to the bottom line. In a world known for profligate extravagance and over-generosity, to be merely careful with money is to invite the reputation of a Scrooge. Jagger was always one of the most famously careful ones, along with Paul McCartney and Ronnie Wood's former frontman, Rod Stewart.

It was a peculiarly macho Sixties trait that he most resented spending money on women, especially those he happened to be casting away on to the scrapheap. Marianne Faithfull, the breathtakingly lovely ex-convent girl with whom Jagger spent four years – and who contributed incalculably to his cultural education and social advancement – left the relationship with little more than a heroin habit. Actress-turned-author Marsha Hunt who bore him a daughter, Karis, had to wait eight years before he was compelled to recognize the girl. Bianca was faced with a prenuptial agreement on her wedding morning, and received a divorce settlement of only around £500,000. Ironically, one of Jerry Hall's initial attractions, apart from her yee-haw Texan looks, was her considerable wealth in her own right from modelling and ranching. Jagger found it restful to be with a woman seemingly above suspicion of wanting to get her hooks into his fortune.

His attitude to money owes something to the American r & b stars who were the Rolling Stones' first heroes and role models. Performers like Chuck Berry and Ike Turner are notorious for their almost pathological meanness, the reaction to having been exploited in their early years. British pop bands of the Sixties – even one as big as the Stones – suffered much the same fate. Two successive managers, Loog Oldham and Allen Klein, failed to secure the band wealth anywhere near commensurate with their status. Despite having dominated the decade, along with the Beatles, they ended it owing huge sums in income tax and were forced to become tax exiles in France.

Since casting off Allen Klein in the early Seventies, the Stones have had no manager in the old paternalistic sense. What they have is a financial adviser who happens also to be a sprig of old European royalty, Prince Rupert Loewenstein. And they have a chief executive who combines his role with that of lead singer, giving equal focus and dedication to both.

It was the Jagger-led Stones who evolved the concept of big-stadium rock and tours that rolled around the world like giant boulders, earning millions first, then tens, then hundreds of millions. Rolling Stone tour statistics are in a class of hyper-inflation unseen since the Weimar Republic. Their 1996 Voodoo Lounge tour grossed somewhere around $250 million – a final grand looting, so it was mistakenly thought, that would persuade them at last to hobble away into retirement. But eighteen months later, they were off again on the Bridges to Babylon tour, destined to last two years and circumnavigate the globe twice. Between the official end of Bridges to Babylon in late 1998 and their delayed UK shows a year later came the No Security tour-within-a-tour which found them playing 'smaller' (i.e. 15–20,000 seat) arenas across the US at ticket prices ranging between $100 and $900. American rock critics dubbed it the Millionaires Watching Millionaires show.

Other rock dinosaurs of the Sixties and Seventies confine themselves to cranking out their old hits onstage and make no effort to compete in the contemporary music market. But the Stones sell as many records today as they ever did. In 1992, they signed with Virgin, choosing it as the major label with the most avant-garde output (and deaf to the wild inappropriateness of its name so far as they were concerned). Their albums since have maintained a steady average sale of between five and six million. A hot new band might sell eight million with their debut album but would be unlikely to pull it off half a dozen times in a row.

Concert promoters like Harvey Goldsmith who were thought to be getting rich off the Stones in fact found themselves squeezed down to ever smaller percentages. In recent years, the band has stopped dealing with individual promoters and assigned world rights in their tours to an American company, TNA, which designs and oversees the whole globetrotting machine (although the ultimate control freak Jagger still personally approves early detail). More and yet more billions are creamed off the sponsorship of their tours by commercial brand names, as if they are some cash-strapped arts or sporting institution rather than the world's highest-grossing performance band. Over the two-year span of Bridges to Babylon, concertgoers had three different trademarks rammed in their faces: Sprint communications, Tommy Hilfiger clothes and Castrol oil.

As might be expected from past, bruising encounters with British income tax, the Stones' main corporate assets rolled out of their native land long ago and are securely rolled up in a network of tax-sheltering foreign companies distributed across the world.

Three Dutch-based companies, for instance, are thought to control the Rolling Stones trademark, the lapping-tongue logo and the publishing rights to Jagger's song output in partnership with Keith Richards. Another Stones company, Marathon Music, one of the last to linger in Britain, was recently acquired by the Prudential Corporation of America.

Jagger's estimated personal wealth of $150 million is constantly topped up by royalties from thirty-five years' worth of Rolling Stones hits, most of them written by Richards and himself. He is said to have £40 million invested in stocks, a fine-art collection valued at £30 million and a fleet of classic cars worth £2 million. Giving Downe House, their £4 million Richmond home, to Jerry hardly left him without a roof over his head. He still has La Fourchette, a chateau in the Loire Valley near Amboise, valued at £1.2 million; a brownstone house in New York's Upper West side, valued at £2.5 million; and Stargroves, his Japanese-style house on Mustique (named after a Gothic folly he once owned in Berkshire), valued at £3.6 million and periodically to let at £7,000 per week.

The recent hyperactive touring years have also seen him embark on a vigorous programme of personal expansion and diversification. His career as a screen actor wisely on hold (remember *Ned Kelly*? And *Freejack*?) he has set up a production company, Jagged Films, whose initial projects included a Dylan Thomas biopic and the screen adaptation of Robert Harris's Second World War novel, *Enigma*. His passion for cricket has been channelled into an Internet provider company, Jagger Internetworks, which is acquiring rights to major matches all over the world, notably the Champions Trophy in Sharjah. His growing status as an art collector has brought an association with Charles Saatchi, the ex-adman who has fostered a generation of young British painters as iconoclastic and over-hyped as young rock stars used to be. Jagger is believed to have profited from Saatchi's guidance and to be an investor in a Saatchi holding company, Landau Enterprises.

The energy and resourcefulness with which Jerry Hall sought a wifely share of these varied treasures made her into something approaching a national heroine. Here was glorious proof of the new ethos that a woman jettisoned in her forties, by even the most powerful man, had other options than just shrivelling up in despair. Indeed, although privately resorting to therapy, the public Jerry positively bloomed. She made the cover of *Hello!* magazine, was painted nude by Lucian Freud, signed contracts to renew her modelling career and became the face of Thierry Mugler perfume, joined *Tatler* as a contributing editor, became a judge of the Whitbread literary awards and announced plans to market replicas of the engagement ring Mick had given her via the American TV shopping channel QVC. Far from moping at home over tear-stained Stones albums, she was noted out and about with property developer Guy Dellal and old Harrovian film producer George Waud. Perhaps her most stylish flourish came when Jagger first claimed that their marriage had no legal standing and therefore no divorce settlement was in order, Jerry faxed his lawyers a synopsis of the memoirs she intended to write unless paid enough to suppress the literary imperative.

Whatever strings or garrotting wires she pulled, they were indubitably the right ones. Her settlement from Jagger is believed to have been worth £10 million, made up of a £4.3 million lump sum and £105,000 per year in maintenance. In addition, their four children, Elizabeth, James, Georgia May and Gabriel, will each receive £25,000 per year until they reach the age of twenty-five. Jagger had the, for him, novel experience of hearing a woman he was parting from describe him as 'very, very generous'.

The whole parting process, indeed, had an amicability to which Jagger was entirely unaccustomed. During the summer-long tussle between their lawyers over the financial settlement, they were constantly seen around together, not only as dutiful parents with their children but at clubs, restaurants and first nights. Jerry even accompanied Jagger when he returned to his unloved alma mater, Dartford Grammar School, to open a new arts centre bearing his name. Directly after the court decision annulling their marriage, they left with the children for Jerry's house in the South of France, a tiny place whose sleeping arrangements could not possibly have kept them that far apart.

Although Jerry remained mistress of their Richmond house, Jagger kept his own apartment there for several months and continued to preside over family meals and outings. According to friends, he telephoned Jerry two or three times daily and plied her with gifts and flowers. It did not seem to bother him that public sympathy remained firmly with Jerry, nor that she seemed increasingly adept at stealing the limelight from him. In the summer of 2000, she made her acting debut when she replaced Kathleen Turner in the West End production of *The Graduate*. The part of the older femme fatale Mrs Robinson required Jerry to appear nude onstage, and was perhaps her most resounding declaration that life after Jagger went bustlingly on. He turned up to support her on her first night, and was observed to be cheering and clapping lustily. According to one report, he even offered to stay at home and babysit for her during the play's run. 'He's wonderful kind and supportive,' Jerry told Radio 4's *Woman's Hour*, adding with a resigned chuckle, 'He just isn't very much of a husband.'

No one denies, however, that he's an excellent father – if a little inclined to the same Victorian strictness as his own father, Joe – and that he dotes on the granddaughters who are only a little younger than his youngest daughter, Georgia. Despite the humiliating court orders and the DNA test which eventually obliged him to recognize his son by Luciana Morad, he could not resist meeting Morad in a London park, and pushing little Lucas around in a buggy. He was always a generous, attentive son to his unshakably straight parents and was devastated by the death of his mother, Eva, early in 2000. He is widely read, hugely well informed about current affairs, witty and charming, and a model employer – 'except', says a former aide, 'on the days when he looks through you as if he's never seen you before'.

The most infamous chapter in his career, the episode that may ensure Sir Cliff, Sir Paul and Sir Elton are never joined by Sir Mick, however nice he makes himself, paradoxically sprang from impulses worthy of Sir Galahad. In 1967, after a police raid on Keith Richards's Sussex cottage, Jagger was tried and briefly imprisoned for possession of illegal amphetamine tablets. The tablets actually belonged to Marianne Faithfull, who had hidden them without Jagger's knowledge in a pocket of one of his jackets. He took the rap to save Marianne's career.

On the road he is seen as an unregenerate despot, ruling the Stones' organization with an iron hand while Richards remains ever the lovable, easy-going old rock 'n' roll reprobate who cares for nothing but the blues and his next bottle of Jack Daniel's. Onstage, Richards plays his 'elegantly wasted' role to the hilt, staggering about with his headdress of metal clips and his driftwood guitar like a drunken Medusa in a mid-Channel gale, sometimes lurching to the mike to delight the crowd with yet another rasping aphorism about his own wickedness. 'It's nice to be here . . . Hey, it's nice to be anywhere, y'know?'

Jagger, as chief executive, was always held responsible for the long-time inequality within the Stones that saw Richards and himself, the so-called Glimmer Twins, lord it over the others like officers and other ranks. Bill Wyman's resignation from the band in 1994 was no sudden fit of pique but the culmination of thirty-four years as a bass-playing lance corporal. Ronnie Wood, who joined as lead guitarist in 1974, was kept merely on a salary and at one point became so hard up that he had to fall back on his original vocation as a painter and illustrator. It wasn't until the 1989 Steels Wheels tour that his fellow second-rankers Wyman and Charlie Watts persuaded the high command (i.e. Mick) to grant him a share in the profits, so allowing him to maintain his

Richmond hunting lodge, his stud farm in County Kildare and his own private pub.

But insiders – on recent Stones tours at least – portray a somewhat different dynamic to the Glimmer Twins. They say that Jagger, for all his surface arrogance, is essentially decent and reasonable, as befits someone who seldom took drugs and now even refuses to drink on tour. But anyone who crosses Keith, an abstainer in neither area, risks unleashing dark and frightening forces. Even Ronnie Wood, his best mate and tireless fellow carouser within the band, admits to having been 'thumped' by him in the past. The film director Julien Temple, who made the Stones' *Undercover* video in 1984, describes a harrowing encounter with the Human Riff in a cloakroom of the George V Hotel in Paris. 'Keith got me up against a wall and put a swordstick to my throat. The point he was making was that he didn't think he featured enough in the video.'

Rather like former iron regimes in eastern Europe, the old order within the Stones has yielded to irresistible pressure from the young. Jagger's daughter Jade, by his second wife Bianca, is utterly unlike her cautious father, a let-it-all-hang-out beauty who combines a career as a jewellery designer with parenting two small daughters, dating eligible young men like the publishing heir Dan Macmillan and posing for magazines wearing nothing but knickers, a necklace and a pair of alligator-skin boots. One journalist who interviewed Jade found her 'rather cross' and offered to come back later, but – shades of 1967! – was told, 'Let's go upstairs and smoke a joint and it'll be okay.'

A second wave of children, borne by Jerry, Pattie Richards and Jo Wood, turned Stones tours into gemütlich affairs, with nannies and governesses in tow. The chirpy Jo, a former pin-up model, became in many ways the most successful Stone wife apart from Shirley Watts (who wisely stays at home at her Arabian stud farm in Dolton, Devon). On tours, the Woods' suite is always known as 'Party central'. Jo turns each soulless master bedroom into a miniature home, bringing her own pillows and bath towels, arranging Ronnie's art materials, personal hi-fi and favourite ornaments, setting up a portable stove as a healthier alternative to room service with a supply of organic soups, pasta and cereals.

Ignoring all previous social distinctions, the children have grown up to be good friends, especially Elizabeth Jagger, Keith's son and daughter by Pattie, and the Woods' spectacular daughter, Leah. Some are already filtering into the organization. Jo Wood's son Jamie, by a former marriage, runs the backstage furnishing company that assembles the Stones' peripatetic backstage area, the pub-like 'VIP lounge' and the twilit inner sanctum where Ronnie and Keith play twelve-bar blues and smoke themselves into inaudibility before each show. (Woe betide Jamie if everything isn't in exactly the same place, from the scarf over Keith's lamp to the ashtray at his elbow.) Leah Wood has matured into a promising singer and during the Bridges to Babylon tour did a guest-spot onstage with her father and surrogate great-uncles.

Almost every Rolling Stones tour in history has kicked off with a scandal, real or manufactured. Since they became pop's founding anti-heroes by urinating on garage forecourts or turning up tieless at the Ritz, negative press has been the band's natural rocket fuel. But with the Jerry affair came headlines that, suddenly, were no longer a turn-on but a put-off, or even a throw-up. As Bridges to Babylon rolled forth with its huge capital investment, there were concerns that anti-Jagger feeling among feminists of both sexes could have a serious effect on ticket sales.

It may, of course, be pure coincidence, and Jagger himself would doubtless vehemently deny having sought to protect his band's revenues by making himself less supercool, Sixties-sneery, snobbish and opaque, more gracious, humble and accessible. But the sea of newsprint and TV footage around Bridges to Babylon suggested otherwise. Everywhere you looked, the old devil seemed to be assiduously courting sympathy. Gone was the effete figure, lounging on the couch at a hundred uninformative press conferences. Gone was the bleating, up-and-down voice, so brilliantly captured by Phil Cornwell on BBC2's *Stella Street*. Gone were the sullen pout, the tossing head, the air of amused disdain towards those who adored him just as much as those who detested him.

Instead we had the Jagger who, after the Stones' 1998 British concerts were called off, went to extraordinary diplomatic lengths to dispel the media view of them as unpatriotic misers. The decision followed Gordon Brown's scrapping of the Foreign Earnings Deduction, which had allowed tax-exiled Britons a flexible quota of working days back in the UK each year. The plugged loophole would not only have penalized Jagger, Wood and Watts (Richards is a US resident) but also many among their 270-strong road crew, wiping in all some £12 million off the tour's books.

The one-time Street Fighting Man was tact incarnate as he besought Tony Blair's rock 'n' roll-loving government to relax what was a retroactive penalty, offering that rare thing a Stones charity concert in the UK by way of exchange. Indeed, it was Blair's treasury spokesmen who came across more like surly, macho Stones of old as they declined to be 'lectured by millionaire tax exiles'. The controversy even brought Jagger to the *Independent*'s Right of Reply column, taking his turn with Robin Cook's ethical foreign policy and the new one-way traffic system in Hampstead.

Nowhere was the New Jagger more cleverly sold than in the interview he gave Chris Evans on Channel 4 just prior to the British tour. It was a brilliant Jagger media coup, bypassing the middle-aged broadsheet pop pundits and aiming straight for a young, stroppy audience that might have been most likely to mock the Stones as pathetic has-beens. In a *TFI Friday* special, shot in edgy black and white, Evans was allowed moments of lese-majesty to make any old-time Stones follower gasp. He was allowed to follow Jagger around backstage, given a conducted tour of his wardrobe, treated to an impromptu piano number and an earnest homily about projection that would have done credit to Sir Henry Irving. To Jagger's myriad accents were now added that of modern teenage Slop English ('Yeah, it's quih a loh of sho-yoos if you think abouh ih.') Evans was there as the modern Stones ran offstage, to be wrapped in white bathrobes and spirited away as if to some health spa rather than time-honoured mischief in hotel rooms. At one point, Jagger's interviewer teasingly showed him Polaroid pictures of humbler figures among his road crew and offered him $50 if he could identify them. Jagger won the $50.

His ultimate rehabilitation, of course, was the only one that really mattered. The Stones' British concerts, when they did finally happen, were superb. Anyone who doubted that a rock gig at grotty old Wembley could hold any surprises had to eat their words along with their rubbery hot dogs. The best moment came halfway through, when a sort of Meccano drawbridge snaked out from the stage to a smaller one, about the size of a boxing ring, in the crowd's midst. The Stones swaggered over the bridge like a troupe of strolling minstrels to play an in-the-round set of joyous, ragged-arsed blues.

And here was Jagger, the shameful old roué, the grandfather, demonstrating yet again that the newest, hottest young rock star of today can never be anything more than his apprentice. Here was the new, nicer Jagger persona which, alas, fell apart in the first line of every song. Here was the 'man of wealth and taste', replete once again with his opera cloak, cloven hooves and forked tail. Here, in the Seventies oldie Some Girls, was even a sarcastic nod towards Jerry, Luciana and the baby boy with outsize lips: 'Some girls give me children I never asked them for . . .' From the audience came not a single girl-power boo or catcall, only a ripple of complicit laughter. Maybe we don't want him to change all that much.

PART ONE

One

'I was schooled with a strap right across my back'

When the black man was alone and destitute, he played the blues. With a roof over his head, however leaky, he played rhythm and blues. The difference is as great as between the country and the city; between Southern cotton fields and Eastern ghettoes; between fatalistic old age and vigorous, upwardly mobile youth. It is the difference between a guitar powered only by its own mournful echo, and a guitar belligerently amplified, played with aggressive slides and swoops along the fretboard by a switchblade knife or broken bottle neck. It is the difference between bleak, dusty, desperate noontide and pulsating, pleasure-seeking night.

While the blues stretch back into vague infinities of work gangs and prison cells, rhythm and blues can be given an approximate time and place of genesis. It grew up first during and just after the Second World War, amid the mass redistribution of American blacks into their country's war machine. Its sound was of newly explored streets and unfamiliar alleys; of cheap neon, soda-fountain sugar and wafting gasoline; of the old, sleepy twelve-bar blues reacting in astonishment, delight – and sometimes fury – to all the varied stimuli of big-city life.

Nowadays, there are expensively illustrated books to familiarize us with r & b's golden postwar age. There are the photographs of Muddy Waters, Jimmy Reed, Otis Rush or T-Bone Walker, in their white shirts and gabardine trousers, singing against heavy silver microphones, perspiring over huge guitars with pearled fretboards, in clubs, bar lounges or juke joints, some tropic Forties night below the Mason-Dixon line. There are the show bills – usually from the Apollo Theatre in Harlem – which depict the young B.B. King, Bo Diddley or Fats Domino, wearing demure tuxedos and tiny bow ties, and smiling with a strained, reassuring politeness.

The smile of an r & b artist circa 1949 was the smile of someone expecting to be beaten up at any moment. The blues – stigmatized since the Twenties as 'race' or 'specialty' music – had been generally too esoteric for whites to understand. Rhythm and blues, with its flash suits, flaunted saxes and unrepressed sexuality, seemed to offer the most blatant threat to respectable – that is to say, all-white – society. It was denounced as lewd, ungodly, demented, a corrupter of children. Its clubs were raided and wrecked by white vigilantes; its performers attacked and, in not a few cases, lynched. Up to 1956 or so, every blues band travelling in its own country was a band on the run.

Throughout the Forties and early Fifties, its greatest creative period, the music remained segregated and submerged. Though r & b songs often appeared in the American hit parade, they were bowdlerized versions, purged of their sexual content by all-white crooners and dance bands. Roll With Me, Henry, an overt sexual challenge, for instance, became Dance With Me, Henry, an invitation to foxtrot. The original artists, with a few exceptions, were unknown to the general record-buying public. They could perform only in black clubs, record only on obscure black-owned labels, have their discs played only by the handful of radio stations controlled by blacks. When Bo Diddley finally got a booking on nationwide TV in 1958, it was stipulated that, to preserve decency, he must perform completely motionless. On camera,

Diddley forgot his promise, lapsed into a shuffling *pas seul* and was docked his entire fee.

'Help save the youth of America!' – so ran one anti-r & b pamphlet of the early Fifties. 'Don't let your children buy or listen to these Negro records. The screaming, idiotic words and savage music are undermining the morals of our white American youth . . .'

A prophecy of things to come if ever there was one.

It is a journey further than any bluesman could imagine from Beale Street, Memphis, to Bexley in deepest Kent and the playground of Maypole infants' school, where, one sunny day in 1950, teacher Ken Llewellyn called a group of his favourite pupils together for an informal photograph. The boys who assembled were the brightest and liveliest in Mr Llewellyn's class. They included Robert Wallis and John Spinks and Michael Jagger, the least likely of all to stand still for a photograph. The others reined him in with arms around his shoulders, neck and waist. They stood together in their flannel shorts, their elastic school belts with metal S-clasps, English schoolboys at their apotheosis, laughing into the warm, safe, quiet Fifties sky.

Kent as a county begins in London, south-east of the Thames, in ranks of suburbs barely distinguishable from one another, crossed by railway bridges, whose names are synonyms for dullness and decorum – Bexley, Bromley, Beckenham, Dartford, Sidcup, Sevenoaks and the rest. One must travel far on grubby trains, crossing many bridges, to discover what is still called 'the Garden of England', with its apple orchards, hop fields and oast houses. It is a large and bewilderingly imprecise county, ranging from the miles of drab dockland around Chatham and Rochester to the Regency splendours of Royal Tunbridge Wells; from the medieval majesty of Canterbury Cathedral to the faded Victorian seaside of Margate and Broadstairs, where Charles Dickens wrote *Bleak House*. Somewhere in the sprawling landscape is the field in which Mr Pickwick lost his hat while watching military manoeuvres, the bucolic landscape, bespoken by Alfred Jingle, of 'apples, hops, cherries, women'.

Least romantic of all Kentish suburbs is Dartford, where, on December 7, 1940, Basil Joseph Jagger married Eva Scutts. The bridegroom was a slight, quiet-looking man whose wiry frame betrayed his calling as physical-training teacher. The bride was a pretty young woman with a wide smile and that air of determined gentility which sometimes goes with slight foreignness. Eva, in fact, had been born in Australia and had emigrated to Britain with her family in her early teens. The best man was Basil's more ebullient brother, Albert. Afterwards, there was a reception for fifty guests at the Coneybeare Hall.

Basil – known as Joe to his family and friends – was not merely a drill sergeant in white singlet and gym shoes, exhorting local schoolchildren to lift up their knees and swing their arms. He subsequently became a lecturer in physical education at Strawberry Hill College, Twickenham. Horace Walpole's sumptuous mock-Gothic mansion was – and still is – the nucleus of this teacher-training institute, run by a Catholic order, the Vincentians, to supply Catholic schools all over the world. Joe Jagger's job was to give a grounding in physical education simple and comprehensive enough to be passed on to student priests or mission children in the wilds of Africa or Asia.

He also worked as a lecturer with the nascent British Sports Council. His speciality was basketball, an American sport not much in vogue in mid-Fifties Britain. Joe Jagger was among the pioneers of the British basketball movement and was the author of what remains the definitive book on the subject, published by Faber and Faber in 1962.

His wife Eva was a lively and energetic person whose vivacity at times seemed to verge on the domineering. Eva had always been secretly rather ashamed of her Australian origin, with its implied stigma of roughness and unsophistication. Marriage to

Joe, with his markedly superior social standing and education, increased her determination to show herself the equal of any true 'Brit'. Their small house, in Denver Road, Dartford, was scoured by Eva into a spotless state the equal of any neighbour's. Joe and Eva's whole life as a young married couple was dictated by consideration of what those ever-vigilant neighbours might think.

Their first son, Michael Philip, was born on July 26, 1943. The tide of the Second World War had long since turned in the Allies' favour, but Britain was still an embattled redoubt of air-raid precautions, white-helmeted wardens, clothing coupons and butcher-shop queues. Though the RAF nightly pounded Hamburg and Essen in 'thousand-bomber raids', attacks by the German Luftwaffe on London continued. The Kent suburbs heard the distant thunder and saw the horizontal flashes as the poor old East End caught it from the sky again.

Michael Jagger was a child of absolutely conventional beauty, with chubby cheeks, guileless eyes and hair that assumed a reddish tinge. As a toddler, he proved amiable and obedient, though prone to boisterous spirits that could sometimes go too far. Once, on holiday at the seaside, his mother remembers, he marched along the beach, deliberately kicking down every other child's sandcastle in his path. His reign as an adored only child lasted until 1947, when Eva presented him with a younger brother, Christopher.

Home life for the Jagger brothers was pervaded by their mother's house-proud fastidiousness and their father's devotion to physical fitness. Their Denver Road neighbours were accustomed to seeing the small back garden of the Jagger house littered with sports equipment – weight-training barbells, cricket stumps and archery targets. Other children asked home to tea by Mike or Chris were somewhat intimidated by the schoolmasterly regimen, which included Grace before meals and a system of fixed penalties and punishments for misbehaviour.

Mike's physical prowess showed through early at Maypole infants' school and afterwards at Wentworth County Primary, to which his Maypole teacher, Ken Llewellyn, an expatriate Welshman, had also transferred. Mr Llewellyn remembers him fondly as one of an outstanding junior class whose ascent to grammar school and university seemed assured. 'It was a joy to teach them. They were full of life, full of all sorts of questions. I took them for games as well. Mike was already looking like a useful cricketer. If I remember him at all, it's running in from the playground with both knees grazed and a great big smile on his face.'

John Spinks lived in Heather Drive, Dartford, not far from the Jaggers in Denver Road. He was Mike's playmate in the sandpit that lay between their houses. When Mike accidentally impaled a hand on a spiked metal railing, it was John Spinks who, with praiseworthy coolness, pulled it free. To John, he seemed at times almost too conventionally law-abiding and obedient. 'I always thought he was a bit of a mother's boy. He did *everything* he was told at home. He was an indiarubber character, really. He could bend any way to stay out of trouble.'

Even as a small boy, his other friend Robert Wallis remembers, he had a strangely remote, abstracted quality – a sense of being preoccupied with matters far weightier than their schoolboy games together. Joe Jagger was currently acting as adviser to a commercial TV programme called *Seeing Sport*, designed to promote physical fitness in children. Once a week, he would take his elder son with him to the studios, to act as model for instruction about athletics or camping. 'Mike is going to show you know to light the fire,' the voiceover would say, or: 'Here's Mike, getting into the tent.' 'He became a bit of a star for doing that,' Robert Wallis says. 'He always had some interest outside the ones we had as a group. He gave the idea the he'd sooner be somewhere else than with us, doing far more glamorous things.'

Robert, John and Mike took the eleven-plus exam together,

passing it as effortlessly as Ken Llewellyn had predicted. This crucial step determined whether they would go on to receive a mundane basic education at a secondary modern or be admitted to the far superior privileges of Dartford Grammar. Eva Jagger had every reason to be proud of her boy in his smart new uniform of gold-trimmed maroon blazer and cap.

Dartford Grammar School, when Mike Jagger arrived there in the early Fifties, possessed most features of an English public school – masters in gowns, house captains, societies, ceremonial Speech Days, ritualized athletics and sport. As its school magazine, *The Dartfordian*, attests, scholarship was generally excellent, yielding an unusually large annual export to Britain's redbrick universities. Prominent in the school curriculum was the Army Cadet Force, designed to cushion the shock of the two years' compulsory National Service each boy would face before embarking on his chosen career.

At Dartford Grammar, Mike Jagger's academic promise – and his buoyant enthusiasm – mysteriously evaporated. From the first form to the fifth he merely coasted, doing only enough work to stay out of trouble. It became a sore provocation to the several teachers in whose subjects he was obviously gifted. The senior languages master, Dr Bennett, particularly resented his indifference, for – aided by unusual powers of mimicry – he showed all the signs of a first-class linguist. 'There was one occasion when I spoke to him about his attitude very severely,' Dr Bennett says. 'He was so deliberately insulting that I simply knocked him down.'

His apathy extended even to sport. He seemed to lose interest in cricket after discovering he was not the deadly spin bowler he had supposed himself at Wentworth. The only sport he played regularly was basketball, his father's speciality. Joe Jagger, in fact, introduced the sport to Dartford Grammar and helped coach the Basketball Society, of which Mike was Hon. Sec. 'He was most keen on that, I think, because it was American,' Robert Wallis says. 'Mike was the one who had *real* American basketball boots to play in when the rest of us only had gym shoes.'

His appearance, from the age of fourteen onward, seemed to reflect his slack and insubordinate attitude. The chubby, laughing schoolboy of Ken Llewellyn's class had grown into an adolescent whose skinny frame, hovering on the edge of effeteness, caused uniform distaste among his teachers. Likewise his face, with its somnolent eyes, its retroussé nose; most of all, the wide, sagging lips, set in what seemed a permanent grimace of either scorn or dumb insolence.

As he moved higher in the school, he became adept at flouting its dress regulations. Instead of the prescribed black lace-up shoes, he would arrive for class in French slip-on moccasins. In place of his blazer, he acquired a black, gold-threaded 'Teddy boy' jacket, which, to Dr Bennett's annoyance, he wore even to the annual Founder's Day ceremony.

He was already a source of much discussion at the nearby girls' grammar school, where opinion as to his attractiveness remained sharply divided. In terms of conventional handsomeness he was obviously a non-starter. Yet some of the very girls who dismissed him as ugly or 'a weed' still looked for him in the after-school swarm and made bold attempts to talk to him – since he seemed uninterested in talking to them. It became almost a competition to pierce that scornful reserve and bring forth that rare smile which could split open the sullen face, making him look still the happy schoolboy who had laughed into the sun.

In 1955 came the plague called rock 'n' roll. Bill Haley and the Comets invaded Britain's sleepy hit parade with Rock Around the Clock, See You Later, Alligator, Everybody Razzle Dazzle and Rockin' Through the Rye. Britain's regimented teenage boys awoke to the sound of a braying sax, a slapping, spinning double bass, a voice that did not croon but jerked and jogged and hiccupped and jumped. What Haley was in fact playing was black rhythm and blues, purged of its bite and wit and wrapped in a swing or country-western beat. The very phrase 'rock and roll' was black slang for energetic fucking. Even in America, its origin had scarcely been realized. In Britain it was simply the most exciting noise that ever confused an adolescent's glands. A British tour by Haley and the Comets in 1956 left a trail of wrecked theatres and slashed cinema seats. Music became, for the first time, a source of conflict between the young, who adored this outrageous new noise, and their parents, who loathed it and strove to extinguish it by every possible means.

A few months earlier, the British Decca label had released a record which, though quieter than Haley's joyous gibberish, was destined to transform many lives more permanently. The record – one of the newfangled 'long playing' kind – was *New Orleans Joys*, by the Chris Barber Jazz Band.

Barber, twenty-five, led Britain's most commercially successful Dixieland band. He remained, however, principally an archivist, devoted to keeping alive sources and style that might otherwise have been overlooked in the current 'Trad' boom. His *New Orleans Joys* LP included two blues songs played in the 'skiffle' style evolved in the Depression years, when musicians were often reduced to instruments extemporized from household utensils. The songs, Rock Island Line and John Henry, were performed by a primitive rhythm section of double bass, kitchen washboard and banjo, the last played by a skinny Glaswegian named Tony Donegan who had changed his name to Lonnie in honour of the American bluesman Lonnie Johnson.

The two songs, released on a single in 1956, became a stupendous British Top Ten hit. Haley and his group, in their plaid jackets and bow ties, owed their appeal to outlandish remoteness. But Donegan, with his nasal whine, his ex-serviceman's haircut and backing of mundane domestic implements, made comparably exciting sounds that anyone could reproduce. Within days of Lonnie Donegan's first appearance on national television, acolyte skiffle groups had sprung up all over Britain. The craze centred on London's Soho, its jazz cellars and newly fashionable espresso coffee houses, into whose gloomy recesses record-company talent scouts now plunged in a hectic search for ersatz Lonnie Donegans. For the first time ever, musical talent was held to be of secondary importance to looks. Any boy who played a guitar and wore a plaid shirt with the collar turned up, if he sat around long enough in coffee bars like the Heaven and Hell, the Gyre and Gimble or the 2 I's, could hope to follow the starry path of Lonnie Donagan or 'Britain's First rock 'n' roller,' Tommy Steele.

All over Britain, in suburban living rooms, boys crouched together with their matchwood guitars, their mothers' washboards and basses improvised from tea chests and wire, struggling to learn the blues songs made popular by Donegan and his successors, grateful for the easy chords and pattered tempo, blissfully unaware that the lyrics, as Woody Guthrie or Huddie Leadbetter had written them, were violent political tracts; that Midnight Special was a cotton slave's suicidal lament or that Lonnie Johnson's plaintively sweet Careless Love was a song about syphilis, ending with murder.

Eva Jagger remembers that even as a very small boy her elder son would stand in front of the family wireless set, singing along to music with words made up in his head. Most of all he seemed to like Latin American rhythms, which he would accompany with a stream of Spanish-sounding nonsense. At the age of ten, on a Spanish holiday with Joe and Eva, he posed for a snapshot in a straw sombrero, playing a toy guitar. Sombrero tipped back, guitar flourished flamenco-style, the pose was, even then, self-consciously theatrical.

The skiffle craze swept through Dartford Grammar as through almost every other British school. Two of Mike's friends, Bob Beckwith and Alan Etherington, acquired guitars and began practising together. But Mike, though he too had a guitar, joined none of the ad hoc classroom skiffle groups that would strum together, perched on desks during break time.

He never really liked Bill Haley, or even Elvis Presley, after the gold-suited, magical lout had superseded Haley as the corrupter of Britain's youth. His first fan worship, significantly, was for Little Richard, the original *black* rock 'n' roll star whose r & b beginnings were now camouflaged in a demented scream, a wobbling drape suit and an aura – though few perceived it then – of sexual ambiguity.

He did succumb, as most did, to the charm of Buddy Holly and the Crickets. Holly is blessed by countless guitar demigods for having first showed them the way from skiffle to rock 'n' roll, in simple but inventive chord sequences through G and E. As his enormous output shows, he was a stylistic chameleon, equally at home with Texas rockabilly and black r & b. Soon to die, he visited Britain on tour only once, in March 1958. Mike Jagger went with another Dartford Grammar School friend, Dick Taylor, to see the Holly stage show at the Granada Cinema, Woolwich. Buddy Holly that night played one of the more esoteric items in his repertoire – a song called Not Fade Away, set to a halting, staccato beat invented by the blues star Bo Diddley. Dick Taylor remembers what an impression that song in particular made on Mike Jagger.

A wispy, amiable boy, son of a plumber in nearby Bexleyheath, Dick Taylor came nearer than most to penetrating the Jagger reserve. For Dick knew about American music far more exotic and exciting than Elvis and Little Richard. What Dick Taylor liked was *real* blues – the scratched and blurred master sketches that the rock 'n' roll industry had turned into glib cartoons. It was at Dick Taylor's house that Mike Jagger listened to Muddy Waters, Jimmy Reed, Howlin' Wolf, giants of the urban blues with heart-shivering voices, calling and answering their virtuoso guitars, that could change the view beyond the lace curtains from Kentish suburbia to the dark and windy canyons along Chicago's Lake Shore Drive. From then on, the blues became Mike's consuming passion.

Part of the music's attraction was its sheer unavailability. Simply hearing it was complicated enough. You could not buy blues records in the Dartford or Bexleyheath record shops. As with all truly worthwhile things, it involved a trip to London. Mike and Dick would spend their Saturday afternoons at the jazz record shops in Charing Cross Road, thumbing through the blues 'import' stock in sleeves already dog-eared and thumbed in their wandering journey across the cultural hemispheres. The very label logos excited them – not boring British Decca and Philips, but Okeh and Crown and Chess and Sue and Imperial and Delmark.

If listening to blues was difficult, seeing it was virtually impossible. Though famous bluesmen like Big Bill Broonzy did perform in Britain during the late Fifties, news of their coming did not percolate down the line to Dartford. The only glimpse given to Dartford Grammar School's secret blues caucus involved sitting through *Jazz on a Summer's Day*, a film documentary about the American Newport Jazz Festival. Almost at the end, a lanky young black man got up onstage and sang through a derisive grin and played a red guitar that dangled almost to the level of his wildly knocking knees. That, for Dick Taylor, Mike Jagger and countless other British boys, was their first tantalizing sight of Chuck Berry. The film sequence ended with Berry dodging a hail of flashbulbs thrown by photographers in fury that the pure jazz had been so disrupted.

Mike Jagger's earliest attempt at blues singing was at the house of a boy name David Soames in Wentworth Drive, Dartford. David was trying to form a rhythm and blues group with Mike Turner, another ex-pupil of Wentworth County Primary School. Both quickly decided that Mike Jagger sang in far too strange a fashion to be their vocalist. He accepted the decision without rancour and afterwards walked home with

Mike Turner, discussing their forthcoming GCE O-Level examinations.

Dick Taylor owned a second-hand drum kit, which gained him admittance to several small amateur groups otherwise top-heavy with guitarists. By his last year at Dartford Grammar, he was practising regularly with Bob Beckwith, Alan Etherington and Mike Jagger. It was hardly a group at all, since they had no equipment – only the Etheringtons' radiogram to amplify the guitars – and because Mike Jagger, their singer, refused to play a guitar himself, as was customary. He just stood or sat there and sang, diffidently until his powers as a mimic came to his aid. 'The first song I remember him doing was Richie Valens's La Bamba,' Dick Taylor says. 'Mick used to come out with this stream of words that sounded just like Spanish. He'd just make them up as he went along.'

The group was called Little Boy Blue and the Blue Boys, in order that there be no mistake concerning their musical intentions. From first to last in their two-year history, Little Boy Blue and the Blue Boys never played to an audience other than Dick Taylor's mum. 'She dug Mick right from the start,' Taylor says. 'She always told him he'd got something special.'

Their repertoire was limited to the precious store of blues import discs Dick Taylor had collected – Howlin' Wolf's Smokestack Lighting; Don and Bob's Good Morning Little Schoolgirl; Dale Hawkins's Susie Q. 'We never even *thought* of playing to other people,' Dick Taylor says. 'We thought we were the only people in England who'd ever *heard* of r & b.'

After *Jazz on a Summer's Day*, Chuck Berry dominated their thoughts. It was Mike Jagger who found out you could get Berry records by writing direct to the Chess record company in Chicago. Berry's voice, light and sharp and strangely white-sounding, had a pitch not dissimilar to his own. Singing along with Sweet Little Sixteen or Reelin' and Rockin', he suddenly felt something more than just a mumbling impersonator. And

Chuck Berry was the first intimation that rhythm and blues might be an expression of youth. Each Berry song was a novel in miniature about American teenage life, teeming with brand-name cars, sassy high-school queens and anarchic exhortations to forsake the classroom in favour of car-driving, singing and dancing.

Practice sessions took place at Alan Etherington's house – because of the radiogram – or in Dick Taylor's bedroom at Bexleyheath, seated on the bed around a big old-fashioned tape recorder. Dick remembers an anxious moment when Mike turned up to rehearse for the first time after accidentally biting a piece out of his tongue in the school gymnastics class. 'He was terrified it was going to affect the way he sang. We all kept telling him it made no difference. But he did seem to lisp a bit and sound more bluesy after that.'

His own home, though welcoming to his friends, did not suggest itself as a practice place for Little Boy Blue and the Blue Boys. Eva Jagger was not discouraging. She had nothing against their music, she told them – it was just that the neighbours might mind the noise. Joe Jagger's main concern, as always, was keeping his son up to the mark in physical education. Once, when Mike was going off with Dick Taylor, his father called out, 'Michael – don't forget your weight training.' Mike turned back obediently, went into the garden and exercised with barbells for a conscientious quarter of an hour.

He had passed his GCE O-Levels in a respectable enough seven subjects, and had qualified for entry into the Sixth Arts form to do Advanced Level English, History and French. He also became a school prefect, despite the headmaster's manifest disapproval. The head, Mr Hudson, had never quite forgiven him for leading what seemed like an organized insurrection by lower-school boys against compulsory enrolment in the school Army Cadet Force.

He stuck out the two-year A-Level course with no idea what

he was working for, beyond a vague notion that journalism might be interesting. For a brief time, too, he toyed with the idea of becoming a radio disc jockey. A London record producer named Joe Meek was currently advertising for would-be deejays to submit demonstration tapes. Robert Wallis remembers copying out Meek's address from a newspaper and passing it on to Mike Jagger. But the project languished, apparently under parental discouragement.

His A-Level passes in English and History were only mediocre but by then it did not matter. He had already secured himself a place at the London School of Economics, to follow a two-year course in the subject that seemed best suited to his indecisive talents. 'I wanted to do arts but thought I ought to do science,' he says now. 'Economics seemed about halfway in between.'

So, each morning, from the autumn of 1961, Mike Jagger, in his striped student scarf, joined the daily crowd of business people at Dartford railway station, his face turned towards a future that still seemed to lie only a little way up the commuter line to Victoria.

Each morning, from the top deck of the green Kentish bus, Dick Taylor would see the same thin, slouching figure trailing reluctantly up the long hill to Sidcup Art College. Winter or summer, Keith Richards wore the same tight blue jeans, Italian pointed shoes, denim jacket and the violet-coloured shirt that never seemed to be given a rest or a wash. In summer as well as winter, he contrived to look pinched and cold, his bullet head accentuating protuberant ears, his nose red raw, his mouth specked with teenage pimples. In one hand, he held a Player's Weights cigarette; in the other, his only possession, a guitar. Dick Taylor knew it would be another day of abandoned study, and of rock 'n' roll practice in the college lavatories.

Guitars, and loving them, are among Keith's earliest

memories. His mother's father, Theodore Augustus Dupree – the family were originally Huguenots from the Channel Islands – led a small semi-professional dance band in the 1930s and himself played several instruments including saxophone, violin and guitar. The guitar still stood in 'Grandfather Gus's' house, in a corner of the sitting room. Keith remembers with what excitement, even as a tiny boy, he would approach it and draw his hands with a soft thrum across its untuned strings.

'He was a great character, my grandfather Gus. At that time, when I was small, he had a job in some tailoring sweatshop – he'd always be bringing little squares of felt out of his pocket and showing us. He carried on playing music, too, right up to the Sixties – touring the American air force bases with a country band. He'd got a job as janitor at Highgate School where Yehudi Menuhin's son was a pupil. My grandfather, in the end, got to know Yehudi; they'd even have a bit of a scrape together on their violins. What a fantastic hustler!'

Bert Richards, Keith's father, was a very different character, quiet and cautious with a reserve that – his son thinks now – was created largely by overwork and exhaustion. Bert worked as a supervisor at Osram's light bulb factory in Hammersmith. He got up each day at 5 a.m. and did not come home in the evening until six. 'He'd have something to eat, watch TV for a couple of hours, then go to bed, absolutely knackered,' Keith says. 'He must have been horrified to see what a thug he'd produced in me.'

The boy born in December 1943 thus grew up closest to his mother, Doris, a warm and jolly woman who had inherited the Dupree fondness for music and romance. Keith remembers how, as Doris did the housework, the radio would constantly pour out American big band music. When he first started school and was too nervous to walk there, Doris carried him all the way, bundled lovingly in her arms. From his earliest childhood, she encouraged him to do, and be, exactly what he wanted.

As a small boy, Keith had a beautiful soprano voice, good

enough to be heard in Westminster Abbey itself. 'Only three of us, in our white surplices, used to be good enough to do the hallelujahs. I was a star then – coming up by coach to London to sing in the inter-schools competition at the Albert Hall. I think that was my first taste of show business: when my voice broke and they didn't want me in the choir any more. Suddenly it was "Don't call us, we'll call you." I think that was when I stopped being a good boy and started to be a yob.'

Doris and Bert Richards lived in Chastillian Road, Dartford, just a street or two away from the Jaggers in Denver Road. Keith attended Wentworth County Primary School and was taught by Ken Llewellyn. He had met Mike Jagger, too, briefly, in the scream and jostle of the infants' playground. Jagger, who customarily affects to remember nothing past, can none the less recall what a strong impression Keith made on him. 'I asked him what he wanted to do when he grew up. He said he wanted to be a cowboy like Roy Rogers and play a guitar. I wasn't that impressed by Roy Rogers, but the bit about the guitar *did* interest me.'

That first acquaintance was to be short-lived. Doris and Bert moved soon afterwards from Chastillian Road to a house on a new council estate on the other side of Dartford. Thereafter, Keith Richards became the very last kind of companion Joe and Eva Jagger could have wished for their elder son.

The Richardses lived on the Temple Hill Estate, in a small semi-detached house, 6 Spielman Road, the estate was brand new, dumped down on raw new tarmac roads without amusements or amenities. Bert Richards, as before, got up at five each morning to go to work at Osram's in Hammersmith. Doris worked part-time in a Dartford baker's shop. And Keith, between his father's indifference and his mother's over-indulgence, began to go resolutely to the bad.

It was not that he lacked ability – even talent. He could be, Ken Llewellyn remembers, a bright, attentive boy, responsive especially to words and language. He enjoyed cricket, swimming and – most surprisingly – tennis. He was, besides, good-natured and open, with a mischievous wit that made even schoolmasters unbend towards him.

What he could not do was accept discipline in any form. It was a lawlessness partly compounded of running wild on the estate; partly of his mother's soft-hearted pampering. Doris did not mind if he failed to do his homework or went AWOL from cross-country runs or – as increasingly happened – if he failed to turn up for school altogether. She would leave him money at home to buy fish and chips for his lunch. Even when he dumped the fish and chip leavings in the kitchen sink, newspaper and all, Doris cleared up after him without complaint.

By the time he was thirteen, ordinary teachers despaired of educating him. It was decided he should go straight to Dartford Technical School, where his father hoped he might succumb to learning a useful trade.

Now, however, the long-suffering Bert Richards faced an additional vexation. 'Every time the poor guy came in at night,' Keith says, 'he'd find me sitting at the top of the stairs with my guitar, playing and banging on the wall for percussion. He was great about it, really. He'd only mutter, "Stop that bloody noise."'

Doris had bought Keith his first guitar, for seven pounds, from her wages at the baker's shop. 'I never knew what make it was,' Keith says. 'The name had been painted out.' The only stipulation Doris made, supported by Grandfather Gus, was that he must learn to play *properly*. Soon afterwards, she gave him more money for a record player, from Dartford Co-Op shop, so he could learn by listening to the skiffle and rock 'n' roll hits.

Now was the time of British rock 'n' roll – of Tommy Steele and Terry Dene and the 'cover' versions of American songs put out on a label called Embassy that was sold only at Woolworth's. Embassy records were the first that Keith Richards tried to copy, sitting at the top of the stairs at 6 Spielman Road. 'I always sat on the top stair to practise. You could get the best echo that way – or standing in the bath.'

He soon realized that what made British rock 'n' roll so tinny and false was not the vocal so much as the backing – the staid guitars played by bored 'session men', and sounding just as plumply complacent. Better by far to scrape up the full six shillings and fourpence for the original American version with guitars that shrilled and echoed as from a separate universe. Keith's next idol, after his grandfather Gus, was Scotty Moore, Elvis Presley's session guitarist. He still thinks Moore's solo on Presley's I'm Left, You're Right, She's Gone the most exciting thing ever recorded. 'I could never work out how he played it, and I still can't. It's such a wonderful thing that I almost don't *want* to know.'

His guitar, allied with the life of a Dartford Teddy boy, became the final, irresistible temptation to play truant. In 1958, he was expelled from Dartford Technical School. A sympathetic teacher suggested there might be one last hope in the art college in the neighbouring dormitory town of Sidcup.

Sidcup Art College sounds immeasurably grander than it ever was. It existed, in fact, to give just such last chances to those whose inglorious school careers had fitted them for nothing better than what was then belittingly called 'commercial art'. Sidcup's art college was remarkably similar to the one in Hope Street, Liverpool, which – also in 1958 – admitted a similar habitual truant named John Lennon.

For Keith, Sidcup Art College was a first introduction to authentic blues music, never captured on a Woolworth's Embassy label. A group of students – including Dick Taylor – would meet in an empty room next to the principal's office, and play Little Walter and Big Bill Broonzy songs among the drawing boards and paste pots. It was from one of them Keith acquired his first electric guitar, swapping it for a pile of records in a hasty transaction in the college 'bogs'.

So far as Dick Taylor was concerned, Keith Richards was just an incorrigible and hilarious distraction from the business of studying graphic design. 'When I think of Keith at college, I think of dustbins burning. We used to get these baths of silk-screen wash, throw them over the dustbins and then throw on a match. The dustbins used to explode with a great "woomph".

'We were all popping pills then – to stay awake without sleep more than to get high. We used to buy these nose inhalers called Nostrilene, for the benzedrine, or even take girls' period pills. Opposite the college, there was this little park with an aviary that had a cockatoo in it. Cocky the Cockatoo we used to call it. Keith used to feed it pep pills and make it stagger around on its perch. If ever we were feeling bored, we'd go and give another upper to Cocky the Cockatoo.'

One morning, on his railway journey from Dartford to Sidcup, Keith happened to get into the same dreary commuter carriage as Mike Jagger, en route to the London School of Economics. They recognized each other vaguely from Wentworth County Primary School and a subsequent meeting when Mike had a holiday job selling ice cream outside Dartford Library. This meeting might have been as casual as the previous ones were it not that Mike had under his arm a pile of import blues albums he had got from America by mail order. Keith noticed the sacred names of Chuck Berry and Little Walker, and, with some incredulity, asked the striped-scarfed LSE student if *he* liked that kind of music, too.

Chatting further, they discovered they had a common friend in Dick Taylor. Dick had already mentioned to Keith that he was rehearsing with a group sworn to play nothing but blues and r & b. By the time their train reached Sidcup, it was half-arranged that Keith Richards should come along and try rehearsing with Little Boy Blue and the Blue Boys.

He brought with him his semi-solid Hofner cutaway guitar and what seemed to the others a stunning virtuosity. Sitting on the stairs at home, he had managed to master nearly all Chuck Berry's introductions and solos, even the swarm of notes running through the Berry classic Johnny B. Goode that created an effect like two guitars at once. He understood that even this complex break, like two guitars in unison, required something more than simply playing notes fast. 'Keith sounded great – but he wasn't *flash*,' Dick Taylor says. 'When he came in, you could feel something holding the band together.'

Keith's arrival, even so, did not advance the fortunes of Little Boy Blue and the Blue Boys. They continued to practise as before, with no thought of any audience beyond Dick Taylor's mum – no inkling that r & b music was a secret vouchsafed to anyone in Britain but themselves. The nearest they came to a public performance was playing together for a snapshot outside the Taylors' back door. The snap shows Dick and Keith with their guitars parodying Chuck Berry's duck walk, and Mike Jagger, in his student's button-up cardigan, striking a dramatic pose against the background of drainpipe and pebbledashed council house wall.

Music in that era forged many friendships between personalities that might otherwise have remained polar opposites. It had happened three years earlier between cynical, trouble-prone John Lennon and cautious, conservative Paul McCartney in Liverpool. It happened now, when Keith Richards, the 'Ted' from a council flat on the wrong side of Dartford, started to go around with Mike Jagger, the economics student from middle-class Denver Road.

Though the LSE in 1961 was not the political hotbed it later became, a mild radicalism was as de rigueur among its students as the prevailing 'bohemian' look. For Mike Jagger it was to be little more than a look, expressed in his new leather tie and knitted cardigan. Just the same, armed with new words like 'capitalism' and 'proletariat', he seemed intent on rejecting his careful upbringing and sliding down to the class his mother so abhorred.

At the LSE, he dropped the 'Mike', which now seemed redolent of bourgeois young men with sports cars. 'Mike Jagger' would henceforward be a creature only in the memory of his earliest friends. It was Mick Jagger who hung around with Keith Richards, talking in broad Cockney and affecting some of Keith's chaotic nonchalance and street-tough recklessness.

The mimicry was not completely one-sided. Keith on occasion could become thoughtful, self-effacing, even shy. It was as if each provided the other with a role he had desired but never dared assume before. Dick Taylor noticed what was to become a regular interchange of identities. 'One day, Mick would become Keith. But then on another day, Keith could go all like Mick. You never knew which way round it would be.

'But from then on, Mick and Keith were together. Whoever else came into the band or left, there'd always be Mick and Keith.'

Before Alexis Korner and his wife Bobbie went to bed in their flat in Moscow Road, Bayswater, they would be careful to leave the kitchenette window slightly ajar at the bottom. Next to the window was a table positioned in such a way that the late-arriving or unexpected guest could enter by rolling sideways across it. When Alexis and Bobbie got up next morning, four or five sleeping figures might be peacefully disposed under the table, against the cooker legs or among the food bowls of the Korners' several cats.

The sleepers were American blues musicians on tour, for whom Alexis and Bobbie Korner provided refuge and hospitality in an otherwise bewildering land. Big Bill Broonzy, Muddy Waters, T-Bone Walker, the guitar giants so often visualized by Mick Jagger and Keith Richards in their windy and harsh Chicago heaven, might be sitting barely twenty miles from Dartford in that Bayswater kitchenette, eating the Southern-style ham hocks that Bobbie Korner had learned to cook.

Alexis Korner's antecedents were as richly cosmopolitan as the syllables of his name suggest. His father was Austrian, a former cavalry officer, and his mother was Greco-Turkish. By his father's first marriage he had a Russian step-grandmother. He himself was born in Paris and spent his early childhood in Switzerland and North Africa. There was something more than a little Moroccan in his dark skin and tightly curled hair, and the vibrant, husky voice which only accidental circumstance was to bend into the brogue of suburban West London.

His father, the former cavalry officer, was an autocratic, distant figure, vaguely connected with high finance and – Alexis later thought – international espionage. 'I know he lost a lot of money in the Twenties, when Britain went off the gold standard, and he couldn't live as well as he had before. He was also supposed to have had something to do with the scandal surrounding the Zinoviev Letter. I'm sure he'd done something pretty major to earn the gratitude of the British government. When war broke out in 1939, we were living in England; my father could have expected to be interned as an enemy alien. Instead, he got his naturalization papers as a British subject virtually overnight.'

One Saturday in 1940, Alexis, a pupil of St Paul's School, went from his home in Ealing to nearby Shepherd's Bush market to indulge in the boyish pastime of pilfering from the stalls. His haul that morning included a record by the blues pianist Jimmy Yancey. 'From that moment,' he remembered later, 'I only wanted to do one thing. I wanted to play boogie-woogie piano.'

When he attempted to do so on the family piano, his father would come along in a fury and slam down the lid. Nor was the elder Korner any better pleased when Alexis brought home his first guitar. 'My father used to say the guitar was a "woman's instrument". He imagined it in operettas, tied with pink ribbon.'

Two years' military service brought relief from this parental prejudice. Alexis served with the British Army in West Germany and – as well as playing football for his regiment – became a part-time announcer over the Forces' radio network. He could saturate himself, not only in the music played to British troops, but also in the far more exciting output of AFN, the American Forces Network. As surreptitiously listening German boys already knew, AFN broadcast the very best in jazz and swing and even types of black music not available to civilians back home in the States. So the blues took root, on NATO bases and, later, in local clubs, amid pornographic bookshops, strip joints and mud-wrestling pits.

Back in London, working in the shipping firm owned by his mother's Greek family, Alexis gravitated naturally to that first postwar 'younger generation', which haunted the Soho cellars, avid for politics and traditional jazz. 'We were elitist – and *highly* political. We used to speak quite seriously in those days of founding a "fourth class". There'd be the upper class, the middle class, the working class and us. That was how the blues came into it. When we heard a Leadbelly song or a Woody Guthrie song, we knew we were listening to a powerful political protest.'

The principal jazz bandleaders of the period did what they could to bring blues to the larger Dixieland audience. Humphrey Lyttelton, trumpeter, Old Etonian and friend of royalty, had brought Big Bill Broonzy to Britain as early as 1953. Ken Colyer, most pure of all the jazz and folk purists, featured some of the greatest American bluesmen at his London club, Studio 51, just off Leicester Square.

Chris Barber remained the music's most passionate, consistent champion – the only one, in Korner's words, to 'put his money where his mouth was' and plough actual cash into keeping blues alive. Barber, in the early Fifties, had been the moving spirit behind a formal conservation body, the National Jazz League. The league flourished, acquiring sufficient capital to buy its own Soho club, the Marquee in Wardour Street.

Alexis Korner joined the Barber band as banjoist during

Lonnie Donegan's absence on National Service. When Donegan returned and Rock Island Line became a hit, Korner was well placed, had he desired, to participate in the nine days' skiffle wonder. He almost joined another successful skiffle group, the Vipers, signed up at the 2 I's coffee bar by a then obscure EMI-label executive called George Martin. Instead, he formed his own group, bowing to commercial pressure with the word 'skiffle' only for its first extended-play record. Thereafter, the group was to be known as Alexis Korner's Blues Incorporated.

The first band in Britain to play nothing but blues was a curious amalgam of fervent fantasy wedded to unlikely and incongruous human shapes. Its chief member, after Korner himself, was Cyril Davies, a fifteen-stone panel beater from South Harrow, a virtuoso on blues harmonica and twelve-string guitar, whose every waking moment was clouded by chagrin that he had not been born a black man. On saxophone there was Dick Heckstall-Smith, who in aspect and manner bore a passing resemblance to Lenin. On double bass there was the future bass guitar maestro, Jack Bruce. The drummer – when Alexis could persuade him to sit in – was a sad-faced boy called Charlie Watts. 'I'd met Charlie at the Troubadour in Brompton Road, and always liked his playing. I'd said to him, "If I ever form a blues group, would you come in as drummer?" But he'd only do it part-time. He was too busy, studying commercial art in Harrow.'

It was Korner's plan from the beginning to start his own club, as Ken Colyer and other musicians had, to protect their chosen music from the jibes or hostility of rival factions. Soho cellars or pub backrooms in those days could be hired for a few shillings a night. Alexis Korner's first such venture, grandly styled the London Blues and Barrelhouse Club, was a room at the Round House pub in Wardour Street. The residency was sometimes interrupted by disputes between Korner and Cyril Davies, which led one or other to storm off and play in some rival club like the Troubadour.

As Blues Incorporated became more established, they started to receive bookings further and further outside London. One night, towards the end of 1961, Alexis found himself playing the blues to a rapturous crowd at a municipal hall in the genteel spa town of Cheltenham, Gloucestershire.

After the performance, a boy came up to Alexis in the pub across the road and talked to him earnestly – but with evident authority – about the blues and bluesmen. The boy was short but broadly built, and looked well-to-do in his smart Italian suit, white tab-collar shirt and Slim Jim tie. He spoke in a soft, well-mannered voice, lisping slightly. He said his name was Brian Jones. He was a musician himself, playing saxophone semi-professionally in a rock group called the Ramrods. What he really wanted to do, he told Alexis, was play Delta-style slide guitar with a band like Blues Incorporated. Alexis said – as Alexis always did – that if Brian Jones ever came to London, he was welcome to sleep on the Korners' kitchen floor.

In March 1962, tired of battling against the prejudice of the Soho jazz crowd, Alexis Korner decided to see how a new blues club would go in his own West London suburb, Ealing. The venue was a small room under the ABC teashop, just across the road from Ealing Broadway station. The first session, March 17, was announced by a small display ad in the *New Musical Express*.

The ad caused astonished excitement twenty miles away in Kent, among a self-defeatingly modest group called Little Boy Blue and the Blue Boys, to whom it still had not occurred that anyone else in Britain shared their musical fixation. The following Saturday, crammed into Alan Etherington's father's Riley 'Pathfinder' car, they set out for Ealing to investigate the extraordinary possibility that other people were playing the blues, to an audience, for money.

Two

'Well, the joint was rockin' . . .'

It truly was happening, in a poky downstairs room between the ABC bakery and a jeweller's shop: their secret music, the contraband repertoire of Muddy Waters, Otis Spann and the Chicago bluesmen, translated from inconceivable distance to deafening propinquity by the oddest imaginable group of men. Blues Incorporated performed, like jazz musicians, with almost professorial seriousness. Alexis Korner, curly-haired and moustachioed, in a white business shirt and tie, occupied the foreground with his Spanish guitar, seated on a chair. Cyril Davies stood next to him, sucking and coaxing the blues 'harp' with a breathy passion that made his pleated trousers wobble. Their audience stood around the tiny recessed stage in equal formality, nursing half pints of beer. As 'Squirrel' ended his harp solo, snatched the silver slide from his mouth and mopped his streaming brow, he received a round of polite applause like a speaker at a temperance meeting.

The instant success of the Ealing club proved to Alexis what he had always suspected – that the blues music, for some reason, had its most devoted following in suburban West London. After the second or third night at Ealing, something even more satisfactory happened. Alexis had brought Blues Incorporated away from Soho partly to escape the hostility of the traditional jazz faction. Now, the very clubs that had rejected him were starting to lose business, as more and more of their customers made the long Saturday night trek to Ealing. Even the purist National Jazz League could not ignore the commercial possibilities implied. Harold Pendleton, manager of the league-owned Marquee Club, came out to Ealing to hear Blues Incorporated, and afterwards offered Korner – whom he had previously not admired – a regular Thursday night engagement at the Marquee.

The band, at that time, had no regular vocalist. 'I'd sing lead – or Squirrel would,' Korner later remembered. 'But we didn't really believe in words. We were *instrumentalists*. The words just got in the way.'

Each Saturday night audience, in any case, was filled with young men, eager to exchange their world of Magicoal electric fires and Bournvita cocoa for the blues shouter's world of tin tenements and dance-hall queens. Anyone who wanted to sing with Blues Incorporated was welcome to try, though Alexis knew from long experience that the results were generally terrible. Then one night, a 6 foot 7 inch, sandy-haired and pink-faced youth got up and sang in a voice so black and raw, it was like having Chicago there in the room. The boy's name was 'Long' John Baldry. He became Blues Incorporated's first featured singer at the Ealing club on Saturdays and on Thursdays at the Marquee.

A few days after the first Ealing session, Alexis Korner received a letter with a Dartford postmark enclosing a small spool tape. The letter, from someone called Mick Jagger, solicited Korner's opinion of three songs by a group named Little Boy Blue and the Blue Boys. The material offered was Reelin' and Rockin', Bright Lights Big City, and Around and Around. The tape was subsequently lost; all Korner could ever remember of it was that it sounded 'absolutely terrible'.

The tape served a useful enough purpose, introducing Little Boy Blue himself to an established musician, known for unusual kindness towards musical beginners. Mick Jagger received the same invitation as everyone else to Ealing, to join Blues Incorporated on the bandstand for what singers, too, called a 'blow'. So, the next Saturday, taking all his courage, Jagger stepped on to the little stage, with its grubby tarpaulin canopy, and sang in public for the very first time.

He did so looking every inch the LSE student in his white poplin shirt, half-unknotted tie and chunky 'bohemian' cardigan, glancing nervously behind him as the dignitaries of Blues Incorporated began to vamp the – for them – absurdly simple chords of Chuck Berry's Around and Around. He himself has only a hazy recollection of standing there, half drunk, off key, forgetting his words and almost paralysed with fright. 'The thing I noticed about him wasn't his singing,' Alexis Korner said. 'It was the way he threw his hair around. He only had a short haircut, like everyone else's. But, for a kid in a cardigan, that was moving quite *excessively*.'

The song died into silence. Then – to the singer's vast astonishment – there was a burst of applause. Even tetchy 'Squirrel' Davis was prepared to clap someone whose love of blues could take him so far beyond the embarrassment barrier. The fact that he had copied Chuck Berry's phrasing note for note was further proof of being a true disciple.

The next time Mick Jagger sang for Alexis Korner, it was for a fee of fifteen shillings, plus beer. Within a month, he had become Blues Incorporated's second-string vocalist, singing with Korner for that same modest stipend whenever Long John Baldry was not available.

On Saturdays, it became a habit for the Dartford boys, Mick, Keith, Alan and Dick, to call at Alexis's flat in Bayswater and spend a couple of hours with the Korners before going on to Ealing together. Bobbie Korner would give them tea while Alexis told them stories of what Muddy and Broonzy had said in that very same kitchen – how Big Bill could never pronounce his fellow bluesmen's names (he called Fats Waller 'Fat Wallace') or how T-Bone Walker, fuddled by distance and drink, had once enquired, 'Is this Paris, France?'

The Korners both remembered Jagger in this period as quiet and polite, though with political pretensions that Alexis found mildly aggravating. 'We were talking about the blues one day and Mick said, "Why are you playing our working-class music?" I said, "Mick – you're at the *LSE*! What could be more middle class than that?" '

Keith, by contrast, was instantly sociable and engaging. 'He'd sit at the kitchen table and talk to Bobbie for *hours*. I remember how he loved words. I didn't really know him as a musician then – only that he played guitar in that group of theirs in Dartford. He never pushed himself forward as a musician. He just seemed happy to be around Mick.'

By this time, the hospitable Korners had another young visitor regularly sleeping on their kitchenette floor. It was the boy Alexis had talked to in Cheltenham, little realizing how that morsel of encouragement had ignited the boy's fierce desire to be in London, playing blues. So, late at night in Moscow Road, the kitchenette window would slide up. A dim figure would roll sideways across the table, down to the floor. Like Muddy Waters and Big Bill Broonzy before him, Brian Jones would fall asleep somewhere between the cats' bowls and the legs of the electric cooker.

Hatherley Road, Cheltenham, lies just outside that smugly elegant Gloucestershire spa town which will be ever associated in the English mind with retired army colonels and colleges for genteel young ladies. Hatherley Road is a long suburban avenue of identical 1930s houses, each with a single bay window, a neat front law and a wrought-iron 'sunrise' gate. Here and there, beyond a uniform creosote-covered garage, one can see the terraces of Cheltenham's exclusive district and beyond, the soft green Cotswolds, striding away towards Wales.

That Lewis Jones was a Welshman could not be doubted by his colleagues at Dowty and Co., Cheltenham's aeronautical engineering works. Short, straight-backed, severe in manner, he possessed the inflexible virtues of Welshness in exact measure with its irreproachable faults. He was, in other words, respectable, decent, hard-working, religious, conventional, puritanically intolerant of those less strong-minded than himself. Like many of his countrymen, he regretted the advance of the twentieth century almost on principle. 'Times change but *I* don't,' he would say, adding a heartfelt 'Thank God!'

The Welsh have almost an obligation to be musical. Lewis Jones played the organ at his local parish church for some years, until his dislike of petty ecclesiastical politics led him to resign. His wife Louisa – also Welsh – possessed a more pronounced talent, and supplemented Lewis's income from Dowty's by giving piano lessons to local schoolchildren.

Their first child, Brian Lewis Hopkin Jones, was born on February 28, 1942. Of the two daughters who followed, only one – Barbara, born in 1946 – survived. The other, Pauline, died of leukaemia when Brian was three. Brian thought his parents had given her away and, for a long time afterwards, lived in terror that the same would be done to him.

He was, his father said, a thoroughly normal and happy small boy, healthy but for childhood ailments and an attack of croup which left him prone to bronchitis and chronic asthma. At his first school, Dean Close, he worked well, enjoyed sport – particularly cricket and badminton – and became an excellent swimmer and diver. Sea air aggravated his asthma, however; after a single day at the beach, he would be confined to bed, wheezing and croaking piteously.

Like his parents, and the race from which he sprang, Brian Jones was instinctively musical. Louisa started giving him piano lessons from the age of six; he afterwards took up the recorder and clarinet. Though able to read music, he mastered the reed instruments by ear and intuition, stumbling on melody by means he himself did not fully understand. So marked was his talent as a small boy that Lewis Jones thought he might be destined for a career as a classical musician.

He passed the eleven-plus exam without effort and went on, as his parents had hoped, to Cheltenham Grammar School, down in the exclusive district of 'The Promenade', the retired generals and the Ladies' College. This exclusive seminary, in fact, stood immediately adjacent to Cheltenham Grammar School and daily provided its senior boys with an unreachable fantasy as the young ladies ran forth, squealing, for their mid-morning break.

Brian began well at Cheltenham Grammar, getting good marks for work, especially science and languages, excelling at cricket and swimming and winning a place as a clarinettist in the school orchestra. 'Then, all of a sudden,' Lewis Jones said bleakly, 'he became very difficult. He started to rebel against everything – mainly me.'

The trouble began when Brian ceased practising classical pieces on piano and clarinet, and began listening to a kind of music that Lewis Jones abhorred. At thirteen, he discovered jazz and, at fourteen, the saxophone-playing of Charlie Parker. He sold the clarinet his parents had bought him and used the proceeds to buy a second-hand alto sax. Within a few days, to his parents' horror, the sound of a first, shaky solo brayed through the quiet house in Hatherley Road.

He was soon good enough to sit in with local bands playing the trad jazz of Chris Barber and Humphrey Lyttelton. Even Cheltenham had its bohemian quarter, centred on the art college, on coffee bars like the Aztec, the Patio and the Waikiki, or pubs like the Wheatsheaf Inn, Leckhampton, where the 66 Jazz Club convened, with Brian Jones as membership secretary.

At Cheltenham Grammar, meanwhile, he became known as a troublemaker, able to disrupt a whole class by his blandly outrageous behaviour. A classmate, Peter Watson, remembers how

Brian would sit in class in football boots, claiming they were more comfortable than shoes. 'Brian said it was boring to drink the regulation milk at break time, so he started the fashion of drinking brown ale instead. It became a whole fashion to drink brown ale at break time instead of milk.'

At break, according to immemorial custom, the whole class would crowd at the window and gaze longingly down on the Cheltenham young ladies as they frolicked on the grass below. Brian Jones, it was well known, belonged to the select few Grammar School boys whose sexual adventures had gone beyond mere kissing and 'petting'. It was known, too, that he scorned the Durex contraceptives that other boys carried symbolically in their wallets. 'Bareback' was the best way, he would insist, smiling a smile so lascivious, yet so mischievous, no one knew whether to believe him.

They believed him when, in 1958, a fourteen-year-old pupil at the girls' Grammar School became pregnant and named Brian Jones as the father. The news caused a scandal in Cheltenham and even got into a Sunday newspaper, the *News of the World*, where Brian was destined to feature many times more. The baby was born but put out to adoption. All that could be hoped, after bringing such disgrace on his family and himself, was that Brian had well and truly learned his lesson.

The scandal brought about his premature exit from Cheltenham Grammar School, despite nine passes at GCE O-Level and Advanced-Level passes in Physics and Chemistry. For the next eighteen months, he worked variously as a shop assistant, a coalman and a trainee in the Borough Architect's office of Cheltenham Council. A boyhood passion for buses led him to a brief career on Cheltenham municipal transport, as conductor and driver. He continued to play alto sax in various trad bands, then in a rock 'n' roll combo called the Ramrods, which enjoyed some local fame until its lead singer went away on honeymoon and choked to death while eating a chip.

In 1961, Brian made a second girl pregnant. Her name was Pat Andrews: she had met Brian at the Aztec coffee bar during one of his spells of unemployment. He had left home by now and was living with a friend named Dick Hattrell at a flat in Cheltenham's art college district. This time, he seemed resigned to marrying the girl he had put 'in the club'. After the baby was born, he visited her in hospital, bringing a vast bouquet of flowers he had bought by selling some of his precious LPs. On his insistence, the baby was named Julian, after the jazz musician Julian 'Cannonball' Adderley.

Brian did not marry Pat Andrews. Instead, shortly after his conversation with Alexis Korner, he took off for London suddenly, accompanied by Dick Hattrell, to start a job his father had found for him with a firm of opticians. Lewis and Louisa Jones heard no more from him until he had become nationally notorious.

He continued to write to Pat Andrews, assuring her he still loved her and would be sending for her and the baby soon. Pat grew increasingly restive after learning he had several girlfriends in London. Finally, one day in 1962, she bundled Julian Mark in her arms and, with just one pound note in her purse, set off from Cheltenham by long-distance bus to track the baby's father down.

He had left even his name behind in Cheltenham. It was not Brian Jones but 'Elmo Lewis' who made his first guest appearance with Blues Incorporated at the Ealing club. He had changed instruments, too, from alto sax to electric guitar, a brand-new, shiny Gibson, bought with money half saved, half stolen, and mastered by his usual blend of intuition, willpower and desire.

No greater contrast could have been imagined between the middle-aged, rather beery-looking blues sidesman and the boy who stepped up beside Alexis in his neat Italian suit, holding the shiny new Gibson with one finger pointed stiff across its pearled fretboard. His debut was the Elmore James classic Dust My Blues. In his West London bedsitter, he had taught himself to play it exactly as James did, with a metal 'slide', swooping the metal bar along the guitar neck to lengthen each note into almost a second angry, sarcastic voice. The sudden appearance of Pat Andrews and baby Julian had only temporarily interrupted the transfiguration of Elmore into Elmo.

Even then, Alexis remembered, his stage presence was subtly but unmistakably flavoured with aggression. The fact that he stood absolutely still somehow intensified an air of challenge to all comers, even as his eyes remained studiously downcast, his wide mouth pursed in virginal tranquillity. 'He'd learned how to *bait* an audience, long before anything like that occurred to Mick. You should have seen those kids' reaction when Brian picked up a tambourine and gave it one tiny little shake in their faces.'

Even the Korners, his best London friends, knew almost nothing of Brian beyond what he inadvertently betrayed. He told them nothing of his home or family, and only under gravest sufferance mentioned the detested word 'Cheltenham'. Alexis and Bobbie, as surrogate parents, came to realize in time that frustration and unhappiness of an abnormal depth lay beneath Brian's driving wish to become famous by any means whatever.

He had abandoned his traineeship as an optician by now, and had a job as an electrical-appliance salesman at Whiteley's department store in Queensway, just a block away from the Korners' flat in Moscow Road. Alexis would sometimes see him after work, crossing the road to meet a girl waiting reproachfully for him in the doorway to the MacFisheries shop. Though Pat Andrews and the baby had moved into Brian's tiny Notting Hill bedsitter, she saw little more of him now than she had in Cheltenham. Eventually, she was forced to take a part-time job to support the child Brian now scarcely acknowledged as his.

To the Korners and the Ealing club crowd, he presented the aspect of a young bachelor, interested only in clothes and in forming a blues band that would take the world by storm. Each time he arrived at the Ealing club he seemed to have a new suit, a new tab-collar shirt, a new bouffant-haired girlfriend admiringly in tow. The money for both, more often than not, would have come from Pat Andrews's minuscule pay packet or from robbing the till in Whiteley's electrical department.

He stayed always one jump ahead of retribution, buoyed up by belief in his destiny and by that way he had of looking as if butter wouldn't melt in his mouth. When Brian fixed anyone with his big baby eyes and spoke in his soft, lisping, well-brought-up voice, it was impossible to imagine such chaos accumulating behind him. 'He had a way of talking that was all his own,' Alexis Korner said. 'It was a most beautiful mixture of good manners and rudeness.'

Ostensibly still living with Pat, Julian and Dick Hattrell, he contrived to lead a semi-nomadic life in London and outside, travelling from town to town, reconnoitring the music clubs, sitting in with local groups in the hope of finding musicians for a band of his own. One of his regular haunts was Guildford, where he would play at the Wooden Bridge Hotel with a scratch band called Rhode Island Red and the Roosters, featuring a pale and – it then seemed – deeply unpromising guitarist named Eric Clapton.

In Oxford, a city catacombed with student-run jazz and blues clubs, he became friends with an English undergraduate named Paul Pond who led a blues group called Thunder Odin's Big Secret. Paul Pond subsequently became Paul Jones, singer with the Manfred Mann group, 'Brian was *terribly* smart in those days,' Jones says. 'Italian box jacket, winklepicker shoes, never a hair out of place. Whenever he passed through Oxford, he'd sleep on my couch. I remember waking up one morning to hear this awful wheezing and snorting from the next room. Brian was lying on the couch, hardly able to breathe. He gasped out that he'd got asthma and had left his inhaler at the party we'd both been to the night before. I had to jump on my bike and go dashing off to get it back for him.'

After sitting in with Thunder Odin's Big Secret a few times, Brian decided that 'P. P. Pond' was the blues partner he needed. The two made a tape which impressed Alexis Korner so much he gave them the job of interval band at the Ealing club. It happened that P. P. Pond was singing Dust My Blues, accompanied by Elmo Lewis on slide guitar, when Mick Jagger, Keith Richards and Dick Taylor walked through the door together.

On Keith especially, the effect was instant hero worship, heightened by Keith's tendency to mix up one name with another. 'It's Elmore James,' he kept whispering to the others. 'It is, man – really! It's fuckin' Elmore James!'

They met up with Brian, afterwards and, over half pints of beer, talked blues for the rest of the night. To the Dartford boys, he seemed a raffish figure, only a year older than Mick and Keith but already a 'semi-pro' and – it emerged – the father of a baby. Keith remembers how, at close quarters, Brian's slight body seemed to thicken on his short and powerful legs. 'He was like a little Welsh bull,' Keith says. 'He was broad, and he looked very tough.'

That first conversation produced only an exchange of views. Brian, interested mainly in jazz-influenced blues, had not yet discovered Chuck Berry. He listened intently to what Keith told him about Berry and Jimmy Reed. He made it clear, though, that his ambitions went somewhat higher than Alexis Korner's part-time student vocalist and a red-nosed, pimply guitarist whose only public appearance to date had been in the garden of a Bexleyheath council house.

The partnership between Elmo Lewis and P. P. Pond lasted only for that one engagement. Paul Pond returned to Oxford to resume his studies and await his destiny with Manfred Mann. Elmo Lewis, on the lookout for partners again, placed an advertisement in *Jazz News*, Soho's club information sheet, grandly inviting prospective sidesmen to audition with him in the back room of a Berwick Street pub, the Bricklayer's Arms.

The first recruit, Ian Stewart, arrived by racing cycle, looking anything but the part of the blues pianist he claimed to be. Thick-set and muscular, with a long, pugnacious jaw, he entered the rehearsal room in leather shorts, carrying a pork pie he had bought for his lunch. When he sat at the piano, however, all such visual reservations vanished. Pumping with one burly leg, he could make even those nicotine-yellowed keys give out the hectic, tinny airs of ragtime and barrel-house. He then sat back, took out his pork pie and began to eat it nonchalantly.

'Stew' became the nucleus of Brian's group, together with an accomplished solo guitarist, Geoff Bradford. Over the next few days, Mick Jagger, Keith Richards and Dick Taylor also drifted in and auditioned to Brian's satisfaction. Stew recognized them from the Ealing club, but rated none of them as musicians in his or Bradford's class. Tough and short-spoken as he was, there was something about Keith, especially, that put him on his guard. 'I think Keith was very shy in those days. Mick had got very friendly with Brian, and that seemed to make Keith edgy and uncomfortable.'

Soon there were arguments between Geoff Bradford, a pure blues guitarist in the Muddy Waters style, and Keith, the Chuck Berry acolyte. Bradford refused to have anything to do with 'rock 'n' roll rubbish' like Roll Over Beethoven and Sweet Little Sixteen, and walked out, never to return. By this time, Elmo Lewis, the three Dartford boys and the lantern-jawed Stew had found enough in common to carry on together.

Practice sessions at the Bricklayer's Arms took place three times a week, even though the embryo – and untitled – group still had no prospect of a booking. 'It was a seven o'clock start, and we'd all be there sharp at seven,' Ian Stewart remembered. 'The one you could never depend on was Brian. He'd suddenly disappear for a few days, then he'd turn up again and want to get another rehearsal going. I never really trusted Brian – mainly because he was always saying, 'Trust me, Stew.'

The solid Stew had a steady daytime job as a shipping clerk with Imperial Chemical Industries in Buckingham Gate. His first impression of Mick and Keith was of semi-vagrants, permanently broke, shabby and ravenous. Mick had no money but his seven pound per week student grant, plus the few shillings he got for singing with Alex. Keith, at the point of expulsion from Sidcup Art College, was entirely dependent on handouts from his mother. 'They looked like they were going to starve together. But Mick *was* rather better off. Every so often, he'd leave Keith and go off to a slightly better caff. Mick always was very fond of his stomach.'

The first spark of originality in the group was struck by spontaneous interaction between Brian on his Gibson guitar and Keith on his Hofner. They would play, not as lead and subordinate rhythm, but as a duet, matching one another solo for solo, merging in a natural two-amp harmony, one zigzagging down the bass notes as the other climbed into treble register. This emergence of a 'two-guitar band' seemed an infinitely more exciting prospect than the skinny LSE student who sat about patiently, awaiting his chance to sing. Even then, in the trio of Mick, Keith and Brian, the joining of two inexorably left the third one out in the cold.

The sound they made could be heard in the main pub and, one night, fell on appreciative ears. Later, in the bar, a middle-aged man came up and introduced himself by visiting card as 'David Norris, Artists' Representative, Cockfosters'. He told them he'd liked what he'd heard, and could get them some engagements in ballrooms and dance halls – perhaps even at military bases on the Continent – provided they got themselves some decent instruments and stage suits. Mr Norris, for his pains, was firmly snubbed. All five had vowed they would never sell out their music to the commercial world, even if it meant they never got a single engagement.

Alexis Korner remained the only real star in the blues firmament. And, in the summer of 1962, it seemed as if Korner's meteoric career was about to leave Mick Jagger behind. Blues Incorporated had been offered their first nationwide broadcast, on the BBC Light Programme's *Jazz Club*. There were, however, two drawbacks. The first was that the BBC appearance, on July 12, clashed with Korner's regular Thursday booking at the Marquee. The second was that the BBC, with typical frugality, would pay for five musicians only. Korner must therefore shed the most dispensable one in his line-up, the vocalist.

Jagger did not mind being dropped. He was, on the contrary, anxious for Korner to seize this chance to bring blues to a national audience. It was arranged that the Marquee date should be filled by Korner's original Ealing vocalist, Long John Baldry. For an intermission band, the Marquee's manager, Harold Pendleton, agreed to give a chance to the group which had been rehearsing at the Bricklayer's Arms, though with so little hope it did not yet have a name.

The engagement was sufficiently important to merit a paragraph in the July 11 issue of *Jazz News*.

> Mick Jagger, R & B vocalist, is taking a rhythm and blues group into the Marquee tomorrow night while Blues Inc. is doing its Jazz Club gig.
>
> Called 'The Rolling Stones' ('I hope they don't think we're a rock and roll outfit,' says Mick), the line-up is: Jagger (vocals), Keith Richards, Elmo Lewis (guitars), Dick Taylor (bass), 'Stew' (piano) and Mick Avory (drums).

The name was chosen by Brian, in honour of the Muddy Waters song Rolling Stone. Ian Stewart, for one, objected strongly to it. 'The Rolling Stones – I said it was terrible! It sounded like the name of an Irish show band, or something that ought to be playing at the Savoy.' Mick Avory, the drummer they had recruited, felt equally dubious, but accepted – as the others did – that, since Brian had formed the group, he could call it what he liked.

So on July 12, 1962, with a playing order written on a page of Ian Stewart's pocket diary, the six Rolling Stones faced their first audience. Mick wore a sweater, Brian a cord jacket and Keith a skimpy dark suit which left his shirt collar and cuffs exposed like the surplice of the angelic choirboy he formerly had been. Behind them, Dick Taylor, Ian Stewart and Mick Avory glanced at one another ominously. 'You could hear people saying "Rolling Stones . . . Rolling *Stones* . . ."' Dick Taylor remembers, '"Ah . . . rock 'n' roll, are they . . ." Before we'd played a note, we could feel the hostility.'

Britain in 1962 was a nation still predominantly interested in recovering from 1939. The only generation that mattered was the one which had survived the war and its scarcely less uncomfortable aftermath, inspired by a common belief that one day butter would cease to be rationed; that coupons would no longer be needed to buy clothing or chocolate. These miracles had come to pass – and more. In British homes, as in American ones seen on the cinema screen, there were now TV sets, washing machines, garages containing cars with fins. There were transistor radios, cocktail cabinets and 'genuine champagne perry'. Harold Macmillan, prime minister since the Suez Crisis, could be believed when he told the country, 'You've never had it so good.' Largely through that powerful superstition, government remained firmly in the hands of an elderly Edwardian whose winged white hair and drooping moustache gave him the appearance of a dilapidated but complacent sea lion.

The decade which still had not defined itself in 1962 was actually starting to form in 1955, with early sightings of that problematical new species, the 'teenager'. It was a species, however, which for the next five years caused little profound effect on

British life. For it sprang almost wholly from what was still dismissively called the 'working' class. Rock 'n' roll music, skiffle, long hair and coffee bars were condemned all in one as a deviation of the lower proletariat. 'Pop', the rock sound watered down, figured not much higher in the social register. Its most successful British exponent, Cliff Richard, owed his survival to having exchanged the grubby aura of the Rocker for that of a conventional show-business personality.

Change was coming, even now, in a battered van making its way to London from the unregarded northern city of Liverpool. In June 1962, the head of an obscure record label, Parlophone, gave an audition to four young Liverpool musicians who had, up to then, been rejected by all the major companies. Their first record – chosen with difficulty from an eccentric and uncommercial repertoire – was not released until the following October. The record was called Love Me Do; the group was the Beatles.

For the Rolling Stones, in October 1962, the most pressing question was whether they could survive another week. It scarcely mattered that their debut at the Marquee Club had gone better than any of them dared hope. To the club's jazz and pure blues crowd, merely the sight of Dick Taylor's bass guitar had been reason enough to detest them. But there had also been a contingent of Mods, up on the town from Wembley or Shepherd's Bush, who loved Chuck Berry and Bo Diddley as much as Keith did, and – being Mods – had conclusively drowned out the jazz fans' disapproval. That endeared the new group still less to Harold Pendleton, who ran the Marquee on behalf of the National Jazz League, and loudly disapproved of their music, their clothes, their attitude and – as it seemed to Ian Stewart – their perversely ill-chosen name.

The only further bookings Harold Pendleton would offer them were as dogsbodies, filling in for other bands that had not turned up. Often, after booking them, Pendleton would telephone Brian Jones and say he didn't want them after all. On the nights when they did make it to the Marquee stage, Pendleton would indulge in sarcasm at their expense. Keith Richards was a frequent target, gawky and shy, with his skinny black suit and pimple-chapped face, playing the Chuck Berry guitar riffs that Pendleton so despised.

The slights they continually received from the jazz faction led Brian Jones, in his capacity as leader, to compose a long, erudite letter to *Jazz News*, complaining of 'the pseudo-intellectual snobbery that unfortunately contaminates the Jazz scene . . . It must be apparent,' Brian continued weightily, 'that Rock 'n' Roll has a far greater affinity for r & b than the latter has for Jazz, insofar that Rock is a direct corruption of Rhythm and Blues whereas Jazz is Negro music on a different plane, intellectually higher but emotionally less intense . . .'

Harold Pendleton had some cause for complaint. The Rolling Stones, though top-heavy with guitarists and their non-playing singer, could persuade no drummer to throw in his lot with them. While anyone could buy a guitar and strum at it, a drummer, with his vast capital investment of fifty pounds or more, conferred instant professionalism and permanence. Mick Avory, on that first Marquee night, had sat in only as a favour. All the drummers they had tried since then were from jazz bands, unable or unwilling to find the r & b backbeat. The only exception was Charlie Watts, Blues Incorporated's part-time drummer, who sat in also with a Soho band called Blues by Six. Charlie, despite his jazz background and long, glum face, always gave them just what they wanted. But he seemed altogether too well set up and prosperous to consider joining them for good. 'We were all a bit in awe of Charlie then,' Keith says. 'We thought he was much too expensive for us.'

Brian Jones's double life as a reluctant family man and fancy-free London bachelor took on a new complexity, late that summer, when he, Mick Jagger and Keith Richards rented a flat together in Edith Grove, Chelsea. The three shared two rooms halfway up a shabby house racked by the noise of lorries thundering through to Fulham Road. The flat was squalid even by London bedsitter standards, with its damp and peeling wallpaper, grubby furniture, filthy curtains and naked light bulbs that functioned at the behest of a single, iron-clad electric coin meter. The lavatory was communal, on the staircase to the flat above. Those who visited it after dark did so with a supply of newspaper, matches and a candle. Keith spoke of buying a revolver, so that he could sit there and shoot at the rats.

The minuscule rent was paid by the pooling of Mick Jagger's student grant with Brian's wage as a shop assistant at Whiteley's. Keith – apart from one brief stint as a Christmas relief postman – contrived to remain unencumbered by any job but playing his guitar. His contribution was a supply of food parcels sent up from Dartford by his mother. Doris Richards would also descend on the flat once a week and take away mounds of dirty underwear and shirts to wash.

To help with the rent, they found a fourth tenant – a young printer whom they knew only as 'Phelge'. 'He was the sort of madman you'd meet around Chelsea then,' Keith says. 'You'd walk in through the front door and there would be Phelge, standing at the top of the stairs with his underpants on his head.'

For Mick, the Edith Grove flat was a chance to break free of the constraints of home and his mother's reproaches for the opportunities he was wasting. He remained, even so, primarily an economics student, tacitly acknowledging that he must one day give up blues singing to work for his degree. Up all night at the Marquee, and Chelsea's perpetual bottle parties, he would still go off next morning to the London School of Economics in Aldwych. His father's waning influence could not altogether remove the habit of exercise. The pale, languid Chelsea layabout still turned out at regular intervals to play soccer in the LSE second eleven.

Keith, jobless and almost penniless, spent most of his days at the flat with no other company than the coin meter and his guitar. Brian, at the outset, still had a job at Whiteley's and, it was presumed, an alternative home with Pat Andrews and the baby. The Whiteley's job vanished when Brian was caught pilfering from the cash register. The link with Pat and the baby was similarly broken – although his friend, Dick Hattrell, remained a faithful follower. After that, Brian also had nothing to do, and would sit around the Edith Grove flat all day with Keith, practising their guitar duets, working out on the harmonica he had almost mastered and plotting where their next meal was coming from. He taught Keith the trick, learned in his Oxford wanderings, of creeping into neighbours' flats on the morning after bottle parties, collecting all the empty beer bottles and returning them to a pub or off-licence to collect the twopence deposits.

A tiny trickle of money came from dates arranged by Brian at venues he had already reconnoitred on his travels outside London. The venues were mostly weekend dances, put on in church halls or suburban sports pavilions. The fee – seldom more than a couple of pounds a night – would be received by Brian, then shared among the other five. They did not know, since Brian thought it not worth mentioning, that he had invariably obtained an extra payment for himself as their leader and – he would also say – their manager and booking agent. Brian, in those days, was always ahead by a tiny, surreptitious percentage.

One of their regular dates was at St Mary's Parish Hall, in Hotheley Road, Richmond, playing in alternation with a group from Shepherd's Bush called the High Numbers, later transfigured into the Who. Another was in a dilapidated wooden dance hall on Eel Pie Island in the River Thames at Twickenham, crossed by a footbridge that levied a sixpenny toll. They would go there by public transport, by bus or by tube, accompanied by Dick Hattrell, whom Brian seemed able to persuade to do almost anything. Hattrell acted as their road manager until he left London for a stint of part-time soldiering in the Territorial Army.

At the Marquee, meanwhile, Harold Pendleton's sarcasm continued unabated. Even Cyril Davis, who had liked the Stones at first, now joined the jazzers against them, brusquely sacking them from a bill on which his band was headlining. No one in those days knew Keith Richards well enough to recognize the warning signs. One evening, late that autumn, after carefully considering something Harold Pendleton had said to him, Keith picked up his guitar like a caveman's club and swung it at Pendleton's head.

After that, there could be no more Marquee dates for a while. There was even less hope at Ken Colyer's Studio 51 or Giorgio Gomelsky's Piccadilly Club, where they had had one disastrous flop. The Rolling Stones therefore decided to do what Alexis Korner had when snobbery and prejudice were threatening to extinguish Blues Incorporated. They set out to start a club and a following of their own.

The club was a peripatetic one, convened on Saturday nights or Sunday afternoons in a succession of pubs in Sutton, Richmond, Putney and Twickenham. Each date along the meridian would display the same laconic poster: 'Rhythm and Blues with the Rollin' Stones [sic]. Admission 4s.' Fortunately, Ian Stewart owned a van as well as his racing bike, and could chauffeur them and their equipment to pubs in places even further distant, like Windsor, Guildford and Maidenhead. Stew proved a sterling hand at unloading guitar cases and amps, even though he might not himself always get the chance to play. 'If there was no piano, I'd just settle down in the van and go to sleep. I *did* have to be up the next morning to go to work at ICI.'

The lack of a permanent drummer continued to be vexing. Mick Avory, who sat in with them most often, had little natural feel for r & b. Carlo Little, from Cyril Davies's group, whom they liked much better, had more pressing extra-curricular work with

Screaming Lord Sutch and the Savages. Unable to approach Charlie Watts, they reluctantly settled for a boy called Tony Chapman, who had played in several semi-pro rock 'n' roll groups. But Chapman, a commercial traveller, wasn't always reliable and was frequently out of town on business trips.

Just before Christmas came another setback. Dick Taylor, their bass player, announced he was quitting to begin a course at the Royal College of Art. The others asked Tony Chapman if he knew any bass guitarists looking for work. Chapman said he might know someone, an ex-colleague of his in a conventional pop group called the Cliftons. It was arranged that Tony Chapman's friend should come for an audition with Brian, Keith and Mick at their local Chelsea pub, the Wetherby Arms, one cold, snowy day in December.

Bill Perks had always hated his family name, and wished he could change it to something more in keeping with his nature and ambitions. His grandfather Perks, he knew, had done the same thing fifty years earlier when fighting illegally as a bare-fist pugilist. 'And when he got older and used to breed racing pigeons, he still went on using another name,' the metamorphosed Bill Wyman says. 'He always raced his pigeons under the name of Jackson.'

The son born to William and Kathleen Perks on October 24, 1936, showed little sign of his ultimate destiny for almost the first quarter of his life. As a child, he was thoughtful, steady, quiet, rather pious. His mother remembers how he would spend hours in his bedroom, in Blenheim Road, Penge, just reading the Bible. At Beckenham Grammar School he was proficient in art and mathematics and a useful athlete. With his precise mind and prodigious memory, he would have been natural university material if born just one decade later. Then, amid Britain's post-war and class-ridden chill, the best a bright working-class boy could hope for was respectable clerkship. His father, a bricklayer out of doors in all weathers, was delighted to think Bill might get a comfortable office job.

His first employment was with the City Tote, a firm of multiple bookmakers in London's West End. He was then called up for two years' service as a clerk in the Royal Air Force. Some of that time he spent in West Germany, at an RAF station near Bremen, where he heard rock 'n' roll music for the first time over the American Forces Network. He remembers, too, what a liking he developed for a fellow serviceman called Lee Wyman, not realizing it was the surname that really appealed to him.

He already thought of himself as Bill Wyman when, demobbed from the RAF, he took a job as storekeeper with an engineering firm in Streatham, south London. He organized the stores with fastidious efficiency, cataloguing the stock and recording its level by a neat system of dockets and coloured strings. In 1959, he married a girl named Diane whom he had met at a dance in Beckenham, and moved with her into a flat above a Penge garage.

His first guitar, brought during his RAF service, was a Spanish model, so badly made he could hardly hold down the strings. He played with scratch groups, in and out of the service, for the next year or two. 'I was never much of a guitarist. I was no good at playing chords. That's why I switched to bass as soon as they started coming in.'

In December 1962 he was already semi-professional, playing bass regularly in the Cliftons and, occasionally, in stage shows presented by the great pop impresario Larry Parnes. He had risen as high as backing Parnes's discovery Dickie Pride, a tiny youth then billed as 'Britain's Little Richard'. 'We had to wear stage make-up . . . little suits all the same. Horrible, they were. You always knew they'd been passed on to you from someone else.'

It was, therefore, with no great hope or expectation that Bill Wyman walked into the Wetherby Arms in Chelsea and beheld the group with whom Tony Chapman had arranged for him to audition. His first thought – tinged with working-class resentment – was that they looked off-puttingly 'bohemian' and 'arty'. They, on their side, felt no instant rapport with the hollow-cheeked, unsmiling newcomer, seven years older than Mick and Keith, and whose reserved manner suggested the superiority of a bass player who had once accompanied Dickie Pride.

What made him desirable was the sheer magnificence of his equipment. With his bass guitar, he hauled in *two* enormous black and gold amplifiers. Even the one he airily called his 'spare' was a Vox 850, bigger than Keith Richards had ever seen outside a shop window. Plugging in his bass, he indicated the 850 and said, 'One of you can put your guitar through that.'

'I wasn't sure – I thought I'd just try things out with them for a bit,' Bill says, 'even though I did think they looked too bohemian. Not long afterwards, they decided they wanted to get rid of Tony Chapman as drummer and bring in Charlie Watts. Tony came to me and said, "Well, that's it, Bill. We can form a new group of our own now." I said, 'No – I think I'm all right where I am." I think I made a wise decision.

Initially, it seemed far from wise. Bill Wyamn's recruitment to 'the Rollin' Stones' coincided with heavy snowfalls, which, as they grew steadily worse, prevented them from getting to all but a scattered few of their suburban dates. At those they did manage to reach, attendance was disastrously reduced. Even their large Eel Pie Island following seemed reluctant to brave the toll bridge over the fast-freezing Thames. Wyman, perched on his amplifier rim, a cigarette dangling from his mouth, regretted his folly in exchanging Larry Parnes's stage shows for arty types like this, who did not even stand up to play, but sat on chairs or stools in a semicircle behind their head-shaking vocalist.

The winter, it turned out, was Britain's worst for more than a hundred years. The entire country became submerged in a featureless white plain, swept by unremittingly savage cold which turned milk to creamy granite and made beer explode spontaneously in its bottles. From December to mid-February, the weather was Britain's sole talking point – apart from a brief scandal, reported from Carlisle just after Christmas, when a group called the Beatles was ejected from a Young Conservatives dance for the impossibly tasteless offence of arriving in black leather jackets.

At Edith Grove, the water pipes were now all frozen solid: Mick, Keith, Brian and Phelge could not wash or pull the lavatory chain. What puny room heaters they had barely took the edge off the biting cold. Bill Wyman, the settled married man, could hardly believe the squalor of the conditions. 'They weren't cooking – just living on pork pies and cups of instant coffee,' Bill says. 'I used to get through pounds, just feeding that electric meter of theirs.'

Their diet was mainly potatoes and eggs, which Brian and Keith would pilfer from Fulham Road grocery shops, and stale bread scavenged from the debris of parties given by other tenants in the house. Bill Wyman, when he dropped by, would bring food and cigarettes as well as shillings for their ravenous coin meter. Once a week, Ian Stewart would hand them a supply of six-shilling (30p) luncheon vouchers, bought up at a shilling each from weight-conscious secretaries in his office at ICI.

On many days, Keith remembers, it would not be worthwhile even getting out of bed. 'We hadn't got any gigs. Nothing to do. We'd spend hours at a time just making faces at each other. Brian was always the best at that. There was a particularly horrible one he could do by pulling his eyes down at the corners and sticking his fingers up his nostrils. He called it "doing a Nanker".' Even when every pipe in the flat was frozen, Brian somehow managed to wash his hair every day, and find a shilling somewhere to blow-dry it into its elaborate cresting wave. He seemed, for all his fastidiousness, the most adept of them all at living rough. Even Keith did not have Brian's sublime assurance, as each frozen midday dawned outside their filthy, iced-up windows, that the wherewithal of keeping warm and not starving could always be borrowed, begged or stolen.

An unexpected windfall was the reappearance of Dick Hattrell, fresh from Territorial Army camp, his £80 gratuity in his pocket, and willing as ever to do anything Brian told him. Within a week, Brian had annexed every penny of Hattrell's money for meals, drinks, even a brand-new guitar. On Brian's orders, Hattrell took off his army greatcoat and handed it to the shivering Keith. He would obediently follow them to their local hamburger bar, hand them more money and, at Brian's command, stand patiently in the snow until they came out again. When Dick Hattrell's money ran out, so did his welcome at the flat. One night as he lay in bed, Brian threatened to electrocute him with a guitar lead. Hattrell fled into the snow, terrified, wearing only his underpants. 'He wouldn't come back for an hour, he was so scared of Brian,' Keith says. 'When they finally did bring him in, he'd turned blue.'

The new year 1963 found Britain still snowbound, with villages, towns, even whole counties cut off, most transport paralysed, all sport fixtures cancelled, a whole nation gone to ground and huddled round the fitful blue warmth of its television screen. On January 12, the Saturday night pop show *Thank Your Lucky Stars* provided its snowed-in bumper audience with the spectacle of the Beatles, in the mop-top haircuts and crew-necked suits, miming their new record Please Please Me, not with scowls and prissy dance steps like Cliff Richard's Shadows, but jigging about uninhibitedly, grinning at the camera and each other. To viewers over twenty-one, the interlude seemed no more than faintly comic. But on a million British teenagers, pent up by so much more than cold, that zesty 'Whoa yeah' chorus had an altogether different effect. By February 16, Please Please Me was number one on the *Melody Maker*'s Top Twenty chart.

The Beatles were also beginning to make regular radio

appearances on the BBC Light Programme's *Saturday Club*, giving live performances from their stage repertoire in a far-off Liverpool cellar club called the Cavern. Much of their material was rhythm and blues which they had copied from import discs brought from America to Liverpool by stewards on the trans-atlantic ships. Brian and Keith, listening to *Saturday Club*, huddled under their blankets at Edith Grove, were astonished to hear Chuck Berry and Bo Diddley songs on the stuffy BBC.

Since *Saturday Club* had a reputation for booking groups which had not yet even made a record, Brian sent off one of his prosy letters to the BBC, requesting an audition for the Stones. A fortnight later, they received a summons to report to a BBC rehearsal room. Before they set off, Brian shampooed and blow-dried his hair into a Beatle cut thicker and more eye-enveloping than the Beatles wore. 'It shocked even us a bit,' Keith says. 'He looked like a Saint Bernard with hair all over his eyes. We told him he'd have to be careful or he'd bump into things.'

The audition took place under the eye of the show's producer and of its compere, Brian Matthew. Both men based their musical judgement on the hidebound prejudices of a corporation which, for years, had banned even the phrase 'Hot Jazz' as being sexually suggestive. 'We got a letter back from the producer in the end,' Bill Wyman says. 'He said they liked us as a group but they couldn't book us because "the singer sounds too coloured".'

Wyman still did not quite know why he stayed on in the Stones, especially now that his friend Tony Chapman had left. The country-wide thaw, and consequent improvement in sub-urban club dates, only emphasized their desperate need of a regular drummer even as semi-reliable as Chapman had been. Brian's idea was to bring in Carlo Little, a bravura performer with Cyril Davis. But to Mick, Keith and Ian Stewart, there was only one possible candidate. 'One night, we all just looked at each other and that did it,' Stew says. 'We went up to Charlie Watts and said, "Right, that's it. You're in."'

The boy with the long, thin, dourly soulful face and the neat mod three-piece suit came from several social worlds away. Charlie Watts was a true Londoner, born at least within a rumour's distance of Bow Bells, and with that air peculiar to many cockneys of being older than his years. His father worked for British Railways at King's Cross station as a parcel deliveryman. His mother had formerly been a factory worker. The family lived in Islington, North London, in a house which, however modest, was ruled by Charles Sr's punctilious tidiness. 'My dad made me cover all my books with brown paper,' Charlie says, '– even my Buffalo Bill annual.' He cherished that annual, with its colour portrait of William F. Cody, looming ferociously from a Wild West that was – and remains – Charlie Watt's abiding passion.

Charlie, at twenty-one, seemed set on a promising professional career. Since leaving Harrow Art College, he had worked as a lettering and layout man for the Regent Street advertisement agency Charles Hobson and Gray. It was a prestigious and – for that time – well-paid job which Charlie was reluctant to jeopardize, even for his beloved jazz. He had, indeed, recently given up playing with Blues Incorporated for fear that too many late nights would impair the daytime steadiness of his hand.

For the Stones, it was not simply that Charlie Watts owned a handsome set of drums and played them with an unobtrusive skill that held each ramshackle blues song together like cement. He was also warmly liked by each of them. He seemed to get on best with the group's shyest and most uncertain member, Keith. Dapper as Charlie himself was, something in Keith's incorrigible raggedness stirred him to wistful admiration. He would sit for hours at Edith Grove, listening to Keith play guitar duets with Brian, listening to their accumulated wisdom concerning Chuck Berry B-sides and, every so often, putting another shilling in the electric meter.

The drawback, in Charlie's eyes, was that he loved jazz above everything, and saw no prospect, via these hard-up student types, of realizing his ambition to visit New York and see Birdland where Charlie Parker used to play. At the time the Stones pounced on him, he was also considering the offer of a regular place in the far more respectable Blues By Six. 'He came to me, agonizing about it,' Alexis Korner said. 'I told him I thought the Rolling Stones were likely to get more work than the others, in the long run.' So at last, with that resigned shrug – that look of placidly expecting the worst – Charlie Watts was in.

On Sunday evenings in the sedate Thames-side borough of Richmond, crowds of teenage boys in corduroy jackets and peg-top trousers, accompanied by white-faced, bare-kneed, shivering girls, could be seen emerging from the railway station and streaming up a narrow passageway by the side of a Victorian pub. At the end, under an improvised sign, CRAWDADDY CLUB, a black-bearded young man, somewhat like Captain Kidd in the comic books, stood guard on the door into the pub's mirror-lined committee room, chaffing his customers in an accent exotically and indeterminately foreign. 'Any girls who want to come in . . .' Giorgio Gomelsky would say, 'we're so full, you'll have to sit on your boyfriends' shoulders.'

Giorgio was a twenty-nine-year-old Russian emigré, born in Georgia, exiled to Switzerland, educated in Italy and Germany, and now one of the best-known figures on the London jazz scene. He had worked for Chris Barber in the Fifties, helping to set up the National jazz league and, later, organizing the first of the League's annual Jazz Festivals at Richmond Athletic Ground. He had discovered blues while working as a courier, escorting American blues singers on from London to Continental dates booked for them by Barber's organization. 'Sonny Boy Williamson lived in my house for six months. I travelled all over with him. We were in Liverpool when the Cavern was still only a Trad Jazz club.'

In the early Sixties, Giorgio combined the role of assistant film editor and West End Jazz Club manager, running the old

Mississippi Room, with earnest attendance at classes to study Stanislavsky's Method acting. Among this fellow students in the class was a young Irishman named Ronan O'Rahilly, whose family was rumoured to own the greater part of County Cork, and who was also trying to crash into the London entertainment scene by managing Alexis Korner's Blues Incorporated.

Gomelsky's first blues club was the Piccadilly, set up on a Russian shoestring in the old Cy Laurie folk cellar. The Rolling Stones played there just once, shortly before Harold Pendleton and Cyril Davies squeezed them out of the Marquee. Much as Gomelsky liked them as individuals, he thought their playing 'abominable'. Counting Mick Jagger's younger brother, Chris, only twenty or so people turned up that night to see them.

In early 1963, the Piccadilly Club had closed and Giorgio needed a new venue that could be hired with the single five-pound note he had in his pocket. He knew the landlord of the Station Hotel in Kew Road, Richmond, and knew that the pub's substantial back room had not been in use since its regular trad jazz sessions had petered out. 'I said, "Let me try blues here, just for one night . . ."' The club was called the Crawdaddy, after a Bo Diddley song, Do the Crawdaddy. Sessions took place on Sunday nights within the Station Hotel's licensing hours, 7 to 10:30 p.m. Its first resident attraction was the Dave Hunt Group, featuring Ray Davies – who would one day lead the Kinks – and playing in Louis Jordan's 1940s 'jump band' style.

Brian Jones had long been pestering Giorgio to do something to help the Rolling Stones. 'He had that little speech impediment – kind of a lisp. It used to be part of his charm. "Come and lithen to us, Giorgio," he'd plead with me. "Oh, Giorgio, *pleathe* get us some gigs."'

Since their first disastrous tryout at the Piccadilly Club, Giorgio had seen the Stones again – at the Red Lion in Sutton – and had noticed a vast improvement. 'But what could I do? Dave Hunt's group already had the Richmond gig.

'It was the weather, really, that got them their chance. Dave Hunt's band couldn't make it, because of the snow – and anyway, I didn't go so much for that jump-band stuff Dave was playing. So, Monday, I rang Ian Stewart – it was so funny: to get the Stones you had to go through to ICI. I said, "Tell everyone in the band you guys are on next Sunday." '

That first Sunday night when the Rolling Stones played the Crawdaddy instead of Dave Hunt's group, attendance was disastrously reduced. 'I even went through to the main pub to try to round some more customers up,' Giorgio says. 'Anyone who'd buy a ticket was allowed to bring in another person for nothing.'

Giorgio himself stood in the half-empty room, watching a group that, in the few weeks since their Red Lion date, had changed almost beyond recognition. The principal change was Brian Jones with his new, heaped, yellow Beatle cut, coaxing and caressing the blues harp in his cupped hands to produce sounds like silvery minnows darting in and deftly out of Keith's guitar riffs. Another change was the boy in the dapper three-piece suit, seated behind his drums with all the pleasure of a convict trying out an electric chair, yet playing with an impeccable, light-handed touch that pulled every loose thread together and closed up every crack. Everything had come right behind the lead singer who was so far from right, but compulsively wrong, in the sweater that slipped off one shoulder like a teagown, his smear of a mouth parroting a black man's words as his opaque eyes searched for his reflection in the mirrors all round him. That snowy Sunday night, behind a Thames-side pub, where bottles clashed into basketwork skips and feathered darts thudded against targets, the Stones began to be brilliant.

Within three weeks, they had attracted a huge following, of whom r & b enthusiasts were only a minor part. Richmond, Twickenham and Surbiton on a Sunday night offered little enough excitement of any kind. The larger and larger crowds that converged on the Station Hotel and flooded down its side passageway contained samples of every teenage faction that had ever done battle on Brighton or Margate beach. There were Mods in high-button suits, newly dismounted from Lambretta scooters. There were black-leather Rockers, in studs and cowboy boots. Unified by the bond of the polo-neck, there were art students and shop assistants and well-brought-up boys and girls from middle-class riverside homes at Putney, Hammersmith and Strand-on-the-Green. 'And do you know – there was never one fight in that place,' Gomelsky says. 'All that glass on the walls, and not even a mirror broken.'

At first, the Crawdaddy crowd behaved like jazz fans, merely standing and watching the Stones in the red-spotlit dusk. Then one night, Giorgio's young assistant, Hamish Grimes, jumped up on a table top and began to leap and flail his arms with the music like a dervish. From Hamish's impromptu outburst there evolved a dance peculiar to the Crawdaddy Club, partly derived from the Twist and the Hully-Gully but unique in that it could be performed by single males or even pairs of males, locked in a strange, crablike embrace, each gripping the other's elastic-sided ankles. The climax of each Stones session was a Bo Diddley song, either Do the Crawdaddy or Pretty Thing, when, at Giorgio's encouragement, the whole 300 would form a solid mass of corduroy, op-art strips and red-spotlit shirt collars, jumping and gyrating together for as long as twenty minutes at a time.

Giorgio Gomelsky became the Rolling Stones' first manager, mainly through his own reluctance to be considered anything so bourgeois. 'It was always a *partnership*. I used to divide the door receipts from each Sunday equally with them. They would help me keep the club going. For instance, we never paid to advertise the Crawdaddy Club. The Stones and I would put illegal fly posters all over. I got them printed for four pounds a thousand, and the Stones mixed up the paste in the bath at Edith Grove.'

From the moment they began pulling in the crowds at Richmond, Giorgio had been urging his contacts in the London music press to come to Richmond and see the Stones perform. He also began shooting 35mm film of them onstage at the Crawdaddy and arranged for them to make a soundtrack of two Bo Diddley songs at a small studio in Morden. It was typical of the idealistic Russian that, while working to launch the Stones, he never attempted to put them under exclusive contract to himself. His advice, on the contrary, was to let no one have control over them but themselves. 'I kept telling them, "Wait. Get strong, so that you can handle all of it yourselves and don't have to ask anyone for anything. Don't run the risk of someone walking in here and taking you over." '

Giorgio, in fairness, had a somewhat larger project on his mind. Two years previously, while living in West Germany, he had visited Hamburg's sleazy St Pauli district and had seen the Beatles in their earliest incarnation as black-leather rockers, pouring out bowdlerized r & b and their own primitive compositions to an audience of whores, transvestites and merchant seamen. Watching them now, in their crew-necked suits, bobbing and frolicking on the torrents of ever wilder hysteria, Giorgio Gomelsky realized they were something more than merely the biggest pop attraction since Cliff Richard and the Shadows.

The tiny world of London impresarios soon brought Giorgio Gomelsky into contact with the Beatles' twenty-seven-year-old manager, Brian Epstein. 'I would be there when dance hall promoters rang up Epstein, offering him £50 for one appearance by the Beatles. He'd say, "I don't know . . ." and start looking in his diary. So then the promoter would offer him £60. "I don't know . . ." he'd still say. The promoter would offer £70, thinking Epstein was stalling for more money. He wasn't. He just couldn't find the right date in his diary.'

Giorgio approached Brian Epstein in his role as avant-garde movie director, proposing a film that would bring out the still unperceived wit and knockabout charm of the Beatles' offstage characters. He was now working on a rough script, helped by Ronan O'Rahilly, his fellow Method-acting student, and the jazz writer Peter Clayton. With the Beatles themselves he was on good enough terms to invite them to the Crawdaddy one Sunday after their appearance on *Thank Your Lucky Stars* at the ABC-TV studios in nearby Twickenham.

As the Stones played that night, they were astonished to see all four Beatles, in expensive leather overcoats, being escorted by Giorgio to a special vantage point beside the stage. Still more astonished were they, later, to be approached by people they looked on as big-time celebrities, and to be told in thick, pally Liverpool accents that their music was 'fab' and 'gear'. John Lennon, in particular, looked at Brian Jones with something like hero-worship. 'You really play that harmonica, don't you,' he said. 'I can't really play – I just blow and suck.'

A lengthy and amicable conversation ensued. For the Beatles, it had been a poignant experience to see a group so much like their former selves, before Brian Epstein cleaned up their music and appearance. The Stones, on their side, recognized blood brothers in the r & b cause who had only reluctantly dropped Chuck Berry in favour of original compositions the pop public increasingly demanded. It fascinated Mick Jagger, especially, to learn that John Lennon and Paul McCartney had already written more than a hundred songs together and that, after just one Top Ten hit, they had a share in their own music-publishing company. For a brief while, Mick cast aside his reserve and quizzed the Beatles closely about how much per song one could earn in royalties.

A week later, the Beatles appeared in their first major London concert, a Pop Prom run by the BBC at the Royal Albert Hall. The Rollin' Stones received front-row tickets and access to the Liverpudlians' embattled dressing room. Later, Giorgio and Brian Jones helped the Beatles' two road managers, Mal and Neil, to load their stage equipment into their van. Some girls, spotting

Brian's blond dome of hair, mistook him for a Beatle, crowded round him, despite his protests, and clamoured for autographs.

The incident, Giorgio remembers, had a transfixing effect on Brian. 'As we walked away from the Albert Hall, down the big steps at the back, he was almost in a daze. "That's what I want, Giorgio," he kept saying. "*That's* what I want."'

Knowing the Beatles was all very nice – but it did not help Giorgio in his efforts to interest powerful London people in a group whose venue, ten miles from the West End, might as well have been another hemisphere. For record company talent scouts, the only worthwhile journey, if not to Soho, was 200 miles north to Liverpool, in their frenzied search for new groups in the Beatles' image. It was a quest pursued with especial fervour by Decca, whose head of A & R, Dick Rowe, was celebrated as The Man Who Turned The Beatles Down. A letter from Giorgio Gomelsky about a new blues group in Surrey did not even reach Dick Rowe's in-tray.

The Stones themselves knew only one person connected with the record industry. This was a school friend of Ian Stewart's named Glyn Johns, who worked at IBC Studios in Portland Place. Part-owned by the orchestra leader Eric Robinson, IBC had very little to do with pop music. But Glyn, a talented engineer, was allowed to record any artists he thought promising. At his invitation, the Rolling Stones came to IBC and, in a single evening, recorded four songs for their stage act, including Chuck Berry's Come On.

The excitement of being in a real studio, supervised by a young engineer who was also a Crawdaddy fan, rather tailed off, since IBC carried little weight with the major record companies. A colleague of Glyn's knew someone at Decca – but on the classical music side. It seemed just more effort wasted on a world whose ears were deaf to all but the Beatles' second number one single, From Me to You.

On April 13, when the Stones' spirits were at their lowest ebb, Giorgio Gomelsky's hustling of newspapers, small as well as large, finally began to pay off. The weekly *Richmond and Twickenham Times* devoted a full page to the blues club behind the Station Hotel and its effect in taking custom from trad jazz clubs in the area. 'The Rolling Stones' – the 'g' once more reinstated – received a somewhat incidental mention: "Save for the spotlit forms of the group on the stage, the room is dark . . . A patch of light catches the sweating dancers and those who are slumped on the floor, where no chairs are provided . . .'

A few days later, Peter Jones of the *Record Mirror* succumbed to Giorgio's entreaties and agreed to give up his Sunday lunchtime to watch Giorgio's group being filmed onstage at their Richmond pub club. Jones was a prescient as well as a prolific journalist, the first to interview the Beatles in any national music paper. He watched the Stones perform on camera, and afterwards met them in the Station Hotel's saloon bar. 'They were hungry, and they were very bitter,' Peter Jones says. 'They told me no one had even been bothered before to drive ten miles out from London to see them. I promised to do my best to get a story about them into the *Record Mirror*.'

Jones was as good as his word. He persuaded the *Record Mirror*'s star reporter, Norman Jopling, to go out to Richmond with a photographer the following Sunday. Jopling – a blues and soul fanatic – was even more impressed than Peter Jones had been. 'The Stones had got the *real* r & b sound, not just a copy of it,' Jopling remembers. 'When they played a Bo Diddley number, it *sounded* like Bo Diddley. And the whole scene around them in that room was unbelievable.'

Norman Jopling's feature article in *Record Mirror*, the following Thursday, surpassed Giorgio's wildest hopes:

> As the Trad scene gradually subsides, promoters of all kinds of teen-beat entertainments have a sigh of relief that they've

found something to take its place. It's Rhythm and Blues, of course. And the number of R & B clubs that have suddenly sprung up is nothing short of fantastic.

At the Station Hotel, Kew Road, the hip kids throw themselves about to the new 'jungle music' like they never did in the more restrained days of Trad.

And the combo they writhe and twist to is called the Rolling Stones. Maybe you haven't heard of them – if you live far from London, the odds are you haven't.

But by gad you will! The Stones are destined to be the biggest group in the R & B scene, if that scene continues to flourish . . .

It was, indeed, an astounding plug for unknown musicians in a paper read throughout the tight community of agents and A & R men. As Norman Jopling recalls, the feedback was instantaneous. '*Record Mirror* hit the streets at about one p.m. in the West End. By four o'clock that afternoon, three different record companies had phoned me, saying "Where can we get hold of these guys?" ' Jopling supplied particulars, although fully aware – as Peter Jones was – that the guys had by now been well and truly got hold of.

Three

'I belong to you and you belong to me, so come on'

At the age of eleven, Andrew Loog Oldham was already incorrigibly addicted to glamour. While other boys read the *Eagle* comic or swapped matchbox labels, Oldham walked the Soho streets, breathing in with delight the mingling scents of coffee beans, salami, striptease and primitive rock 'n' roll. Glamorous as these surroundings were, they paled next to the glamour he already perceived in himself. From an even earlier age, he had visualized his own life as an epic film of which he was both the star and the rapt audience. 'It was the only way I could get to school in the morning. As I walked in through the gates, I'd see the opening credits start to roll . . .'

The name which in later years seemed so typical a product of its owner's imagination was, in fact, genuine. Andrew Loog Oldham was the son of a Dutch-American air force officer, killed on a bombing mission over Germany in 1944. Born out of wedlock, the baby received both parents' names. His Dutch origins were always faintly manifest in a pink complexion, butter-coloured hair and eyes whose myopic pallor gave Oldham, even at his most uppity and outrageous, the look of a rather studious small boy.

A private boarding school to which his widowed mother sent

him provided an early object lesson in the relation of fantasy to profit. The school – in Witney, Oxfordshire – was run by an ex-army officer, a dashing figure whose frequent absences were rumoured to be connected with vital work for the government. The head was, in fact, a prisoner on parole who moved around the country, setting up small schools, collecting fees, running up bills, then vanishing without trace. That headmaster was Andrew Loog Oldham's first lesson in the principle that, provided you had nerve and style enough, you could get away with almost anything.

In 1955, the pink-faced Hampstead schoolboy was a familiar figure among the teenage crowd at Soho's famous 2 I's coffee bar. Norah, the doorkeeper, knew him well and would let him downstairs into the skiffle cellar without paying the usual one-shilling cover charge. His taste in pop heroes was eccentric even then – Wee Willie Harris, green-haired and wizened; Vince Taylor, an early American rocker, afterwards famous in France. 'It was always the sex in rock 'n' roll that attracted me . . . the sex that most people didn't realize was there. Like the Everly Brothers. Two guys with the same kind of face, the same kind of hair. They were meant to be singing together to some girl, but really they were singing to each other.'

From the age of thirteen or so, Oldham saw himself as an amalgam of two movie roles, both portrayed by his screen idol, the suave if faintly reptilian Laurence Harvey. He wanted to be Harvey's version of Joe Lampton, ruthless working-class hero of *Room at the Top*. He wanted just as much to be the jive-talking young Jewish hustler whom Harvey played in *Expresso Bongo*, sashaying round Soho in Italian box jacket and rakish trilby hat, scouring the pasteboard streets for any quick way to a dividend.

He left Wellingborough College at sixteen with three GCE O-Levels – in English, divinity, and, he claims, rifle shooting – and at once set about making his way in the world as Laurence Harvey had shown him. His first coup was to go to Chelsea, walk into Mary Quant's clothes boutique and ask for a job in any capacity whatever. Mary Quant and her husband, Alexander Plunkett-Green, were amused by the blond-haired youth and his barefaced effrontery. They agreed to take him on as an odd-job boy, teamaker and messenger.

He worked for Mary Quant throughout the period when her plungingly simple black and white dresses, short skirts, sailor necks and oversized bows altered the look of haute couture, and of London, forever. In February 1962, the first issue of a colour supplement by the hitherto stuffy *Sunday Times* featured a Quant dress worn by a new young model, Jean Shrimpton, and photographed, not by the customary middle-aged society acolyte but by a young man, David Bailey, who came from London's East End and – still more outrageously – made no attempt to conceal it. This first 'in crowd', as defined by the *Sunday Times*, did not, of course, include anyone named Andrew Loog Oldham; still, he was happy. 'I was where I wanted to be – around stars.'

At this stage, the only way of achieving stardom himself, as his mental scenario had dictated, was to become a pop singer. The fact that he could neither sing nor play an instrument seemed hardly relevant. Over a period of months, London agents and managers would be intermittently persecuted by the same blond, bespectacled, unmusical youth, posing under such aliases as 'Chancery Laine' and 'Sandy Beach'.

By working for Mary Quant all day, and by night as a waiter at Soho's Flamingo Club, he saved enough to migrate to the French Riviera. There, for several months, he worked in sea-front bars and as an itinerant window dresser. There, too, in company with two freelance journalists, he concocted his first great money-making scheme. The plan was to kidnap a wealthy heiress. Andrew would keep her, drugged, in a flat in Monte Carlo while the journalists sold the story to the London *Daily Express*. It would give the story a piquant twist, they said, if Andrew were subsequently to marry the heiress. This he was quite willing to do. Unfortunately, the scheme foundered after the, not unwilling, girl had been taken to the Monte Carlo flat. Her father had friends in the British government, and got an official D-notice issued, prohibiting any newspaper from running the story. Andrew Loog Oldham thus failed to become nationally famous either as a kidnapper or as a cad.

Back in London, a job with the Leslie Frewin publishing house provided an entrée into the decidedly glamorous world of public relations. He left Frewin to join a PR company whose clients included the pop singer Mark Wynter. Handsome, blow-waved and insipid in the prevailing American style, Wynter was following what seemed an inexorable course from Top Twenty hit to low-budget 'exploitation' feature film. One of Oldham's jobs was to accompany him on location to Twickenham studios and share a bedroom with him at a nearby small hotel. 'Every morning, Mark used to get up very early and creep off to the bathroom to wash and shave and fix his hair. Then he'd come and get back into bed. A bit later, he'd sit up and say "Well, Andrew – time to set off for the studios." He was convinced I thought he always woke up looking like that. I thought that was great – that really *was* looking after your image.'

Two major pop impresarios, Larry Parnes and Don Arden, between them controlled all the singers and groups for whom Oldham hoped to work as publicist. Parnes ran a menagerie of exotically named singers from offices in Cromwell Road, opposite the headquarters of the Boy Scout movement (at which, in spare moments, he liked to gaze through binoculars). Don Arden, an authentically frightening figure, rivalled Larry Parnes in promoting pop package tours, cobbled from the hitmakers of the moment. Andew Loog Oldham joined Arden for a while but was fired after inviting journalists to view cinema seats which, during a particularly well-appreciated package show, had been slashed with razors and drenched with female urine.

He was by this time a well-known figure around ABC-TV's

studios in Aston Road, Birmingham, where *Thank Your Lucky Stars* was recorded. In February 1963, he stood and watched the Beatles give their first nationwide performance of Please Please Me. He later approached Brian Epstein, and offered himself as publicist for Epstein's company, NEMS Enterprises. Brian Epstein, it happened, was preparing to launch two other Liverpool acts, Gerry and the Pacemakers and Billy J. Kramer and the Dakotas. He agreed to hire Andrew Loog Oldham to promote the two groups on a monthly retainer of £25.

The arrangement was somewhat hampered by Tony Barrow, a London-based Liverpudlian already writing press releases about the Beatles and sleeve notes for their first album Brian Eptstein ordained that Barrow should concentrate on written handouts while Oldham – by now running his own PR company – dreamed up stunts to get paragraphs into the papers. The Beatles themselves, watched over with obsessive jealousy by Epstein, remained always tantalizingly out of reach. His NEMS work was for the advancement of Gerry Marsden and Billy J. Kramer, each awaiting Top Twenty success in cardboard shoes and cheap little shortie overcoats.

Oldham's journeys north, though chilly and unglamorous, brought one further big advance. In Manchester, he met Tony Calder, a young agent handling local groups like the Hollies and Wayne Fontana and the Mindbenders. Manchester groups were by now starting to benefit from London's obsession with the Mersey Sound. Tony Calder also took on Oldham as publicist for his firm, Kennedy Street Enterprises. 'It felt just like tiddlywinks. I'd already got Liverpool sewn up, with Epstein and NEMS. Now I'd got Manchester as well.'

A chance PR assignment for the American record producer Phil Spector, early in 1962, altered Oldham's conception of how he might seize his still unspecified destiny. Up to then, in pop music, celebrity had come only to performers – the singers first, then the star guitarists and, latterly, the groups. No fame, or even credit, was given to the A & R men who arranged and supervised even the biggest hit recordings. Phil Spector was the first A & R man to be as well known as the artists he recorded – to produce each three-minute disc in his individual and unmistakable style of complex multitrack effects and cavernous echo: the Spector Wall of Sound.

Phil Spector became the epitome of all Andrew Loog Oldham wished to be. His persona was that of a semi-gangster, riding round in dark-windowed limousines, protected by ugly bodyguards with bulges under their arms. While Spector was in London, Andrew Loog Oldham rode round with him, devoutly questioning him about the secret of his success. Instead of the hoped-for technical hints, Phil Spector imparted a piece of advice which Oldham at the time found rather disappointing. If Oldham ever found a group to record, Spector said, he should on no account let them use the record company's studio but should instead pay for an independent studio session and afterwards sell or lease back the tapes to the record company. That way, you had control and you had much more money.

In April 1963, the Beatles were number one in every chart with From Me to You. Gerry and the Pacemakers were Number Two with How Do You Do It? Oldham lost his retainer from NEMS Enterprises, and began looking around for something else to make up that monthly £25. Calling in at the *Record Mirror* office – a habitual haunt of his for picking up tips – he found Peter Jones enthusing over an unknown blues group whose fortunes Norman Jopling was about to change with a eulogistic article. As Oldham listened, the pop singer and the publicist faded; a brand-new incarnation of himself took shape on his mental Cinerama screen.

He drove to Richmond the very next Sunday. In the narrow passageway beside the Station Hotel, he met a boy and girl coming out into the warm spring dusk. Neither Mick Jagger nor his girlfriend Chrissie Shrimpton noticed Andrew Loog Oldham, for the simple reason that they were having a furious argument.

The Crawdaddy that night was anything but the wild spectacle Norman Jopling had described. Giorgio Gomelsky had been called away to Switzerland by the death of his father. Without Giorgio to enliven it, the club was in a torpid mood. The Stones had even resumed their old purist habit of playing seated on a ring of bar stools. 'There was no production,' Oldham says. 'It was just a blues roots thing . . . "Here I am and this is what I'm playing." Even so, I knew what I was looking at. It was Sex. And I was maybe forty-eight hours ahead of the pack.'

Suffering an uncharacteristic fit of shyness, Oldham did not approach the Stones that first night. For all his hubris, he knew he was in no position on his own to try to manage a pop group. As a PR man he could exist on the wing, using other people's office desks and telephones. As a would-be manager, he could not function unless connected to the crucial network of tour promoters, song pluggers and record company talent scouts. He realized there was no alternative – his discovery would have to be shared.

His natural first choice was the PR client who happened to be Britain's most famous pop manager. Oldham went to Brian Epstein and said he would be leaving NEMS Enterprises as he'd found this great group out at Richmond and wanted to have a shot at managing them. He offered a deal whereby, in exchange for some office space and minimal funding by NEMS, Epstein could have 50 per cent of the Rolling Stones. But Epstein felt that, with the Beatles and his other Liverpool acts, he already had enough and more to think about. He thus passed up the chance to manage what would become the two greatest supergroups of all time.

Oldham's next approach was to Eric Easton, an agent handling such middle-of-the-road acts as guitarist Bert Weedon, singer Julie Grant and the pub pianist Mrs Mills. A former electronic organist, bespectacled and quiet, he seemed the least likely of all patrons for a shaggy r & b band. None the less, he agreed to go with Oldham and see them the following Sunday night, even though it would mean missing his favourite television programme, *Sunday Night at the London Palladium.*

For a second time, Oldham watched the Stones play their 'blue-roots thing' behind their diffident, loose-lipped vocalist in his sloppy student pullover. At the end, Eric Easton, who also hired out electronic organs to Butlins holiday camps, gave Oldham a look that was only the faintest 'maybe'. Oldham approached the group's drummer, a sad-faced, smartly dressed boy, and asked who their leader was. Charlie Watts pointed to Brian Jones. Oldham remembers with what determination Brian headed him off from talking to either Mick or Keith. "Brian was a really weird shape with that big head, broad body and short legs, like a little Welsh pony. But he had incredible magnetism. He could make you focus on just his face."

There were subsequent meetings at Eric Easton's London office, at which the cautious agent said he might be able to do something for the Stones though he was making no promises. His one creative suggestion, to Oldham privately, was that Mick Jagger's voice might not be strong enough to stand the pressure of performing night after night. When Brian, as 'leader', was brought into the discussion, he seemed quite amenable to dropping Mick if necessary. But Oldham, for reasons he himself still did not quite understand, insisted that the vocalist was irreplaceable.

While Easton pondered overall strategy, Oldham applied himself to getting on friendly terms with the six Stones in a way that might have warned his older colleague of things to come. It was, indeed, the most brilliant self-selling job the nineteen-year-old had yet pulled off, expertly mixing audacity with intuition. He came on to Brian, Mick, Keith, Stew, Bill and Charlie as a London big shot who could give them anything they wanted and get anywhere they cared to go. At the same time, he was one of them, a rebel, an outsider who shared their quasi-Marxist ideals and evangelistic zeal for bringing pure blues and r & b to a wider audience. Without being able to play or sing a note, Andrew in effect joined the band.

When Giorgio Gomelsky returned from Switzerland early in May, he found that the Stones had signed an exclusive management agreement with Andrew Loog Oldham and Eric Easton. Brian Jones broke the news to Giorgio, mysteriously claiming that Oldham was a schoolfriend of his. Brian, in fact, had signed the agreement on behalf of all the Stones and had, additionally, done a private deal with Easton to receive £5 a week over and above what the others were paid in salary.

In 1962, the most unenvied figure in British pop music was Dick Rowe of Decca Records, The Man Who Turned The Beatles Down. It made no difference to remind himself – as Rowe constantly did – that his decision at the time had seemed entirely logical. Two auditions, in Liverpool, then London, had failed to detect any noticeable merit in a quartet of juvenile eccentrics singing Besame Mucho, Your Feet's Too Big and other items perversely unsuited to current teenage fashion. So, in January 1962, Dick Rowe passed on the Beatles, instead signing up a group with the altogether more desirable and commercial name of Brian Poole and the Tremeloes.

Ten months later, the calamity of Dick Rowe's decision confronted him each day of his working life. The Beatles had become the biggest thing in teenage entertainment since Elvis Presley. Dick Rowe had let them slip through his fingers and into the waiting clutches of Decca's deadly rival, EMI.

For twenty years, these two companies had controlled British popular music, producing 95 per cent of all discs on their myriad labels as well as manufacturing the wireless sets, record players – and even needles – required to bring their product to life. Of the two,

Decca seemed more wholeheartedly devoted to entertainment. The blue Decca label, the white Decca factory at Wimbledon, were synonymous with the age of the wind-up gramophone. Decca introduced the first long-playing record into Britain when EMI was still mainly an electrical company, manufacturing TV sets, radiograms and weapons systems for the then War Office.

Decca was the creation – and, substantially, the property – of Sir Edward Lewis, a white-haired, gangling man who, even on days that paid high dividends, was seldom observed to smile. For Sir Edward, recorded music was a commodity little different from soap or safety pins, and only really in tune if it harmonized with a good showing on the Stock Exchange, Sir Edward Lewis's favourite place in the world. 'I only ever knew of one person who could make him laugh,' Dick Rowe remembered later. 'That was Tommy Cooper. If Sir Edward ever left the office early, you could be sure Tommy Cooper was on television that night,'

Decca's pre-eminence as a record company ended in 1954 with the arrival of Sir Joseph Lockwood, a successful flour miller, to the EMI chairmanship. Lockwood instantly halted EMI's decline, ending the manufacture of radiograms and investing in new record-pressing plant just in time for the first pop music boom. Sir Edward, for his part, took Lockwood's success as a personal insult, and would speak of him only in the most slighting manner. He took some comfort from the fact that Lockwood, unlike himself, owned no substantial part of his company's stock and was, therefore, 'just an employee'.

Now, thanks to Dick Rowe, Lockwood had carried off the greatest prize of all. Not only the Beatles but all other northern groups and their new money-spinning sound seemed to have been engorged by EMI. No one wanted Decca after the preposterous mistake of its hapless A & R chief. 'Things got so bad,' a former Decca employee says, 'that if a boy with a guitar had just walked along Albert Embankment past our office, the whole A & R staff would have rushed out to sign him up.'

Rowe's only consolation was that no group, however big, could possibly appeal to British teenagers for longer than six months. He might have lost the Beatles, but he had a sporting chance of finding the *next* Beatles. It was to this objective that Rowe's entire A & R department was now frenziedly devoted. Like every other record company, Decca had sent teams of talent scouts up to Liverpool to scour the Merseyside clubs and ballrooms. The fact that the Beatles' home town was a seaport acted powerfully on the A & R men's overheated minds. The search for new Beatles was widened to other seaports, Cardiff, Bristol and Southampton.

Dick Rowe himself was still drawn back, with remorseful fascination, to Liverpool. He was there again in the first week of May 1963, hoping to find the next Beatles in a talent contest he had been asked to help judge at the city's Philharmonic Hall. To add to his discomfort, a Beatle, George Harrison, sat with him on the judging panel. Rowe remarked to George with a brave show of lightheartedness that he was still kicking himself. Though John Lennon had been heard to say he hoped the Decca man kicked himself to death, George seemed to cherish no animosity. 'In fact,' Rowe said, 'he told me I'd been right to turn the Beatles down because they'd done such a terrible audition.'

Halfway through the talent contest, the next Beatles still had not materialized. George Harrison remarked to Dick Rowe that there was a group down in London he should consider signing; a group called the Rolling Stones who played each Sunday night at the Station Hotel, Richmond . . . When George turned round, he found he was talking to himself. Rowe's chair was empty.

He remembered that, as he drove through Richmond after his headlong journey down from Liverpool, the sun was low in the sky, red and warm like a portent of redemption. 'The sun was so bright that when I got into the club, I could hardly see anything at all. Just crowds of boys – I couldn't see any girls. Crowds of boys, rising and falling on the balls of their feet.' Unannounced – unnoticed in the Crawdaddy's Sunday night crush – Dick Rowe stood and watched the five figures who were about to rescue his reputation.

Elated as he was, he forced himself to follow A & R protocol. 'I'd *never* speak directly to a group that interested me. It was *always* to their agent or manager. I couldn't find anything out in the club about who managed the Stones. Next morning, I was in my office at eight o'clock ringing round all the main agencies. No one I spoke to seemed to have heard of the Rolling Stones. Eventually someone said, "Try Eric Easton." I knew Eric, of course. Once I'd spoken to him, the whole deal went through in a matter of days.'

Before the Stones could sign with Decca, one small difficulty had to be overcome. The tape of five songs they had recorded with Glyn Johns at IBC studios was still held by IBC, and could thus be termed a prior recording commitment. Eric Easton's advice was that the Stones themselves should approach IBC, saying they had now split up and wanted to buy the tape back as a souvenir. An unsuspecting IBC agreed to return the tape for what it had cost in studio time: £109.

Within less than a week, Easton and Dick Rowe were concluding what Decca's A & R chief presumed would be a straightforward two-year recording contract. If anything, Rowe considered, it showed largesse on Decca's part. When Brian Epstein signed the Beatles with EMI, he had been forced, after many previous rejections, to accept a miserly rate of one old penny royalty per double-sided record, rising in yearly increments of one farthing. Rowe, therefore, felt it almost a point of honour to offer the Rolling Stones, however unknown and untried, the standard record royalty rate, five per cent of the retail price of each copy sold.

Thus far, Dick Rowe's dealings had been with his pleasant and obliging contemporary, Eric Easton. The familiar process, of doing deals quietly over the heads of inexperienced boys, was now rudely shattered by Easton's nineteen-year-old associate. Before Andrew Loog Oldham even walked into Decca he had imagined the film cameras starting to roll on yet another version of himself. 'I'd decided I was going to be a nasty little upstart tycoon shit.' At his first meeting with Decca's managing director, Bill Townsley, Oldham sat down, uninvited, and coolly put his feet up on Townsley's desk.

Dick Rowe gazed just as expressively at the fair-haired youth who had peremptorily cut across his genial suggestions to Eric Easton about possible dates for the Stones to cut their first record at Decca's West Hampstead studios, and which of Decca's staff producers might supervise them. Oldham replied that the Stones would not be using Decca studios and, while Rowe was still goggling, added that they did not need a producer. They already had one, named Andrew Loog Oldham.

Oldham had never forgotten the advice imparted to him in the depths of Phil Spector's limousine. That advice was, simply, that all material taped in the studios of a record company remained the company's copyright. By recording the Stones independently, then leasing the record 'masters' back to Decca for manufacture and distribution, Oldham would retain the copyright and, simultaneously, rob Decca of control over what was recorded. Such a deal had not been proposed in the whole history of British recorded music. It was a measure of Decca's desperation to launch the 'new Beatles' that Oldham's conditions were accepted.

The sunglasses through which Andrew Loog Oldham blandly surveyed his disgruntled new associates were a further ploy borrowed from Phil Spector. Through his mind's movie camera, he saw himself already as an English Spector – an entrepreneur as famous and glamorous as any performer in his care. So Oldham, despite never before having set foot in a record studio, announced to Dick Rowe and Decca that the Rolling Stones' first single would be under his exclusive direction.

It was a simple matter, anyway, to hire a studio at Olympic Sound, just off Baker Street, at a fee of five pounds per hour. There, on May 10, 1963, Oldham met the six Stones under the slightly bemused eye of the single engineer, Roger Savage, whose services were included in the price.

Oldham had instructed the Stones to choose what they considered the five best numbers in their repertoire. He himself would then decide which would be the A-side and which the B-side of the single. That decision proved more troublesome than he had expected. The Stones' best stage numbers were Roll Over Beethoven, Dust My Blues, Roadrunner – rhythm and blues standards, now so widely in use among other groups they could have little impact on the commercial record charts.

The final choice for the A-side was Come On, the Chuck Berry song they had already taped at IBC studios. As a number, its chief virtue was its obscurity. Few of Berry's British fans had heard the original version with its uncharacteristically ill-humoured lyric and odd rumba beat. The B-side – which did not have to be so commercial – was another song already taped at IBC, Willie Dixon's I Want To Be Loved.

For three hours or so, the Stones worked to polish a version of Come On, which, even at its best, would still betray for all time their sense of uneasy self-compromise. Chuck Berry's perverse rumba was stripped down to bare guitars and bass, played at the tempo of rapid feet pattering in and out of a wah-wah harmonica riff. Mick Jagger's vocal similarly purged the lyric of its exasperation at ramshackle cars and crossed telephone lines. Where Chuck Berry sang of 'some stupid jerk', Jagger felt it more judicious to say 'some stupid guy'. Even with a key change, allowing much of the song to be repeated, the finished track lasted barely a minute and three-quarters.

As producer, Andrew Loog Oldham confined himself to watching the studio clock, fretting that another hour had passed and another five pounds had been spent. The final take was finished at just before 6 p.m. Unwilling to spend five pounds more, Oldham said that one would do and began to walk out of the studio. 'What about mixing?' the engineer asked in bewilderment. Britain's putative Phil Spector had not realized that, after a song was taped, its separate vocal and instrumental tracks were then 'mixed' for internal balance. 'You mix it,' Oldham said airily. 'I'll drop in and pick it up in the morning.'

The result, even after mixing, was clearly far below even the very moderate standard of a 1963 pop single. Dick Rowe said so, and the Stones agreed. They were now as keen as Rowe that the single be recorded under experienced supervision in Decca's own studios. There, at last, both Come On and I Want to Be Loved reached a standard satisfactory to musicians and A & R man. Then it was decided to go with the IBC version after all. The release date was fixed as June 7.

The Stones were now Decca recording artists, part of a galaxy of talent that included Little Richard, Tommy Steele, Duane Eddy and the works of Buddy Holly. For all that, while Eric Easton worked on their future career, present circumstances remained much as before. They continued playing the same few club dates for the same few pounds each – Giorgio's Crawdaddy, the Marquee, Ken Colyer's Studio 51. Even that former nest of folk purists was now so packed out each Sunday afternoon that girls could reach the lavatory only by letting themselves be lifted up and passed along over people's heads.

One Sunday at Studio 51, the crush was so fierce that a girl named Shirley Arnold fainted. She came to in the band's changing room, under the solicitous gaze of the Stones and their young manager. Shirley was a passionate blues fan, then going out with a member of another r & b group, the Downliner Sect. She got talking to Oldham who, after very few minutes, offered her the job of organizing the Stones' embryonic fan club. 'I said I'd give it a go. There and then, Andrew handed me about three hundred postal orders that girls had sent in as subscriptions and said, "Okay, get on with it."'

Decca, meanwhile, prepared to launch their new acquisition with all the fire and verve of civil servants on a Friday afternoon. Decca's promotional strategy – in common with everything else – came directly from the chairman's office. Sir Edward Lewis did not believe in publicity. In his experience, greater profits accrued from artists whose private lives remained obscure. So it had proved in the case of Ted Heath the bandleader, whose very death had gone largely unnoticed by his sizeable American public, thus allowing Decca to go on recording the Heath band as if he were still conducting them.

As Andrew Loog Oldham knew from his months as a publicist, there was only one sure way of pushing a debut single by an unknown group into the national Top Twenty charts. The group must appear on ABC-TV's hugely popular Saturday night pop show, *Thank Your Lucky Stars*.

It seemed a great stroke of luck that Brian Matthew, compere of *Thank Your Lucky Stars* – and of BBC Radio's equally influential *Saturday Club* programme – was also one of Eric Easton's clients. Unfortunately, Matthew had so far reacted adversely to the Stones, criticizing Mick Jagger's vocal style and their general scruffiness. To get a booking on *Thank Your Lucky Stars*, the Stones must conform to the pattern for all pop groups that the Beatles had ordained. They must wear matching stage suits, and look neat and clean and amiable.

Whatever outrage the Stones felt at his proposal was subdued by their eagerness to get in front of the TV cameras. They allowed themselves to be presented to Matthew and his producer, Philip Jones, in uniform outfits whose Carnaby cuteness might better have suited a team of chorus boys. The jackets were houndstooth check bumfreezers, high-buttoning, with velvet half-collars. With the jackets went round-collar shirts, slim ties and Cuban-heeled Beatle boots. The ensemble had been financed – and chosen – by Eric Easton, and earned nods of approval from all but those compelled to button and tab themselves into it. The humiliation, though, was more than worthwhile. The Stones were booked to mime their single on *Thank Your Lucky Stars* on the day of its release, June 7.

The alterations did not stop there. Keith Richards, to his eternal mystification, was told to drop the 's' from his surname to give it a 'more pop sound', like Cliff Richard. And Ian Stewart, the Stones' piano player, chauffeur and provider of luncheon vouchers, was dropped from the stage line-up. Six in one group was too many, Andrew Loog Oldham had decided. And Stew, with his short hair, beefy arms and pugnaciously sensible face, looked 'too normal' for what Oldham's mental movie camera was already starting to run.

'It wasn't done very nicely,' Stewart remembered. 'I just turned up one day to find the others had stage suits and there was no stage suit for me. None of them even mentioned it to me – apart from Brian. "You're still a full member of the group, Stew," he kept telling me. "You'll still get a sixth share, I promise you."'

The Stones, however, did not ditch Stew with the amnesiac finality with which the Beatles had ditched their first drummer, Pete Best, in favour of Ringo Starr. Oldham's request was that Stew should stay on as their roadie, driver and packhorse and occasional back-up pianist. He agreed, though his pride was badly hurt. 'I thought, "I can't go back to ICI after this. I might as well stay with them and see the world."'

Thank Your Lucky Stars on June 7, 1963, offered Britain's teenagers the customary spectacle of records mimed by their artists, not always accurately, dwarfed by elaborate stage sets and half-drowned by pre-recorded female screams. Top of the bill was Helen Shapiro, a sixteen-year-old got up to look forty, in bouffant hair and flouncy petticoats. The Viscounts, an English close-harmony trio, sang their cover version of the American novelty hit Who Put the Bomp? Two disc jockeys, Pete Murray and Jimmy Henney, delivered judgement on new singles with all the fatuous disinterest of men in their late thirties, aided by a local girl named Janice Nicholls, whose invariable adjudication, 'I'll give it five' – or, in Birmingham dialect, 'Oi'll give eet foive' – had become a national catch phrase.

The Stones were bottom of the bill and, as such, merited only a simple, two-sided set, decorated with cut-out playing-card shapes. Mick stood on a low plinth, just to the rear of Brian and Bill. Keith, seated on a stool, and Charlie at his drums were seen in profile. Their spot in all lasted barely a minute and a half. As the cameras moved up and back, and pre-recorded screams raged around them, the houndstooth-checked, velvet-collared Rolling Stones tried as hard as they could, or ever would again, to be a conventional pop group.

A minute and a half proved enough for many viewers, when the recorded show was broadcast the following weekend. Afterwards, ABC-TV's Birmingham switchboard was jammed with calls protesting that such a scruffy group had appeared on *Lucky Stars*, and hoping they would not be invited back.

First review of Come On in the trade press new release columns were not much better. *Record Mirror*, the most enthusiastic, commended 'a bluesy, commercial group which could make the charts in a small way'. For the pop-oriented *Disc* and *New Musical Express*, Come On fell between two stools, being neither 'Mersey Sound' nor imported American ballad. What little radio play the single received made it sound thin and anaemic. A month after its release, the *New Musical Express* chart showed it at number twenty-six, only one place higher than the Beatles' From Me to You, issued almost three months earlier.

The only significant piece of publicity, apart from *Thank Your Lucky Stars*, came about thanks to Giorgio Gomelsky's good nature. Giorgio bore the Stones no ill will for his peremptory squeezing out, and had gone on plugging them enthusiastically to his friends in Fleet Street. Patrick Doncaster, the *Daily Mirror*'s rather elderly pop columnist, was at length persuaded to come to

Richmond and write about the Crawdaddy Club, the Stones and a new young group, the Yardbirds, whom Giorgio now promoted.

Doncaster's full-page *Mirror* piece on June 13 set the scene only too well. The Ind Coope brewery – which had not previously been aware of the frolics conducted on its property – summarily evicted Giorgio Gomelsky from the Station Hotel's back room. Thereafter, the Crawdaddy Club convened in the open air at Richmond Athletic Ground. The Stones, the Yardbirds, Cyril Davies and Long John Baldry played on a rugby pitch in front of the main grandstand, to promenading audiences of up to a thousand.

Eric Easton, meanwhile, laboured to set the Stones on the path ordained for an aspiring beat group – the dreary round-Britain path of the pop package show. It was no mean achievement, after the poor chart performance of Come On, for Easton to book them into a nationwide tour beginning on September 29, headed by America's famous Everly Brothers and featuring the Stones' own r & b hero, Bo Diddley.

The prospect was one alluring enough to make up Mick Jagger's mind, at last, about the direction he wanted his life to take. Even after the Stones had signed with Decca, he had continued to hover between music and the London School of Economics, keeping all options open to a point where the other Stones became irritated hardly less than Joe and Eva Jagger, and even threatened to drop him as vocalist if he were not available to go on tour. So Mick Jagger went to the LSE registrar and announced he would not be completing his economics course. To his surprise, and relief, no obstacle was put in his way. 'The registrar said I could go back later if I wanted. It was all surprisingly easy.'

On August 12, the Stones made their last appearance on their Richmond home turf, playing at the *Evening News*-sponsored National Jazz and Blues Festival with Acker Bilk, Cyril Davies and Long John Baldry. It was to be almost their only London booking prior to leaving on tour with the Everly Brothers. The next step in Eric Easton's strategy was to launch them into a practically non-stop schedule of one-nighters at ballrooms in remote East Anglian towns like Wisbech, Soham, Whittlesey and King's Lynn.

For most of Britain throughout that unseasonably wet summer, interest had centred on the developing scandal of John Profumo, a Conservative cabinet minister, Christine Keeler, his twenty-two-year-old mistress, and the subsequent lurid press exposures which had revealed Britain's High Tory establishment to be sexually linked with an underworld of call girls, Mayfair pimps, property racketeers and even – it was suggested – Russian spies. For once, Britain suspended disapproval of its renegade young to contemplate the possibility that senior government ministers indulged in public fellatio; that 'up to eight' High Court judges had been involved in a single sex orgy; that at a fashionable London dinner party, another eminent politician had waited at table naked and masked and wearing a placard which read 'If my services don't please you, whip me.'

By contrast with Profumo, Christine Keeler, Stephen Ward and Mandy Rice-Davies, the preoccupations of teenagers seemed positively wholesome. The exact nature of that preoccupation was earnestly sought by London's commercial TV company, Associated-Rediffusion, in planning a new weekend pop music show to pre-empt *Thank Your Lucky Stars*. The A-R show was to be called *Ready, Steady, Go* and be introduced – unprecedentedly – by people the same age as its audience. The producer, Elkan Allan, auditioned each applicant for the job by asking one question: 'What do you think young people in this country care about most?' A girl named Cathy McGowan was hired for answering, simply, 'Clothes.'

It was the clothes of its audience – not confined to seats as before in such shows, but thronging a large, high-ceilinged, multi-level studio – which established *Ready, Steady, Go* as the epitome of a new pop style, a fashion changing almost as quickly as did the Top Ten sounds. Hipster trousers, flared jeans, leather jackets, op-art dresses, the girls' Quant crops, the boys' Beatle cuts, seethed all around Cathy McGowan and the deliberately exposed TV hardware. The atmosphere was that of a King's Road party where the performers themselves had just chanced to drop by. It was an atmosphere powerfully established by the show's Friday-night slogan 'The weekend starts here'; a feeling projected to millions that all belonged to the same quintessentially fashionable club whose only qualification was that you must be under twenty-one.

The Stones, to their great chagrin, spent those same Friday nights packed into Ian Stewart's van, heading out through the East End to Hertfordshire, Bedfordshire or the Cambridgeshire Fens. It irked them particularly to think that the Beatles, mere northerners, were kings of the new London while they themselves suffered this provincial banishment. In Stew's van, Bill Wyman always insisted on the front passenger seat as safeguard against the travel sickness from which he claimed to have suffered since childhood. Not for years did the others realize that was Bill's way of securing the van's most comfortable seat.

The town halls and ballrooms of Whittlesey, Soham and Wisbech were about as far as one could travel from *Ready, Steady Go*: big, draughty vaults, filled with boys in Fifties cowlicks and girls in twinsets and ballooned petticoats. The Stones' r & b repertoire was greeted with puzzlement, if not downright hostility. Better things happened when they tried American songs in the pop-soul idiom – Lieber and Stoller's Poison Ivy; Arthur Alexander's You Better Move On. Even after Come On became a minor hit, the Stones were so ashamed of their performance on record, they refused to do the song on stage.

Somewhere between Whittlesey, Cambridgeshire, and the Everly Brothers tour, Eric Easton's houndstooth-check jackets were cast off for good. It was a discreet rebellion, led – surprisingly – by Charlie Watts, the first to abandon his stage suit in some Fenland dressing room. Keith Richard made his unwearable by multilayered whisky and chocolate stains. The group photograph taken for the tour poster shows them restored to their corduroys and polo necks, standing on a jetty beside the Thames, not far from Edith Grove. A short pre-tour feature in *New Musical Express* began: 'They are the group who prefer casual wear to stage suits and who sometimes don't bother to change before going onstage . . .'

The tour that opened at the London New Victoria Cinema on September 29 was an odd mélange assembled by its promoter – the frightening Don Arden – to attract all possible levels of the pop listening public. The Everly Brothers were fading legends of the rock 'n' roll Fifties. Bo Diddley was a cult r & b star. The Flintstones were a heavy saxophone combo. Julie Grant – another Eric Easton client – was a middle-of-the-road ballad singer. When, after barely a week, the mixture proved insufficiently powerful at the box office, Don Arden hastily flew in a second rock 'n' roll legend Little Richard, to co-star with the Everlys.

For the Stones – given small-type billing equal to Julie Grant – what mattered most was the honour of appearing on the same programme as their idol, Bo Diddley. To show their respect, they dropped all Bo Diddley material from their tour act. Diddley was flattered by the homage of his five shaggy acolytes and was so impressed by Bill and Charlie's playing he asked both to appear with him as session men on BBC Radio's *Saturday Club*.

From its opening London date, the tour headed out into the dim, dark hemisphere beyond Watford which, in pre-motorway Britain, was referred to with vague foreboding as 'the North'. 'A few miles out, and it was all new to me,' Keith says. 'Up to then, I'd never been further north than north London.'

Derby, Nottingham, Sheffield, Birmingham, Manchester, Bradford, Newcastle and twenty other cities – ancient and important and even beautiful cities, as yet undespoiled by planners – all clotted indistinguishably into the Stones' first experience of the road. Shows, twice nightly, in some huge old art deco circuit cinema, a Gaumont, a Regal or Odeon. Dark alleys, scratched stage doors and freezing backstairs passages. Dressing-rooms littered with beer bottles and old fish and chip wrappings. Hooks for coats, squalid lavatories, naked light bulbs. A peep through dusty plush curtains into the buzzing, twilit auditorium. Managers and under-managers, short-haired and nylon-shirted, hovering in anxious hostility. Sound systems as a rule no more elaborate than the same two stand microphones used in last Christmas's pantomime. The curtains parting on shrieks as from damned souls, and plush darkness bejewelled with green Exit signs, smudged here and there by the white crossbelts of the St John Ambulance Brigade.

Cinema managers, fearful of riots and torn seats, had looked sufficiently askance at pop groups who invaded their backstage region in mock sharkskin suits and ruffle-fronted evening shirts. 'When we used to walk in,' Bill Wyman says, 'some manager guy would look at us and say, "Go on, get down to your dressing room. You've only got ten minutes to get changed for the show." We'd say, "We're ready to go onstage *now*. We're ten minutes *early*."'

The initiation was also into cities still walled in Victorian darkness, where the only restaurants open late were Indian or Chinese; where hotels smelled of cabbage and beer slops, heat in the rooms was available only by coin meter, and bedclothes passed on a rich legacy of fleas, ticks and scabies. For most of the tour – thanks to another private deal he had done as self-styled leader of the group – Brian managed to stay in slightly more expensive hotels than the others.

On Sunday, October 13, at the Odeon Cinema, Liverpool, Little Richard, the Everly Brothers, Bo Diddley, Julie Grant and the

Rolling Stones performed to a barely half-filled house. That same night, the Beatles topped the bill of ATV's variety show *Sunday Night at the London Palladium* after a day in which their fans had kept the Palladium virtually under siege. An audience of fifteen million watched the four little figures in halter-neck suits, with wide grins and bouncing-clean hair, who in that moment ceased to be a teenage fad and became a national treasure.

It was with some nervousness, later on, that the Stones played the Cavern Club in Mathew Street, the Beatles' now celebrated Liverpool home. They need not have worried. The Cavern crowd, urged on by Bob Wooler, the resident disc jokey, gave the visitors a tumultuous welcome. Later, they sampled the pleasures of an all-night city, first at Allan Williams's Blue Angel Club, then with some local girls who concluded the entertainment by inviting them home to breakfast.

On October 16, it was announced that the Beatles would take part in the 1963 Royal Command Variety Show in the presence of the Queen Mother, Princess Margaret and Lord Snowdon. Fleet Street had found the ideal antidote to Profumo, Keeler, that whole summer of upper-class sordidness. With the encouragement of the press, Britain gulped down the Beatles like a reviving tonic. Even those who found their music loud and their hair ludicrous could not help but be charmed by their freshness and cheekiness, the sharp-witted yet amiable back-answers – uttered mainly by John Lennon – which seemed to reassert the essential honesty and integrity of the working man.

The Rolling Stones, like everyone else on the Everly Brothers package tour, grew even more conscious that the centre of the world was far from the Gaumont Cinema, Bradford. Nor did a visit from their nineteen-year-old co-manager greatly bolster up their self-esteem. Andrew Loog Oldham, having breezed in, made perfunctory enquiries and looked aghast at the encircling grimness, wished them good luck and disappeared again.

Oldham went straight to Liverpool, and the more promising company of John Lennon and Paul McCartney, both simultaneously visiting what was still their home base. The three afterwards drove back down to London. 'It was a very weird journey,' Oldham remembers. 'I don't know if we were drunk or stoned, or both. John and Paul started talking about getting themselves disfigured so that the fans could never recognize them and chase them any more. They were talking about all the different ways their faces might be mutilated. "We could get caught in a fire," Paul said. "We could have special rubber masks made, like skin . . ."'

Oldham's main worry on the Stones' behalf was finding them something to record as a follow-up to Come On. He had ransacked the entire catalogue of the American Chess and Checker r & b labels for something which was neither too well known in its original version or covered already by the proliferation of new British blues groups. It was an unsuccessful search which made Andrew Loog Oldham wish even more fervently, as he sat in John and Paul's black-windowed limousine, that the Rolling Stones could knock off their own hit songs with the same nonchalant ease as the Beatles.

The final choice, agreed with Decca's Dick Rowe, was a cover version of the Coasters' semi-comical Poison Ivy and, for the B-side, Benny Spellman's Fortune Teller. At Rowe's suggestion, the session was entrusted to one of Decca's younger staff producers, Michael Barclay. 'It was a disaster,' Dick Rowe remembered. 'The Stones thought Mike was a fuddy-duddy; he thought they were mad.' The result was a version of Poison Ivy which Decca and the Stones hated in almost equal measure. The single appeared on Decca's schedule of new releases but was then cancelled.

A further long discussion-cum-rehearsal at the Studio 51 Club in Great Newport Street produced nothing else that Andrew Loog Oldham considered remotely promising.

Exasperated, he left the Stones to their tinkering and arguing and started mooching round the Soho streets like Laurence Harvey in *Expresso Bongo*, hoping – as that inspirational film idol had hoped – that something or other might turn up.

Miraculously enough, something did. A London taxi stopped next to Oldham, and out jumped John Lennon and Paul McCartney. The Beatles, that day, had been at the Dorchester Hotel, receiving awards from the Variety Club of Great Britain. John and Paul were now on the loose together, looking for more excitement.

'The dialogue,' Oldham says, 'really did go like this, "'Ello, Andy. You're looking unhappy. What's the matter?" "Oh, I'm fed up. The Stones can't find a song to record." "Oh – *we've* got a song we've almost written. The Stones can record that if yer like."'

The song was I Wanna Be Your Man, one of a clutch of new Lennon-McCartney numbers written for their forthcoming second album *With The Beatles*. Susceptible to fashion as ever, and natural mimics, they had produced their own two-minute blast of rhythm and blues. As it was still not quite finished, John and Paul went back with Oldham to Studio 51 and put the final touches to it while the Stones waited.

This casual gift from pop music's hottest songwriting team provided the lethargic Stones with a rush of adrenaline. It required only an hour or two at Kingsway Sound Studios, Holborn, to produce their own Chicago Blues interpretation of I Wanna Be Your Man, replacing winsome Beatles' harmonics with the belligerent simplicity of Mick Jagger's voice and Brian Jones's slide guitar. For a B-side, it was enough to tape a twelve-bar blues instrumental, hastily ad-libbed, as was its title: Stoned. Plagiarism as it was (of Booker T's Green Onions), this counted as an original composition. Andrew Loog Oldham set up a publishing company to handle such collective efforts, its proceeds to be divided between the five Stones and himself. The company was called Nanker Phelge Music, combining Brian Jones's word for a grotesque facial contortion with the name of their Edith Grove flatmate, Jimmy Phelge, the youth who at unexpected moments used to wear his underpants on his head.

I Wanna Be Your Man was released on November 1. The Stones were still on tour with the Everly Brothers and Little Richard, playing two shows at the Odeon Cinema, Rochester. Two nights later, the tour finally wound itself up at the Odeon, Hammersmith. Here at last the Stones were on home territory. The show's compere, Bob Bain, had to plead with the audience to stop shouting, 'We want the Stones' and instead shout, 'We Want the Everlys.'

To the rest of Britain, however, even big-name groups like the Searchers and the Shadows hardly impinged on an obsession born in the trickery of Fleet Street but now rampant beyond any newspaper's manipulation. On November 4, the Beatles captivated the Royal Command Variety Show by suggesting that a blue-blooded audience containing both the Queen Mother and Princess Margaret should either clap or 'rattle yer jewellery'. On November 22, their second album, *With the Beatles*, launched them, looking like soulful art students, into the upper as well as lower social sphere, selling enough copies on advance orders to push the whole album into the Top Twenty *singles* chart. In early December, the *New Musical Express* chart showed yet another Lennon-McCartney song, I Wanna Be Your Man by the Rolling Stones, at number thirteen. For influential critics like Brian Matthew, more interest lay in the song's composers than in the group which had been lucky enough to record it. 'Do you realize,' Brian Matthew repeatedly asked his BBC radio audience, 'how many songs in the current Top Ten are written by, if not sung by, the Beatles?'

Four

'Beatle your Rolling Stone hair'

We owe this intimate backstage visit to one of Britain's last surviving cinema newsreels, in happier days devoted exclusively to sport and royalty but now, in 1964, bravely attempting to fathom an uproar more raucous, to its elderly editors, than the cry of their own screen emblem, the Pathé cockerel.

We follow as the camera tracks uncertainly down a dark passageway, round a corner and through a suddenly opened door into the Stones' dressing room. It is, however clumsy, an attempt at *cinéma vérité* – a pop group on tour, caught between performances. The camera settles first on Keith Richard, leaning forward, a cigarette clamped between his lips, to fasten a shirt collar as high as a Regency beau's hunting stock. Beyond Keith, Brian Jones, in black coat and snow-white jeans, holds up his lozenge-shaped guitar, the better to show the complex chord he is shaping. His hair is now peroxide blond, an aureole of metallic gold covering his eyes, almost encircling his face. The camera moves to Mick Jagger, in a matelot-striped jersey, then it moves on somewhat hastily. His face wears an expression not wholly welcoming; besides, he isn't holding a guitar.

The stage sequence filmed by Pathé shows how undeveloped Jagger still was as a performer or personality. The song is the

Stones' old club standby, Chuck Berry's Round and Around. Jagger sings it, hunched around the old-fashioned stand-mike, his face turned diffidently into one matelot-striped shoulder. His lips open just enough to moisten themselves. His eyes seem cloudily preoccupied. At intervals, he claps his hands flamenco-style above his head. Beside him, Keith Richard jigs around, wearing a happy, rather dizzy grin. Far on the other side, with heaped gold hair shutting out his eyes, Brian Jones stands, motionlessly provocative. The camera cuts away to girls with Beatle fringes, alternately screaming and stuffing handkerchiefs into their mouths. Now we see the full stage, empty but for the Stones, their vestigial equipment and a red-curtained backdrop. Jagger leaves the microphone and – the only word is – waddles like a duck shaking water from its tail.

On January 6, they were out on tour again, in the George Cooper Organization's 'Group Scene 1964' show. By now they were big enough to merit equal top billing with the Ronettes, an American girl group, highly successful on Phil Spector's Philles record label. Spector had already sent his acolyte Andrew Loog Oldham a telegram, sternly warning 'Leave my girls alone.' As both individual Stones and Ronettes have since corroborated, that warning was to no avail.

The combination of svelte, sinuous black girls and snarling, scruffy white boys attracted much interest in a music press jaded equally by Christmas indulgence and Beatle overkill. In *New Musical Express* under a heading 'Girls Scream at Stones, Boys at Ronnettes'. Andy Gray praised the show's 'vocal volume and body action'. Gray's review – which set the seal of box-office success on the tour – is revealing as a sample both of 1964 pop journalism and also the pitifully short performances given by even top-of-the-bill attractions:

> Two packed houses greeted with cheers, screams and scarf-waving the local lads who have made good – the Rolling

> Stones. Fever-pitch excitement met compere Al Paige's announcement of them, and they tore into their act with Girls, followed by Come On. This group certainly is different – members wear what they like, from shirts to leather jackets, but they have long hair in common.
>
> Lead singer Mick Jagger whips out a harmonica occasionally and brews up more excitement while the three guitars and drums throb away in back. Hey Mona was another R & B compeller before a quiet number, very appealingly sung by Brian Jones [sic], You Better Move On. Back to the torrid stuff for the last two numbers, Roll Over, Beethoven and I Wanna Be Your Man, taking the act to encore applause . . .

Decca's release of an EP – extended play – record on January 17 redoubled the nightly pandemonium. The EP, with its handful of tracks and cheap picture cover, was a well-tried device for getting additional mileage from a pop act whose success did not yet warrant a full twelve- or thirteen-track LP. The Stones' first EP was in this catchpenny tradition, offering their cancelled A-side Poison Ivy, together with versions of Chuck Berry's Bye Bye Johnny and Berry Gordy's much imitated Money. The exception was an Arthur Alexander song, You Better Move On, sung by Mick Jagger with care and almost without affectation. You Better Move On proved popular enough to take the entire EP into the Top Ten singles chart barely a week after its release.

The Stones' third single, it was already decided, would be a cover version of the Buddy Holly song Not Fade Away – which Mick Jagger had first heard with Dick Taylor at Woolwich Granada back in 1957 – but drastically rearranged by cross-breeding with an equally important stylistic source. On to the mild, reflective Holly song, Keith Richard had grafted guitar chords played in the shuffling, stop-start Bo Diddley beat. 'To me,' Andrew Loog Oldham says, 'when Keith sat in the corner and came up with those chords, *that* was really the first song the

Stones ever wrote.' The result was played at twice the speed of the Holly original, flashed across, each second verse, by a whinny from Brian Jones's harmonica.

The taping of Not Fade Away, at Regent Sound, towards the end of January 1964, was an occasion that would have horrified conventional A & R men like Dick Rowe. Oldham and the Stones had hit on the ideal way of escaping interference from Rowe or anyone else from Decca. They recorded by night, not even starting until long after all A & R men were safely back in their suburban mock-Georgian villas, tucked up between their nylon fitted sheets.

Not Fade Away was taped as the culmination of a drunken studio party at which the Stones and Oldham were joined by Phil Spector and two members of the Hollies, Alan Clarke and Graham Nash. Later on, the American singer Gene Pitney also dropped in, bringing with him an outsize bottle of brandy. The final Not Fade Away take featured the two Hollies, appropriately, on back-up vocals and Phil Spector shaking the maracas of which the rhythm track is mainly composed. Spector also cobbled up a B-side song called Little By Little, a pastiche of Jimmy Reed's Shame, Shame, Shame, dashing it off in minutes, with Mick Jagger's help, in the corridor. Little By Little was recorded as a simple jam session of guitar, harmonica, piano – played by Gene Pitney – and a Jagger vocal, like the maracas, audibly plastered. At frequent intervals, the session disintegrated into tomfoolery, with Jagger rudely mimicking Sir Edward Lewis, the Decca chairman, and Phil Spector ad-libbing an obscene recitative under the title Andrew's Blues.

On February 4, at New York's Kennedy airport, the Beatles emerged from their aircraft to behold a 5,000-strong crowd, keening and howling in the grip of that European virus which the *New York Post* had predicted would definitely *not* spread to America. Their appearance, four nights later, on NBC-TV's *Ed Sullivan Show* – for a knockdown fee of $3,500 – was watched by an estimated 70 million, or 60 per cent of the American TV audience.

The Beatles' conquest of America took them out of the orbit of mere pop. In Britain, those who had once damned and denounced them now commended them as an invaluable addition to the export drive. Their name took on almost a talismanic quality, securing newspaper headlines impartially for anyone who invoked it. Members of Parliament, peers of the realm, archbishops, even royalty itself, now talked and talked about the Beatles. To their teenage audience this was, of course, the most gratifying turnabout from last year's parental ridicule. Just the same, to find one's idols shared by one's mother, and even one's grandmother, made pop seem suddenly rather tame.

No one's mother or grandmother liked the single, released on February 27 and now climbing up the Top Twenty, spurred on by alternate kicks of delight and hostility. The Stones' late-night carousings with the Hollies and Phil Spector had produced a noise which sold itself, both as instant hit material and instant anti-heroism, from its first chaotic, maraca-shaking chord. Phil Spector's presence is widely supposed to have brought about the Stones' vastly improved cohesion in Not Fade Away – guitars sharper, harmonica more savage, the general onslaught resembling a miniature wall of sound.

The national press was quick to spot the new fad – or, in other words, to take up Andrew Loog Oldham's suggested story angle. 'They look,' said the *Daily Express*, 'like boys whom any self-respecting mum would lock in the bathroom. But the Rolling Stones – five tough young London-based music-makers with doorstep mouths, pallid cheeks and unkempt hair – are not worried what mums think . . . For now that the Beatles have registered with all age groups, the Rolling Stones have taken over as the voice of the teens.'

Last year's Beatle crowds, it was becoming clear, had behaved moderately in comparison with those who followed the new voice of the teens. The Stones' third tour, early in February, played each night to an uproar, not merely of screaming girls corralled in cinema seats, but also of spontaneous battles between Mods and their sartorial foes, the Rockers. Other groups to whom this happened would hug their precious guitars to them and hurry from the stage. But the Rolling Stones played on. Brian Jones in particular loved to see trouble starting and to encourage it subtly by brief, goading shakes of his hair and tambourine. It was largely from this trick of Brian's that Mick Jagger learned how small, tantalizing body movements could tease up conventional screams to a banshee-like howl. He, too, began to experiment, slipping off his Cecil Gee Italian jacket and dangling it on his forefinger like a stripper's G-string.

The Stones' television appearances, on *Lucky Stars* and *Ready, Steady, Go,* had precipitated a blizzard of hate mail. 'The whole lot of you,' wrote a typical correspondent, 'should be given a good bath, then all that hair should be cut off. I'm not against pop music when it's sung by a nice clean boy like Cliff Richard, but you are a disgrace. Your filthy appearance is likely to corrupt teenagers all over the country . . .'

One feature of those TV appearances, above all, had caused adult Britain to recoil with almost speechless revulsion. The Beatles, for all their mop-top fringes, had always been assiduously barbered and groomed. The Stones' hair, its length, its volume, its wild lack of shape, made the Beatles' look decorously short by comparison. Not since the early Victorian age had young British men been seen with hair that hung down their necks and curled over their shirt collars, half obliterating their eyes and ears. To a nation whose collective memory of military life was still strong, the Stones' hair signified almost rabid uncleanliness. And, indeed, the voice of adult Britain rang out like so many sergeant majors. The president of the National Federation of Hairdressers, offering to give the next number one pop group a free haircut – and, by implication, a disinfecting and de-lousing – added: 'The Rolling

Stones are the worst. One of them looks as though he has got a yellow feather duster on his head.' Brian Jones was deeply offended, especially since he nowadays washed his newly golden hair on average *twice* each day and was known within the Stones as Mister Shampoo.

All who attacked the Stones fondly imagined themselves to be part of a process that must ultimately consign the ugly little upstarts to ear-burning oblivion. A great many worthy citizens might have held their peace if they had realized what Andrew Loog Oldham did by early 1964: that the more ferociously grown-ups attacked and derided the Stones, the more their teenage fans would love and support them.

Coverage of the Stones from spring 1964 onwards testifies to Oldham's artful success in making their name synonymous with surliness, squalor, rebellion and menace. Newspaper reporters then were usually middle-aged, baffled by pop music and only too glad of the phrases which Oldham provided. Almost every story began in the same way: 'They are called the Ugliest Group in Britain . . .' Other stories described the Stones' habit, when exasperated by pressmen's questions, of sticking their fingers up their noses and dragging down their eyes in a collective version of Brian Jones's 'nanker' grimace. Perhaps Oldham's greatest thematic coup was a headline in *Melody Maker*: WOULD YOU LET YOUR DAUGHTER GO WITH A ROLLING STONE? The words mutated into what became almost a national catch-phrase whenever the Stones appeared on television. 'Would you let *your* daughter marry one?' people said to each other, or, 'Mothers turn pale . . .'

To the fans, they were presented in the mode of Elvis Presley a decade previously – as rebels who were nice boys when you got to know them. No less an authority than Jimmy Savile confided to his pop column audience in the *People* newspaper that 'they're a great team for having a laugh, and dress very clean and smart when they relax'. Oldham ensured that they did everything that pop fans expected, posing as lurid colour pin-ups for teen magazines like *Rave* and *Fabulous 208*, grouped in uniform leather waistcoats or jumping up together in zany Beatle style. Their clothes – Brian Jones's especially – were discussed at inordinate length. Like every other group, they filled in their 'Life Lines' for *New Musical Express*, tempering sarcasm with what was usual, including the ritual white lie about their ages. Mick Jagger ('born 1944') gave his Favourite Colour as 'red, blue, yellow, green, pink, black, white', and his Favourite Clothes as 'my father's'. Keith Richard gave his Year of Birth as '1944', his Parents' Names as 'Boris and Dirt', his Favourite Actor as 'Harold Wilson', his Miscellaneous Dislikes as 'headaches, corns, pimples, gangrene'. Brian Jones ('born 1944') gave his Sister's Name as 'Hashish' and his Biggest Career Break as 'break from parents'. Though Bill Wyman subtracted the largest amount from his age – five years – he admitted the existence of his wife, Diane, and his four-year-old son, Steven. Only Charlie Watts did not lie about his age or his Hobbies: 'collecting antique firearms and modelling in plaster'.

The 'voice of the teens' no longer needed their manager to whip up notoriety for them. On March 27, under a headline BEATLE YOUR ROLLING STONE HAIR, the *Daily Mirror* reported that eleven pupils at a boys' school in Coventry had been suspended for imitating the Stones' hairstyle. The headmaster had refused to reinstate them until they returned to school with hair 'cut neatly, like the Beatles'.'

By April 1964, they had spent so many consecutive weeks on tour that when Bill Wyman finally went home, his dog mistook him for a burglar and tried to bite him.

Bill had moved with his wife and son from their flat in Penge to a modest house in Farnborough. He was still conspicuously the older man of the group, weighing the pleasures of stardom against the need to support a family and pay off a mortgage. That was only just possible on the wage each of the Stones drew from Eric Easton, pending Decca's first payout of royalties – which, their contract now revealed, might not be for up to a year after the actual record sales. When Bill drove home to Farnborough, he did so in the mood of an overworked commercial traveller, minus commission.

Mick, Keith and Brian had left the Edith Grove flat and gone separate ways which, at the time, seemed dictated by Brian's eternally complicated love life. He now wanted nothing to do with Pat Andrews and baby Julian, being deeply involved with a pretty young model named Linda Lawrence. Within a matter of only months, the inevitable happened. Linda, too, discovered that she was pregnant.

Mick and Keith were now sharing a flat with Andrew Loog Oldham in Willesden, North London. 'We had two rooms between us,' Oldham says. 'And we had to share a bathroom. It was rather a quiet place, really. Half a bottle of wine in that flat was a big deal. And anyway, all three of us were going steady.'

Mick Jagger was 'going steady', in almost every sense of that winsome Fifties phrase, with Chrissie Shrimpton, seventeen-year-old younger sister of Jean Shrimpton, the famous new face of *Vogue* and Sunday colour supplements. A year earlier, watching the Stones play at a basement club in Maidenhead, a friend of Chrissie's dared her to go up to Jagger and ask him to kiss her. The encounter was symbolic of the new kind of Sixties girl Chrissie Shrimpton was no less than the kind of Sixties man Jagger would shortly become. He did kiss her and afterwards invited her out to a cinema in Windsor.

Chrissie's father was a prosperous builder in the Buckinghamshire town of High Wycombe, with a substantial house and farm a few miles into the country. Mr Shrimpton did not at first care at all for the thin, spotty boy his younger daughter had been bringing home after excursions to music clubs in the neighbourhood. The fact that he was an LSE student, a cut above the usual pop-group type, somewhat mollified Chrissie's parents. And Mr Shrimpton, self-made man that he was, perceived that, under the hair and spots and sullen lips, there was an acute and calculating intelligence.

Though Chrissie did not share her sister Jean's cool, unfussed beauty, she was in every way an improvement on Mick's Dartford girlfriends. She was also, despite her elfin appearance, strong-minded and forthright, with a temper that Mick soon provoked by his cool and careless attitude to the obligations of a steady boyfriend. Their romance from the beginning was punctuated by fights like the one Oldham had witnessed in the Crawdaddy Club passage.

They were, even so, genuinely and often happily in love, and had made plans to marry as soon as Mick earned enough money to support a wife. This was in the days when he still planned to finish his economics degree course and choose some respectable career in business, or – he once told Chrissie's father – perhaps even politics.

The Shrimptons, with their substantial country house, gave Mick Jagger his first social step up from suburban Dartford. Still more attractive was the connection through Chrissie's famous sister with the world of fashionable young London – David Bailey, Mary Quant, the *Sunday Times*, Whipp's and the Ad Lib. Though Chrissie herself was at secretarial college, her name sometimes appeared in magazine stories about Jean. Mick, though hardly even semi-famous, liked to imagine their romance to be the stuff of newspaper gossip columns. So he would refer to it, in tour interviews with provincial journalists, sitting on the cold back stairs of some northern Gaumont of ABC, sniffing with the faint flu that plagued all the Stones and tilting a Pepsi bottle against his lips. '. . . there's all those lies being written about me and Chrissie Shrimpton . . .'

He was now palpably a being apart from the other Stones, in

his cable-stitched fisherman's sweater, his languid eyes appraising his interviewer's cheap suit as he dismissed this or that question as 'too much of a drag to talk about'. Offstage, he seemed the most antisocial and isolated: a rebel against his home and background, more vehement even than was Brian Jones. For weeks on end, Joe and Eva Jagger down in Dartford would hear nothing from him. Keith, by contrast, kept in touch with Doris Richards and showered her with gifts to delight her eccentric heart. Charlie Watts was a model of filial affection who presented his mother with a coffee gateau religiously every Friday night. When buying a gateau for his girlfriend also, Charlie would take the walnut from the centre of the girlfriend's cake and put it on his mother's, so that she'd have two walnuts.

In those days, there were people who could talk to Mick about his apparent rejection of two very pleasant, if deeply ordinary, parents. Paul McCartney had a long talk with him about it one night when the Beatles and Stones were out together. McCartney got on well with his widower father, and all old people, and was depressed by Mick's dogged insistence, against much evidence to the contrary, that parents were 'a drag'. Everything was 'a drag', it seemed, which did not supply lustre to his still undecided image.

To so natural a mimic, those early road shows as supporting attraction to big American stars were like a series of lessons in pop idol behaviour and deportment. He had watched the Everly Brothers, singing to one another like blow-waved, cooing narcissists. He had seen Little Richard, a rock 'n' roll master whose music had always been strangely ambiguous of gender, and who now took to the stage in full make-up, complete with nail varnish. It was on the Little Richard tour that Jagger asked a Liverpool musician, Lee Curtis, how he could find out about theatrical make-up. Curtis's brother, Joe Flannery, sat him down backstage and showed him how to apply actors' pancake and rouge.

Chrissie Shrimpton had watched Jagger's growing awareness

of himself as something more than merely a constituent of the Stones' democracy. To Chrissie, he still pretended it was all for a laugh; that the normal, sensible part of him stood back and laughed when little girls screamed for him. But then, if they were out together and girls waylaid them, to Chrissie's great irritation, Mick would pretend not to be with her – even ask her to make herself scarce. The Beatles might have lost followers after the revelation that John Lennon had a wife. It was better for Mick's image – so Andrew Loog Oldham said – if he seemed to have no steady girlfriend.

Chrissie felt slighted by Mick's apparent willingness to let Andre Oldham rule and dominate him – accepting, for instance, Oldham's firm rule that girlfriends were barred when the Stones travelled on tour. Mick's closeness with Oldham was starting to cause comment among Chrissie's friends who saw them together in pubs, deep in purported musical strategy. Chrissie Shrimpton, in no doubt about Mick's virility, was nettled when a female acquaintance asked, 'At that flat, do Mick and Andrew sleep in the same bed?'

Brian Jones was now living in considerably greater comfort than his former flatmates, having managed to billet himself with the parents of his girlfriend, Linda Lawrence, at their house in Windsor. The arrangement was, of course, based on the idea that Brian's intentions towards Linda were honourable. Before the opposite proved to be the case, the Lawrences showed him every consideration. He was allowed to use Mr Lawrence's car whenever he wished. The name of the house was even changed, in Brian's honour, to 'Rolling Stone'. And he did seem infatuated with Linda. On tour, he would shower her with postcards – to 'darlin' Linda' – and on his return buy her expensive presents. These included a French poodle and a goat which Brian liked to take for walks through Windsor on a lead.

His passion for Linda seemed to fade in proportion to the progress of her pregnancy. He was soon on the move again, forsaking the Lawrences' hospitality for a small flat in Chester Street, Belgravia. The birth of a son to Linda completed the alienation process. Brian was seldom other than indifferent to the baby, to whom, in a mood of mischievous malice, he gave the same name as his child by Pat Andrews – Julian Mark. 'He was so rude about that poor little kid,' Shirley Arnold, the Stones' fan club secretary, remembers. 'He used to call it Broad Bean Head.'

As Brian tired of Linda, his indifference curdled into physical cruelty. On her visits to him in Chester Street, he would sometimes knock her about so violently that his downstairs neighbours – another group, the Pretty Things – could hear bumps and crashes through the ceiling.

To Brian all that mattered was the living of his longed-for role as a pop star. He loved being famous, being recognized, pursued and mobbed by girls – for himself now, not as a counterfeit Beatle. He loved having money, having girls, having wine, having clothes. He loved the pop-star night life at clubs like the Ad Lib, the Establishment, Whipp's and Scotch of St James's. He loved the shopping raids on boutiques in corduroy, button-down blocks on either side of Carnaby Street. Brian was the Stone nominated as *Rave* magazine's Best-Dressed Pop Star of the Week. He thought nothing of spending £30 on one French Jacket from Cecil Gee's, £10 on a single silk shirt from Just Men. What he did not buy he would cheerfully steal. The striped jersey, copied by boys all over Britain after Brian wore it on *Ready, Steady, Go*, had in fact been stolen from the wardrobe of one of his Pretty Things neighbours.

The Pathé newsreel film, shot backstage at Hull ABC cinema, shows what a masterly performer Brian was offstage as well as on. In that film, he appears choirboy innocent, concerned only with tuning his guitar. He would sit down with pimply teenage provincial journalists, the soul of amiability, speaking in that voice so soft, it was almost effeminate, his gold-fringed eyes open wide with incredulity at the attitude of the latest hotel to refuse the

Stones accommodation, though – as likely as not – it would have been Brian's own behaviour that precipitated the ban. 'The Scotch Corner Hotel . . . near Darlington . . . ooh, that's a *terrible* place. So *aggressive*.'

Within the Stones, in their claustrophobic tour life, Brian was invariably the source of any disagreement or disruption. They were all waiting in the wings one night when Keith went for him with both fists, shouting, 'Where's my chicken, you bastard?' Brian, before the show, had filched and eaten Keith's portion of the only food they would be likely to get that night.

Brian continued to regard himself as leader of the Rolling Stones, and as such entitled to a higher pay-out and superior hotel rooms, all the time in blissful unawareness that his secret negotiations and subterfuges were well known to the other four. In those heady early days, the others were content to take out their resentment of 'Mr Shampoo' in comparatively harmless ways. Mick and Keith both developed impersonations of Brian based on his physical defects – the too short legs he attempted to hide on stacked-up Cuban heels; the foreshortened neck which made his chin rest, never quite comfortably, on the roll-top of his sweater. The subtle ragging of Brian increased on a trip with Oldham to Northern Ireland to make a documentary film, directed by Peter Whitehead and entitled – in honour of its least willing participant – *Charlie Is My Darling*. 'Brian really went over the top whenever Peter Whitehead's camera was on him,' Oldham says. 'He'd do these long soliloquies to camera. "Why am I a musician . . . and who am I?" He didn't realize the others were sending him up rotten.'

What no one could deny was the strength and drive Brian gave to the Stones by sheer musicianship. His preposterous egotism, his amoral willingness to do anyone down and filch anything, were forgotten as soon as he picked up his slide guitar or played harmonica, his cheeks filling and hollowing with the quick, light, dancing breath that kept the whole sound together.

'Brian was a power in the Stones as long as he could pick up any instrument in the studio and get a tune out of it,' Oldham says. 'As soon as he stopped trying, and just played rhythm guitar, he was finished.'

The process had already begun which was to define the power structure within the Stones, binding Mick and Keith together in their unstoppable alliance and leaving Brian irretrievably out in the cold. It began on the night that Andrew Loog Oldham locked his two flatmates in the kitchen of their Willesden basement and threatened not to let them out until they had written a song.

For Oldham, it was a matter of sheer convenience. He was tired of rummaging through Chappell's r & b song catalogue in the perpetual search for material acceptable to the Stones' purist conscience and to Decca's A & R department. Their two Top Twenty singles seemed to confirm what Oldham told them with ever increasing frequency: 'You can't be a hit group just on rhythm and blues.' Nor – it was implicitly added – could Oldham himself become the teenage Svengali of British pop just by sorting through sheet music and listening to song pluggers' demo tapes.

The necessity of putting together a twelve-track LP, to capitalize on their singles' success, intensified Oldham's fear that the Stones were in imminent danger of running out of material. Yet again, he looked enviously towards the Beatles, whose own original songs had comprised a good 50 per cent of their second, million-selling album, *With The Beatles*. Mick and Keith, too, though far from convinced they could concoct a song together, had been deeply impressed by the exercise in instant Lennon-McCartney composition that had produced I Wanna Be Your Man. So, when their manager locked the kitchen door on them in Willesden, they agreed, for the moment, not to kick it down.

Their first attempts at songs were ballads of a glutinous sentimentality, quite unsuitable for the Stones' repertoire, or for anyone else's, despite all Oldham's bullish attempts at syndication. The first ever Jagger-Richard composition, It Should Be You, was eventually recorded by an obscure white soul artist named George Bean. Slightly more success befell another early ballad, That Girl Belongs to Yesterday, when recorded by Gene Pitney, their erstwhile session pianist. Pitney had a minor hit with the song only after drastic rearrangement to suit a piercing voice which, it was said, hit notes that only record engineers and gods could hear.

Only one Jagger-Richard song, Tell Me, was considered good enough for the album released by Decca in April 1964 (although two more tracks bore the Stones' collective songwriting name, Phelge). Tell Me has curio value as a heavy-handed attempt by Mick and Keith to imitate the Mersey Beat sound of the numerous post-Beatle groups from Liverpool. Strange it is to hear the Stones trying to sound Beatle-ish, with tolling bass drum, minor chords and chocked-up close harmony. Mick Jagger's 'Whoa yeah' rings out in patent embarrassment. Keith Richard descants him, a McCartney made of cigarette ash and Brillo pads.

The other eleven tracks are a belligerently alive memento of the Stones as an r & b band, the way they used to sound at Ken Colyer's or the Crawdaddy. Given the limitations of a tiny, primitive studio, and severely rationed time there, they could do little else but blast out the best of their club repertoire, imagining an audience in place of Regent Sound's egg-box walls and Oldham's agitated eye on the clock. 'Andrew told us we couldn't afford retakes,' Bill Wyman says. 'The only time we broke was for food, or to let Mick run out and get sheet music for the words of Can I Get A Witness?'

The tracks are a squirming medley from the soul and blues bag: Chuck Berry's Carol, Bo Diddley's Mona, Jimmy Reed's Honest I Do, Willie Dixon's I Just Wanna Make Love To You. Even then, they could not find quite enough songs, and were forced to throw in a lengthy instrumental sequence vamped around the chords of Can I Get A Witness? featuring Ian Stewart on electric organ, with instrumental breaks by Keith and Brian.

There is even a comedy number, Walkin' the Dog, with Mick Jagger skilfully mimicking Rufus Thomas's pop-eyed jokiness. The Jagger of this first album is simply a singer with the band, stepping back to allow others their turn. But in every syllable he sings, there are signs of the Jagger to come. There are signs, most powerfully, in Slim Harpo's I'm A King Bee, a slow blues, torrid with sexual warning – 'I'm a king bee, baby, buzzin' round your hive' – intoned by Jagger in a somnolent drawl, his tongue and lips playing an audible, almost visible part.

The album sleeve was an Oldham tour de force. Borrowed unashamedly from the famous black and white portrait on the cover of *With The Beatles*, it had one big difference – the subject of prolonged battle between Oldham and Decca's design department. Even the epoch-making Beatles sleeve bore a title and the artists' name. Oldham, however, insisted that the Stones' sleeve should make no statement other than its pictorial one. The five Stones stood sidelong, glowering from shadows so intense, one could barely see the buttons on their Carnaby Street clothes. It was left to the buyer to know who they were and to peer closer at their faces for evidence of animal sullenness or poetic sensitivity. Twenty years on, the look is still modern, the nerve still coolly audacious. On the back, convention returned with song titles, photographs and a sleeve note by Oldham that began: 'The Rolling Stones are more than a group. They are a way of life . . .'

By the day of its release, the album had sold 100,000 copies in advance orders. The Beatles – as Oldham jubilantly pointed out – had sold only 6,000 advance copies of their debut album, *Please Please Me*. He had further cause for glee when the Rolling Stones, climbing up the trade press album charts, displaced *With The Beatles* on its way down. Oldham, naturally, dismissed the fact that the Beatles album had been in the charts since the previous November. Everywhere he went, to everyone he met, he uttered the same cry of triumph: 'The Stones have knocked the Beatles off.'

London (AP) Americans – brace yourselves.

> In the tracks of the Beatles, a second wave of sheepdog-looking, angry-acting, guitar-playing Britons is on the way.
>
> They call themselves the Rolling Stones and they're due in New York Tuesday.
>
> Of the Rolling Stones, one detractor has said:
>
> 'They are dirtier and are streakier and more dishevelled than the Beatles, and in some places they're more popular than the Beatles.'
>
> Says Mick Jagger:
>
> 'I hate to get up in the morning. I'm not overfond of being hungry either.'
>
> From Keith Richard:
>
> 'People think we're wild and unruly. But it isn't true. I would say that the most important thing about us is that we're our own best friends.'
>
> More than the others perhaps, Brian Jones likes clothes. He puts his philosophy this way:
>
> 'It depends on what I feel like really. Sometimes I'll wear very flamboyant clothes like this frilly shirt. Other times I'll wear very casual stuff. I spend a lot of my free time buying stuff.'
>
> Then he adds:
>
> 'There's really not much else to do.'

Misgivings about this first trip to America were by no means all on America's side. The Stones took off from Heathrow airport on June 6 almost as unhappy about the whole idea. They knew only too well that when the Beatles had reached America four months earlier, it was on the strength of a single lodged firmly at the top of *Billboard* magazine's Hot Hundred. Their own first US single, Not Fade Away, coupled with I Wanna Be Your Man, had, since its mid-May release, barely scraped into the *Billboard* list. Only Andrew Loog Oldham remained unperturbed. The Beatles, he reminded them, had taken two years and three flop singles to 'break' in America. Oldham believed he had the contacts and the nerve to make things happen a lot faster than that.

The Rolling Stones were to be launched in America, not as r & b iconoclasts but – in the subtitle of their US debut album – as 'England's Newest Hitmakers', overtly exploiting the craze for British pop which the Beatles had started and which was now too great for even the Beatles to satisfy alone. In this so-called British invasion, the Stones were following some of the groups they most despised – Herman's Hermits, Billy J. Kramer, the Searchers. 'Everyone we really hated seemed to be doing far better in the States than we were,' Bill Wyman remembers. 'They'd had a number one record, done a good tour, good TV. We'd got nothing like that to look forward to. No wonder we were depressed on the way over.'

What few newspaper reports of their coming had appeared in America all picked up from the line from Associated Press – that the Stones' chief characteristic as a group was barely believable 'dirtiness'. The only exception was *Vogue*, a magazine then under the inspired editorship of Diana Vreeland. *Vogue* devoted a full page to David Bailey's portrait of Mick Jagger, looking upward from his penny-round collar with big-eyed, schoolboyish winsomeness. 'To the inner group in London, the new spectacular is a solemn young man, Mick Jagger,' *Vogue* reported. 'For the British, the Stones have a perverse, unsettling sex appeal, with Jagger out in front of his team-mates . . . To women, he's fascinating, to men a scare . . . quite different from the Beatles, and more terrifying.'

The scene at John F. Kennedy airport, when the Stones landed on June 2, was all too obviously an attempt to recreate the Beatles' famous touchdown four months earlier. A crowd, numbering hundreds rather than thousands, screamed somewhat wanly as a bevy of girls came forward to greet the arrivals, accompanied by four symbolically shaggy Old English sheepdogs. The screams were over well before the Stones entered the terminal, watched by US Customs and Immigration officials whose thunderstruck revulsion suggested them to be irregular readers of *Vogue*. That first walk down the synthetic red carpet unloosed, on every side, a cry which would be repeated in scales of horror and derision throughout almost every state in the Union: 'Why dontcha get ya goddamned hair cut?'

With no hit single to their credit, the Stones merited scant promotional help from their US record label, London. It was left to Andrew Loog Oldham to whip up a rather pallid semblance of the Beatles' celebrated imprisonment inside the Plaza Hotel. The London *Daily Mirror*, next day, was persuaded to run a story that the Rolling Stones were barricaded inside their – much less grand – Manhattan hotel for fear of girls with nail scissors, threatening to cut off lumps of their hair. The tale was rather spoiled by an agency picture of Brian Jones strolling down Broadway in a loose silk shirt and sleeveless bolero but producing no more public reaction than any other freak encountered at noon in midtown Manhattan.

For the Stones' American TV debut, Oldham could arrange nothing grander than the Les Crane programme, an obscure talk show transmitted in competition with the Late Late Movies, whose semi-somnabulistic host contrived such penetrating questions as 'You guys all dress different – how come?' 'Because we are all different persons,' Mick Jagger answered in the lisping public school accent he had adopted for transatlantic use.

Worse was to come in Los Angeles two nights later, when the Stones appeared on Dean Martin's *Hollywood Palace* TV show, sharing the bill with circus elephants, acrobats and rhinestone-studded cowboys. As the show was pre-recorded in separate segments, the Stones could not know that Dean Martin's script was full of ponderous attempts to be funny at their expense. 'Their hair isn't long,' quipped the crooner. 'It's just smaller foreheads and higher eyebrows . . .' 'Now don't go away, everyone,' he pleaded humorously as the show broke for commercials. 'You wouldn't want to leave me with these Rolling Stones, would you?' Later, introducing a trampolinist, Martin quipped, 'That's the father of the Rolling Stones. He's been trying to kill himself ever since.'

The West Coast pop fraternity, by contrast, provided good friends and still better object lessons. As protégés of Phil Spector, the Stones were received as VIPs in what was, after New York, the world's recording capital. Spector's advice to Oldham at the Not Fade Away session had been to get the Stones with all speed into an American recording studio. In addition to touring, they were booked for a session at RCA's Hollywood studio and, later in Chicago, at Chess Records, the self-same studios used by Chuck Berry, Muddy Waters and virtually every other blues master they had ever idolized.

A good friend on the West Coast was Sonny Bono, soon to find fame with his wife as Sonny and Cher, but at this time merely an energetic music PR and promotion man. 'Sonny met us at the airport in these way-out clothes – striped trousers and scarves and bangles,' Oldham says. 'The Stones had never seen clothes like that before. When Sonny opened the boot of his car, there were *stacks* of records in there – about a thousand. That blew our minds as well. In England, you never *saw* the records like that, actually on their way to the punters.'

From the West Coast, the Stones embarked on what was not so much a tour as a series of random one-nighters, booked by Eric Easton in London, often with no knowledge of the event, the promoter or the venue. Their first American performance, at San Bernardino on July 5, was in an old-fashioned pop jamboree, sharing the bill with Bobby Goldsboro, Bobby Vee and the Chiffons. Here, the omens seemed promising. They easily outplayed their competition and finished their show fronted by kneeling, crash-helmeted police to fend off hundreds of entreating arms. 'It was a straight gas that night,' Keith remembers. 'The kids knew all the songs and sang along with them. Especially when we got to Route 66 – they roared out 'San Bernardino' like a football crowd.'

That euphoria was to be short-lived. At the Stones' next date – a 'teen fair' in San Antonio, Texas – they were required to play standing on the edge of a water tank full of trained seals. In a 20,000 capacity arena, only a few hundred seats were filled. The London *Daily Mirror* reported that the Stones had been booed – although an acrobatic act and a performing monkey on the same bill were both called back for encores. The *Mirror* quoted a local seventeen-year-old's scornful remark about the 'New Beatles': 'All they've got that our school groups haven't got is hair.'

In Omaha, Nebraska, the arrival of the New Beatles was taken ludicrously in earnest. The Stones were met at the airport by a squad of twelve motorcycle cops and delivered, with wailing sirens, to a 15,000-seat auditorium where approximately 600 people awaited them. 'We couldn't see it at the time, but all that was really doing us some good,' Keith says. 'In England, we'd been used to coming onstage, blasting off four numbers and going. America, that first tour, really made us work. We had to fill up the spaces somehow.'

In New York and Los Angeles, the Stones had seemed wild enough. In the American Midwest in 1964, their effect was literally traumatizing. Incredulous revulsion, on the faces of policemen, town sheriffs, hotel clerks and coffee-shop waitresses, greeted them wherever they went. 'I've never been hated by so many people I've never met as in Nebraska in the mid-Sixties,' Keith says. 'Everyone looked at you with a look that could kill. You could tell they just wanted to beat the shit out of you.'

The bright spot of their journey was to be their recording session at Chess Studios in Chicago. Oldham had been determined not to waste this precious opportunity on run-of-the-mill r & b material, and had succeeded in finding the Stones a first-class soul song to record at Chess as their next single. The song, It's All

Over Now, had already been a minor hit for its composer Bobby Womack and his group the Valentinos. The publishing rights, Oldham learned, were controlled for Womack by his business manager, a New York accountant named Allen Klein.

Chicago was all but poisoned for the Stones by the spectacle of themselves on the *Hollywood Palace* TV show, recorded a week previously. Even after doing the show, they had not realized the extent to which they had been just fodder for Dean Martin's boozy jokes. Jagger was particularly outraged that they should have been set up as stooges, and at once telephoned Eric Easton in London to scream at Easton for having booked the spot. In fact, as Oldham said, the Stones probably gained fans as a result of Martin's behaviour.

Next day, they arrived at Chess Studios, on South Michigan Boulevard. As they walked in, so did a black man with a chubby, kindly face and a small Oriental moustache. 'It was Muddy Waters,' says Bill Wyman. 'He helped us carry our gear inside.'

Two formative days passed at Chess, under the supervision of Ron Malo, a house engineer responsible for some of the greatest work ever recorded by Chuck Berry and Bo Diddley. What Malo had done in the Fifties for Berry and Diddley, he now did for the Rolling Stones, cutting back their native looseness and disorder, focusing tight on the essentials which they themselves still could not see. Under Malo, for the first time, they played, not as a scrabbly rhythm section but in the broken-up style developed by blues masters who had sung and played lead guitar simultaneously. The first few seconds of It's All Over Now, with Keith Richard's bass tremolo growling like the bark of a large dog against Brian Jones's country pizzicato, represents the start of the Stones as, above all, an irresistible compulsion to dance.

No less formative was the mood of the song itself: a lyric about losing love, sung by Mick Jagger with a triumphant and delighted sneer, released at last from the tedious affair and its tiresome 'half-assed games'. Perfectly in counterpoint with the fang-sharp sound, that callow voice grimaced its poison-pen phrases, uncertain – as it would ever be – whether it spoke as victor or victim. The mimic was becoming his own man at last.

Muddy Waters dropped in frequently to talk to the Stones during their session. So did two more of their great Chicago blues idols, Willie Dixon and Buddy Guy. The bluesmen were naturally full of benevolence towards the young Britishers who had given their songs a new lease of life. Later on, even the great Chuck Berry came in to inspect them. Rock 'n' roll's poet laureate, though not best known for charity towards young musicians, thawed considerably in the light of the composer's royalties the Stones were earning him. He praised their version of Reelin' and Rockin', stayed to watch them work on an EP track, Down the Road Apiece, and invited them to visit his nearby estate, Berry Park.

The session concluded, the Stones euphorically called a press conference outside the Chess building on South Michigan Avenue. Several dozen screaming girls turned the occasion into a riot which ended only after a senior Chicago police officer strode up to the Stones and snarled, 'Get outta here or I'll lock up the whole goddamned bunch.'

They had been back on tour only a day or two when Phil Spector, in New York, picked up his office telephone to hear Mick Jagger's voice, speaking from a hotel room in Hershey, Pennsylvania. 'Everything here,' Jagger moaned, 'is fuckin' *brown*!' The Stones that night were performing in a town named, and largely decorated, in honour of its principal product, the Hershey chocolate bar. 'The phones are brown,' Jagger wailed, 'the rooms are brown, even the fuckin' *streets* are brown . . .'

The tour's last weary leg through Pennsylvania and New York State was interrupted by some cheering news from home. In *Record Mirror*'s annual popularity poll, the Stones had pipped the Beatles as Top British Group. Mick Jagger had been named Top British Group Member. The Beatles held their lead only in the Year's Best Single category, She Loves You winning narrowly from the Stones' Not Fade Away.

With the release of another US single, Tell Me, and strategic plugging of their 'England's Newest Hitmakers' album, the Stones, at long last, seemed to be penetrating the consciousness of teenage America. The tour ended in New York on a definite high note with two concerts at Carnegie Hall, scene of the Beatles' triumph six months earlier. Both concerts were promoted by Murrary 'the K' Kaufman, the influential New York disc jockey whom John Lennon had first introduced to the Stones (largely to get the egregious deejay off the Beatles long-suffering backs). Thanks to Murray the K's promotion, the Carnegie Hall concerts were each an immediate sell-out. At the first, Stones fans started running wild before a note had been played. The police forbade the Stones to close the show as planned: instead they were forced to appear halfway and escape during the first interval.

Their return to London, just as America was waking up to them, struck converts like Murray the K as perversely ill-advised. The truth was that Oldham could not afford to keep them, or himself, in New York a minute longer. Oldham had already calculated that, for the whole tour, he and the Stones would receive earnings of approximately ten shillings (50p) each. The story for the British press was that the Stones were returning – £1,500 out of pocket in air fares – to honour a booking, made months earlier when they weren't famous, to play at the annual commemoration ball of Magdalen College, Oxford.

At Heathrow, they were met by a hundred girls and a bevy of newspapermen whose interest was now something more than perfunctory. To one reporter, Keith ingenuously showed the handgun he had bought in America, he said 'as easily as candy floss'. Mick Jagger was met by his girlfriend Chrissie Shrimpton and on enquiries about how he felt at having been placed sixth in *Record Mirror*'s Best Dressed Pop Star list. 'It's a joke,' Jagger replied, speaking in a cockney accent once again.

It's All Over Now was released in Britain on June 26. Advance orders of 150,000 copies put it instantly into every trade paper's Top Ten. Within a week it had risen through the Merseybeat barrier, to challenge and then displace that summer's big surprise hit single, the Animals' House of the Rising Sun.

The organizers of the Magdalen College ball were therefore not a little astonished when, halfway through the night's open-air junketings, it was reported that the Stones had turned up as arranged and were bringing in their equipment. Even the Beatles, generally honourable about bookings, had, the previous year, accepted £500 to play at Christ's College May Ball and had then failed to appear. The Stones' fee had likewise been settled months earlier when they were still only semi-famous. None the less – for reasons never fully apparent – they insisted they must keep their word. It doubtless weighed with them that a major blues artist, Howlin' Wolf, was also due to appear at the Magdalen event, and that they ought not to give ground to its other main pop attraction, Freddie and the Dreamers.

The writer John Heilpern was one of Oxford University's few dedicated Stones fans who purposely crossed the floodlit college lawns, uproarious with patrician cries and steel-band music, to the marquee where the Stones were setting up their equipment in a mood of evident disenchantment. 'They were all deeply pissed off about having to play,' Heilpern remembers. 'They'd been booked to do an hour, so they managed to spend at least the first forty minutes tuning up. Brian Jones already looked zonked out of his mind. There was a sense of vague leadership from Mick Jagger. When he started, everyone did. At first, they didn't try; they were hissed and booed, which obviously delighted them. Then, all of a sudden, they all snapped into it.'

It was a moment, for Heilpern and many others, signifying the start of what would one day be termed 'the counterculture' but what, that night at Oxford, seemed more a question of class turned upside down. The surly, middle-class boys, playing

American r & b, were patently a new aristocracy, just as the dinner-jacketed throng, jigging up and down before them, would become part of a willing new proletariat. The noise spread, through the canvas walls, across grass strewn with debs and duckboards, drowning the steel band. More and more young men in tailcoats, clutching girlfriends and champagne bottles, came in to hear the Stones, and dance.

PART TWO

Five

'My client has no fleas'

Until the 1960s, the Berkshire industrial town of Reading was one of the quietest, most boring places to be found in the entire British Isles. Its only notable architectural feature was the grim Victorian prison where Oscar Wilde was incarcerated and wrote his famous *Ballad of Reading Gaol.* Huntley and Palmer's biscuit factory, itself rather resembling a prison, wafted rich, jammy scents over a drab redbrick townscape whose only other notable literary appearance was in Patrick Hamilton's comic novel *Mr Stimpson and Mr Gorse*. Reading was the very last place on earth one would have looked for an Austrian baroness, let alone the girl fated one day to become Britain's most notorious scarlet woman. Yet there they both were, living in modest Millman Road – Eva Sacher-Masoch, the Baroness Erisso, and her daughter, Marianne.

The Sacher-Masochs are an ancient and illustrious Austrian family dating back to the reign of Charlemagne. Europe's *Who's Who*, the *Almanach de Gotha*, testifies to almost nine centuries of Sacher-Masoch involvement in warfare and the arts, culminating in the nineteenth-century novelist who first described the giving of pain for sexual pleasure, and used his own name to define it: Masochism.

Eva's childhood was dominated by her father, an Austrian

count of the old school, who went off to the Great War much as his forebears had accompanied Charlemagne, with a silver helmet, a cloak and a string of seven Arab chargers. The count survived, with his grandeur almost all intact. Eva spent her girlhood in surroundings of nineteenth-century splendour, albeit tinged with the growing menace of Nazism. A gifted dancer, and very beautiful, she won a place with the famous Max Reinhardt company in Vienna. But for the war in 1939, she would have joined Max Reinhardt in Hollywood and would, undoubtedly, have become a major film star.

It was to be her destiny, instead, to live out the Nazi terror, and so meet and fall in love with an Englishman, Glyn Faithfull, whose peacetime study was research into ancient words and languages. As a philologist, Glyn had been drafted into British wartime intelligence and was in Yugoslavia as a liaison officer with a unit of Tito's partisans that included Eva's brother, Alexander. The story in the family goes that Glyn Faithfull saved Alexander's life. He, in gratitude, recommended the Englishman to the affections of his beautiful sister, herself active in the Viennese Resistance attempting to save Austrian Jews from extermination.

The war over, Glyn Faithfull married his Austrian baroness, brought her home to England and resumed his academic career with a teaching post at Liverpool University. Their only child, Marianne, was born in 1947 and first came to consciousness in the unlikely surroundings of Ormskirk, Lancashire.

Marianne's first real memories begin after the age of six, when her parents separated and Eva took her to live in Reading, in a tiny house which, even so, contained rich reminders of her high-born Austrian heritage. There were the ceremonial dinner plates, from banquets long unaffordable, and leather books from private libraries long dispersed. There was the discovery that Eva spoke in a voice quite different from other girls' mothers; that her speech, her gestures, her very posture belonged to somewhere far from Millman Road. 'Eva had to adapt her whole body to that house,' Marianne says. 'She'd grown up in rooms so big you could just *sweep* across them. At Millman Road there was no room big enough to sweep across. She'd trained herself to be very careful and contained, to suit the size of the rooms we had.'

Marianne remembers with what grande dame style Eva used to invest even the most mundane parts of their life in Reading. 'She'd go round the shops, talking to everyone as if she was touring her estate. One must always be gracious, she said. She told me I had to smile at everyone. And the poorer they were, the nicer I had to be to them.'

The dour Reading shopkeepers were, if anything, more captivated by the little girl who would, in time, do her mother's shopping, carefully repeating Eva's ceremonious: 'One pound of tomatoes – not too big. One ni-ize lettuce . . .' 'Millman Road wasn't in the worst part of Reading, but it was near the worst part. There was one very frightening street I had to go down to the shop where I used to buy my mother's Woodbine cigarettes. "Darleeng . . ." she'd say, "you go out and get me some Voodbines . . ."'

The baroness was a cultivated as well as formidable woman. From her mother, at the earliest age, Marianne learned to read voraciously and appreciate paintings and music. Though money was short, Eva took her back to Vienna to show her where she had come from and visit the city's great museums and galleries. 'My mother taught me something else as well at an early age. She taught me that to be beautiful – as I knew I was – shouldn't be a passive thing. It was something to be put to use, the way that, in the past, she'd put her own beauty to use. I was trained by a highly trained professional.'

A local Catholic convent, St Joseph's, agreed to accept the baroness's daughter as a weekly boarder on semi-charitable terms. 'When I first brought a friend home to Millman Road, I got this terrible shock,' Marianne says. 'I realized that my home wasn't the same as other girls'. I realized my mother was quite different from everyone else's.'

St Joseph's was run by an order of nuns, on principles of medieval strictness. When bathing, the girls had to wear shifts, to avoid the sin of looking at their own nude bodies. It was a system which Marianne, a non-Catholic, found especially repressive and fought against with the enquiring mind her mother had fostered in her. At home, none of the bookcases was ever locked. Marianne and a schoolfriend set about methodically reading through the entire index of books forbidden to Catholics.

At sixteen, both beautiful and intelligent, her future seemed overburdened with promise. Her academic prowess – especially in languages – would have gained her admittance to any of Britain's top universities. Her talent for drama, allied to her looks and pure mezzo-soprano singing voice, would likewise have taken her to the best academies of either drama or music. 'There was no doubt, in my mind or my mother's, that I'd go on the stage. The only question was, how?'

Meanwhile, to use her own wistful phrase, Marianne Faithfull 'lived in a Renoir painting – long blonde hair, sunny days, straw hat with ribbons . . .' She had begun to sing semi-professionally – folk songs, with guitar accompaniment, in a Reading coffee bar to an adoring circle of local college boys. 'I'd learned my lesson from Eva – that beauty was something I had to put to use. I knew things *must* happen to me – that my looks and my voice together were a devastating combination.'

As sixteen, she began going steady with John Dunbar, a Cambridge undergraduate studying fine art at Churchill College. She remembers standing for hours outside the telephone box near her house, waiting to talk to John until her money ran out. He was the first boy to make love to her – in her innocence, she thought he would be the only one. The centre of her world moved from Reading to Cambridge, where she would visit Dunbar at his college, and in London, where his family lived and where he had many friends among the new pop in-crowd.

In the early summer of 1964, Marianne went with John Dunbar to a party in London, given to launch a new girl singer named Adrienne Posta. Many of the in-crowd were there – among them an old friend of John Dunbar's, whose sunglasses and puff-sleeved silk shirt made it hard for Marianne to believe John had first met him through a shared interest in left-wing politics. So she was first introduced to Andrew Loog Oldham while at the same time, across the noisy room, receiving her first sight of her future lover, supporter and nemesis Mick Jagger.

Just then, Jagger's glance was only one in the swarm that settled on honey-blonde hair and the face it framed, in which virginal innocence co-existed with a kind of helpless sensuality, brimming of its own accord in her wide blue eyes and a mouth as tender, as bruisable, as soft, red fruit. Marianne was well aware she had captured the attention of every man in the room. 'I knew I was at that party just as a beautiful woman, to go to the highest bidder,' she says. 'I knew I had to use my looks, the way Eva had said, to create a situation; to make things happen that I wanted to happen.'

What happened was that Andrew Loog Oldham came swaggering up and, on being introduced to Marianne Faithfull, said: 'With a name like that, you ought to be making records.' The name added to the lovely, misty face had set wheels awhirl in Oldham's mind, even before Marianne told him she was already singing semi-professionally. Within literally minutes, Oldham informed her she could become a big star, provided she placed herself under his exclusive management.

She met Mick Jagger, with Keith, a few minutes afterwards, but was not impressed. She disliked Mick's pallor, his spotty face and the studied crudeness of his voice and manner. Jagger's invariable approach to girls he considered 'high class' was ''Ello, darlin'. 'Ow yer doing?' Their first brief conversation ended with

Jagger deliberately slopping wine down the front of Marianne's dress.

Oldham, it transpired, had been absolutely serious. Within a few days of the party, Marianne found herself offered a formal management contract and a recording test with the Stones' label, Decca. Since she herself was only seventeen, all contracts had to be endorsed by her mother, the baroness. 'Eva signed everything, even though she didn't really know what it was about,' Marianne says. 'Her one stipulation was that when I went out on tour, I must always have a chaperon.'

Oldham's real plan, as always, was for the greater expansion of Andrew Loog Oldham. The manager of the pop group which had outraged Britain now saw his chance to perpetrate an even greater surprise. What more surprising contrast could there be to the shaggy, surly Rolling Stones than a sweet-faced ex-convent girl whose voice was softly elegant and whose mother was an Austrian noblewoman? With a chaperon thrown in as well, Oldham's promotional script was practically writing itself.

To launch Marianne Faithfull on record, Oldham planned to use a song by Lionel Bart, a composer of stage musicals then at his apotheosis. The B-side was to be Greensleeves, with slight modifications that would allow Oldham, not King Henry VIII, to claim the composer's credit.

The Lionel Bart song, unfortunately, did not suit Marianne's voice. Oldham therefore had no alternative but to order a song from a composing team whose efforts thus far had been confined to sentimental ballads – Mick Jagger and Keith Richard. 'I told them, Marianne's a convent girl. I want a song with brick walls all around it, and high windows and *no* sex.'

These tight restrictions, paradoxically, set free the creative chemistry between Mick and Keith that they had almost despaired of discovering. As Time Goes By – subsequently retitled As Tears Go By – was their first *real* song in the sense that it sprang wholly from within themselves, stamped unmistakably with a shared character. Simple, even elegant, imbued with overtones of Tennyson's Lady of Shalott, its qualities startled no one more than its two composers. For weeks afterwards, Mick remembers, they would rack their brains in fruitless attempts to write something else as good.

Marianne went into the Decca studios under much the same strictures, performing the song in the most muted possible version of her rich mezzo voice. The result was what Oldham had wanted: a convent girl singing sweetly and shyly, with high walls and no sex. In August 1964, As Tears Go By was number nine in the charts. Marianne Faithfull was Britain's latest female singing star. 'Greensleeves goes Pop,' the *Daily Mirror* said.

To this day, Oldham carries around with him a letter he received from Marianne just prior to her debut television appearance on *Ready, Steady, Go*. With almost painful shyness and politeness, she asks directions to the studios in Kingsway and hopes the show will be over in time for her to catch her last train back to Reading.

Caliban's island was not more full than Great Britain, in August 1964, of the sound of voices and 'twangling instruments', beamed from insecure moorings three miles distant, their harbinger a watery ship's bell.

Giorgio Gomelsky's fellow Method actor Ronan O'Rahilly was the first – by a cat's whisker – to get the big idea. For years, British entrepreneurs had dreamed of starting pop radio stations in the American style, but had always been thwarted by the BBC's legally enforced monopoly. O'Rahilly's wheeze was to fit out a ship as a radio station and begin transmitting off the Essex coast, outside Britain's three-mile territorial limit. Radio Caroline announced itself over the 1964 Easter bank holiday, with a record clearly chosen to echo its own piratical effrontery: Not Fade Away by the Rolling Stones. Almost simultaneously, a rival ship, Radio Atlanta – fitted out in the same Irish port, despite heavy sabotage from O'Rahilly's supporters – began pouring the same heady mixture of continuous pop, American-style commercials and station identification jingles into Britain's radio sets.

Within a few weeks, the two pirate stations, as they were instantly dubbed, together had an audience numbering hundreds of thousands. Official attempts to ban them under the Wireless Telegraphy Acts revealed that they were indeed beyond parliamentary jurisdiction. It became evident also that Radio Caroline and Radio Atlanta were providing something the public wanted, despite years of BBC insistence to the contrary. The pirates therefore could continue, and multiply. Soon there was Radio London; Radio Scotland; Radio Clyde; Radio Sutch; Radio Invicta; Radio City. Transmitter ships littered the North Sea, locked in a wavelength war that occasionally spilled into actual violence. A man was even killed in a night attack on the disused Thames Estuary fort which housed Radio City.

The muffled creaks of pirate ship timbers, and groans of their intermittently seasick young disc jockeys, are an essential element in recalling the 1964 'Beat Boom'. The sounds were the more exciting for rising and falling somewhat, as the vessel did; being smuggled into the radio dial, like so much contraband.

With those thousand twangling instruments – bought usually on the instalment plan – came voices, multifariously accented. Following Liverpool's glorification, other far-flung provincial capitals could also now pride themselves on emitting a competitively fashionable sound. As well as Mersey groups (Pacemakers, Searchers, Mojos, All Stars, Chants, Undertakers, Flamingoes) and Manchester groups (Hollies, Dakotas, Mindbenders, Hermits, Dreamers), there were Birmingham groups (Applejacks, Fortunes, Ivy League); there were Tyneside groups (Animals, Bluechips); Scotttish groups (Luvvers, Poets) and Irish groups (Bachelors, Them). London restored its dented cultural superiority with groups mingling club r & b with aggressive Mod culture

(The Who, Small Faces, Kinks). There were all-instrument groups (Jaywalkers, Blues Inc) and all-vocal groups (Four Pennies, Walker Brothers). There were earnest groups (Manfred Mann, Yardbirds) and comical groups (Fourmost, Rockin' Berries, Barron Knights). There were, in short, dozens, if not hundreds of groups. And, presumably, that Decca executive who had pronounced guitar groups to be on the way out was still in his Albert Embankment office, trying to kick himself to death.

Whatever the passing allegiance for this or that newly fashionable group, being a pop fan in 1964 Britain depended on one fundamental question: 'Are you Beatles or are you Stones?' asked with the searching ferocity of rival factions in a football crowd. Even football factions, though, had scarcely been as rife with implications of reflected character.

To answer 'Beatles' implied that one was oneself similarly amiable, good-natured, a believer in the power of success to effect conformity. To answer 'Stones' meant, more succinctly, that one wished to smash up the entire British Isles. On June 24, a Stones concert in the Winter Gardens, Blackpool, provoked a riot that seventy policemen could not contain. The Stones themselves came under heavy attack, from hails of spittle and grabbing hands that eventually succeeded in pulling a Steinway grand piano off the stage. The journalist Roy Carr – then a musician in a back-up band – remembers with what deep gratification he saw Keith Richard persuade an over-eager fan to retreat from the stage rim by sinking one pointed boot toe in his face. Afterwards, Ian Stewart, the imperturbable, came round to their dressing room to distribute various chips of splintered wood, saying, 'Here's your guitar . . . and here's your amp . . .'

On July 3, a Stones concert in Belfast was cancelled for fear of some similar outbreak. What Belfast avoided, Holland received in double measure eight days later, when the Stones caused the virtual destruction of a cinema in The Hague. Next day, when they arrived back in Manchester for a *Ready, Steady, Go* appearance, a door was wrenched bodily from their hired limousine. So it continued, in Liverpool, Manchester, Carlisle and Edinburgh, the splinter of chairs and woodwork threatening to drown even the chart success of their new EP, Five by Five. Their progress, viewed on old newsreels and TV film, shows what a change was coming over pop concerts. More police, more 'stewards' of more and more doubtful provenance, massed along the stage front. More foolhardy lunges at Mick Jagger by desperate girls. More nonchalant violence in the seizing of such girls by their arms, legs, even their hair, to toss them back into the crowd.

The virus was spreading into parts of Europe where even Beatlemania had not taken root. On October 18 – despite an attempt to ban them by Belgium's Minister of the Interior – the Stones played to a howling sea of heads at the Brussels World's Fair ground. Two nights later, in Paris, the pop concert in its old, innocent, sedentary form was finally laid to rest. The Stones' show at the Olympia Theatre ended in running fights between gendarmes and youths who ran amok through the boulevards, breaking shop windows, slashing at newspaper kiosks, overturning café tables and hurling customers on to the pavement. The *Daily Mirror* reported that 150 arrests had been made.

On October 23, the bacillus was once more reported en route to the American continent. America's worst fears were confirmed by a publicity photograph, showing the Stones apparently in an advanced state of destitution, Mick Jagger engaged in scratching himself like a baboon while Keith peered with absorption inside the waistband of his jeans. 'The Rolling Stones, who haven't washed for a week . . .' the caption began.

At Kennedy airport, girls who broke from the crowd barriers were felled by policemen with flying football tackles. One of them, pulled forth for a random TV interview, proved surprisingly lucid in answer to the stock question, 'Why do you like the Stones?'

'Because . . . Keith is beautiful, and because . . . they're so ugly, they're attractive.'

Their appearance on the Ed Sullivan TV show on October 26 presented Sullivan's coast-to-coast audience with the interesting spectacle of a studio apparently being torn to shreds by its audience. Sullivan issued a statement, disclaiming responsibility for the Stones' engagement and vowing they would never pollute his air time again. 'I promise you, they'll never be back on our show . . . Frankly, I didn't see the Rolling Stones until the day before the broadcast. They were recommended by my scouts in England. I was shocked myself when I saw them.

'Now the Dave Clark Five *are* nice fellows. They're gentlemen and they perform well. It took me seventeen years to build this show. I'm not going to have it destroyed in a matter of weeks.'

Another TV clip shows Mick Jagger being interviewed, next to an anxious-looking Charlie Watts. The usual establishment interviewer, bald and bow-tied, speaks devoutly into his microphone, then thrusts it outward as if only half convinced Jagger is capable of speech. 'Er, Mick . . . er, how are you all enjoying your first trip to the States? I'm sorry: your *second* trip.'

'Yes, our second trip,' Jagger replies. 'Yes, it's been very enjoyable. Highly enjoyable, yes.' His voice is deliberately polite and hushed to semi-audibility.

'But that's not the way it was the first time you came over.'

'Oh, *no*,' Jagger says, contriving in the same moment to be both emphatic and utterly uninterested. 'When we first came over here, it was just to get ourselves known about, so to speak.' His voice softens to a sing-song, little-boyish lisp, like Brian's. 'And then we went back. And things started happenin' for uth.'

'And, uh . . . why was that?'

'Dunno.' Jagger smiles his shy smile and shrugs. 'Some . . . chemical reaction.'

On the West Coast, between studio sessions at RCA,

Hollywood, the Stones appeared on a TAMI (Teenage Music International) pop package show, filmed at Santa Monica Civic Auditorium and shown later in cinemas throughout America. Technically, they topped the bill, headlining above Gerry and the Pacemakers, Jan and Dean, Chuck Berry, the Beach Boys, Marvin Gaye and Smokey Robinson and the Miracles. Even James Brown, grand master and autocrat of all black soul singers, had his name in smaller type than the Stones. 'We were all terrified about appearing on the same bill as James Brown,' Bill Wyman says. 'He'd told everybody that when he went onstage, he was going to make the Rolling Stones wish they'd never set foot in America.

'We were all in the dressing room beforehand, really scared. And Marvin Gaye and Chuck Berry came in to see us. Marvin Gaye said, "Are you guys nervous?" We said, "Petrified." He was really nice. He said, "Hey, go out there and just do your best. Nobody wants to know if you're better than anybody. They only want to know that you're on."'

They stood in the wings, a little comforted, watching James Brown steal the show as expected with his frantic energy and whooping lust, with shrieking and pleading and impossible preening, a sweat-shiny dynamo trapped on the moving staircase of his own feet. They watched the bizarre multi-encore finale in which Brown, on his knees, was forcibly wrapped in a cloak by bodyguards and strong-armed towards the wings, before turning and throwing off the cloak – exact to a drum roll – and starting to sing and dance and sweat anew.

The Stones did not expect to surpass that. But they still gave a performance impressive enough for 'Mr Dynamite' to grant them an audience in the dressing room where he sat, surrounded by black retainers and stage shoes and tubs of champagne on ice. It was the first time that Mick Jagger had realized that a musician could be a monarch and despot also. Jagger, indeed, returned to London having learned the most crucial object lesson of his life.

To Chuck Berry's voice and Rufus Thomas's grimaces were now added James Brown's dance steps – the very way Brown boogied up to unclip his microphone.

'That was when the Mick Jagger we know began,' Giorgio Gomelsky says. 'After that second trip to America. When Mick got off the plane back in London, he was doing the James Brown slide.'

The presentation of the Rolling Stones' new single, Little Red Rooster, on *Ready, Steady, Go*, had an avant-garde audacity which would have done credit to Samuel Beckett. At first, all the viewer saw was a mouth, unmistakable for its sullen and insolent, overstuffed lips. 'I am the little red rooster,' sang this oracle wetly, 'too lazy to crow for days . . .' The mouth on its own sang a full chorus before the camera pulled back to show Jagger's face and, at length, the other Stones behind him, misty and subservient in the sleepwalking beat whose only ornamentation was the tremulous swoops and shocks of a lone bar slide guitar.

It had seemed like a gamble for the Stones to follow up a pop hit like It's All Over Now with an unreformed blues classic, written by Willie Dixon and first recorded by Howlin' Wolf. In the event, Little Red Rooster proved the ideal vehicle, both for the Stones as blues purists and for Mick Jagger as an increasingly audacious purveyor of sexual innuendo. It was a production as compulsive instrumentally as vocally, with Brian Jones's slide guitar see-sawing from a low throb, like blood through an artery, up to its palpitant, quivering high.

Jagger, performing the song on *Ready, Steady, Go*, seemed less like a pop vocalist than a young lord posing for some Mayfair portraitist with barely good grace. It confirmed what the pop audience was beginning to suspect – that he and the Stones inhabited a world more private and privileged than even Associated-Rediffusion's Kingsway studios. The fact was corroborated by the London *Daily Express*'s William Hickey column, hitherto the exclusive preserve of society hostesses, playboys and debutantes. 'There's no harm these days in knowing a Rolling Stone,' the Hickey columnist wrote. '. . . some of their best friends, in fact, are fledglings from the upper classes . . .'

Robert Fraser, the London art dealer, was such a friend, though scarcely a fledgling. The son of a Scots merchant banker, he had been educated at Eton and then taken a commission in the army, serving with distinction in the Kenya Mau-Mau emergency. In 1964, he already enjoyed high standing in the London art world for his prescient championing of American pop artists like Andy Warhol and Jim Dine. Slight and dark and nervous-looking, he combined formidable taste with a passion for novelty, adventure and low life. With these the Rolling Stones would furnish Robert Fraser in all too great abundance.

He had met them first in Paris after their Olympia concert, while police were still scooping up rioters from the debris of wrecked pavement cafés. 'I'd bumped into Teddy, the disc jockey from the Ad Lib, who'd come over specially to see the Stones. They knew Teddy well, of course, because he was so into their black music. Through Teddy I got talking to Brian Jones – who even then seemed very paranoid. Later on, I took them all to a party at Donald Cammell's studio.'

Cammell, an American painter and would-be film-maker, would also figure prominently in the Stones' social conversion. That night in 1964, he was simply host at a party where five British pop musicians were the very least glamorous and fashionable guests. 'They all looked very ugly, very scruffy,' Robert Fraser later remembered. 'Mick was just a rude slob. You could tell it was the first time any of them had been to a place like Donald's or to a party like that – big studio . . . low lights, wonderful-looking women . . . drugs . . .'

Fraser subsequently introduced them to his Old Etonian friend Christopher Gibbs, a young antique dealer whose Chelsea shop was credited as source of the current mania for Moroccan decor in fashionable Mayfair and Belgravia homes. Gibbs was nephew of the Governor of Rhodesia, a friend of Cecil Beaton, whose diary describes him as 'a most cultivated young man'. He was also a unique mixture of modern wit and old-fashioned courtliness. With Fraser and Cammell, he was the Stones' initiator into an older metropolitan clique whose raffish doings had titillated society columns during the middle and late Fifites. Brian, Mick and Keith, as modern counterparts – with the added attraction of money to burn – were welcomed with open arms into the 'Chelsea Set'.

John Lennon, with his infallible gift for an apt phrase, said that fashionable young London in 1964 was 'like a gentleman's smoking club'. The in-crowd, yearningly celebrated by pop song and newspaper report, in fact consisted of no more than a dozen faces, moving in a pack around the same tiny circuit of late-night West End clubs. And no club was truly 'in' until its high-priced darkness could disclose the chalk-pale face of a Beatle or a Rolling Stone or – in the innermost in-ness – a Beatle and a Stone conversing together.

The deadly rivals of the Top Twenty and music press popularity polls were, in private life, very good friends. The Stones readily admitted that without George Harrison they might never have got their Decca contract, just as without Lennon and McCartney, they would never have had a hit single. The Beatles, on their side, felt sneaking envy of the Stones' refusal to compromise themselves with stage suits and insincere smiles, the way even John Lennon had been forced to do.

The Stones' challenge to the Beatles as a pop attraction had, if anything, increased the bond between them. Being so famous that one constantly risked being torn limb from limb was a predicament that no one else understood quite so well. Likewise, the predicament of being showered with pocket money while, at the same time, vaguely realizing one was not half so rich as one might think. In the expensive darkness of the Ad Lib, Beatles and

Stones first compared notes about their record contracts and royalty rates. The surprise was that the Beatles, for all their international money-spinning, actually earned less per copy of each single and album than did the Stones.

Robert Fraser was a friend of both Beatles and Stones – one of many they had in common. Andrew Loog Oldham's crony Peter Asher was the brother of Paul McCartney's actress girlfriend, Jane Asher. Paul had for some months lodged at the Ashers' Wimpole Street house, in an attic room occupied by a bed, a wardrobe, two Cocteau drawings and a cache of Gold Discs. Paul was friendly with John Dunbar, boyfriend of Oldham's protégée, Marianne Faithfull – herself the strongest infusion of gentility into the Stones' background. When Marianne broadcast a charity appeal on Radio Caroline in the winter of 1964, it was with all the quiet, self-effacing dignity of minor royalty.

The Beatles were now making their second feature film, *Help!*, in a state of helpless hilarity which even their director, Richard Lester, did not recognize as their first high from smoking marijuana. Bob Dylan, a rising American folk singer, had introduced them, in New York, to this traditional resort of American jazz and blues musicians. Illegal in Britain, it was supposed – by the police as much as anyone – to have died out with the novels of Sax Rohmer. The small, draggled cigarette thus carried minimal risk, passing from the Beatles to their friends the Rolling Stones, the next novelty after hipster trousers or tinted sunglasses or Mateus rosé wine or Scotch and Coke.

Those little transparent packets of grass added the merest wavelet to a narcotic ocean which, long before 1964, had made London the drug capital of the Western world. It had begun in Victorian times, when Britain's imperial possessions encompassed the Chinese opium trade, and every local tobacconist sold 'opium lozenges' as a cough remedy available to all. Narcotic substances, long outlawed in other countries, continued to be present in mundane British products like nose inhalers, stomach mixture, even laughing powder from joke shops. Britain was the only country where pure heroin was available by prescription from any doctor, and could be bought on the street with considerably less risk than attended the passing of a bet for horse racing. 'I remember when you could buy heroin jacks [tablets] for a pound each,' Robert Fraser said. 'A phial of pure cocaine for fifty pounds. There were smart doctors all over Mayfair who'd prescribe it for you.'

Hard drugs, in other words, had been an upper-class pursuit long before pop musicians started giggling over marijuana. Fraser himself had smoked grass years before, in New York's avant-garde art circles. Like others before, and since, he was not so much hooked by heroin as seduced by it. Long cured from addiction, he still shuddered to remember that first 'rush', so very different from soft-drug fuzziness. 'That's the thing about heroin. It doesn't disorient you. It seems to *stabilize* you. It's a feeling like you've been wandering around in the Antarctic for days, and you suddenly walk into a nice warm room with a bar.'

As Andrew Loog Oldham stood in the howling throng, his bodyguard, Reg – alternatively known as Reg the Butcher – would struggle up to join him, looking cautiously over one shoulder and speaking, as far as possible, in an urgent undertone. 'Don't move a muscle, Andrew,' Reg the Butcher would caution. 'There are eight blokes standing right behind you . . .'

It was the newest of Oldham's fantasies that he needed a muscle-bound protector, like those Phil Spector employed, to shield him from the righteous fury, or murderous envy, of the world on which he had unleashed the Rolling Stones. So Reg the Butcher rode around with him in his powder-blue American Chevrolet and sat in on his business meetings. The idea was that Oldham, whenever thwarted, would say 'Go and thump that guy, Reg,' and Reg would go and thump the guy.

'Actually,' Oldham says, 'he got me into more fights than he got me out of. Like when he'd come up and say "Don't move. There are eight people behind you . . ." "Reg," I'd say. "We're at a concert. This is a crowd. There are *bound* to be eight people standing behind me . . ." '

The Stones' second album, released on January 30, 1965, launched Oldham into a new phase of egotistical fantasy. Once again, Decca's art department had been compelled to accept a front cover devoid of the title artists' name, and adorned by a David Bailey photograph calculated to make every British parent reach for the DDT. Five faces in close-up glowered from deep shadow that still did not hide the many scars and pimples and craters left by former pimples on Keith Richard's face. Mick Jagger stood right at the back, craning his neck to see over the others' heads. 'I put Mick there deliberately,' Bailey says. 'I didn't want the others to think he was getting special treatment because he was a friend of mine.'

On the back of the album was Oldham's literary debut: a sleeve note written in the prose style of Anthony Burgess's *A Clockwork Orange*:

> It is the summer of the night London's eyes be shut tight all but twelve peepers and six hip malchicks who prance the street. Newspaper-strewn and gray which waits another day to hide its dingy countenance the six have been sound ball journey made to another sphere which pays royalties in eight months or a year.
>
> . . . This is The Stones' new disc within. Cast deep in your pockets for loot to buy this disc of groovies and fancy words. If you don't have the bread, see that blind man, knock him on the head, steal his wallet and lo and behold, you have the loot. If you put in the boot, good. Another one sold.

The album itself was rather routine – predominantly r & b in content, yet somehow lacking the manic live quality of its predecessor. The tracks had been made at three different studios, so varied in texture from the discipline of Chess, Chicago – evident on a version of Chuck Berry's Down the Road Apiece which Chuck Berry himself had heard and commended – through rather muted soul gushers, recorded at RCA, Hollywood, with Phil Spector's arranger Jack Nitzsche on piano, to Regent Sound's egg-box echo, featured on a limp Jagger-Richard effort, Grown Up Wrong. Mick and Keith were wholly successful, however, with Left Off The Hook, a bed-sitting room vignette suffused with Jagger's sneering imperviousness to feminine wiles. Conversely, Time Is On My Side – copied from the Irma Thomas version – reminded him of close moments with Chrissie, and became a tender soliloquy more personal than anything he would ever write for himself.

Oldham cannot now remember whether it was a conscious or merely subconscious instinct to galvanize their rather anti-climactic production with a sleeve note recommending people to knock down blind men and steal their wallets. Certainly the ensuing furore had a stage-managed element, not breaking out until a full month after *Rolling Stones No. 2* had hit the shops. Then all at once a Mrs Gwen Matthews, secretary of the Bournemouth Blind Aid Association, was quoted as saying 'They're horrible. It's putting ideas into people's heads. I'm writing to Decca to ask them to change the cover . . .'

Within a week, Oldham had a scandal which, for the first time, caused his name to appear in print as many times as the Stones'. The *Daily Telegraph* quoted him as saying he had written the offending passage 'for fun, in the bath'. Decca, bowing to pressure from Mrs Matthews and others, called back as many copies of the LP as possible, and reissued them in a new sleeve with the offending paragraph deleted. But the scandal would not subside. In the House of Lords, a former Conservative minister asked for the Director of Public Prosecutions to investigate what appeared to be 'a deliberate incitement to criminal action'. A Home Office spokesman replied that there were insufficient grounds, adding: 'If it is any consolation to the noble lord, research I made at the weekend supports the view that, even when they are intelligible, the words of a pop song are not considered important, and teenagers have even less regard to the blurb on the envelope.'

On their first Australasian and Far East tour earlier in January, Oldham had definitely cast himself as the sixth Stone – if not the first. 'The boys and I,' he told pressmen, with mock-regal sarcasm, at Sydney airport, 'were moved as we stood on the steps of the airliner which had brought us to this distant land, receiving a tremendous welcome from these warm-hearted and wonderful colonials.' The warm-hearted colonials, 3,000 of them, were even now tearing down a chain-wire perimeter fence and wrenching up rails from their steel floor bolts.

The thirty-day tour of Australia and New Zealand established the Stones as a menace to antipodean stability, with newspaper headlines like SHOCKERS! UGLY LOOKS! UGLY SPEECH! UGLY MANNERS! on the one hand and on the other, hysteria-sodden concerts in Sydney, Melbourne, Brisbane, Perth, Adelaide and Wellington. By the end of the tour, the Stones had four records in the Australian Top Ten, including their weak cover version of the Drifters' Under the Boardwalk. A disbelieving Britain had meanwhile seen wire service photographs of them immersing themselves in Auckland's hot springs and all five – even Keith Richard – apparently enjoying the sunshine and open air.

On February 26, Decca released a new Stones single that was to prove to Oldham beyond all doubt that he could make hits happen by the mesmeric power of his will. With The Last Time, Mick Jagger and Keith Richard, under duress from their manager, had at last written something good enough for an A-side. The song itself was basic and Bo Diddley-esque. What lifted it out of the ordinary was a four-note guitar phrase by Keith Richard that slithered through the lyric with a malign, unignorable persistence, like migraine rendered into sound.

The Last Time went to number one in Britain eight days after its release. With the top-selling British single as well as top LP *and* EP (Five By Five), the Stones might reasonably have expected a rest. Instead, Oldham and Easton launched them afresh on a British tour, itself to be turned into a further EP, Got Live If You Want It, engineered by their IBC friend, Glyn Johns, and containing scream-rent versions of Pain In My Heart and Everybody Needs Somebody to Love. One track consisted solely of the audience chanting 'We want the Stones.' It was *technically* a song,' Oldham says. 'So we thought Nanker Phelge might as well cop the proceeds from the publishing.'

Oldham's ambitions had by now outgrown any simple group of five. From January 1964, he began recording for Decca in his own right as director of 'the Andrew Loog Oldham Orchestra'. Studio session men in huge numbers – sometimes including individual Stones – would be assembled periodically to perform such Oldham orchestral compositions as Funky and Fleopatra; 365 Rolling Stones; and the tortuously punning Theme for a Mod Summer Night's Ball.

Only one obstacle remained between Oldham and total fulfilment. This was, alas, not something which Reg the Butcher could arrange by going over and thumping somebody. It could only come in a letter such as Paul McCartney in his Wimpole Street bedsitter had just received from his Mayfair accountants. Andrew Loog Oldham, despite his hold over Britain's number one hit-making pop group, still, somehow or other, had not managed to become a millionaire.

The Stones, despite selling something like a million singles and albums for Decca, remained victims of an accountancy system which did not pay artists their royalty earnings for anything up to a year. Decca saw no reason to change this practice, even though the Stones' initial two-year recording contract was due to expire in May 1965, and several other major labels – notably American CBS – had already expressed passionate eagerness to sign them.

The present British tour, though sold out at all its seventy shows, was still resolutely failing to make anyone's fortune. Oldham and Eric Easton were in legal dispute with their co-promoter, the Australian Robert Stigwood, for allegedly not paying their agreed percentage of the box-office receipts. Keith, in particular, felt so strongly about the £10,000 involved that he confronted Robert Stigwood at a London club and – in the words of journalist Keith Altham – 'started to beat the shit out of him. Every time Stigwood tried to get up, Keith would belt him again. "Keith," I said, "why do you keep *on* hitting him?" "Because he keeps getting up," Keith said.'

The Swinging Summer of 1965 found Oldham still eager and eagle-eyed for every possible farthing. It was his reason, that August, for going to London's Hilton Hotel to have breakfast with the New York accountant Allen Klein. Klein was Sam Cooke's manager, and also proprietor of the song-publishing company which held copyright on the Rolling Stones' recent big hit, It's All Over Now. Oldham, as usual, hoped to obtain a share of the song's publishing royalties.

At the Hilton – after brief general pleasantries – Klein asked Andrew Loog Oldham a simple but devastating question. 'Andrew,' he said. 'How'd you like to be a millionaire?'

Oldham replied that he would, very much.

'Okay,' Klein said. 'Whaddaya want for now?'

'I want a Rolls-Royce,' Andrew Loog Oldham replied.

'You got it,' said Klein.

It was the summer when British life broke up and rearranged itself on a kaleidoscopic array of seeming brand-newness. Everywhere, there seemed to be new clothes, new trends, new wounds, new looks, new promises for the future. Matters far more important than mere pop music had come to be computed in terms of image. National euphoria reached its highest point in 1965 when almost everyone seemed to have got their image just right.

Harold Wilson had brought the Labour Party back to power after thirteen years in exile, with a slogan borrowed from teenage culture (Let's Go With Labour) and promises of national revival, after decadent Toryism, administered by clean, bright, classless young ministers, 'forged in the white heat of the technological revolution'. So stupendously successful had been Harold Wilson's verbal gimmickry that the Conservatives, too, now looked to their image, dismissing the skeletal Scottish laird who had been their last prime minister and choosing as leader a middle-class, ex-grammar-school boy whose recreations were not grouse-shooting and port drinking but yachting and playing the church organ. Amazing as it must seem to posterity, Edward Heath was intended to fire the imagination of the young.

The Tories, colouring Heath's shirt a shade darker blue on campaign posters, did not yet realize they were competing with a master. In May 1965, the Queen's Birthday Honours list – drawn up by her Prime Minister – created each of the four Beatles Members of the Most Excellent Order of the British Empire. By that brilliant stroke, Harold Wilson's Socialist government and the bigger and bigger booming youth market became synonymous. Those who had feared Labour's restoration would mean a return to postwar austerity saw with amazement that it meant op-art dresses, Carnaby Street boutiques and pop stars skipping into Buckingham Palace like an extra scene from *A Hard Day's Night*.

Throughout that whole deluded summer, Britain could be said to contain only one genuinely and unapologetically wicked element. One stubborn obstacle to Harold Wilson's yeah-yeah Utopia reaffirmed its disruptive presence on July 22 at West Ham Magistrates' Court, in a case which was to arouse comment and disgust across the nation.

Mr Charles Keeley, manager of the Francis service station in Romford Road, Stratford, testified that late on the night of March 18, a chauffeur-driven Daimler had pulled on to his garage forecourt and a 'shaggy-haired monster' – identified in court as Bill Wyman – had got out and asked 'in disgusting language' whether he could use the lavatory. Mr Keeley – whose whole testimony suggested that before he took up garage work he had been resident in a monastery – replied that the public washroom was out of order, and refused to allow use of a staff one inside. At this, he said, 'eight or nine youths and girls', including Mick Jagger and Brian Jones, got out of the car and Jagger pushed him aside, saying, 'We piss anywhere, man.' The phrase was taken up by the others in what was described as a 'gentle chant', with one of the party even dancing in time to it. Jagger, Jones and Wyman, it was alleged, then walked across and urinated in a line against the forecourt wall.

Convicted for 'insulting behaviour', they were fined three pounds each, with fifteen pounds court costs. 'Because you have reached exalted heights in your profession, it does not mean you can behave in this manner,' the chairman of the magistrates said, speaking against female uproar from the public gallery which suggested precisely the opposite.

The story of Charles Keeley's midnight ordeal was splashed in every national newspaper, accompanied by pictures of the five Stones (Keith and Charlie had appeared as character witnesses) emerging from the court in handy juxtaposition to headlines like the *Sunday Express*'s LONG-HAIRED MONSTERS. Buried deep in each spun-out narrative was the significant fact that the prosecution had not been a police matter, but had been brought privately by Mr Keeley and a garage customer, Mr Eric Lavender, 'former chief warden at the Dunning Hall Youth Club'. Both asked to give their addresses to the court in writing for fear of reprisals from Stones fans.

The incident at Charles Keeley's service station was a moderate retaliation to what the Stones themselves had suffered, from garage attendants and many others intent on striking some similar ad hoc blow for common decency. Wherever they stopped, however well-mannered their behaviour, they still faced persecution, in open insults and arbitrary bans from roadside hotels, restaurants and cafés. A scattered few places like the Ram Jam Inn or the Blue Boar café – as their food-splattered walls bore witness – catered specifically for travelling pop groups. Otherwise, the Stones had no choice but to use lorry-drivers' pull-ups and motorway service areas, which brought them into direct contact with a public literally thirsting for their blood.

Loudly insulted from almost every surrounding table in one particular motorway restaurant, they managed to consume a greasy, over-priced breakfast, showing no reaction whatever. 'When we got up to leave,' Bill Wyman says, 'we went and ordered one fried egg to be served to everyone in the place. All the people who'd been abusing us suddenly got a single fried egg each put in front of them and were told that it was from us. This really British thing took over – everyone started nodding at us and smiling and saying "Oh – thanks very much . . ." '

Police patrol cars were simultaneously waking up to the fact that enormous black limousines with dark-shaded windows did not transport only cabinet ministers and foreign diplomats. From mid-1964, the Stones had to contend with ritual police checks and exuberant prosecutions for minor traffic offences, pumped up by press headlines into yet further evidence of Britain's moral disintegration. When, in late 1964, Mick Jagger was summonsed on three such minuscule charges at Tettenhall, Staffordshire, his solicitor felt obliged to deliver a long and eloquent plea that the length of Jagger's hair should not count as an additional offence. 'The Duke of Marlborough had hair longer than my client, and he won several famous battles. *His* hair was powdered, I think because of fleas. My client has no fleas . . .'

The Stones' tour of America and Canada, in April and May 1965, brought them up against police methods hurriedly evolved under the joint stimulus of pop and civil rights movement. At their Ottawa concert, a fifty-strong police cordon stood on the stage with them, literally blotting them from sight. In London, Ontario, the police stopped the show after fifteen minutes by turning on the house lights and cutting off the power to the Stones' amplifiers. 'We felt sorry for the fans, not getting a proper show,' Mick Jagger says, 'so we *did* sort of gang up on the police.' CRUDE AND RUDE ROLLING STONES HURL INSULTS AT POLICE was the next day's banner headline. Hundreds of calls to local radio stations, however, made it clear whom the audience blamed for the shambles.

Sometimes, backstage, Keith or Brian would be approached by a mountainous cop with a Rolling Stones album in his hand, and words to the general effect: 'Sign this, ya long-haired sissy pervert, or I'll bust ya goddamned head open.' Other officers made it clear that, though they might regard the Stones as semi-human, they were still prepared to be insulted by a sufficiently large bribe. 'That happened when we first went on the *Ed Sullivan Show*,' Bill Wyman says. 'Hundreds of girls were screaming and yelling outside the theatre. The police came and told us that if we wanted protection, we'd have to pay them off. Every hour, they came back and told us we'd have to give them more money or they'd go away.'

With The Last Time at number eight in the *Billboard* Hot Hundred, there was naturally no more talk of their being banned from the Sullivan show. They made a return appearance on May 2, looking slightly smarter, at their host's earnest insistence, and even agreeing to be cooped up in the studio for eight hours before transmission. This time they appeared twice, playing The Last Time, then coming back for an unprecedented four-song encore. Sullivan afterwards sent them a conciliatory telegram. 'Received hundreds of calls from parents complaining about you but thousands from teenagers praising you. Best of luck on your tour . . .'

Their other main TV spot was on *Shindig*, a nationally popular music show directed by the emigré British pop promotor Jack Good. 'Howlin' Wolf had come up from South California or somewhere to be with us on *Shindig*,' Keith says. 'I'll always remember Jack Good's voice on the set, very English, calling out, "Er – Howlin', could you do that again?" and "Er, Mr Wolf . . ." '

It was on the tour's Southern leg – at a small motel in Clearwater, Florida – that Keith played over to Mick Jagger a guitar riff which, he thought, might be the basis of a makeweight track for the Stones' next LP. 'I'd woken up in the middle of the night, thought of the riff and put it straight down on a tape. In the morning, I still thought it sounded pretty good. I played it to Mick and said, "The words that go with this are *I can't get no satisfaction*." That was just a working title. It could just as well have been Auntie Millie's Caught Her Left Tit in the Mangle. I thought of it as just a little riff, an album filler. I never thought it was anything like commercial enough to be a single.'

Even after Jagger had gone away and written words developing this basic 'hook', Keith could not be persuaded that he'd hit on an inspirational new Stones A-side. 'I think Keith felt it was too basic . . . just a silly kind of a riff,' Jagger says. 'And he was afraid it would sound like folk rock. Doing Satisfaction was the only real time we ever had a disagreement.'

The song was tried out on tape, first at Chess Studios, Chicago, then at RCA, Hollywood, under Dave Hassinger's supervision and in the stimulating atmosphere of having recently escaped being crushed to death together in a limousine. After the Long Beach concert, 10,000 fans surged forward, through security barriers and around the Stones' black Chrysler motorcade. For some minutes they were entombed by bodies and wrenching fingers and faces upside down, silently screaming, until police managed to clear a path ahead.

At RCA, Keith worked on his silly little riff some more, feeding it now through a Gibson fuzzbox that lacquered each note into the malign darkness of ink or ebony. The result, as mixed by Dave Hassinger, struck everyone – but Keith – as the best thing the Stones had ever done in a studio. Keith still argued with Mick that (I Can't Get No) Satisfaction was too weak for an A-side, and that people would recognize his intro as a copy from Martha and the Vandellas' Dancing in the Street.

Proof of this internal dissent was the single's appearance in America in May, three full months before its British release. Within two weeks, it had jumped sixty places in the *Billboard* chart, from 64 to 4. On June 15, (I Can't Get No) Satisfaction became the Stones' first American number one.

It also became the target of scandalized attack from the adult world, unparalleled even in the early days of the anti-rock 'n' roll crusade. Up to then, moral outrage against pop music had centred on its alleged suggestiveness – the veiled suggestions and innuendoes beyond which no song lyricist dared go and few teenage listeners dared imagine. Here, for the first time, a pop song turned from the vocabulary of calf love to the vocabulary of sex. Since duellists ceased to meet each other on parade grounds at dawn, there had been but one, universally recognized source of 'satisfaction'.

No song in history, probably, has gained so much notoriety from its title. Few enough people realized then – and few realize now – that (I Can't Get No) Satisfaction was not about sex (or, as many believed, about male masturbation). It was Mick Jagger's reaction against the Stones' American tour life, penned in motel rooms or streaming along endless interstate highways. The non-providers of satisfaction are not promiscuity or playing with oneself, or being unable to piss against garage walls. They are men on TV, advertising detergent, and voices on car radios, giving out 'useless information', and the general, head-whirling emptiness of 'drivin' round the world – doin' this and signin' that – and tryin' to make some girl' (the song's one overt sexual reference). Satisfaction was a blues song transferred to the pop idiom: a hymn of hate against a world not oppressive but over-indulgent; a lament on the empty feeling of having too much, whose cosseted fury every over-indulged Western teenager could instantly recognize.

Not that such a definition occurred to anyone in 1965. What took Satisfaction to the top of the British and American charts was the guitar phrase whose guttural malevolence makes it still probably the best-known intro in pop. Bound up with the venomous noise, and the editorial uproar it provoked, there is the black and white image of the Stones performing Satisfaction on the *Ed Sullivan Show*, when Sullivan's censors ordered a bleep to cover the reference to 'tryin' to make some girl'; as if that absurd squibble of sound could purge the sight of Mick Jagger, in his cuddly sweater and Rupert Bear checked trousers, wide-eyed and whispering mayhem.

Six

'Everybody's got something to hide'

In 1964, shortly after the Beatles' conquest of America, Brian Epstein received a visit which caused that elegant, doomed young man considerable amusement. Allen Klein, the New York accountant, took advantage of a trip to London to call on Epstein and offer his client, Sam Cooke, as a possible supporting act on the Beatles' next American tour. It soon became obvious, however, that larger matters were on Klein's mind. Halfway through the meeting, in his hoarse and homely New Jersey accent, he made an outrageous suggestion, which was basically that he, Allen Klein, should manage the Beatles' finances instead of Epstein. Touching his foulard scarf with a too-well-manicured hand, Brian Epstein smiled at the preposterous notion.

People about to do business with Klein would often smile in just that tolerantly patronizing way. One could easily laugh at the short, squat figure, in shape so much like a tenpin bowling pin, which would stump into executive boardrooms wearing only jeans and sneakers and none-too-clean turtleneck sweater. One could smile at the podgy face, topped by a cowlick of greased hair and jammed down ferociously on a chin that had already published a second edition and seemed to be contemplating a third. One could smile – one was positively encouraged to do so – with the sidelong quirky mouth and the dark brown, button-bright eyes, which, despite their fixed stare, moved from side to side continually as if studying the columns of invisible balance sheets.

Klein's appearance, in short, was as completely at odds with his reputation as is the outward aspect of the bright-eyed, cheerfully striped piranha fish. And indeed, as anyone could testify who had conducted negotiations with Klein or survived one of the lawsuits with which he pursued his heart's desires, a piranha might conceivably have the edge in politeness.

Much about Allen Klein may be explained by an early life of almost Dickensian hardship and lovelessness. He was born in 1932 in Newark, New Jersey, the son of a neighbourhood kosher butcher. His mother died when he was small and his father, unable to cope with both shop and family, put him and his two sisters into the care of the Hebrew Shelter Orphanage. Allen remained there for ten years, growing up in conditions of austere orthodoxy.

The many contenders for the title of Allen Klein's worst enemy could not gainsay the solitary virtue he claimed for himself – his astonishing capacity of work. It was a virtue instilled in him in early childhood. As an accountancy student at the Lutheran Uppsala College, he completed a four-year course in three years, paying for his own tuition with two simultaneous part-time jobs. In class, he would frequently collapse forward on to his desk with exhaustion. Half-asleep as he was, he could still do a mental arithmetic sum quicker than any other student, rattling off the answer without lifting his head from his arms.

On graduating from Uppsala College, Allen Klein took his first ever holiday, in Miami. There he met a girl named Betty, a student of political science, and there and then decided he must marry her. The proposal was made with typical Klein abruptness. 'When I took her home that first time, I told her I'd never hurt her,' he remembered later. 'She started to cry. "Don't tell me you love me . . ." she's saying. "Don't tell me you want to marry me . . ."'

They were married in 1958. Klein's income as a junior in a firm of New York accountants was $182.50 per month. Banished from his father's home by an unsympathetic stepmother, he had lately been reduced to sleeping at seamen's hostels, in genuine danger from a nightly cast of drunks, homosexuals and psychopaths.

His income sank further when, shortly after marrying Betty, he took a one-room office and set up as the newest and hungriest in the swarm of Manhattan's accountants. Despite their poverty, Berry remembered, he would always take cabs to meetings across town. 'To be successful, you gotta *look* successful,' was another of his axioms. 'Who's going to put any trust in a guy who arrives on the subway?'

His big break came when he accepted a small retainer to handle the affairs of Buddy Knox, a teenage pop singer who had enjoyed huge success in 1957 with a song named Party Doll. Klein discovered that Buddy Knox's record company, from a mixture of inefficiency and contempt for one so young, had failed to pay over a substantial part of what they owed him in royalties. A more interesting discovery was the worried confusion on the faces of record-company men whom Klein confronted with these discrepancies. The upshot was that Buddy Knox got what he was owed. Klein received $3,000 commission – enough to buy him and Betty their first new car.

To each of his subsequent clients from pop music and show business, Klein's offer was bluntly simple: 'I can find you money you never even knew you had.' He would find it, as for Buddy Knox, trapped and forgotten in ponderously slow accounting systems, or in unpaid performance fees or miscalculated box-office percentages. He would then confront the miscreant company in the role of avenging angel, armed with writs and warrants and, occasionally, real live federal marshals. In a business traditionally fuelled by fuzzy bonhomie, the Klein experience was traumatic. Even record companies that treated their artists well and paid them properly could never feel completely sure that Klein's intervention would not cause pain and embarrassment. 'If a corporation is big, it *has* to make mistakes,' was his dogged maxim. 'There's no corporation in the world that doesn't have something to hide.'

The technique worked with spectacular success in the early Sixties on behalf of Steve Lawrence, Eydie Gorme, Bobby Darin and, most notably, Bobby Vinton, an adolescent crooner whom Klein approached at a mutual friend's wedding with the unnerving enquiry: 'How would you like to make $100,000?'

'What do I have to do?' the startled crooner asked.

'Nuthin',' Klein answered. 'It's what *I* have to do.' Shortly afterwards, a cheque for $100,000 in ferreted-out fees and back royalties was delivered to Vinton.

It was a devastatingly simple way, not only of attracting big clients but also of achieving power over them immeasurably greater than any conventional theatrical agent. 'It's natural . . .' Klein's nephew and ex-employee, Ronnie Schneider, says. 'You hand someone a cheque for $100,000 and you're a hero . . . you work miracles. After that, the guy is going to do anything you tell him.'

Klein's other reputation in the music business was as a contract-buster, peerlessly adept in the extrication of his clients from seemingly iron-clad recording agreements in order to sign them to rival companies for large advances. Klein in negotiation could draw on an immense store of disconcerting devices, from cab-driver obscenity to lofty hauteur; from little-boy false naivety to conspiratorial winks and nudges; from predatory exultation to pained surprise that the world could be so indelicate. Two things sustained him through these marathons of boardroom bluff, bile and bad-mouthing. One was the unshakable belief that he, Allen Klein, was the very fount of all honour and square-dealing rectitude. The other was a readiness to engage in lawsuits that practically amounted to collector's mania. At the peak of Klein's career, his company was involved in some fifty lawsuits, their plaintiffs ranging from the US Internal Revenue Service to Diner's Club.

Klein's ambitions to expand into film production date back to a company with the odd name of Hunger Incorporated and a film entitled *Without Each Other*, whose appearance in the 1962 Cannes Film Festival resulted from a remarkable piece of hype. The film somehow got itself tipped in the American entertainment press as a winner of five awards, despite not having been seen by the voting jury or, for that matter, entered officially in the festival. 'What I did at Cannes,' Klein would frequently chuckle nostalgically. 'That really was *fantastic* . . .'

Unable to make headway as a film mogul, despite a growing hoard of movie corporation stock, Klein devoted himself to a pop music market that had expanded beyond even his expectations. In 1964, he took over the affairs of Sam Cooke, a talented black soul singer then riding high on the twist craze. Klein negotiated an unheard-of million-dollar advance for Cooke from the RCA label against royalties which, unhappily, would never be earned. In December 1964, Cooke was shot to death in a lonely motel while with a lady other than his wife.

Klein's failure to annexe the Beatles in 1964 he accounted but a momentary setback. He continued to boast that he would have Brian Epstein's treasure, even setting the deadline as Christmas 1965. Meanwhile he applied himself to wooing the Beatles' temporary chart rivals, a group of white-trousered Londoners called the Dave Clark Five. His next conquest was the young South African impresario Mickie Most, who had built up a roster of British group such as the Animals and Herman's Hermits.

His acquisition of the folk singer Donovan served as a foretaste of Klein's awesome effect on the amateurish and ingenuous world of British pop management. Donovan, a gipsyish seventeen-year-old, had been discovered playing his guitar on the beach at Westcliff-on-Sea, and successfully launched by two young agents as Britain's answer to Bob Dylan. In 1965, Allen Klein decided he wanted Donovan, and flew to Britain in person. Within days, both of Donovan's managers and his record label, Pye, had lost him forever. 'Did I steal him from Pye? I stole him from Pye,' Klein admitted afterwards. 'But at that time, he didn't even have a contract with them – or with Hickory in America.'

The British Invasion thus ceased to originate in London but became, as it were, short-circuited back to New York, into a lofty office suite in the Time-Life building, and a chunky thirty-two-year-old who smoked a statesmanlike pipe and quaffed incessant Coca-Cola, and who backed up his prodigious feats of mental arithmetic with portable file-cabinets, hauled incessantly back and forth across the Atlantic; whose hair was dressed with heavy oil, in defiance of all current fashions and whose favourite casual wear was woollen cardigans with mock leather facings.

The Rolling Stones met Allen Klein just a day or so after he had promised Andrew Loog Oldham a Rolls-Royce with darkened windows, exactly like the one owned by John Lennon. 'We all went down with Andrew to the Hilton to meet him,' Keith says. 'In walks this little fat American geezer, smoking a pipe, wearing the most *diabolical* clothes. But we liked him. He made us laugh. And at least he was under fifty.'

Klein, at that one short meeting, managed to stoke up all the vague dissatisfaction the Stones felt over an income that remained so little commensurate with their success. It was Keith Richard who largely persuaded the others to go along with the deal that Oldham wanted to do with Klein. 'I said we ought to try to turn everything around . . . to get right out of the cheapo English scene. Klein was big – he had the Animals and Herman's Hermits, who were monster then. I said, "Let's go along with someone who could turn everything round or fuck things up once and for all."'

According to Keith's biographer Barbara Charone, the deal

was mostly worked out in the high-priced darkness of Scotch of St James's. At one point, Klein barked across at Oldham, 'Which one makes the records?' Oldham pointed at Keith and said, 'That one.'

The arrangement was that Klein should act as Oldham's business manager, leaving Oldham free for creative activities, as he put it. Oldham would retain responsibility for the Stones' recorded output and for the more outrageous of their publicity stunts. Contracts, tour schedules, all the mundane details connected with the millions he promised to reap, would be in the charge of Allen Klein.

The flaw in this strategy was Eric Easton, Oldham's managerial partner, who had largely financed the Stones as a professional act and whose office in Argyll Street, W1, was their London base and mailing address for their official fan club. Klein had brusquely intimated that Easton had no part in the deal.

Easton was informed, with all the cavalierness available to his twenty-one-year-old partner, that the Stones no longer wanted him, and that Oldham and a new associate were prepared to buy out his contractual interest. His response was to start legal proceedings against Oldham for breach of their original management agreement, and against Klein for bringing out that breach. His first attempt to serve court papers on his young opponent was thwarted – Oldham simply turned and bolted like a rabbit. 'You'll have to accept them sooner or later, you naughty boy . . .' Eric Easton called after him.

Klein's approach to Oldham had been made with his customary impeccable timing. The Stones' two-year contract with Decca had expired in July 1965 and by mid-August was still not fully renegotiated. The new royalty deal, about to be concluded by Easton and Oldham, would have given the Stones 24 per cent of the wholesale price, or about 4p per disc sold. The situation gave scope for a classic Klein move – the 'let me prove myself before I take a cent' ploy. He offered to intervene in the

Decca deal before Oldham and the Stones had officially hired him, to show what infinitely better terms he could get for them.

Decca's executives were amazed, at what they presumed to be the final discussion of the new contract with Eric Easton, to behold instead Allen Klein's squat figure leading all five Stones into the conference room. Klein's tactic on that occasion was Olympian hauteur. He flatly refused to discuss anything with anyone but Decca's chairman, Sir Edward Lewis.

The subsequent encounter between Klein and Sir Edward by all accounts presented the distressing spectacle of an elderly English greyhound trying to dislodge a mongrel terrier from its jugular vein. The upshot was that Lewis, in return for keeping the Stones, agreed to part with $1.25 million in advance royalties. The money was to be paid via Decca's US subsidiary into the Stones' collective company, Nanker Phelge Music.

To fill Eric Easton's role of booking agent for the Stones Europe, Oldham nominated Tito Burns, a former dance-ban_ leader whose organization was best known for handling Cliff Richard. Tito Burns, in fact, had known Andrew Loog Oldham in days long before he became a teenage tycoon. 'I'd met him around 1960, when I was on holiday in Juan-les-Pins,' Burns remembered. 'We always used to go to an English café called Butler's Tea Rooms. Andrew used to be a waiter there.'

Tito Burns was in California when he received the call to meet Oldham and Allen Klein in New York. 'I'd first run across Allen a few years earlier when, right out of the blue, he offered me $25,000 for a little music-publishing company I'd started. I could never understand why he'd wanted it so much. He told me it was just to get *any* sort of foothold in the English scene.

'I was in two minds whether to go up to New York and meet him, but eventually I did. As soon as I walked into the room, Allen barked across at me, "Howdya like to be the Rolling Stones' agent?" "Not particularly," I said.'

On August 28, the London *Evening Standard* reported that the

Rolling Stones had a new manager, Allen Klein, and a new agent, Tito Burns. The story added that, under Klein's supervision, the Stones were to make five feature films over a three-year period, mainly financed by their record company, Decca, whose chairman had outbid 'two overseas companies' for the privilege. The first of these films, provisionally entitled *Only Lovers Left Alive*, was said to be already at the scripting stage.

To Fleet Street's pop music writers, the story made perfect sense. The Stones, propelled by their new American mentor, clearly were about to follow the Beatles' path from Top Twenty to cinema box-office smash. Scarcely anyone bothered to report Decca's subsequent indignant denial that they had agreed to finance five Rolling Stones films (although rights to a film and soundtrack album were included in the $1.25 million advance). Nor did anyone notice, as the months passed, that *Only Lovers Left Alive* – which was to have portrayed a devastated world, inhabited only by teenagers – seemed to hover at the scripting stage indefinitely.

The Stones accepted their destiny as film stars as they had accepted their two new protectors: without serious murmur or dissent. Tito Burns they remembered with vague goodwill for having said encouraging things to them after an early Albert Hall concert. 'None of them ever gave me the slightest problem,' Burns remembered. 'It was all "'Ello, Teat," or "See you later, Teat," or "Sure, Teat, we won't let you down." And I can honestly say they never did. Charlie Watts, of course, used to sit and talk to me for hours about jazz and my days with the big bands.'

Only one feature of the new arrangement slightly puzzled Tito Burns. On the Stones' next European tour he had strict instructions from Allen Klein to receive all concert earnings in person and pay them directly not into the Stones' English bank account but into a company in Delaware, USA.

*

The first that New York heard of Allen Klein's takeover was a hundred-foot-high Times Square billboard showing David Bailey's album-sleeve portrait of the Stones in a blow-up 60 feet by 40 and bearing an inscription whose author could easily be guessed even before he himself appeared below it, staring up proudly through tinted glasses, along with numerous baffled Broadway citizens.

'The sound, face and mind of today,' ran Andrew Loog Oldham's message to New York, 'is more relative to the hope of tomorrow and the reality of destruction than the blind who cannot see their children for fear and division. Something that grew and related. Five reflections of today's children. The Rolling Stones.'

Oldham's new partner had insisted that a Stones album be rush-released in America only to absorb all possible benefit from the lingering aftershock of Satisfaction. The Times Squa billboard was an Allen Klein device already employed on beha of the late Sam Cooke. The album, *December's Children*, was much less spectacular: a cobbled-together set of earlier LP tracks and studio out-takes which – as Keith was heard to mutter discontentedly – they would never have dared foist on their British public.

All their music press poll awards and gold and silver discs had not lessened the pressure to stay ahead of other groups in the ceaseless scramble for the next Top Twenty hit. Their third British album, *Out of Our Heads*, though a vivid enough sample of the Stones' developing fondness for soul music (most notably in a version of Sam Cooke's Good Times), contained nothing as strong as Satisfaction. It was thus dismissed as 'samey and boring' by music papers like *Disc* whose lofty teenage pronouncements even Mick Jagger took as gospel. *Disc* insinuated, so it must be true, that the Rolling Stones were starting to slip.

'It's difficult to realize what pressure we were under to keep on turning out hits,' Keith says. 'Each single you made in those days had to be better *and* do better. If the next one didn't do as well as the last one, everyone told you you were sliding out. After Satisfaction, we all thought, "Wow – lucky us. Now for a good rest . . ." and then in comes Andrew saying, "Right, where's the next one?" It got to be a state of mind. Every eight weeks, you had to come up with a red-hot song that said it all in two minutes, thirty seconds.'

The new single, Get Off My Cloud, was an upbeat dancer, with chords cribbed unashamedly from Twist and Shout, and a lyric – bawled by Jagger purposely in double time – which must represent the earliest attempt to infiltrate the British Top Ten with marijuana smoke. The vision of sitting 'on the 99th floor . . . imagining the world had stopped' and of a little flying man 'dressed up like a Union Jack' evoked all the apparently hilarious and harmless sensations of 'highs' as they were in 1966. One could write and sing about such things in absolute safety in a time when, to most English people, 'stoned' still meant tipsy; and even the starchy panellists on *Juke Box Jury* could be seen jigging up and down in delighted agreement with Bob Dylan's exhortation that 'everybody must get stoned . . .'

Allen Klein's influence was powerfully evident throughout the American tour that began on October 29 with the now customary warm-up shows in Canada. That same week, Klein's office announced an expected gross of $1.5 million, the largest box-office sum in pop touring history. Only the Beatles, in 1964, had touched a million dollars (and in the process caused such alarm to the US Internal Revenue that much of the money remained frozen in a protracted wrangle over the Anglo-American tax treaty).

Klein himself was present at most of the tour dates, dressed in a button-up cardigan with leather facings that caused Oldham much amusement behind his chubby back. In Klein's absence, tour business was administered by his nephew, Ronnie Schneider, a young accountant whom all the Stones liked for his volatile humour and squeaky, excitable voice. Obedient to Uncle Allen's instructions, Ronnie Schneider received each night's box-office percentage in person and put it for safe keeping under his bed.

Also present on the tour was Klein's personal promotion man, Pete Bennett – an individual whose immaculately Mafia-like aspect undoubtedly played a part in his legendary powers of persuasion over radio disc jockeys and producers. It was Pete Bennett who had implanted Get Off My Cloud in the American Top Ten within a fortnight of its release. That much could already to be said for Allen Klein's management. There was also the benefit – most keenly enjoyed by Oldham – of being escorted in public by a gigantic, Sicilian-looking man in a black sharkskin suit who would, from time to time, reflectively pat what seemed to be a handgun bulging under his left armpit.

The British photographer Gered Mankowitz – whose playwright father had written Oldham's seminal fantasy, *Expresso Bongo* – travelled across America with the tour, adding to an excellent portfolio that had begun with the sleeve photograph for *Out of Our Heads*. Mankowitz shared a hotel room with Pete Bennett, whom he remembers sitting on the toilet with the door wide open, in old-fashioned sock suspenders, describing what trouble he had getting shoes hand-made for his oddly paddle-shaped feet.

'A lot of that tour was quite depressing,' Mankowitz says. 'Mick was very down – he seemed to be missing Chrissie Shrimpton a lot. Charlie Watts missed his wife, Shirley. He'd be on the phone to her in Sussex every night, and hang up practically in tears.'

During their stay in New York, girls constantly invaded their hotel, the Sheraton City Squire, bribing bellboys and floor waiters for access by giving 'head' in stairwells and service elevators. Shortly after the hotel management insisted that the Stones transfer to the Sheraton Lincoln Square, New York was plunged into a total blackout. At the height of this, Bob Dylan arrived to pay Brian Jones a visit, accompanied by members of the electric band with which he had lately outraged his pure folk fans. Brian, Dylan and his guitarist Robbie Robertson drank, smoked and played together by candlelight, until someone knocked a candle over and set fire to one of the beds.

'Brian saw a lot of Dylan in New York,' Gered Mankowitz says. 'Where the other Stones were concerned, he seemed to be getting more and more remote. I remember a terrible scene with Brian one day when we'd all stopped on the road to eat. Brian said he wasn't hungry, and just sat in the car. When everyone else came out of the restaurant, Brian decided he *was* hungry and marched inside by himself. "Come on, Brian," the others were saying. "We're running late. We've got to go." Brian just sat there, taking no notice.

'Finally, someone – I think it was that huge guy, Pete Bennett – just picked him up by the scruff of the neck and the seat of his pants, carried him out to the car and dumped him in.'

Outwardly, at least, Brian continued to personify the Stones' dangerous, irrepressible glamour. Brian had been first to adopt the new London fashion of frock coats, flowing scarves and floppy-brimmed hats such as were previously seen on the heads of society women at Ascot. Cameras zoomed in avidly on this exotic figure, like a character in a Grimms' fairy tale, who seemed bent on extending the Stones' decadence to actual transvestism, with his wild white fedora and pressed-down gold fringe, his capes and furs, striped trews and high-stacked alligator boots. Brian made news again in Los Angeles when he appeared in public with a stunningly long-legged girl of exactly matching blondeness, just arrived from London to join him. Her name, the press discovered, was Anita Pallenberg: she was a German film actress and fashion model. According to some reports, Brian had already announced their engagement.

America's revulsion, although it remained strong in the faces of individual policemen, had been somewhat moderated on a civic level by respect for the Stones' dollar-earning power. Denver, Colorado, thus commemorated their coming with an official 'Rolling Stones Day'. Even Boston, that sepulchre of East Coast conservatism, was moved to present them with the Freedom of the City.

These blandishments did nothing to soften the truculence with which the Stones continued to delight their American audiences. In America, even more than Britain, they had become the perfect antidote to the Beatles' impish good manners. 'The Beatles want to hold you hand,' wrote Tom Wolfe in a famous epigram, 'but the Stones want to burn your town.' Though Wolfe had swallowed not one but two PR myths, his judgement confirmed the Stones' appeal to an audience for whom pop music was very far from a question of simply having fun. This second 1965 tour took place against a background of increasing turbulence throughout America's formerly peaceful schools and university campuses, and increasing student protest against the now palpable horrors of America's war in Vietnam. It was a revolt fuelled by pop music – by the bitter, tongue-twisting polemics of Bob Dylan, the sweet-voiced reproaches of Joan Baez. To the American establishment, long hair, Mod clothes and guitars ceased to be merely absurd and became, quite possibly, subversive. Nor could there be any doubt who the ringleaders were. Find an anti-war demonstration, a march or sit-in, and you would find a Rolling Stones song somewhere near. The fact that the Stones themselves, through Mick Jagger's cautious tongue, abstained from all political comment, could hardly be accounted relevant. Their music was the missile: with every play of Satisfaction or Get Off My Cloud, another life of steady dates, early nights, short hair and fraternity meetings went up in flames.

The final concert, before an audience of 14,000 at Los Angeles Sports Arena, went ahead despite real fears that only four Stones might be available to take the stage. On December 4, onstage at Sacramento, Keith had idly touched a live microphone with his metal-inlaid guitar neck and received an electric shock which left him unconscious for seven minutes.

Later that night in Los Angeles, Keith and Brian underwent further initiation from the new species of Rolling Stones fans, attending the second 'Acid Test' party given by the Acid writer Ken Kesey and his followers, 'The Merry Pranksters'. Keith and Brian both passed the test required, which was to sample a man-made drug so new it had not yet been declared illegal: lysergic acid diethylamid, known for short as LSD.

In the fifteenth century, the Pallenbergs were Swedish, a wealthy clan whose most notable member was painted by Holbein, seated among bags of gold. Anita's great-great-grandfather, Arnold Böcklin, a German Swiss, emigrated to Florence to become a painter renowned in the nineteenth-century neoclassical school. Her grandfather and father were painters also, based in Rome but with family and social contacts in Germany, Spain and France. Anita and her sister grew up fluent in four languages and accustomed to the company of painters, writers and musicians.

As a teenager, she studied picture restoration, medicine and graphic design. In 1963, aged twenty-one, she went from Rome to New York by boat, travelling with her boyfriend, an Italian photographer named Mario Schifano. She had meant to continue studying art, and spent some time in Jasper Johns's studio, observing the great man and washing his paintbrushes. She also helped Schifano and other fashion photographers by standing in for models who were late or indisposed. Pictures began to appear in top fashion magazines of the girl with the cropped blonde hair, the lean thoroughbred body and the snub-nosed, unsettling smile.

By 1965, Anita Pallenberg was accepting magazine assignments in all the major European capitals and had appeared in several films made by the young German director Volker

The Glimmer Twins (front row, right) meet at Wentworth, circa 1954.

Jagger (front row, right) in his junior school cricket team.
(Andre Camara/Rex Features)

Jagger and the Stones' first manager, Andrew Loog Oldham. *(Rex Features)*

Brian's Stones with 'too normal' Ian Stewart (fourth from left). *(Rex Features)*

Brian stealing the limelight, 1964. *(Hulton Getty)*

The Lips on an early outing. *(Ray Green/Hulton Getty)*

Left: On the beer in Paris, 1966. *(Rex Features)*

Right: Brian and Anita when things were good. *(J. Wilds/Hulton Getty)*

Below: Stones in the Park, 1967. *(Hulton Getty)*

Left: Mick and Marianne. *(Rex Features)*

Below: Marianne and Nicholas at the Hyde Park gig. *(Ian Showell/Hulton Getty)*

Right: Brian leaves West London Magistrates Court, June 1967. *(Hulton Getty)*

Centre right: Mick and Keith outside Chichester Magistrates Court, May 1967. *(Ted West/Hulton Getty)*

Below right: Marianne and Mick leave Cheyne Walk for Great Marlborough Street Court, June 1969. *(Hulton Getty)*

Beggars at the Banquet, 1968. *(Hulton Getty)*

Studio session filmed by Jean-Luc Godard for *One Plus One*. *(Hulton Getty)*

Schlöndorff. Her main social sphere, however, continued to be the art world. In London, she knew Robert Fraser and, through Fraser, met the antique dealer Christopher Gibbs. 'Anita in those days was absolutely electrifying,' Gibbs says. 'Whenever she came into a room, every head would turn to look at her. There was something kittenish about her, a sense of mischief – of naughtiness. When I talked to her, I discovered she was highly intelligent and extremely well read. She'd read obscure German romantic novelists like Hoffmann as well as all the usual Hermann Hessery.'

In September 1965, Anita had gone to West Germany on a fashion job. She was in Munich on the night of a Rolling Stones concert and, on an impulse, decided to try to meet them. After the show, she persuaded a Swedish photographer to smuggle her backstage. 'That's how I met Brian. He was the only one of the Stones who really bothered to talk to me. He could even speak a little German. There had been some kind of disagreement within the Stones, Brian against the others, and he was crying.

'He said, "Come and spend the night with me! I don't want to be alone." So I went with him. Almost the whole night he spent crying. Whatever had happened with the other Stones had absolutely devastated him.'

She saw Brian again in Paris, when the Stones played the Olympia, and in London on her fashion-modelling trips. Their one-night stand in Munich became a love affair, even though Brian then had a steady girlfriend – a French model named Zou Zou – and Anita was constantly on the move around Europe. 'I fell in love with Brian – in love all the way. He was a great guy, you know. Talented, funny and with that instant quality of "Let's do it. Let's try anything."'

In those early days, she was conscious that the other Stones regarded her with suspicion. 'You could see them exchanging looks like "Who is this weird bird?" Mick, especially, was very hostile. But he could never make me feel uncomfortable. Even today, I can squash him with just one word. But he was the one most against my seeing Brian and being around the Stones. He told Chrissie Shrimpton she wasn't to have anything to do with me.'

Brian returned from Los Angeles apparently on top of the world, carrying an antique mountain dulcimer and an immense lump of California Gold hashish presented to him by an American well-wisher. Anita had gone back to Munich on a modelling job, but was to rejoin him in a few weeks and live with him at his new mews house, behind the ABC Cinema, Fulham Road.

Even in Brian's absence, this house tended to be somewhat crowded. The spare bedroom was occupied by a young Scots film student named Dave Thomson, whom Brain had befriended the previous year in Glasgow. Frequently, too, there would be visits by Brian's French model girlfriend, Zou Zou. When Anita passed through London en route to join the Stones in Los Angeles, Brian had arranged with Thomson that she should stay for a few days while applying for a British work permit. Shortly before Anita's arrival, Zou Zou had flown in unexpectedly from Paris, intending to use Brian's room as usual. Dave Thomson had managed to get rid of her in the nick of time.

A few days after the Stones' return, Thomson was astonished to find himself taken on one side by the normally taciturn Charlie Watts. According to Charlie, Brian had been so full of pills and drink in America that he'd missed playing on several studio sessions, including the one for Satisfaction. In Chicago he had been admitted to hospital – where only Charlie and Bill Wyman had troubled to visit him. An American doctor had afterwards told Charlie that if Brian continued to drink at his present rate, he could kill himself within a year.

Even before the tour, as Thomson well knew, Brian would routinely drink two bottles of whisky a day, and swallow handfuls of pills, mostly the uppers that were indispensable to any pop star's all-night life. A doctor he used was among London's most bountiful providers of drugs on prescription, the model for the

Beatles' in-joking song Doctor Robert. 'And there was hash and grass,' Thomson says, 'just lying on tables all over the house.'

Dave Thomson's regard for Brian was something exceptional in the Stones' retinue of hangers-on and gofers. And he had good reason to believe that Brian's insecurity came from definite, as well as wildly indefinite, sources. He remembers, after their first meeting in Glasgow, going back to see Brian at the Central Hotel, and finding him listening at the door of a room where Oldham and the other Stones were talking. 'They're all in there,' Brian had whispered. 'They're trying to get rid of me.'

'I thought he was just being paranoid,' Dave Thomson says. 'Then, one time, I got a lift down to London in a car with Andrew, Mick and Keith. All the way down, Andrew was talking about how they could sack Brian from the Stones, and making catty remarks about him.'

Thomson was also privy to Brian's frequent, and futile, attempts at writing the original songs which, he believed, would give him back equality in the Stones with Mick and Keith. The knack eluded Brian, even when Oldham tried shock therapy on him as with the other two, locking him in a hotel room with Gene Pitney and a piano. All Brian's musical intuition, his natural command of half a dozen instruments, could not conjure up the requisite facile pattern of chords and rhymes. Under Dave Thomson's influence he began to think, instead, about composing for films. The two were now collaborating on a surrealist scenario, to be shot in Scandinavia and the French Camargue.

Brian and the Stones' power axis were not entirely estranged. There would still be times when, for inscrutable reasons, Keith would go off Mick and swing back to his old partner in bedsitter guitar duets. Keith still had no steady girlfriend or settled home, and would stay for lengthy periods in Brian's spare room relegating Dave Thomson to the living-room couch. Thomson remembers that Keith was there, and at his most mischievous, during a surprise visit by Brian's ex-girlfriend Linda Lawrence, infuriated by his involvement with Zou Zou and his failure to provide for his third son, the second Julian.

'Linda suddenly marched past me into the house. Brian was upstairs, hissing, "Get rid of her, man!" Keith just thought the whole thing was a laugh. He kept teasing Brian about how ugly the kid was and what a big head it had.'

If Brian could remain indifferent to his three illegitimate offspring, he was none the less haunted by terror that their existence might be discovered and exposed in some newspaper like the *News of the World*. 'Brian really wasn't that much worse than other people in the music business,' Dave Thomson says. 'All the groups had the same attitude to the girls who ran after them. They were just pieces of meat.

'Brian was always terrified that the girls he went with on the tours might be under age. After every tour, he used to worry about being hit by paternity suits. Remember, there was no Pill in those days. The girls just used to tell the guys to pull out at the last moment. I remember Brian telling me how he'd come all over some girl's hair.'

At times, there seemed to be something else gnawing at Brian – an anxiety deeper even than what was happening to him in the Stones. At the Fulham mews house, for several months, he would not go out of doors until after dark. A ring of the telephone late at night would make him deeply agitated. 'I remember once,' Thomson says, 'when Bob Dylan rang through from the States at about three in the morning. Brian wouldn't believe it was Dylan until Albert Grossman [Dylan's then manager] came on the line to say it was.

'Brian once said to me, "They're out to get me, Dave – someone in America and someone over here. I don't know who they are, but they're out to get me."'

With Anita Pallenberg's arrival in London to be his live-in girlfriend, Brian seemed to recover his old, arrogant spirits. 'He took me with him to meet her at Heathrow,' Dave Thomson says. 'We drove out there in the Rolls-Royce Silver Cloud Brian had just bought from George Harrison. The idea was that we'd go straight on down to see his parents in Cheltenham, to show them the car. Brian had to prove to his father that there *was* a future in being a musician. I got the impression that he still desperately wanted his family's good opinion.'

As Brian led Anita from the Heathrow arrivals building, an airport photographer stepped forward. That picture, of the gold-haired, wide-eyed pop star and his stunning new possession in her fun fur coat, flowered miniskirt and long, suede-booted legs, nestling submissively against him, would seem to be the very essence of a young man's blessed good luck. 'We didn't drive down to Cheltenham after all,' Dave Thomson says. 'We drove straight back to the mews, so that Brian and Anita could go to bed.'

Brian's transformation continued in the weeks that followed. The morose outsider whom Dave Thomson had seen slumped in an armchair, endlessly playing Nina Simone albums, now sat demurely upstairs before a multifaceted mirror while Anita tinted his hair to a pallor indistinguishable from hers. To her, as to some sympathetic nurse, he confessed his many neuroses about the way he looked. Did it matter that his legs were so short? Could one see the caps he had on his teeth?

Anita meant more than beauty to Brian: she meant restoration of power. She was an instant boost to his sagging morale within the Stones. For not even Mick Jagger could show off a bird like this. Brian had seen Mick's unease in Anita's company; his wariness of her ability to deflate him with a single sultry look or offhand phrase. Mick might not like Anita, but he could not help but be impressed with her standing with people like Robert Fraser and Christopher Gibbs, and Tara Browne, the young heir to the Guinness millions, and almost everyone on that high social level where he himself still felt so very far from comfortable.

Formerly, Brian's closest friends had been musicians, like Spencer Davis, Pete Townshend and George Harrison. Now, with Anita, he, too, was swept into the world of art galleries and dinner parties in tapestried Chelsea rooms. Anita found most pop musicians boring and their wives crushed almost into inaudibility by northern male chauvinism. 'When John Lennon used to come to the house, he'd bring his wife, Cynthia. As soon as they arrived, Cyn would go upstairs, lock herself in the bog and not come out for the rest of the evening.'

As well as a stunningly beautiful girl, Brian had found an accomplice whose penchant for mischief was more than a match for his own. Ronnie Schneider remembers what havoc the two of them caused in California when the Stones were having a day out at the beach, and everyone hired miniature power boats. 'Anita in that power boat was *deadly* – she'd ram everyone into splinters. After a while, Brian turned his boat around and just headed out to sea. The lifeguards were ringing bells – the Coast Guard was about to be alerted. Brian just kept on going and going.

'I said to him later, "Why did you *do* that, Brian?" He just grinned and said, "I was following the seagulls." '

As one unwilling eavesdropper can testify, Anita's was the dominant role in the sex sessions that could last for days at a time. Dave Thomson, still occupying Brian's spare room, heard noises which suggested Anita was initiating him into the more arcane sexual pleasures. 'I actually saw her one night going into their room with a bloody great whip. I could hear her whipping Brian.'

Brian, for his part, had one deviant taste which surprised even Anita. He enjoyed setting fire to model cars and toy trains. The train-spotting craze of his boyhood was perpetuated by an elaborate miniature track layout, with which he would cover the entire living-room floor. Anita would photograph him as he crawled around, dousing miniature locomotives in lighter fluid and setting fire to them.

Anita was behind the darkest of all their escapades. When Germany's *Stern* magazine wanted to feature Brian on its cover, Anita persuaded him to be photographed in Nazi SS uniform, grinding a doll beneath one jack-booted heel. *Stern* rejected the cover and a furore broke out in the British press which Brian could not much appease by claiming he had meant to make an 'anti-Nazi protest' or, privately, that he'd been high on LSD at the time. 'It was all my idea,' Anita says. 'It *was* naughty, but what the hell . . . He looked *good* in SS uniform.'

Anita evidently brought out in Brian the latent femininity he had suppressed in relentless sexual buccaneering and his almost wilful fathering of children. 'There was a legend that he broke out once, and jumped into bed with Mick. And one night, he got me to do him up in drag. You remember Françoise Hardy the French singer? Brian said "Can you do me up like Françoise Hardy?" So I gave him the full thing with make-up, clothes, a wig . . .'

Anita would still go away on fashion jobs in France or Germany, arousing Brian to transports of jealousy – either devastated tears, such as he had wept to her in Munich, or the sudden peevish rage that could seize him. Like other girls before her, Anita suffered physical attacks, with his fists or any weapon that came to hand. 'He would pick up anything – a tray of sandwiches, a whole table – and just throw it.' When Anita accepted a film part with Volker Schlöndorff, Brian grabbed the script from her and tore it to shreds. She calmed him that time by suggesting he should compose the film's musical score.

To this inherent emotional instability was now added the effect of the LSD which Brian had regularly taken since his initiation in late 1965. The drug was already known to have a Russian-roulette quality, offering the entirely unpredictable alternatives of a good trip, when the world could shimmer like crystal, or a bad trip, through all the horrors of purgatory. For Brian – as some snapshots taken in a Soho basement show – a good trip meant grinning and cavorting like a little blond leprechaun. A bad trip brought hallucinations which left him crumpled up and whimpering with fear. 'He'd see monsters,' Anita Pallenberg says. '"Can't you see them?" he'd ask me. "They're all coming out of the wardrobe! They're horrible!"' At the album session, he refused to go into the studio where the other Stones were waiting. In his dazzled, horrified mind, the whole place was swarming with black beetles.

Seven

'It's down to me; the change has come . . .'

The place is a busy roundabout in west London, opposite the Sixties landmark, the Cherry Blossom boot polish factory. A black Rolls-Royce detaches itself from the traffic and sweeps to a stop on the forecourt of the Talgarth service station. Half a dozen pairs of eyes idly settle on the figure that alights from it and walks, with tentative, tripping steps towards the air-supply line. '. . . Mick Jagger, isn't it?' someone whispers. His companions stare incredulously at the meagre body, festooned with fashionable scarves and bangles like a hurriedly dressed doll; at the mounds of hair combed down around cautious eyes and drawn-in lips; at the spindly legs on too-high boot heels, almost stumbling. Can it be only *this* which threatens their daughters, girlfriends and young wives? The notion is so confusing that Jagger is not molested, shouted at or even overtly recognized. The moment passes in embarrassed conspiracy not to see or be seen.

Not since ancient Greece had gods formed so visible and numerous a class as in Britain in 1966 under the pullulating Olympus of the pop music industry. And, as in those mythical times, the gods came in every shape and size. There were tall ones, short ones, fat ones and skinny ones. There were some with fresh faces, and others afflicted with scrofulous acne. There were even those in the mop-top multitude with thinning hair or clumsily positioned toupees. There were those who received the rites of worship accorded all under twenty-five, despite having the raddled and debauched appearance of middle-aged child molesters.

Fan adoration made allowance for these varieties, oddities and mutations. Behind the screams lay remembrance that the hit-makers of the moment were, after all, only quartets of lads from Liverpool, Manchester, Birmingham or Stoke Poges. Screams were emitted as much on principle as anything: they stopped as suddenly as they began, leaving only drenched mascara behind. Doctors and psychologists who analysed them – usually for a fat fee in a Sunday tabloid newspaper – were unanimous in pronouncing them fundamentally harmless.

Where Mick Jagger was concerned, however, the doctors and psychologists could offer no such comfortingly simplistic diagnosis. Elvis Presley at his most scandalous had not exerted a power so wholly and disturbingly physical. Presley, while he made girls scream, did not have Jagger's ability to make men feel uncomfortable. The effect was more akin to a male ballet dancer with his conflicting and colliding sexuality: the swan's neck and smeared harlot eyes allied to an overstuffed and straining cod-piece. Small wonder that lorry drivers at the Talgarth service station, that day in 1966, stared uncomfortably off toward the boot polish factory.

Combo, the male pop fan magazine, expressed the prevailing confusion as early as 1964 with a story 'categorically denying' rumours that Mick Jagger was about to go to Sweden and have a sex-change operation.

That conundrum continued throughout the personality which Jagger offered to his public. On the one hand, there was the loutishness, assiduously cultivated: the Christian name cut down to its curt proletarian root; the surname, so befitting jagged doings, derived – or so he like to claim – from an old English word for 'knifer' or footpad. On the other hand were the teasing intimations of sensitivity, intelligence, even intellect; the sense that, even as he climbed the hit parade, Mick Jagger was also steadily scaling the ladder of society.

No one better illustrated how the ancient redoubts of the British class system had dissolved under pressure both from without and within. Trendy magazines like *Nova*, *Queen* and *London Life*, teemed with stories about youthful peers and baronets, prised from a stately heritage, democratized in Carnaby Street and launched into the King's Road as hustling impresarios, gentlemen's outfitters or restaurateurs. Just as potent were the tales of working-class boys, propelled upward by fashion or photography to mingle, unabashed, with the international jet set. The word of the moment was 'classless', applied without discrimination to the clothes and hairdos and, above all, the curious, teeth-clenching accents common to those whom hopes of cashing in on the seemingly endless youth boom had moved upwards or downwards. Classlessness was simply degrees of affectation and, as such, produced snobbery more rigid and hierarchical than any it claimed to replace. Mick Jagger, alternately slurring Cockney and lispingly public school – with both incarnations clearly directed as social betterment – was classlessness incarnate.

Jagger's face seemed to express the sensation, common to so many, of finding oneself young, beautiful and rich in an era increasingly inclined to worship youth, beauty and spending power. What made his expression so piquant was that it responded to such idolatry, not acquiescently, as young gods and Beatles should, but with indifference, even hostility – a smouldering ill-will which silk clothes, fine food, wine, women and every conceivable physical pampering somehow aggravated. The real pleasure of being Mick Jagger, one felt, was in having everything but being tempted by nothing: a drained and languorous, exquisitely photogenic ennui.

It was an attitude richly conveyed by the Stones' new single, 19th Nervous Breakdown. The song was a lampoon of upper-class girls at upper-class parties – 'dismal, dull affairs' – and, by implication, their foolish efforts to insinuate themselves into the queue trying to catch Jagger's eye. 'It seems to me that you have seen too much in too few years,' he sang, doubtless with the same mock psychoanalysis he used in real life to deflate some luckless, pushy deb.

Glimpses of the other Jagger, sensitive, poetic and vulnerable, were positioned among the Stones' recorded output with tripwire delicacy. The B-side of 19th Nervous Breakdown was As Tears Go By, the song originally written for Marianne Faithfull, now scored for strings – in obvious imitation of Paul McCartney's Yesterday – and lisped by Jagger with all the pathos of Tiny Tim in his chimney corner. Choirboy innocence featured also on Lady Jane, a mini-madrigal written by Jagger for the Stones' next album, even though the title had been inspired by *Lady Chatterley's Lover* (it was Mellors's word for Connie's vagina) and the chorister in question seems to be addressing various members of an Elizabethan seraglio.

The fourth Rolling Stones album, *Aftermath* – released in April 1966 – confirmed Jagger's new individual eminence while apparently preserving the Stones' interior democracy. The difference was that all fourteen tracks were Jagger-Richard songs, with lyrics written almost entirely by Jagger. Even Andrew Loog Oldham's presence was diminished, owing to sudden independence of spirit on Decca Records' part. Decca had refused to accept the album's original title, *Could You Walk on the Water?*, and the accompanying sleeve photograph of the Stones immersed up to their necks in an urban reservoir. Oldham's customary sleeve-note extravaganza was dropped also, in favour of straightforward commentary by Dave Hassinger, the RCA studio engineer. Oldham's credits were limited to 'producer' and, under his old alias 'Sandy Beach', designer of a bright-pink substitute cover.

On *Aftermath*, Jagger's shifting poses of scornful misogyny and little-boy winsomeness mingled with virtuoso playing by Brian Jones on a range of instruments seldom seen before in a pop recording studio. The opening track, Mother's Little Helper – a satire about a pill-addicted housewife – featured Brian on Indian sitar, an instrument also adopted by George Harrison, but played here with a feel for its strange, hot, jangling dissonance that Harrison could not bring to the Beatles' Norwegian Wood. On two tracks, Lady Jane and Waiting, Brian played dulcimer, a tiny stringed instrument, half-mandolin, half-harp, given to him by the American folk singer Richard Farina. On two more, Out of Time and Under My Thumb, he played marimba, the African xylophone.

Brian's intros and solos and inter-verse embroidery gave *Aftermath* a visual quality that no Stones album would ever quite recapture. Through Brian, Jagger's songs of callow male triumph took on the chameleon colours of 'Swinging London' six months in advance of the Beatles' *Revolver*. Most evocative of all was – and still is – Under My Thumb, with its marimba notes circling downward to a strange pot-pourri of electric keyboard, asymmetric drum brushes and offkey guitar.

Under My Thumb, with its crowing victory over a recalcitrant female ego, was not a song likely to gladden the heart of Chrissie Shrimpton. Still less, Out of Time, insistently taunting, 'You're obsolete, my baby. My poor old-fashioned baby . . .' Now that Mick was so famous and fashionable, he felt he should be seen with a girl more famous and fashionable than Jean Shrimpton's younger sister. Jagger the pop star wanted no part now of the commitment which Jagger the less cautious economics student had made eighteen months before, and which Chrissie regarded as still binding. Even in its happiest phase, their relationship had been stormy. Now the battles went on continually, often before an audience uncomfortably aware, as she was not, that Chrissie's time was running out.

Their lives were intertwined in a way that Jagger still shrank from trying to unravel. They had lived together for almost a year, first in a cramped basement in Bryanston Mews, subsequently in Jagger's much plusher £50 per week flat at Harley House, a Marylebone Road mansion block. Chrissie had even left her secretarial job at Decca to work for Andrew Loog Oldham. As Mick Jagger's girlfriend, she was herself something of a personality. *Mod*, the latest American fan magazine, ran a regular column by Chrissie, 'From London With Luv', describing the Stones-Beatles social circle in terms of cosy domesticity. 'Mick and I went down to visit George and Pattie Harrison last week . . . We sat in John's private cinema, had hot chocolate and watched a film called *Citizen Kane* . . . I think Stevie Winwood is the best singer we have. (Ouch! Mick has just hit me.) . . . Recently I had my 21st birthday. Mick gave me a huge rocking horse which I named Petunia . . .'

A picture spread of Jagger in another American teen mag tells a somewhat different story. We see Jagger variously seated before a gilded Victorian mirror, lounging against a G-Plan shelf unit (on which a claret bottle basket is deliberately visible) and at breakfast, surrounded by 'outsize cups of Cantonese design'. The scene is worthy of one of those Edwardian young men about town whose only domestic companion would be a discreetly gliding gentleman's gentleman.

The monocled young rakes who would leave their Mayfair eyries to sport in the mire of Soho or Seven Dials had not enjoyed female flesh in as much quantity, and with such small regard, as this pale London lordling in his Harley House 'pad'. The fastidious sneer to be seen on Jagger's face in almost any female company hinted at how easily sex presented itself to him, and how little he esteemed the girls who offered their bodies, in any position, for however brief a proprietorial grip on his arm. It was part of his peculiar appeal, that aura of sexual surfeit so intense as to produce a kind of exhausted virginality.

On tour, Chrissie could not help but guess, Mick was as active as any of the Stones in the sexual orgies that filled out time between one concert and the next. Their latter American tours had witnessed the advent of the groupie: a type of girl who would tenaciously follow this or that English group, intent on bedding one of them, or all of them (or, in some spectacular cases, all simultaneously). Brian Jones told the story of going into another group's hotel suite to find its four members occupied with a single groupie. 'Come on, Brian,' one of them had shouted. 'There's room for you as well . . .'

Mick hid such things from Chrissie as he hid them from the world, behind the impenetrable mask of his cool. Journalists who interviewed him noticed his growing adeptness at side-stepping questions, or else answering them with an open-faced candour which only later revealed itself as the vehicle for no information whatever. This convenient amnesia blanketed his home and school background and all specifics of his time at the LSE. As far as the world could gather, Mick Jagger had been born and bred a star and, under the closest scrutiny, remained just as bright, remote and featureless.

The mask could slip – as when, in a fit of rage against Sir Edward Lewis, he called the Decca chairman 'a fuckin' old idiot'; or when, on the Stones' 1965 European tour, he outraged the German press by goose-stepping around the stage in time to Satisfaction. There were also the moments when his cautious and self-conscious nature gave way to something altogether different, feline and outrageous – in the recently revived theatrical term, 'camp'. He had once let himself be photographed in a BBC make-up department, sitting under the dryer with his hair in a net like some middle-aged housewife. When the Stones took over a whole edition of *Ready, Steady, Go* as hosts, Mick appeared with Oldham, miming to Sonny and Cher's I Got You Babe, exchanging fond smiles and stroking each other's hair.

His closest friend outside the Stones was David Bailey, the

young cockney photographer, who had become almost as famous – and outrageous – as a pop star. When Bailey shocked Britain by getting married in a pullover, Mick Jagger was his equally untailcoated best man. Bailey's photographs in American *Vogue* had long since taken him to the heart of the, rather older, New York in-crowd ruled by Andy Warhol and Baby Jane Holzer. The Stones played for Baby Jane's birthday party at the New York Academy of Music, prompting Tom Wolfe to an early effusion of New Journalism on the subject of Jagger's mouth. Warhol remembered the style Jagger could get with ordinary cheap Carnaby clothes, 'putting together pants and jackets that no one else would think of doing'.

There was another side to Jagger's cautious nature, seen only by those select few friends he would agree to meet in pubs and restaurants. He hated, in almost any circumstances, to part with money. His extreme thrift was all the more noticeable in a milieu where wild spending, on clothes and cars and country estates, was part of the glamour passed on to fans. 'The Mojos shared out £100 to go shopping,' ran a typical fan mag piece, '– and that's not peanuts!' Jagger's income already equalled all the Mojos' combined, yet he remained studentishly frugal, offering a sort of quasi-Marxist indifference to money as his alibi for always letting others pick up the tab. Even in this outwardly affluent post-Klein period, when all the Stones were following Beatle precedent and investing in country houses, Jagger remained the sort of person who would call round at David Bailey's studio and ask if he could sleep on the couch.

Charlie Watts had already bought a sixteenth-century house in Sussex, originally designed as a hunting lodge for the first Archbishop of Canterbury, and latterly occupied by a one-time Attorney General, Lord Shawcross. (Establishment figures, though they might officially deplore the Stones, never objected to selling them houses.) It proved the perfect hideaway for Charlie's deeply private life with his wife, Shirley; for her sculpture studio and horses and his collections of silver, jazz records, model soldiers and American Civil War memorabilia. His father, the former parcel deliveryman, approved of the property, though Mrs Watts wished he could have chosen something 'a bit more modern'.

Keith decided next, showing what a vein of English romanticism lay under his gipsy exterior by choosing 'Redlands', a fifteenth-century moated cottage in the Sussex village of West Wittering. A fan magazine journalist, paying the first of several unexpected visits to the property, found the front door wide open, all five half-timbered bedrooms still unfurnished, the kitchen a sea of dirty dishes and a burnt sausage in the frying pan.

Mick, however, stayed on at the same London mansion flat, half living with the same unsatisfactory girlfriend. Brian Jones's affair with Anita Pallenberg had increased his discontent with Chrissie. Anita was exactly the kind of 'classy bird' he had picked out for himself a hundred times from glossy magazines and films. And Anita, though she affected to despise him, seems to have given him more than one lingering glance, over Brain's golden head. 'I always got the feeling with Anita that Mick was the one she *really* wanted,' Dave Thomson says. 'I felt she was working her way through the Stones to get to Mick.'

There was, of course, another girl in the Stones' circle who more than measured up to Mick's ideals of beauty and class. She had always seemed out of his reach and, with her marriage, seemed now more so than ever. Just the same, through that hot, hectic summer of 1966, as the rows with Chrissie increased in violence, and as he couldn't get a date with his first choice, Julie Christie, Mick Jagger began to see more and more of Marianne Faithfull.

Swinging London had reached Cambridge University early in 1965, when assorted Fleet Street journalists laid siege to Churchill College, waiting until its most envied undergraduate, John Dunbar, should attempt to enter or leave the Fine Arts faculty.

After several days on the run, Dunbar wearily threw up his hands and gave the story to the *Cambridge Daily News*'s Paul Buttle. MARIANNE FAITHFULL WEDS CAMBRIDGE STUDENT ran the newsbills posted that night among free-wheeling throngs in Petty Cury and Trinity Street.

For Marianne, it was a time of almost schizophrenic contrasts. On the one hand, she was still the seventeen-year-old convent girl, intent on marrying the first boy who had ever made love to her. On the other hand, she was a famous pop star whose virginal beauty made her the target of seduction attempts from almost every man she met. Gene Pitney, the American star, had already made determined attempts to persuade her to run away with him. Then, a week before her wedding, Bob Dylan inveigled Marianne into his suite at the Savoy Hotel and tried to win her in a way that only Bob Dylan would. 'He sat down in front of me and started to write songs at terrific speed. He asked who John was, and when I said, "He's a student," Dylan was terribly contemptuous.

'All the time, he was writing these songs – covering sheet after sheet with them. Finally, when it was clear I wouldn't let him come on to me, he picked up every bit of paper and put them all away. I never even saw what he'd written. I only wish I'd had the chance to nick some of it.'

The public approved of Marianne's wedding and, when a baby son, Nicholas, was born rather soon afterwards, forbore even to count fingers backward through the months of her pregnancy. Her life continued, then, in its continual paradox – on the one hand, the genteel young wife and mother, given increasingly to musicians' slang; on the other hand, the package-show star, seated at the back of the tour bus with her nose buried in a Jane Austen novel.

For John Dunbar, the future seemed to hold comparable brilliance. In 1966, with two young partners, he founded the Indica Gallery in a mews in the heart of London's West End.

The gallery, small but chastely elegant, was to be devoted to the work of new 'swinging' painters and sculptors, while its adjacent bookshop would specialize in off-beat, radical literature from sources already known to some as the Underground.

Dunbar's partners in the venture were Peter Asher, brother of Paul McCartney's girlfriend Jane, and a wispy boy known only as Miles who had grown up with Brian Jones in Cheltenham. The support of pop music's brahmin class was assured from the start when Paul McCartney helped to paint the gallery white before its official opening. Later that year, at an Indica exhibition entitled Unfinished Paintings and Objects, John Dunbar was to introduce the Japanese performance artist Yoko Ono to the renegade Beatle and painter *manqué* John Lennon.

At first, Marianne had been shocked by the Stones – by their scruffiness and spottiness and surly indifference to the gifts life was heaping upon them. Marianne remembered only too well what it had been like to ask for credit at the Reading shops. Part of the Stones' new stardom was unlimited credit, offered by boutiques whose trendiness would increase a hundredfold if a Rolling Stone shopped there. 'All the Stones had piles of clothes on credit, and never paid for any of them. I used to tell Mick off about that. It was something I'd been taught by Eva from childhood – however hard up you are, your credit must always be good.'

Of all the Stones, she was initially drawn to Brian; not so much for his looks as for the insouciant malice that still sparkled under his platinum fringe. 'I knew there was a psychic trial of strength going on between Brian and the others, and that Brian was losing it. And there were all these mothers of his illegitimate children in the background. We were all round at Brian and Anita's place in Courtfield Road one day and suddenly this ex-girlfriend of his, Linda, appeared in the street outside with Julian, their child, in her arms. She was standing right under the window, holding the baby up as if to say "What are you going to do about *this*?" Brian just looked down at them and laughed.'

The ex-convent girl had by now herself been initiated into all the pleasures of smart young London society. By 1966, she was habituated to marijuana and the varicoloured pills with which her new friends propped their eyes open through each night's freewheeling pleasure. Then one day at a party, Robert Fraser, the art dealer, beckoned her into another room, pointed to a small white pile of cocaine on the mantelpiece and told her to take a sniff. 'I didn't know what you had to do; I just snorted up the whole lot in one go. Robert was *very* offended.'

The domestic idyll with John Dunbar and baby Nicholas was to be short-lived. Dunbar, though brilliant and imaginative, could not keep up with the affluent pop world Marianne now inhabited, nor maintain herself and Nicholas in the grand style of her hit-parade friends. With a nanny to take care of Nicholas, she began to forsake Dunbar's art gallery circle for the houses, shut in by Moroccan drapes and heavy with camouflaging incense, where Rolling Stones and their courtiers were to be found.

Marianne claims that, before her affair with Mick Jagger, she had slept with two other Stones – by obvious implication, Keith and Brian. The subject is one upon which Keith chooses to remain gallantly silent. In Brian's case, his friend Dave Thomson believes, matters went no further than some exploratory groping. 'Brian told me he'd once been shut in a cupboard with Marianne. But all he did was give her a good feel-up.'

By mid-1966, the pressure of her too-hasty marriage and motherhood was propelling her, almost without her knowledge, into the arms of a person she thought she disliked – a person whose outward crudeness and cockiness, she found, held surprising depths of sensitivity and sympathy. 'I went to Mick because I needed a friend. Mick was a friend who also happened to be a millionaire.'

Her young assistant, Jo Bergman – a future power in the life of the Stones – puts it rather more simply. 'Marianne was living in this freezing cold flat. When Mick started to come and see her, suddenly there were electric heaters everywhere.'

Jagger, at the time, was said to be suffering from 'complete exhaustion', due mainly to a schedule that had brought the Stones back to Australia and New Zealand in February, and then packed them off again with barely a respite on a new European tour more chaotic and violent than any yet. At their Paris Olympia show, police used batons and tear gas against the 3,000 rioters. Twelve gendarmes were hurt, including one suffering from bites. At the Musicorama in Marseilles, a chair sailed out of the audience, opening a two-inch cut above Jagger's right eye.

Hardly a month elapsed before yet another US and Canadian tour. Jagger began it still in a state of exhaustion, descending the aircraft steps as one reporter noted, 'smiling lamely, supported by the brassbound epaulets on his shoulders'. He seemed to be living out the neurosis of the Stones' current single, Paint It Black, in which the singer was portrayed as a palpitant wreck, turning his head away from pretty girls, like Joyce's Stephen Daedalus, 'until my darkness goes . . .'

The tour began on a note of high fashion with the Stones featured among back-combed American debutantes on the cover of *Town and Country* magazine, and a press reception thrown by Allen Klein on a yacht in New York harbour, when fan magazines were excluded in favour of journalistic gentry (like *Town and Country*'s own Linda Eastman). The Stones were noticeably more stand-offish, as one disgruntled guest wrote. 'There's a feeling of "Don't touch me, I'm a Rolling Stone." Even that manager of theirs is so hung up on himself, it's unbelievable . . . Mick is a hippie in the true sense of the word. When someone says something honest, he goes blank . . .'

Klein's litigation-loving style was detectable in the stunt with which Andrew Loog Oldham launched the Stones on this fifth transcontinental journey. Oldham announced he had filed a five million dollar lawsuit against fourteen New York hotels for turning away the Stones and so casting aspersions on their good name. It was all pure fiction and, as events proved, rather unnecessary. Headlines after Oldham's heart were already burning the Stones' progress across the American map like one of those old movie sequences symbolizing a country given over to fire and plunder.

The opening concert, in Lynn, Massachusetts, was stopped by the police after only minutes, and the audience dispersed with a ferocity that turned mere high spirits into mob rage. As the Stones drove away afterwards, their car windows were belaboured with wooden planks torn up from the walkways. In Montreal, the Stones stopped playing to boo the stage-front bouncers for punching and judo-chopping at girls who tried to grab at Jagger. In Syracuse, they were said to have insulted an American flag by dragging it along the floor of the War Memorial Hall. (Brian Jones had merely been trying to take the flag as a souvenir.) In Vancouver, the thirty-six concert casualties included ushers kicked in the groin, women policeman suffering from exhaustion, bouncers with alleged concussion and fans nursing assorted broken bones. In Montreal, where the police had subdued fans by ramming them head first into a wood fence, the Stones came offstage through an aisle of fifty prostrate bodies.

The last American concert – for longer than anyone imagined – was in Hawaii on July 25. The Stones then dispersed for brief holidays before starting a new British tour late in September. Brian Jones, in Morocco with Anita Pallenberg, was reported to have broken his right hand in a climbing accident.

The British tour coincided with yet another single, Have You Seen Your Mother, Baby, Standing in the Shadow? whose convoluted title reflected the pressure on Jagger and Richard to dash off another three-minute smash while simultaneously ducking chairs and being attacked by wooden planks. On this song, tour chaos followed them even into the studio, upsetting the malign tautness they had achieved on Satisfaction, causing

Jagger to gabble the obscure lyric breathlessly as if eyeing up exits, and everyone else to pound and scrub their instruments towards the same quick getaway. Brass and cathedral-like echo were added in a too hurried mix, to get it all finished for unveiling on the next Ed Sullivan TV show.

In America, the single was issued inside a picture sleeve that struck new horror into conservative hearts. The Stones were photographed as a group of ageing transvestites, each one adopting a 'drag' role to which his character seemed only too well suited. Brian Jones ('Flossie') pouted smoke rings in a WAAF uniform and peroxide wig. Keith ('Molly') in befrogged costume and cameo brooch, looked like an archdeacon's wife turned to drink. Jagger, his lips reddened to the size of chipolata sausages, wore a bedraggled cloche hat and Charlie (alias 'Millicent') a ratty-looking fur cape. The centrepiece was a wheelchair in which Bill Wyman ('Sarah') sat, a sullen WAC, with skinny spinster legs almost tied in a knot.

The British tour began on September 29, amid lengthy music press post-mortems as to why Have You See Your Mother, Baby? had not reached number one in America or Britain. If it was 'over the kids' heads', as luminaries like Eric Clapton and Mike D'Abo agreed, no more perfect theme song could have been found for concerts which eclipsed even Vancouver and Montreal in uproar and violence. British fans, deprived of the Stones for almost a year, were intent on making up for lost time. The final show, at the Royal Albert Hall, was halted after three minutes when Jagger was attacked by three girls simultaneously, and the arbitrary collaring, punching and tossing back of half a dozen more still could not stem the screaming tidal wave.

A film sequence shot that night shows the Stones at their most goadingly indifferent – Mick Jagger in Mod crop and flowered shirt; Keith in sunglasses, collar and tie, like a blinded mafioso; Brian Jones, in velvet frock coat and heavy sideburns, laughing hysterically as the power fails, the house lights rise, loose drums roll underfoot, Charlie hastily exits to the rear, and Brian himself is turned around and shepherded away by large official hands.

Swinging London sung to its zenith through that summer season when girls went bare-thighed in wasp-striped mini-dresses and boys, buttoned up in Beau Brummell coats, swaggered down King's Road closely followed by camera crews from *Life* magazine, recording anthropomorphic data for what its sister publication *Time* had momentously – and a year late – dubbed the Style Capital of Europe. The effect of *Time* and *Life* between them had been an American tourist boom not seen since London's last royal coronation. The subculture was now a sub-continent, of boutiques, bistros, bric-a-brac markets, purveying solid versions of the parody Britishness which pop music had made the rage across America. It was a time when fortunes could be made from naming a shop I Was Lord Kitchener's Valet; when the British saw their national colours profitably transferred from imperial flagstaff to Carnaby Street plastic bag. Mass-produced jingoism led inevitably to a resurgence of the genuine article, blossoming still further in weeks of unaccustomed summer sun. When, in August, England beat West Germany to win the 1966 World Cup, it truly did seem as if Britannia was back in business.

The Beatles continued to be Swinging London's foremost citizens. They had ceased live performances in August, with-drawing, shell-shocked, into lives of individual plutocracy, reuniting only to make albums that would chart their ascent into the same iconographic firmament as Portobello Road market and I Was Lord Kitchener's Valet. The Beatles' *Revolver* is held to be the first thematic pop LP, capturing as it does, by random images, the sun-soaked euphoria of London in 1966. The Stones' *Aftermath* can make an equal claim – a better one, even, in its blend of metropolitan arrogance with strange, Eastern-sounding noise.

The era which the Beatles officially announced – and which

Brian Jones had subtly prophesied four months earlier – took shape in the odour of joss sticks, smouldering among twilit tumbles of embroidered caftans, tapestried slippers, prayer beads, leather footstools and beaten-brass trays. The Beatles' (and Stones') experiments with sitars set off a fascination with all things Eastern, passed from Britain to America via the mutually reacting pop industry. In Britain, the effect was merely commercial; in America, it was profoundly cerebral. Rumours began to reach London of young people in California who had thrown off all convention to practise Hinduism, in precept or in spirit, with shoulder-length hair and flowing beards and robes and sandals and flower garlands, barring all activity but Buddha-like goodwill and consumption of those substances with which Eastern sages were said to have attained their wisdom and maintained their repose.

It was, ironically, the Tory London *Evening Standard* which published earliest details of the new 'hippie' communities in San Francisco and on the North California coast, and transmitted their apostate slogan: 'Turn on, tune in, drop out.' The *Sunday Times* soon afterwards introduced Britain to the hippie movement's first leader – or guru – one Timothy Leary, a Harvard academic who had sacrificed his career to explore the 'psychedelic' (literally, mind-expanding) properties of the man-made drug lysergic acid diethylamide. Even the *Sunday Times* did not know, however, that in Pont Street, Knightsbridge, there was already an establishment called the World Psychedelic Centre where liquid LSD was available free to anyone who wanted it, sprinkled on little fingers of bread.

Andrew Loog Oldham was also swinging to a zenith as the youth-obsessed capital's latest big businessman under twenty-four. Oldham, in mid 1966, joined forces with his old PR confederate Tony Calder to form an independent record label, Immediate. The idea had come, inevitably, from Phil Spector's Philles label, with additional inspiration from Berry Gordy's

Motown corporation. Like Motown, Immediate was conceived as a team of songwriters, arrangers and producers, kept in harness to service artists selected by the power of one Diaghilev eye. Like Motown, Immediate would have its own distinctive style, an aura of success that headed its product to the charts before the customers had heard a word. Its hippy winsome slogan was 'Proud To Be Part Of The Industry Of Human Happiness'.

Immediate's chief in-house asset was the songwriting team of Mick Jagger and Keith Richard. To stimulate this all-important commodity, Oldham encouraged both Mick and Keith to make their first essays as record producers. Jagger's debut was with Chris Farlowe, a bulky young r & b shouter, singing Out of Time from *Aftermath*. Farlowe's version, laden with more scornful pity than even Jagger's, became the new label's first number one in August 1966. Keith's first production was the 'Arandbee' (r & b) Orchestra, playing a medley of past Stones hits grandiosely entitled Today's Pop Symphony. The aim was to prove that Jagger-Richard songs made melodies as durable as Lennon and McCartney's.

Immediate Records operated from a small flat in Ivor Court, Marylebone. With Tony Calder established here too, in an office comparably luxurious, the only space available for employees like Shirley Arnold was corners and cubby-holes. 'It was terrible, really,' Shirley says, 'but we put up with it. The worst part of any office job is boredom. With Andrew, at least you knew you'd never be bored.'

Since fainting at Ken Colyer's club and awakening to find herself secretary of the Rolling Stones fan club, Shirley Arnold had become indispensable within the Oldham empire. The Stones all liked her for her cockney good sense, her obligingness and a concern for them far beyond the call of secretarial duty. While they were on tour, Shirley would keep in touch with their parents, relaying messages, delivering assurances that this or that new press scandal was no cause for maternal alarm. 'I never really did much care for Mrs Jagger. She was always complaining. But Doris Richards was great. She was so game and ready for anything. She'd even smoked a joint with Keith, just to see what it was all about.

'The funny things was, the Stones did everything they could to stop me ever taking any drugs. Especially Keith – even at the time when he was pouring *everything* into himself. Someone offered me something in the office once, and Keith forbade me to touch it.'

Shirley had been fond of Eric Easton and had regretted his brutal dumping when Oldham teamed with Allen Klein. Her first sight of Klein was not reassuring. 'I saw him in the office in a T-shirt, swigging from a bottle of whisky. When I got to know him, though, I liked him. He was always nice to the girls in the office, and never missed buying us presents at Christmas. Once, I remember, he gave each of us a rather dainty little china pomander.'

Oldham's new status as music mogul, on theoretically equal terms with Decca's Sir Edward Lewis, had prompted him to change his ferociously casual Mod malchick look for boardroom suits and pebble-lensed spectacles and a downward-turning moustache, such as Mexican bandits had sported in the Saturday morning movies of his boyhood. He had also dismissed Reg the Butcher as his chauffeur-bodyguard in favour of a more upmarket protector named Eddie.

Behind the Zapata moustache and the shawl-like jacket lapels, he was still – as Eric Easton had sorrowfully remarked – a very naughty boy. One of his favourite pastimes while being driven by Eddie in his Rolls was to invite a fellow passenger to open a door, hang out of the speeding vehicle and peep underneath it at Oldham, hanging from the door on the other side. He was playing that game one night with the stage designer Sean Kenny, unaware that a police car was close on Eddie's tail. 'When the cops eventually stopped us, they thumped both of us,'

Oldham remembers. 'I suppose I *had* been a bit cheeky to them as well.'

In addition to the full-size Rolls, he acquired a miniature version, grafted on to a Mini Minor chassis, the ultimate expensive and pointless Sixties toy. 'There were only two of them in the country,' Shirley Arnold says. 'John Lennon had the first one, so Andrew couldn't be happy until he'd got one, too. It had stereo music speakers on the *outside*. Andrew took a couple of us out for a ride in it one lunchtime. I'll never forget zooming round the West End in that little tiny Rolls with the speakers pounding and people leaping out of Andrew's way.'

The Immediate office thronged with youths whose potential as singers and songwriters seemed to matter less than their personal prettiness. 'We never thought Andrew was actually gay,' Shirley Arnold says. 'But he *did* like to have pretty boys working for him.'

As an employer, Shirley remembers, he could veer wildly from outrageous indulgence to almost psychopathic cruelty. 'He came in one day, wearing this beautiful brand-new suede coat. A boy in the office admired it, and Andrew just took it off and gave it to him. "Suede never did suit me," he said. Another time, there was someone in the company he'd decided to get rid of. Andrew waited until this person was out and then went in and wrecked his office.'

Oldham's executive roles as label boss and film tycoon led him increasingly to delegate and dissipate the Stones' management. With Allen Klein booking them in America and Tito Burns handling European tours, there was no longer any need to travel with them. Over the past two years, an entirely separate road organization had grown up around the Stones, responsible for transporting their equipment and, more crucially, preventing their being torn limb from limb. The faithful Ian Stewart was reinforced by Tom Keylock, a hulking Londoner whose eyes swam mistily behind thick bifocal glasses. Keylock's one-man car hire company provided the Stones with the Austin Princess limousine they used for travelling between engagements. From chauffeur, he had progressed to bodyguard, using muscles, and combat techniques, acquired in the army paratroopers.

By late 1966, Oldham found himself too busy even to go on devising the publicity stunts with which he had maintained the Stones' notoriety in the British press. That fictitious five million dollar lawsuit was his PR swansong. Thereafter, he gave the Stones' media image into the charge of Les Perrin, a middle-aged, thoroughly conventional Fleet Street publicist, whose hiring was to prove one of the best things Oldham ever did for the Stones.

His own dealings with the band now tended to be mainly in recording studios, at those unpredictable moments when they could break from touring to work on tracks for a new album. Here, even he began to notice the influence of the bodyguard Tom Keylock, especially over Keith, who had an incurable weakness for tough guys, and Brian, who was pathetically grateful even for so changeable an ally. There was also 'Spanish Tony' Sanchez, a Soho narcotics dealer who was Brian and Keith's chief supplier of hash and pills.

'I got impatient with all that courtier stuff, the chauffeurs and the bodyguards,' Oldham says. 'It was like being back at public school. You had to be in Mick's house or Keith's house or Brian's house. It all started when they got involved with the so-called society people – the Frasers, the Donald Cammells. And I didn't like the drug thing, because it got in the way. It interfered with business.'

Oldham claims that his quick thinking saved the Stones from a drugs bust somewhat in advance of their famous one, when they had met at Olympic Studios in Barnes to work on a track that eventually became Let's Spend the Night Together.

'Everyone was up in the control room, smoking away. You could look out from there, down the whole length of the studio, which was a pretty big, long room. Suddenly, at the far end, I saw about eight policemen come through a door and across the studio towards us.

'I ran out of the control room and stopped the first two. "Quick," I said. "Have you got truncheons?" Both of them brought out their truncheons. "Right," I said, "now hit them together." The coppers hit their truncheons together. "That's perfect," I said. "Just what we need on the track. Could you sit down here and do it when we record?" They all sat down, dead chuffed – forgetting all about trying to bust us – and we recorded two of them, hitting their truncheons together. It even stayed on the finished track, I think.'

It was Christopher Gibbs who first introduced Brian and Anita to Morocco. They would accompany the antiques dealer when he visited Tangier or Marrakesh to buy carpets, fabrics and curios for his Chelsea shop. In Tangier, they would stay at the exquisite Hotel Minzah and spend days with Gibbs in the Grand Socco bazaar, wandering through the noisy labyrinths striped over by a latticework of sun. At night, they ate kebabs and couscous, and watched the acrobats and silver-hung belly dancers, taking turns to draw on a bubbling hookah of dunglike tobacco mingled with the more fragrant ancient Eastern substance which Moroccans were only just learning to call 'shit'.

Morocco in the 1940s was to American literary men what Paris had been in the 1920s. The great William Burroughs, panjandrum of New York's avant-garde, lived in Tangier, ruling over a court of artist-expatriates that included Paul Bowles the novelist and Brion Gysin the painter. The Sixties brought a further influx from America and Europe to sample Morocco's now half-admissible delights of *kif* and prostitutes. On the Tangier seafront, you might see Joe Orton, the young British playwright, sunning himself with his lover and future killer Kenneth Halliwell. In the High Atlas, you might well come across Truman Capote, escaping – or pursuing – his latest drama-ridden love. At the Minzah, you might see the grreat Cecil Beaton, socialite, designer and photographer breakfasting alone beside the fountain.

Morocco affected Brian Jones more profoundly than anything since he had first heard Elmore James. It was not just the hashish, jetted up through a hookah or smouldering in the bowl of an intricately carved pipe. It was not just the clothes, caftans, djellabahs, cloaks and waistcoats, beaded with glass or silver, which Anita and he bought by the trunkful, along with cushions, footstools, copperware, gold and beaten metal lamps for their new studio apartment. In Morocco, Brian found a country whose daily life, both spiritual and secular, is indivisible from music. He was fascinated to see, in Tangier's Grand Socco, in the green and white ceramic city of Fez, especially in the great red clay marketplace at Marrakesh, musicians playing subtle and delicate thousand-year-old Berber melodies on pipes and drums that were the natural descant to trade, conversation, worship and argument. From Brion Gysin he heard of the master musicians of Jajouka, in the foothills of the Rif mountains, whose pipe music, dating from before Islam, had so affected Gysin he swore he could not let even a day pass without hearing it again. Brian had begged Gysin to take him to Jajouka to hear the master musicians and, possibly, learn something from them about making records with the Stones.

Christopher Gibbs remembers that summer 1966 trip chiefly for the constant bickering between Brian and Anita. 'They fought about everything – cars, prices, restaurant menus. Brian could never win an argument with Anita, although he always made the mistake of trying. There would be terrible scenes with both of them screaming at each other. The difference was that Brian didn't know what he was doing. Anita *did* know what she was doing. I think that in a more gracious age, Anita would have been called a witch.'

Among Brian's more unlikely Moroccan holiday chums was the Welsh actor Victor Spinetti, who had appeared in the Beatles' film *Help!*. Spinetti tells the story of finding the Stone red-eyed and sniffing with a mild dose of flu and offering him a Beechams powder. 'Thanks, man,' Brian said, tearing open the packet and inhaling its innocent white powder with one snort. In Tangier he appeared with a bandaged right hand which, the Stones' London office announced, he had broken 'while mountain climbing'. In fact, as Christopher Gibbs remembers, it was the result of another fracas with Anita in their hotel room. Brian had aimed a blow at her, missed and slammed his fist into a metal window frame.

Mick Jagger's love affair with Marianne Faithfull began late that summer, by such cautious and slow degrees that Marianne herself was for some time hardly aware of it. For Mick, even so decisive an act was necessarily hedged about with ambiguity and equivocation. Most of his friends believed that when he broke away from Chrissie Shrimpton, it would be for another girlfriend named Tish. Even when he took the plunge at last and asked Marianne to meet him secretly in Paris, he seemed to be keeping his options still open. Donald Cammell the film producer remembered, at a party there, how Mick strove part of the time to keep up a pretence that he and Marianne were together only by coincidence.

Soon afterwards, he nerved himself to tell Chrissie, at last, that it was all over between them. Chrissie took it badly, at one point even trying to kill herself at Harley House while Mick was out. It would not be the last time that attempted suicide thwarted his desire, at all times, to keep up appearances.

He declared his involvement with Marianne in the most oblique way possible, taking her on an extended cruise in a hired yacht along the French Riviera. At night, they would come ashore and dance, unnoticed, in the seafront discotheques. 'We got very friendly with this particular disc jockey,' Marianne says. 'One night, I asked him if he'd got any speed.' The disc jockey poured a stream of Italian-made amphetamines into her hands.

By the time she returned to London, to move in with Jagger at Harley House, Marianne thought she had finished all the uppers the French deejay had given her. So she had – all but four, which remained where she had hidden the supply, in the pocket of a green velvet jacket of Jagger's. She soon forgot all about them, and Jagger had no idea that they were there.

Eight

'The Oscar Wilde Mistake

Nowadays, sleazy British newspapers are two a penny. But in 1967, Sunday's *News of the World* still occupied a unique position in the mean City of London thoroughfare and dark side alleys known collectively as Fleet Street. Actually, the *News of the World*'s headquarters were in Bouverie Street, just off Fleet Street, immediately adjacent to those of the humorous magazine *Punch*. When Malcolm Muggeridge became *Punch*'s eighth editor in the early 1950s, he would sit in his office, gloomily watching the huge bales of newsprint being hoisted into the *News of the World*'s premises for use that coming weekend. Gloomily, because from time to time Muggeridge tried to parody the paper's style in his magazine, but always had his handiwork effortlessly surpassed by the next edition of the real thing. The *News of the World* was something beyond parody.

Its proud masthead boast of 'largest circulation on earth' was no idle one. Its weekly sale was six million copies, its readership probably four times that figure. As George Orwell noted in the 1930s, it was an almost sacred ritual for some twenty-five million Britons each Sabbath to settle down in after-lunch torpor with a pot of tea stewing on the hob, unfold the old-fashioned broadsheet paper and immerse themselves in that familiar half-world, before newspapers dared call a spade a spade, where scandal and prurient smut co-existed with moral indignation reminiscent of the age of Gladstone.

For three-quarters of a century, the *News of the World* had regaled its vast public with a scarcely changing diet of vicars exposed as 'sex fiends', scoutmasters revealed to be homosexuals, milkmen with seraglios on suburban housing estates and lay-preachers surprised in love nests in Streatham. Disgracing and crucifying these sad little people under the alibi of a concern for public morals was carried out with a gloating relish closer to true pornography than anything Soho's meanest streets could offer. The same was true of the paper's investigations into larger social evils, which had a monotonous tendency to focus on organized prostitution and were carried out by undercover teams using all the apparatus of the agent provocateur. No such enquiry was deemed successful unless a *NoW* reporter could write that, offered some forbidden favour, he 'made an excuse and left'. In those far-off hot-metal printing days, the paper kept its favourite crowd-pulling headline permanently set in type: WE NAME THESE GUILTY MEN.

Though the formula worked as well in 1967 as in 1907, the *News of the World* was always prepared to extend its righteous wrath to more current objects of suspicion, disapproval and envy. In January 1966, Brian Jones's worst fears were realized when his Cheltenham girlfriend Pat Andrews applied to South-West London Magistrates' Court for maintenance payments to their four-year-old son Julian. Next Sunday, the *News of the World* ran a full-page story, THE GIRL WHO LOVED A ROLLING STONE, about Pat in her present straitened circumstances as an eleven pounds per week shop assistant. This prompted the paper's chief muck-raking competitor, the *People*, to a follow-up story (enigmatically headed BRIAN JONES HAS ANOTHER BABY) about Linda Lawrence and the out-of-court settlement Brian had recently been compelled to make to her for support of his second son named Julian.

It had been borne in gradually on the not very powerful minds in Bouverie Street that pop music offered the ingredient of lurid showbiz scandal and sententious moral crusading in one irresistible package. Pop music, to the Sunday newspaper reading public, increasingly meant drugs. It meant a perversion suddenly resurrected from Victorian novelettes to something one could practically hear issuing from one's child's transistor radio. Drugs and their increasing use by 'young people', with pop music's manifest encouragement, had become a common Fleet Street obsession. But as yet the menace remained vague. No specific pop star stood condemned. So in February 1967, in its inimitable way, the *News of the World* set out to name the guilty men.

If the Stones had wanted to set themselves up as number one target, they could hardly have gone about it better. In January, uproar swept through the British popular press over the title of their new single, Let's Spend the Night Together. A suggestive title certainly, but no more so than a dozen other songs proposing nocturnal activity, from Bing Crosby's Blue of the Night to Elvis Presley's One Night With You. The Stones were merely repeating what young boys nowadays found easy to say to girls – and vice versa. One could not, of course, expect Fleet Street to comprehend anything so simple. In America, the outrage was proportionately greater. Performing the song for Ed Sullivan, Mick Jagger had to amend the words to 'Let's spend some time together'.

Respectable society received another stinging slap in the face on January 22 when the Stones appeared on Britain's most popular television variety show, *Sunday Night at the London Palladium*. Something like ten million people each week watched this hour-long feast of jugglers and trampolinists and a concluding star spot that might be filled one Sunday by Frank Sinatra and the next by Dame Margot Fonteyn. In an invariably spectacular finale, the top of the bill star mounted a circular stage among his fellow performers and high-plumed show-girls, interspersed among giant letters spelling out SUNDAY NIGHT AT THE LONDON PALLADIUM. The stage, with its cargo of artistes and giant letters, then slowly revolved, amid swelling violins and cheery waves of farewell.

Since the Beatles' famous appearance in 1963, most major pop acts of the moment had done the Palladium show and waved goodbye from its revolving stage. It was therefore on a simple head-hunting basis that Lew Grade, boss of the ATV network, pressured his old friend Tito Burns to persuade the Stones to appear. 'I had to talk them into it,' Burns remembered. 'They weren't very keen. But it *was* the biggest show on television. Lew Grade was supposed to be grateful to me for evermore.'

Two hours before the show went out, Tito Burns received an anguished telephone call from the London Palladium. At rehearsals, the Stones had flatly refused to stand on the revolving stage and wave goodbye to the audience. Burns hurried to the Palladium to find Mick Jagger, in a floral shirt, engaged in furious argument with Andrew Loog Oldham, the Stones' studio engineer Glyn Johns, and the show's producer Albert Locke. It transpired that Jagger was the one who would not revolve and wave. In his own words, he refused to let the Stones become 'part of a circus'.

'I did my best to persuade him,' Tim Burns said. 'I said it was part of a tradition, it couldn't do any harm.' But Jagger remained adamant. Albert Locke stamped off to devise an alternative finale with the Stones walking offstage while everyone else revolved and waved. Oldham, meanwhile, had disappeared from the theatre. 'He went off to his clinic, I think,' Tito Burns said. 'He used to go to this clinic every so often and get himself put to sleep for three days.'

The story of the Stones' 'insult' to the London Palladium,

their fellow artistes and Lew Grade's revolving stage was prolonged well into the following week. On Thursday, the *Mail* still had enough angry readers' letters to fill a whole extra page. 'Who do they think they are?' wrote a typical correspondent, (Mrs) E. M. Smith of Clive Yale, Hastings, Sussex. 'I have never seen such a repulsive turn.' (Mrs) E. M. Smith would be more astounded still ere long.

On February 5, the *News of the World* published a full page exposé headlined THE SECRETS OF THE POP STARS' HIDEAWAY, and couched in the dramatic, staccato prose of reporters working under cover like ace detectives to penetrate a difficult and dangerous underworld.

The underworld in this case, somewhat surprisingly, was Roehampton, a London suburb best known for a hospital specializing in artificial limbs. According to the *News of the World*, wild LSD parties had taken place in Roehampton at a house rented to a fairly famous pop group, the Moody Blues, but frequented by a much more famous figure, Mick Jagger of the Rolling Stones.

On learning this, the *NoW* sleuths had naturally wished to seek out Mick Jagger and confront him with his heinous crime. They described their long vigil at a club he was said to frequent – Blases, in Kensington – and their triumph when the familiar Rolling Stone came into the club, consented to be interviewed and freely admitted everything they put to him – a confession made all the more spectacular by the *News of the World* team's tendency to confuse LSD with hashish.

'I don't go much on it now the cats have taken it up,' they quoted their – very talkative – interviewee as saying. 'It'll just get a dirty name. I remember the first time I took it. It was on our first tour with Bo Diddley and Little Richard . . .'

'During the time we were at Blases,' the investigators continued, 'Jagger took about six benzedrine tablets. "I just wouldn't stay awake at places like this if I didn't have them," he said . . .

Later at Blases, Jagger showed a companion and two girls a piece of hash and invited them to his flat for a "smoke".'

Confusing LSD with hashish was not, alas, the *News of the World* sleuths' only blunder that night. All the time they thought they were talking to Mick Jagger, they were actually talking to Brian Jones.

Anyone with the remotest knowledge of the real Jagger could have told the luckless hacks how impossible it would have been for him to swallow 'bennies' publicly and pull out lumps of hashish, let alone indulge in the matey confessions quoted. Anyone who knew Jagger knew that his attitude to drugs was as coy and cautious as to women, hairdressers, clothes and the colour of his cars. Though he certainly smoked hash, it was always with the utmost discretion. The irony was that Jagger himself felt uneasy about Brian and Keith's reckless use of LSD, its effect on them as people as well as the obvious risk of a police bust. Just a week earlier, he had left Keith's house in Sussex, muttering dark forebodings to Donald Cammell. 'This is all getting out of hand,' Cammell remembered him saying. 'I don't know where it's all going to end.'

On Sunday mornings at Harley House, it was Jagger's habit to cover his and Marianne's bed with all the newspapers, both heavy and pop. The *News of the World* was the first thing he read, in mild amusement first, then stupefaction and finally outrage so intense as to scatter his usual caution to the winds. That Sunday evening, he was due to appear on the Eamonn Andrews television talk show. When Andrews cautiously touched on the drugs question, Jagger announced that the whole story was a lie and he would shortly issue a libel writ against the *News of the World*.

It was, in Robert Fraser's phrase, 'the Oscar Wilde mistake' – rushing to law to refute a particular allegation of sins one had committed in general. An equal mistake was to imagine the *News of the World*, taxed with a claim that could cost it punitive damages, would simply pay up and apologize.

What the *News of the World* very naturally did was try to establish that, even if Jagger had not taken LSD in Roehampton and swallowed 'bennies' at Blases, he none the less took drugs and was as such a menace to society. If that could be proved, his libel action would not stand a chance. The sub judice law now prevented the *News of the World* from publishing further revelations before the libel case came to court. If, however, the police should discover any of the same pop stars to be taking drugs, there would be nothing to stop a fair and accurate report of the subsequent proceedings. Nor could any libel jury in Britain convict any newspaper for revealing what was proved, however tardily, to be true.

With hindsight, the wisest thing for Jagger to have done at this point would have been to lock himself in his Harley House flat and spend the weeks until his libel case came to court living like a Trappist monk. What he actually did may seem incredibly stupid and arrogant. But, in fairness, he could have no conception of the forces now ranged against him.

The next weekend, he drove with Marianne to spend the weekend at Redlands, Keith's cottage near West Wittering, Sussex. The party also included Robert Fraser, Christopher Gibbs, the photographer Michael Cooper, Beatle George Harrison and his wife Pattie. Along with log fires and country rambles, the main attraction of the weekend was to be a young American named David Schneidermann, who had materialized from California just a few weeks earlier. Fondly known as 'Acid King David' this personage dispensed a rare and sought-after type of LSD called Sunshine, compounded by a noted San Francisco chemist and imbibed in pellets of bright orange. 'I can picture him now,' says Christopher Gibbs. 'A sort of upmarket flower child who knew more about drugs than anyone the Stones had ever met. "What!" he'd say. "You mean you never heard of dimethyl tryptomine!"'

Call it arrogance, call it naivety or just a young Sixties pop star's well-founded sense of being invulnerable. At all events, the drug-hating Jagger hardly could have been in a worse place as establishment Britain was poised to take its long-delayed revenge – in a country cottage among several confirmed drug-users, under pressure from the others to let Acid King David Schneidermann give him his first taste of LSD.

Eleven guests were in the convoy that followed Keith's Bentley down to Redlands that Saturday night for what was supposed to be a quiet, uneventful Sunday. Apart from Acid King David, only two of the party did not rank as trusted friends. One was a Moroccan named Ali who travelled with the gay Fraser as his servant. The other was Nicky Cramer, a King's Road character who had somehow attached himself to the party and whom Keith was too soft-hearted to disinvite.

On Sunday morning, Acid King David went around the guests' bedrooms like a hippie Jeeves, dispensing trays of tea and enough Sunshine capsules to send everyone off into a languorous trip without even the bother of sitting up. It wasn't until early afternoon that people began drifting down to Redlands' high-raftered living room, relaxed and exhilarated by visions their Californian protégé had furnished. The winter's day being mild and sunny, it was decided to go on a tour of the Sussex countryside, stopping off to look at the house of the surrealist art collector Edward James.

They did not find Edward James's house, but still spent a pleasant couple of hours driving round the empty lanes and running through the woods around Keith's estate, down to a small shingle beach. Michael Cooper photographed Keith, in sunglasses and Afghan fur coat, gambolling over the pebbles, seemingly without a care in the world.

The cars came back to Redlands at about 6 p.m. Shortly afterwards, George Harrison decided he was bored, and he and Pattie drove off to their psychedelic bungalow in Surrey. With George gone, it now seems, a lucky talisman was removed from the house. Keith for one is still convinced that subsequent events could not have happened with a Beatle, almost sacredly immune to official persecution, still on the premises.

The eight males in the party assembled in the living room that was part Olde England, part joss-scented Marrakesh bazaar. Marianne Faithfull had gone upstairs for a bath. She had brought only one set of clothes with her, and these were now muddy and crumpled after the day's country ramblings. So, rather than get dressed again, she came downstairs wrapped in a fur rug taken from one of the beds. After supper – a Moroccan buffet, prepared by Robert Fraser's servant Ali – the company gathered round the TV set, listening to Bob Dylan music while they waited for the Sunday night film, Jack Webb in *Pete Kelly's Blues*. It was, in Christopher Gibbs's words, 'a scene of pure domesticity'.

At about 7.30 p.m., a force of nineteen police officers in assorted vehicles made its way up the long wooded drive that separates Redlands from the main Chichester road. The tip-off they had received had left ample time for the raid to be plotted at West Sussex Regional Police Headquarters and a search warrant to be obtained at a special sitting of Chichester magistrates. The force included three policewomen for the searching of women suspects. (Three women, Marianne, Pattie Harrison and Anita Pallenberg, were supposed to have been in the Redlands party.) The force was commanded by Chief Inspector Gordon Dineley of the West Sussex Constabulary, in full uniform and white-braided cap.

No one inside Redlands heard the police convoy arrive. The first sign of intruders was a single face, flashing briefly at one leaded window-pane. 'Keith looked up and said there seemed to be some little old lady outside,' Marianne remembers. 'He thought it must be some fan, trying to get autographs.'

A violent knocking at the front door then began. Keith got up reluctantly from his cushions to answer it. The others, in their gentle, slightly hilarious stupor, looked up a moment later at what seemed to Marianne to be another, this time wholly ludicrous, LSD vision. Chief Inspector Dineley stood in their midst, sombrely magnificent, like some celestial commissionaire, announcing that, pursuant to the Dangerous Drugs Act, 1964, he had a warrant to search the premises.

There ensued a brief pause while the victims gaped up at the police, now pouring in through every crevice, and the police looked upon a scene that was to be described later, under oath, as one of scarcely believable decadence. They looked at the half-timbered walls, hung with Moroccan drapes; at the huge tapestried cushions underfoot; at the TV set, mutely flickering while Bob Dylan's voice wailed and sneered out of twin stereo speakers; at the small, almost child-like figures in embroidered robes, lounging among pillows and wine bottles; at the hair tangled around chalk-white faces turned up to them, still not quite seriously; at the particular face that was engraved like a Wanted poster on the mind of every police officer in Britain. 'Poor Mick – he could hardly believe his bad luck,' Marianne says. 'The first day he ever dares take an LSD trip, eighteen policemen come pouring in through the door.'

Marianne, a girl alone with eight men, wearing only a fur rug, was the detail which was to give the scene its immortality. The rug was, in fact, extremely large; it could – as Keith says – have covered three girls Marianne's size. Nevertheless Detective Sergeant Stanley Cudmore testified later that, as he studied her closer, trying to detect the usual symptoms of cannabis smoking, Marianne made a deliberate attempt to provoke him by letting the rug slip, 'disclosing parts of her nude body'.

Chief Inspector Dineley, meanwhile, was inquiring formally if Keith Richard was the owner of the invaded premises. Keith – whose dignity remained unimpaired throughout – agreed that he was and requested the Chief Inspector politely not to let his raiders walk all over the valuable cushions under their feet.

Most of those present, including Mick Jagger, believed at this stage they had no real cause for alarm. Though all had taken LSD, no one was in possession of a single Sunshine capsule. The entire supply remained in Acid King David's attaché case – which, as it happened, lay in full view in the centre of the living room.

Only Robert Fraser had cause to fear the outcome of the impending body search. In one trouser pocket, Fraser carried a carved wooden box containing twenty-four heroin jacks, supplied to him by Keith's favourite pusher, Spanish Tony Sanchez. In another pocket, he had a lump of hashish and some amphetamine uppers. Despite his muzzy state, Fraser knew he must, if possible, hide the heroin jacks at least. Casually he slipped a hand into his trouser pocket to open the box, and began to shake the small white tablets out into the lining.

Police officers were now all over Redlands, opening cupboards, turning out drawers, peering darkly into book matches and plastic sachets of in-flight mustard and mayonnaise which Keith had collected on various foreign tours. In the bedroom she shared with Mick, a giggling Marianne was being searched – or rather, since she was naked, scanned – by Detective Constable Rosemary Slade. A male detective had already taken charge of the green velvet jacket Mick had brought with him but had not worn since that pre-Christmas cruise with Marianne along the French Riviera.

Down in the living room, Jagger, Richard, Michael Cooper, Acid King David, Nicky Cramer, Ali the Moroccan, Robert Fraser and Christopher Gibbs stood in line to be frisked. The police had by now distinguished between their quarry and the 'gentlemen' present, and indeed treated both Gibbs and Fraser almost apologetically. The first find was on Acid King David – a small tin and envelope full of cannabis, and what the policeman concerned entered in his notebook as 'a ball of brown substance'. When a policeman put out a tentative hand to Acid King David's briefcase, the American shouted, 'Please don't open the case. It's full of exposed film.' The PC respectfully obeyed.

By the time the young officer assigned to search him was patting his pockets, Robert Fraser had managed to shake all twenty-four heroin tablets free of their carved pillbox. The policeman found the box, examined it and asked what the traces of white powder in it were. Fraser replied that he was diabetic; the box contained his insulin supply. The tablets were then retrieved from his pocket lining and shown to a senior officer, who seemed ready to accept Fraser's story that they contained only insulin. 'He handed them back to me. Then he said, "I'd better keep just one back for analysis." At that moment, I knew I'd had it.'

Jagger was then shown his green velvet jacket and the small glass phial that had been discovered in one of its pockets. The phial contained the final four of the amphetamine uppers given to Marianne Faithful three months earlier by her French disc jockey friend.

In a moment of impressively quick thinking, Jagger recognized the pills, realized they were Marianne's and decided to take the blame. He agreed that the jacket belonged to him, and, when asked if the tablets were his also, replied, 'Yes. My doctor prescribed them for me.' He even named a doctor – Dr Dixon Firth – in Wilton Crescent, Knightsbridge. Asked why he needed tablets, he said, 'To stay awake and work.'

The phial was added to the raid's other spoils – two carved pipes, a pudding basin that had been used for a bedside ashtray, Robert Fraser's heroin jack and Keith's American book matches and mustard sachets. Keith was then formally cautioned that if any of these items contained unlawful drugs, he could face additional prosecution for allowing their use on his property. 'I see,' Keith said drily. 'You pin it all on me.' And with mutual farewells – for neither side ever complained of discourtesy on the other's part – Chief Inspector Dineley and his task force left the house and disappeared into the wooded Sussex night.

A moment or so later, the telephone rang. It was Brian Jones, calling from London to say that he'd stopped work on the music for Anita's new film, and they could join the party within a couple of hours. 'Don't bother,' Keith told him. 'We've all just been busted.'

The atmosphere among Keith's house party was curiously calm. Christopher Gibbs remembers 'a rather philosophical feeling – like "It had to happen and it's happened."' They supposed the raid to have come from no other source but the British policemen, wishing to collar a Rolling Stone on any pretext whatever. If anything, they felt they had come off rather lightly. The failure to find Acid King David's LSD store was no more than astounding good luck. Whatever charges might follow the analysis of Marianne's pep pills and the Moroccan hash pipes had to be relatively trivial.

Thus reassured, the party stayed on at Redlands – all but three. Robert Fraser needed to get back to London urgently. With him and Ali in their van rode Acid King David Schneidermann, clutching his attaché case of undisclosed Sunshine.

Fraser *was* in a panic – and with good reason. To be caught in possession of heroin, the deadliest of all illegal drugs, meant almost certain imprisonment. There was, however, one chance based on the anomalous fact that the drug was legal if prescribed by a doctor to a registered addict. Fraser's only hope was to persuade some doctor to give him a backdated prescription. Acid King David, too, was deeply agitated, as well as incredulous that the police had not hauled everyone straight off for interrogation and charging. 'I advised him to get out of the country right away,' Robert Fraser says. Acid King David did so that very night.

When Fraser reached home, he sent an immediate SOS to Spanish Tony Sanchez, the Soho dealer who had sold him the heroin jacks – and had himself very nearly joined the Redlands party. Spanish Tony advised bribing the police analysts to say that the confiscated jack contained only glucose. He offered to sound out the various 'bent coppers' he knew in the West End division to see if the problem could be settled for money.

Spanish Tony's enquiries proved fruitful. All the substances taken from Redlands could be 'lost', he told Mick and Keith, for a bribe of £7,000. Andrew Loog Oldham, in California on other business, still knew nothing of the bust. The two chief Stones, for the very first time, were acting on their own initiative. Together they eagerly shelled out £5,000, and Robert Fraser managed to scrape up the residue. The money was put into a carrier bag and paid over by Spanish Tony to his police contact in a pub in Kilburn.

The following Sunday, February 19, in addition to its continuing series 'Pop Stars and Drugs', the *News of the World* ran a front-page story confirming that insidious social evil with fresh, exclusive evidence. The Redlands raid was then described, without a single name (to observe the sub judice law) but otherwise in the most intimate detail. The story said that one 'nationally known star' had had pep pills taken from him; that 'bottles and an ashtray' had also been seized for analysis; that, as well as the two 'nationally famous names' likely to face drugs charges, a third had left the raided house just in time; and that 'a foreign national' was being watched for at air and seaports in case he should try to leave the country.

Every line in the piece reeked of quid pro quo. It was plain that the *News of the World* had got the story exclusively in return for tipping off the police that the party was to take place. How had the moralists at Bouverie Street possibly got hold of details supposedly known only to Keith Richard, Mick Jagger and the others invited to join them at Redlands? The immediate conclusion was that one of the house party was a traitor. Excluding the staunch friends of the Stones, Christopher Gibbs, Robert Fraser, Michael Cooper and Moroccan Ali, suspicion naturally fell on the two who had come merely as hangers-on: Nicky Cramer, the Chelsea flower person, and Acid King David Schneidermann.

Nicky Cramer's innocence was established with brutal

efficiency. A mutual friend of Mick and Keith's named David Litvinoff visited the unfortunate flower child and beat him up systematically. When Cramer still did not confess, he was pronounced in the clear.

That left only Acid King David, the visitor from America who had become a Stones friend so very quickly, by stages that no one now could quite remember or explain. Elaborated by many theories suited to the drama of the moment, his persona became increasingly bizarre. Michael Cooper remembered looking into Acid King David's luggage for hashish, and seeing he possessed a second passport in the name of 'David English'. Cooper also remembered a strange talk with the American about firearms and espionage . . . 'like he was into the James Bond thing, you know . . . the whole CIA bit'.

With the story of the raid in print, there plainly was little hope that the police could be bribed to forget it. Probably there had been no hope even before Spanish Tony paid his police contact the £7,000, since there was no evidence that the money ever made its way to anyone in the West Sussex Constabulary. Even so, when a further week had passed and still nothing came of the matter, it seemed as if the money might have found its mark.

The wisest thing meanwhile was to get as far away from Britain, and probable further notoriety, as possible. In this at least Mick and Keith were fortunate, finding themselves in a rare professional lull. The Stones had just released an album, *Between the Buttons*, and had no further group commitment until their European tour, beginning on March 25.

Morocco was the obvious choice of sanctuary. To lessen the risk of harassment en route, they agreed to travel separately, meeting up, with Robert Fraser, Michael Cooper and other friends, in Marrakesh. Mick and Marianne would fly from Paris while Keith would drive down, accompanied by Brian Jones and Anita Pallenberg.

A rapprochement between Keith and Brian had lately occurred, thanks mainly to Mick's absorption in his affair with Marianne. Keith still felt it keenly that he had no steady girlfriend, and had, paradoxically, turned back to Brian for the kind of bachelor companionship they used to enjoy at Edith Grove. For some weeks past, indeed, he had been staying with Brian and Anita in their galleried studio apartment in Courtfield Road.

Brian welcomed him, delighted to have Keith back in his gang again, with that implied rejection of Mick; scarcely less pleased at the obvious mutual affinity between Keith and Anita. These weeks before his world disintegrated were a good time for Brian, with Keith and Anita as a new power axis, and his prestige as a musician higher than ever. To allay his jealousy, Anita had arranged for him to write a soundtrack score for the film she was to make with Volker Schlöndorff. The film, entitled *A Degree of Murder*, featured Anita as a female assassin. Brian had thrown himself enthusiastically into the project, hiring Glyn Johns to recruit notable young freelance session men like pianist Nicky Hopkins and guitarist Jimmy Page. His finished score, using an eclectic range of instruments – with eerily atmospheric passages played by Brian himself on dulcimer, sitar and autoharp – was pronounced brilliant by Volker Schlöndorff, Glyn Johns and everyone else who heard it.

In the general Moroccan exodus, therefore, Brian, Anita and Keith travelled as a natural threesome. Keith had a hankering to make the entire trip in the Blue Lena, as he called his sky-coloured Bentley Continental. With Tom Keylock along to share the driving and handle frontier formalities, the 2,000-mile journey down through France and Spain promised fun, relaxation and harmony.

The Blue Lena crossed the English Channel without incident, stopping in Paris to pick up a fifth passenger, Donald Cammell's girlfriend Deborah. They continued southward then, with France only faintly discernible outside the boom of the in-car stereo, Brian and Anita lounging in the back like fur-wrapped, blond Borgias, and Keith up front, laughing indulgently at Tom Keylock's Cockney patter. The chauffeur claimed, while in the paratroops, to have suffered wounds necessitating a skin graft from his bottom to his nose – as he frequently boasted, 'Most of my arse is on my face.' (A quick-witted girl in the Stones' office was once inspired to retort, 'That must be why so much shit comes out of your mouth, Tom.')

All went smoothly until the Bentley reached Toulon. Brian, who had been showing signs of asthmatic unease on the mountainous route, suddenly developed a high fever and was admitted to hospital with pneumonia. He insisted, however, that Anita should go on into Spain with Keith and the other two. When he felt better, he would fly straight to Tangier to meet them at the Hotel Minzah.

It was clear to Tom Keylock, even from the evidence of his rear-view mirror, as the Blue Lena passed Montpelier, Béziers, then Perpignan, that Keith and Anita were becoming something more than friends. Keith by now realized the inevitable, though he tried to avoid it with vague plans for getting off with the other female passenger, Deborah. At Valencia, he and Anita spent the night together but next morning tacitly agreed to treat it as just a pleasant interlude. 'I was still very wary,' Keith says, 'and trying hard not to fuck up the new thing I had going with Brian.'

No journey with Keith Richard could be entirely devoid of drama, as Anita discovered when they stopped in Barcelona and went to a night club. Keith got into a furious row with some waiters who would not accept his Diner's Club card without seeing his passport. While Keylock fetched the passport, Keith, Anita and Deborah were taken to police headquarters and interrogated until six o'clock the next morning. Back at their hotel there was a message from Brian, ordering Anita to return to Toulon and fetch him. She decided to pretend the message hadn't reached her.

They crossed by ferry from Malaga to Tangier a few days later, and checked into the Hotel Minzah. The desk clerk handed Anita a sheaf of Brian's frantic telegrams and telephone messages. Keith – still trying valiantly to play a straight bat – urged Anita to fly back to Toulon with Deborah to collected Brian while he and Tom Keylock went on to Marrakesh.

Mick was already at the appointed hotel, with Robert Fraser and Michael Cooper, waiting for Marianne to join him from Naples. Two days later, Brian and Anita arrived from the airport. Brian had recovered from his pneumonia but looked haggard with fatigue and suspicion. He clearly guessed something had happened between Anita and Keith, but would not – could not – accuse Keith outright. He took out his insecurity in the usual way – by beating Anita up in the privacy of their suite. Her make-up, fortunately, hid the worst of the bruises.

The week that followed put everyone else, as they'd hoped, into a more stable, relaxed frame of mind. The party shopped in the casbah and the big central square, drank mint tea and Scotch and Coke, smoked grass and Gauloises, dropped acid and lounged like ordinary tourists round the hotel pool. To that chlorine-scented court came Brion Gysin, the avant-garde painter and Cecil Beaton, photographer of more conventional royalty, who coveted Mick Jagger as a subject, if nothing else, and whose famous diaries record the scene with penetrating unworldliness.

> On the Tuesday evening I came down to dinner very late and, to my surprise, sitting in the hotel lobby, discovered Mick Jagger and a sleepy-looking band of gipsies. Robert Fraser, one of their company, wearing a huge, black felt hat, was coughing by the swimming pool . . . It was a strange group. The three 'Stones': Brian Jones with his girlfriend Anita Pallenberg – dirty white face, dirty blackened eyes, dirty canary drops of hair, barbaric jewellery – Keith Richard

in eighteenth-century suit, long black velvet coat and the tightest pants; and, of course, Mick Jagger . . .

I didn't want to give the impression that I was only interested in Mick, but it happened that we sat next to one another as he drank a Vodka Collins and smoked with pointed finger held high. His skin is chicken-breast white and of a fine quality. He has an inborn elegance.

. . . By degrees the shy aloofness of the gang broke down. We got into two cars . . . [My] car was filled with pop art cushions, scarlet fur rugs and sex magazines. Immediately the most tremendous volume of pop music boomed in the region of the back of my neck. Mick and Brian responded rhythmically and the girl leant forward and screamed in whispers that she had just played a murderess in a film that was to be shown at the Cannes Festival.

. . . We went to a Moroccan restaurant. Mick . . . is very gentle and with perfect manners. He has much appreciation and his small, albino-fringed eyes notice everything. He has an analytical slant and compares everything he is seeing here with earlier impressions in other countries.

. . . He asked: 'Have you ever taken LSD? Oh, I should. It would mean so much to you: you'd never forget the colours. For a painter it is a great experience. One's brain works not on four cylinders but on four thousand.'

. . . By the time we reached the hotel, it was three o'clock . . . Mick listened to pop records for a couple of hours, and was then so tired that he went to sleep without taking off his clothes . . .

At eleven o'clock, he appeared at the swimming pool. I could not believe it was the same person walking towards us. The very strong sun, reflected from the white ground, made his face look a white, podgy, shapeless mess; eyes very small, nose very pink, hair sandy dark. His figure, his hands and arms were incredibly feminine.

> None of them was willing to talk, except in spasms. No one could make up their minds what to do, or when.
>
> I took Mick through the trees to photograph him in the midday sun . . . He is sexy, yet completely sexless. He could nearly be a eunuch. As a model he is a natural.
>
> Their wardrobe is extensive. Mick showed me the rows of brocade coats. Everything is shoddy, poorly made, the seams burst. Keith himself had sewn his trousers, lavender and dull rose, with a band of badly stitched leather dividing the two colours.
>
> Brian, at the pool, appears in white pants with a huge black square applied on the back. It is very smart in spite of the fact that the seams are giving way. But with such marvellously flat, tight, compact figures as they have, with no buttocks or stomach, almost anything looks well on them.

The Stones' party occupied the hotel's entire tenth floor. Brion Gysin remembers a collective LSD trip in one or another suite, with Elmore James music wailing, Keith strumming along on guitar, Mick pirouetting dementedly round the room and Brian Jones – 'like a little celluloid kewpie doll' – with Tom Keylock murmuring intrigue into his ear. When trays of food were brought in, everyone rode the trays around the floor like toboggans.

As the evening wore on and the trip wore off, Brian and Anita began squabbling again. Anita grabbed some sleeping pills and locked herself in their bedroom. Brian beckoned to Tom Keylock and asked the chauffeur to go out and find him a local whore. The others left him to it, racing off in various cars for an all-night trip into the Atlas mountains.

Next morning, the atmosphere around the pool was electric. Brian, the night before, had gone into town, returned with two tattooed Moroccan whores, and tried to force Anita into a group sex orgy. When she refused, he had beaten her up so severely she thought he meant to kill her.

Anita now sat in a poolside chair, locked in a passionate stare with Keith, ducking up and down in the water. Even Mick Jagger could not detach himself, as he would have much preferred, from the mounting tension. 'It's getting fuckin' heavy,' he kept staying to Robert Fraser in the intervals of packing and complaining about his hotel bill. Then Tom Keylock came in to report that a posse of British journalists was about to fly in from London. The obvious risk was that they would collar Brian and get him to blurt out something scandalous about the case pending against Mick and Keith. So Tom Keylock deputed Brion Gysin to take Brian out into the Djemaa el Fna, the big central square, to record Moroccan music, drink mint tea, buy souvenirs and get lost.

While Brian was away, Keith Richard came to a decision. 'I was so disgusted with the way Brian had treated Anita, I just threw her in the back of the car and split.' Anita tells the same story – not of being stolen but rescued. 'I was in fear of my life. I was hysterical. Keith saved me.'

Tom Keylock drove them back to Tangier, where they boarded the ferry for Malaga. There, the Spanish Customs almost put paid to their escape. Searching for drugs, half a dozen officers stripped the Blue Lena down to the chassis. The small piece of hash Keith had on him was successfully concealed by Keylock in the most obvious hiding-place – under the flap to the petrol tank.

Two nights later in Paris, Donald Cammell was awakened by a frantic knocking on his apartment door. It was Brian, without luggage, babbling, 'They left me. They just went off and left me . . .' Mixed up in the story he poured out to Cammell was something about a carved wooden pipe he'd bought that afternoon with Brion Gysin in Marrakesh. He'd come back with the pipe to find Anita, Keith, Tom Keylock and the Bentley all gone.

The fugitives, meanwhile, had driven back as far as Madrid, then caught a plane for London, leaving Keylock to bring home the Blue Lena at his leisure. They were now at a small flat Keith maintained in St John's Wood, hiding out until Anita could pluck up nerve to go back to Courtfield Road for her clothes.

The hope that Spanish Tony had managed to buy off the police was dashed, virtually at the moment Keith re-entered Britain. On March 18, the *Daily Mirror* splashed the story that Mick Jagger and Keith Richard were to be summonsed on drugs charges arising from a raid on the latter's country house. Once more, through hand-in-glove co-operation with Scotland Yard, Fleet Street could pre-empt the process of the law. Four days later, as the *Mirror* had promised, the summonses came. Jagger was accused, with Robert Fraser and the vanished Acid King David Schneidermann, of possessing substances unlawful under the Dangerous Drugs Act, 1964. Keith was accused of 'knowingly permitting' his house to be used for those drugs' consumption. The case was set down to be heard by Chichester magistrates on May 10, with the option of summary trial or referral to the next West Sussex Quarter Sessions.

An aggrieved Spanish Tony later sought out his police contact and asked what had happened to the £7,000 which Jagger, Richard and Fraser had paid as a bribe. All he could elicit was that the money had not got to 'the right man' before revelation of the bust in the *News of the World* and other papers had made a cover-up impossible. 'That's what I feel most bitter about,' Keith says. 'In America, you pay off the cops as a matter of course. It's business. But in Britain, you pay them off and they still do you.'

Brian Jones was now back in London also, recovered from his hysterics and determined to regain Anita with a bravura display of masculinity. Discovering she was at Keith's 'crash pad', he drove there and hammered on the door, which Keith then suddenly opened. Brian came hurtling in and sprawled on the front hall carpet.

Anita would not go back to Brian – nor was she yet ready to move in with Keith. Another film part – in Roger Vadim's space fantasy, *Barbarella* – was about to take her to Spain on location. Keith had to tour Europe with the Stones, sharing a stage for the next three weeks with Brian and his smouldering reproach.

The tour had been planned as the Stones' farewell to concert performance for the foreseeable future. Like the Beatles, they were weary of incessant touring and the necessity of making records always on the run. Exhaustion had clearly shown in their last album, *Between the Buttons*, in which lack of ideas combined with over-production to produce a curious, limply echoing effect, like a vaudeville show in an almost empty hall. The album offered such aberrant Stones items as Back Street Girl, a French *valse musette* complete with accordions, and Something Happened To Me, gasped out by Keith's nicotine-roughened voice in a ludicrous setting of pithead brass bands. The play-out groove featured Jagger giving facetious road-safety advice. 'Remember . . . if you're going out on your bike tonight . . . wear white!'

It was not a good time to be travelling abroad. The summonses against Mick and Keith in Britain put them automatically on the Red List of suspected drug-traffickers, circulated among all European customs authorities. In France, Sweden, West Germany, Austria and Greece, going through customs meant the same ordeal for all five Stones – even drug-free, innocent Charlie Watts – of ransacked cases and, often, rough strip-searches. Brian, before each airport touchdown, would be terrorized by Tom Keylock into flushing his pills and hashish down the aircraft toilet. 'It was the only way to be safe,' Keylock says. 'I used to tell him, if he said he was clean and he wasn't, I'd chin him.'

The British press was determined there should be trouble – any kind. On April 8, the *Daily Express* reported the controversy between Mick Jagger and the Olympic long-jump champion Lynn Davies about the Stones' alleged bad behaviour at a hotel in Dortmund, West Germany. According to Davies, the hotel's breakfast room had quailed under the stream of obscenities to be heard from the Stones' table. 'I felt sick and ashamed to be British,' the sensitive athlete declared. '. . . They are tarnishing their country's name in a foreign land . . .' The allegations were put to Jagger in Paris, at a press conference called to complain of his continuing harassment by customs officers. 'We deny that we were badly behaved,' he retorted. 'We hardly ever used the public rooms at that hotel. They were crammed with athletes, behaving very badly.'

From Paris, the Stones travelled to Poland to make their first, and last, appearance behind the Iron Curtain. The first of two concerts at the Warsaw Palace of Culture took place before 2,000 hand-picked Communist Party officials and their children, while a mass of ordinary teenagers, who had been unable to buy tickets, waited outside, guarded by units of the Polish army. The Stones, to their great bewilderment, could elicit no audience response beyond polite clapping. Halfway through the first show, Mick Jagger had a brilliant idea. Tom Keylock was deputed to drive round the Palace of Culture, scattering Rolling Stones singles just beyond the army cordons. The entire crowd at once broke through to pick up the precious discs, and were driven back by clubs, tear gas and water-cannon fire. It was only by a miracle that troops stationed on the front steps did not actually open fire with their levelled machine guns.

That night, as the running battles still continued, a Polish photographer handed Tom Keylock several rolls of film, shot as the army prepared to counter-attack. Keylock persuaded Don Short, a *Daily Mirror* reporter, to smuggle the film out when they left Poland the following day. Short, in consternation, hid the film down his underpants; then, at Warsaw airport, he lost his nerve and passed it back to Keylock, who successfully jettisoned it. The Polish customs' only victim was Les Perrin, the Stones' publicist, for neglecting to declare all the currency he was exporting. Perrin could not leave until he had gone into the airport shop and spent his surplus Polish money on a full-length bearskin coat.

Things were hardly less ugly in Athens, when the Stones gave what would be their final performance for more than two years. Greece's new regime of Fascist army colonels had not yet got round to banning rock concerts, but they showed their disapproval with hundreds of armed police, pinning the stadium crowd so far back that Jagger could not hope to perform his final, climatic trick of dancing to the stage edge and tossing out roses from a bowl.

Instead, he handed the basket to Tom Keylock and said, 'Okay, baby – run!' As Keylock sprinted towards the police perimeter, several officers at once made ready to receive him. Keylock swung the basket at them, 'chinning' two or three, then hurled it into the air and, as the roses cascaded down, ran for his life.

Nine

'A Mars bar fills that gap'

On May 10, Mick Jagger and Keith Richard sat with Robert Fraser in the small police court at Chichester, Sussex, waiting for their names to be called among the minor larcenies and traffic peccadilloes that are the normal diet of English provincial magistrates. Both accused Stones wore sober dark suits and the expressions of downcast meekness in which their publicist, Les Perrin, had painstakingly rehearsed them. 'We were all squeezed up together on these little benches – the lawyers, the national press and us,' Keith remembers. 'It was a bit like being back at school. I don't think even at that point we expected anything much worse then a cuff on the side of the head or a ruler across the knuckles.'

Jagger had maintained that optimistic view to Marianne each time she begged him to let her confess that the tablets the police found in his jacket at Redlands really belonged to her. 'Mick kept saying that his career could stand a drug bust but mine couldn't,' Marianne says. 'I could tell it pleased him to think he was playing the English gentleman – that he wouldn't let me be thrown to the wolves.'

Robert Fraser, alone of the trio, was prey to deep gloom and pessimism. Fraser had realized at the outset how prejudicial it must be to his own very serious drug offence to appear in harness with two such notorious co-defendants. The court's refusal to grant him a separate trial had condemned the Old Etonian to forced association with all the Stones accumulated outrage and ill will. It was, moreover, just a few weeks since Fraser had undergone prosecution over the alleged indecency of some Jim Dine paintings exhibited at his Mount Street gallery. Robert Fraser suspected, if Mick and Keith did not, what a wave was preparing to break in that dusty, sunshiny little courtroom.

The court clerk read out the formal indictments. Michael Philip Jagger – using Les Perrin's office address of 'New Oxford Street, London, W1.' – stood accused of possessing four tablets containing amphetamine sulphate and methlamphetamine hydrochloride, contrary to the Dangerous Drugs (Prevention of Misuse) Act, 1964. Robert Hugh Fraser of Mount Street, London, W1., was accused of possessing heroin and eight amphetamine capsules similar to those found in Jagger's possession. Keith Richard – charged in his real surname, 'Richards' – of Redlands Lane, West Wittering, was accused of allowing his house to be used for the smoking of cannabis.

All three pleaded 'Not Guilty'. Mr Geoffrey Leach, counsel for Jagger and Richard, said he wished 'to deny most strongly these allegations and to challenge the interpretation thought to be placed by the Prosecution on the evidence in its possession'. Mr William Denny, for Robert Fraser, said his client 'would welcome the earliest opportunity to make answer to the charges against him'.

The three, having elected trial by jury in a higher court, claimed the right to reserve their defence until their reappearance at West Sussex Quarter Sessions in June. The committal proceedings, even so, allowed a lengthy précis of the police case to be given by prosecuting solicitor Anthony McCowan. Magistrates in 1967 had no power to impose reporting restrictions if the committal evidence seemed likely to engender prejudice before the main trial. The story of Chief Inspector Dineley's swoop could therefore run at length in every national newspaper five weeks before any of the accused had uttered a word in his own defence.

The law, however, went out of its way to protect a fourth, absent member of the Redlands party. Since Acid King David Schneidermann had failed to appear to answer charges of possessing cannabis, the bench ruled it would be unfair for his name to appear in the newspaper reports.

Half an hour later, Mick, Keith and Robert Fraser left the court on bail of £250 each, emerging into brilliant sunshine and the scrum of Fleet Street photographers, amid screams, cheers and scattered boos, escorted by Les Perrin, who could be observed at ticklish moments actually holding Mick Jagger's hand. Nearby in the crowd was a familiar and, as of now, deeply anxious, podgy face. Allen Klein had flown in from New York to attend court that day and remain on hand throughout the trial to come.

At four o'clock that same afternoon, the Scotland Yard Drug Squad raided Brian Jones's flat in Courtfield Road. They found Brian dressed in a Japanese kimono and bleary-eyed, sitting among the debris of an all-night party. The only remaining guest was twenty-four-year-old Prince Stanislas Klossowski de Rola, a Swiss nobleman and would-be pop singer, known within the Stones' circle as 'Stash'.

This was the easiest Stone of all to put into the bag. The entire flat was littered with evidence of drug-taking revelry which Brian had made no attempt to conceal, even though he had received at least two anonymous phone calls warning him that the police were on their way.

A few minutes' work by the raiders among the divans and outsize cushions were enough to produce eleven different items for chemical analysis. They included a pile of hashish, some methedrine and a glass phial containing traces of cocaine. When asked if the cocaine was his, Brian recoiled in horror. 'No, man

– not cocaine,' he stammered. 'That's not my scene. I smoke hash but I'm not a junkie.'

In some uncanny way, the whole of London seems to have known in advance that Brian Jones was to be busted. When he and Stash were brought out, to be questioned further at Chelsea Police Station, crowds of reporters and onlookers were already gathered in Courtfield Road. By 5 p.m., Brian had been formally charged with possession of cocaine, methedrine and cannabis resin. Stash was charged with possessing cannabis, even though no trace of the drug had been found either on his person or on the divan where he had been sleeping.

Next morning, the blond-haired, haggard Stone and the Swiss princeling made a ten-minute appearance before Great Marlborough Street Court's stipendiary magistrate. Both elected trial by jury at Inner London Sessions and were released on bail of £250 each. Brian's first act was to send a telegram to his parents in Cheltenham. 'Please don't worry, don't jump to nasty conclusions and don't judge me too harshly. All my love . . .'

The exquisitely neat alignment of Brian's bust with Mick and Keith's committal for trial, proved beyond any doubt that the Rolling Stones, through their three most prominent and notorious members, were now under systematic attack by the establishment whose sensibilities they had so long carelessly flouted. Not for their own misdemeanours only, but for all the pampered, nonchalant arrogance of Britain's pop generation, they had been marked down for a retribution which, in the ensuing weeks, despite all its judicial pomp and deliberateness, bore marked similarities to a medieval hue-and-cry.

The first hard lesson, for young men cocooned in flattery as much as luxury, was to realize how very few among their immense social circle had the ability, intelligence – or, for that matter, the inclination – to give them the help they now desperately needed.

There would be little help from Decca Records for musicians who had largely secured the company its current multi-million-pound annual profit. Sir Edward Lewis, though he expressed himself 'concerned' at the Stones' plight, and its possible repercussions on Decca shares, remained carefully dissociated from all strategy being prepared for their defence. 'The Stones weren't an in-house Decca act, the way the Beatles were at EMI,' Andrew Loog Oldham says. 'That's why, when the Beatles got into drug busts later, Sir Joseph Lockwood gave them all that support. To Decca, the Stones were just freelances. They had to look after themselves.'

Oldham himself likewise played a curiously small part in the developing drama, giving the reins of management over largely to Allen Klein. But for Oldham, however, there would have been no Les Perrin to choreograph the manners and subdue the wardrobes of his two charges, and in every way mitigate the unfavourable image they would take with them into court. Perrin also used his extensive contacts in the borderland between Fleet Street and Parliament to enlist the sympathy of liberal-minded MPs like Tom Driberg – already a social conquest of Mick Jagger's – and the Home Office junior minister, Dick Taverne. On May 19, speaking in Wales, Taverne cited the Jagger-Richard case as one where the reporting of committal proceedings must inevitably create prejudice against accused who had not yet spoken in their own defence.

Before Mick and Keith even came to trial, most of the papers had agreed this must be the end for the Rolling Stones. So it could easily have been but for Mick, a wholly unexpected tower of strength in this period, both in marshalling his and Keith's defence and, simultaneously, motivating Bill and Charlie, those deeply bemused, innocent bystanders, to get back into the studio and begin work on an album to redeem the failure of *Between the Buttons*. An additional spur was provided, in early June, by the Beatles' psychedelic masterpiece *Sgt. Pepper's Lonely Hearts Club*

Band, combining drug-sparkled mysticism with matey Toytown humour, and packaged in an historic sleeve showing the four Beatles as sateen hussars, set about by pop-art icons, marijuana plants and a doll wearing a sweatshirt saying WELCOME THE ROLLING STONES.

The first tentative studio sessions made clear to everyone that Brian Jones was on the edge of complete disintegration. The bust at Courtfield Road had come only days after his return from the Cannes Film Festival and an anguished week with Anita Pallenberg, as musical director and star respectively of the film *A Degree of Murder*. Brian had stayed in the same hotel as Anita and Keith, and accompanied them on the round of parties and receptions, waiting for a chance to renew his pleas to Anita to return to him. But all that happened when he did get her alone was that old, uncontrollable urge to abuse and hit her.

Since losing Anita, he had had half a dozen girls from the scores who offered themselves. His old Cheltenham schoolfriend Peter Watson remembers meeting him in Tottenham Court Road, bejewelled and bangled, a smut-eyed dolly bird clinging to each arm. At the end of their conversation, Brian proffered the girls to Watson, as one might a packet of cigarettes, and said, 'Here – do you want one?'

He had subsequently acquired a steady girlfriend in Suki Poitier, a fashion model whose blonde hair and facial bone structure were the most like Anita's he could find. Suki had survived the car crash that killed Tara Browne, heir to the Guinness fortune, Brian's close friend and subject of John Lennon's finest song, A Day in the Life. She moved in with Brian shortly after the Courtfield Road bust, and for the next eighteen months bravely endured the ordeal of being a living replica.

Brian was now a haunted and a haunting sight. The face, under its gold fringe, was puffy and sick-pale; the eyes, when not glazed over, wavered back and forth, bleakly reflecting the chaos inside his head. He would sometimes arrive at Olympic Studios so drunk he could do nothing but sit among his guitars and music-stands, and sink into comatose sleep. When he could pick up a guitar, he would sometimes play it without tuning it, or so badly that the whole take was unusable. After a time, the others found it simplest to have his amplifier lead quietly disconnected.

The bust and his impending trial had stopped him using hashish – and, indeed, made him paranoiacally fearful that some-one else might leave some at Courtfield Road where the police could find it. He continued, none the less, to dose himself with barbiturates washed down with brandy or Scotch and, in safe houses, to carry on experimenting with new varieties of LSD. His closest friend in this period was Jimi Hendrix, the young American blues wizard whose stage act was lewder than the Stones had ever dared to be. In June, Brian flew to America to see Hendrix play at the first-ever rock festival, at Monterey, California. Though present only as a spectator, warmly interested in the new generation of American stars like Hendrix and Janis Joplin, he became a festival attraction in his own right, wandering round the hippy bivouacs in his silks and Berber jewellery. 'Brian and Jimi took STP together at Monterey,' Anita Pallenberg says. 'That's the acid which can give you a seventy-two hour trip.'

Barely noticed in the glare surrounding the Jagger-Richard trial, Brian began paying regular visits to a Harley Street psy-chiatrist, Dr Leonard Henry. Dr Henry considered his condition serious enough to warrant residential treatment, and arranged with a Harley Street colleague, Dr Anthony Flood, for Brian to spend three weeks at Flood's private clinic at Roehampton. The beginning of this analysis-cum-rest cure was not auspicious. Brian arrived in full regalia, accompanied by Tom Keylock and Suki Poitier, and demanded a double-bedded room for Suki and himself during his treatment. 'It's not on,' Dr Flood said tersely. 'In any case, the first thing I'm going to do is put you to sleep for two days.'

The psychiatrist's initial diagnosis had much to do with this infantile urge to exhibit sexual bravado, even in a state of manifest desperation. Brian, he noted, was 'anxious, considerably depressed, perhaps even suicidal . . . He is easily depressed and easily thwarted. He cannot sort out his problems satisfactorily because he becomes so anxious and depressed . . . He has not a great deal of confidence in himself . . . He is still trying to grow up in many ways.'

Dr Flood was struck, at the same time, by the intelligence and perceptiveness that could shine through Brian's superstar conceits and tantrums. Psychiatrist and patient became something like friends in hours of conversation ranging from Brian's hypochondriac obsession with all forms of artificial stimulant, through his interest in railway locomotives and London buses, to quite advanced questions of history, philosophy and ethics. At one point, he told Dr Flood he had always regretted not going to university. When told that twenty-five was not too late an age to do so, he seemed to give the matter serious consideration.

The treatment seemed to be working until a day when Brian begged Dr Flood to let him out for the evening, because, he insisted, the other Stones needed him at Olympic Studios. The doctor agreed, on condition he was back in bed by midnight at the latest. Brian appeared at seven the next morning, so full of alcohol and pills that he could hardly walk. Dr Flood had no alternative but to put him to bed and start again from the beginning.

Trial at a regional quarter sessions, under the old English court structure, was nowhere near as burdened with legal pomp and circumstance as the yearly assizes. This lower court – named for its traditional covering each 'quarter day' – featured no grey-wigged judge, walking in state to the courthouse, preceded by mace-bearer and chamberlain. At quarter sessions it was sufficient for a senior lawyer – a Recorder, sitting alone, or Chairman, sitting with lay magistrates – to preside over the case, sum up the evidence and give legal directions to the jury. The Jagger-

Richard-Fraser trial was unusual in that the Chairman of West Sussex Quarter Session happened also to be a judge, sixty-one-year-old ex-Naval Commander Leslie Kenneth Allen Block.

It was not in his metropolitan capacity in the Mayor's and City of London Court, but as a Sussex landowner, dairy farmer and Justice of the Peace that Judge Block found himself charged with conduct of Britain's most scandal-ridden trial since the era of Oscar Wilde. He was to rise to the occasion, even so, as a classic British judge, combining unworldly and fastidious remoteness from the matter he was trying with an intermittent desire to crack jokes for the amusement of the assembled barristers.

The three-day trial, from June 27–29, turned Chichester from a quiet yachtsmen's haven into a scrimmage to glimpse the main defendants that was by no means confined to hysterical little girls. Extra police by the hundred were drafted in to control the mêlée around the court buildings, of fans, reporters, TV crews and casual gawpers. Bright sunshine and abundant hot-dog and ice-cream stalls lent almost a carnival atmosphere. One quick-witted huckster brought a van with silk screen printing equipment to run off T-shirts inscribed 'Free the Stones' and 'Mick is Innocent'.

Counsel for the defence of both Mick and Keith was forty-four-year-old Michael Havers QC, a future Attorney-General, at that time one of the most eminent, and costly, 'silks' at the criminal Bar. Havers had been retained not for his eminence only but for his genuine indignation that Jagger should have been prosecuted so ruthlessly for what seemed a technicality and Keith on such apparently circumstantial evidence. It was disconcerting, none the less, for the two Stones, after fighting their way from their limousine into the court precincts, to observe Havers and the prosecuting counsel, Malcom Morris QC, talking together as amiably as member of the same club, fraternity and family.

Mick Jagger was first to be called from the well of the old-fashioned courtroom into its elevated wooden dock. As the familiar doll-like figure appeared, dressed in a light green jacket, olive trousers, frilled shirt and multi-striped tie, an involuntary gasp came from the eighty-odd girls who threatened to overbalance the narrow public gallery. The police usher bellowed for silence but could not – and would never – still an undercurrent of female anguish like the constant soft rustle of tissue paper or chocolate box wrappings.

The task before Michael Havers that morning was comparatively simple. Jagger's plea of not guilty to illegal possession of amphetamines left only one possible defence. Havers must convince the jury that Jagger had got the four tablets on prescription from a doctor, even though no written prescription could be produced in evidence.

The secondary part of Havers's strategy was to emphasize the extremely marginal nature of the alleged offence. The tablets, though illegal in Britain, were sold openly in other European countries – were, indeed, recommended by their makers, Lepetit of Milan, as a remedy for mundane ailments like travel sickness. A law designed to curb criminal and habitual drug-pushers was being mobilized against someone whose offence, according to the evidence, was purely accidental, and could be repeated by any respectable citizen who bought travel sickness pills abroad and forgot to dispose of them before returning to Britain.

In the quick verbal brush-strokes of what he clearly considered an open-and-shut case, Michael Morris QC outlined the circumstances of the police swoop on Redlands, the search of the upstairs bedrooms and the discovery of the four tablets in Jagger's green velvet jacket. Detective Sergeant Stanley Cudmore then took the stand with his official notebook to testify that Jagger had admitted the tablets were his, and claimed they were a doctor's prescription to help him 'stay awake and work'. Sergeant Cudmore, under cross-examination, agreed that Jagger's conduct throughout the raid had been 'thoroughly adult and co-operative'.

The only witness for the defence was Dr Raymond Dixon Firth of Wilton Crescent, Knightsbridge, Jagger's doctor since 1965. Dr Dixon Firth testified that 'some time before February', Jagger had rung up to ask about some tablets he said he'd bought on his way back from the San Remo Pop Festival, and had been taking to help him cope with a period of intense personal strain. The doctor realized the pills were amphetamines and gave Jagger permission to go on taking them, provided he did so only in an emergency. This, in Dr Dixon Firth's opinion, was a valid prescription which put Jagger in absolutely legal possession of the amphetamines. He added that if Jagger had come to his surgery for something to enable him to 'stay awake and work', the doctor would have prescribed exactly that same drug.

Judge Block turned and conferred briefly with his three fellow magistrates – two more Sussex farmers and a newsagent from Worthing. Then he addressed the jury of eleven men and one woman.

'These [Dr Dixon Firth's] remarks cannot be regarded as a prescription,' he said. 'I therefore direct you that there is no defence to this charge.' The jury retired for a token six minutes before returning its obligatory verdict of guilty. Judge Block turned back to Jagger, now standing and gripping the edge of the dock. 'I propose to defer sentencing you until after the trial of your two friends,' the judge continued. 'In the meantime, you will be remanded in custody.' The police warder who had appeared beside him took Jagger's arm and steered him to a police cell below the courtroom, to await the end of the day's proceedings.

The trial of Robert Fraser lasted an even shorter time. Fraser, on the advice of his counsel, William Denny, had changed his plea to Guilty. All that could be done, therefore, was to plead the mitigating circumstances of Fraser's distinguished military career in Kenya during the Mau Mau emergency and the hard work and flair by which he had afterwards founded his London art gallery. Knowing the layman's view of drug addicts as helpless and spineless beings, Mr Denny took pains to stress how desperately Fraser had wrestled with his heroin addiction – how, after one traumatic cure, he had lapsed back into the habit but had, none the less, found courage and resolution enough to telephone his doctor for help. He was now 'completely cured', his counsel said. 'There is no reason why he should ever go back on to heroin again.'

Fraser's sentence also was deferred until the end of Keith Richard's trial. He, too, was remanded in custody and removed to a police cell, pending his and Jagger's departure to spend that night in prison. A brief period was allowed for each to confer with his solicitor. Keith, still on committal bail, had meanwhile driven at top speed back to West Wittering where Jagger had spent the previous night, to fetch him some clean clothes, a book (on Tibetan philosophy) and a 184-piece jigsaw puzzle.

Jagger and Robert Fraser were then each handcuffed to a prison officer, bundled rapidly into a grey police van with other remand prisoners and driven, through the crowd of distraught girls and craning camera-lenses, to begin the thirty-eight-mile journey to the Victorian prison at Lewes. It was a brutal measure to adopt with individuals who, despite their shocked bewilderment, were never other than peaceful and co-operative.

At Lewes Prison, the two were placed together in a room in the prison hospital. Jagger, as he later admitted, was 'deathly scared and in tears'. Before lights out – at an hour when a Rolling Stone customarily thought of getting up – two visitors were brought in to see him. One was Marianne Faithfull, bringing him sixty cigarettes, a draughts board, newspapers and fresh fruit. The other was Michael Cooper, carrying a miniature camera in the hope of photographing Jagger behind bars. A prison officer spotted the camera as he was leaving and confiscated the film inside.

Next morning, June 28, Jagger and Robert Fraser were awakened before seven, given a meagre breakfast, then handcuffed again for their return to Chichester. Some of the more sympathetic newspapermen were already asking whether the two really had to be led to and from court, manacled like murderers or psychopaths. A prison spokesman eventually replied it had been done because their guards 'had no instructions to do otherwise'.

At Chichester, Jagger and Fraser were put back into a cell under the courtroom, waiting to be brought up and sentenced if Keith Richard's trial should be concluded that day. Though uncomfortable and boring, their eight-hour wait was not devoid of comfort. Permission was given for a local hotelier to bring in their lunch – roast lamb for Jagger and, for Fraser, cold salmon salad. Both finished their meal with a dish of strawberries and cream.

Above them, Keith Richard now sat in the dock, wearing a black Beau Brummell suit and white polo-neck shirt, his well-worn, twenty-four-year-old face expressionless under a heaped black pompadour as ragged as if he, too, had spent the night on a prison bench. Now there was no tissuey rustling from the girls in the public gallery. The court was plunged into spellbound silence, broken only by the voice of Malcolm Morris QC, and the sound of frantic scribbling in the packed press bench. Even the dignified man from *The Times* could let none of this get away.

For the first time, the jury received a full account of the raid on Redlands, the discovery of eight men and 'a young woman' listening to pop music while watching television, and the 'strong, sweet, unusual smell' which the police had at once detected. '. . . In the drawing room where Richard was entertaining his guests, one of them had a large supply of cannabis resin,' Malcolm Morris continued. 'The behaviour of one of the guests may suggest she was under the influence of cannabis in a way that Richard could not fail to notice . . . You cannot have any doubt at all that he was permitting his house to be used for the purpose of smoking cannabis.'

The supplier of 'that large supply of cannabis resin' continued to have an apparently charmed life. 'He is a man not before the court, and, indeed, not now in the country,' Malcolm Morris told the jury. 'You are not concerned with the name or identity of anyone at that party other than Keith Richard.' Only after pressure from Michael Havers – and a little vernacular joke from Judge Block, who observed that the man had 'done a bunk' – was Acid King David Schneidermann's name finally heard in court. Even then, it was his surname only, and rendered phonetically in most reports as 'Snidermann'.

Resuming his major theme, Malcolm Morris told the jury they would hear from a Scotland Yard Drug Squad officer, Detective Inspector John Lynch, that the effect of smoking cannabis was tranquillity, happiness and 'a tendency to dispel inhibitions'.

'You may think it could have had exactly that effect on one of Richard's guests. This was the young lady sitting on the settee. All she was wearing was a light-coloured fur rug which, from time to time, she allowed to fall, disclosing her nude body. She was unperturbed and apparently enjoying the situation. Although she was taken upstairs, where her clothes were, to be searched, she returned wearing only the fur rug and, in the words of the woman detective looking after her, in merry mood – one apparently of vague unconcern.

'*We are not concerned*', continued the QC, 'with who that young lady was or may have been. But was she someone who had lost her inhibitions, and had she lost them because of smoking Indian hemp?'

One can only marvel at this attempt to condemn Keith Richard on a drugs charge by implying he had simultaneously been holding a sex orgy. In doing so, Malcolm Morris was handing the press an already die-stamped banner headline – one of those scraps of smutty innuendo which, once lodged in a million or so minds, make questions of guilt and innocence scarcely relevant. Not even the Christine Keeler case had given Fleet Street what Malcolm Morris QC gave it on June 28, 1967.

At the mention of 'nudity' there had been excitement enough among the journalists present. At the mention of 'a fur rug', there was something not far removed from collective orgasm.

No doubt could exist as to the nude girl's identity. Marianne Faithfull had been in court throughout the proceedings, sitting next to Allen Klein and Les Perrin. Though both sides in the case had agreed she should not be named, every newspaper could use her photograph in quite legal juxtaposition with its story of the raid, the rug-wrapped girl and her shameless attempts to arouse policemen in the course of their duty. Already, by some mysterious means, a rumour was travelling the length and breadth of England that, when the police entered Keith Richard's sitting room, they had interrupted an orgy of cunnilingus in which Jagger had been licking a Mars bar pushed into Marianne's vagina. The Mars bar was a detail of such sheer madness as to make the story believed, then and for ever after. No one needed any explanation of the line that appeared gnomically on *Private Eye* magazine's next front cover: 'A Mars bar fills that gap.'

Four police witnesses for the prosecution gave evidence to support the idea that, in addition to being high on cannabis, Marianne was also a shameless nymphomaniac. Woman Detective Constable Rosemary Slade, indeed, testified that when the search party arrived, 'Miss 'X' – as Marianne was futilely described – had been 'completely naked'. Woman Detective Constable Evelyn Fuller described her 'merry mood' and 'apparent unconcern' when taken upstairs to be searched, and how, once alone with Miss Fuller, she had 'deliberately let the rug fall'.

The rug itself made a dramatic appearance in Michael Havers's cross-examination of Detective Sergeant Stanley Cudmore, after Sergeant Cudmore's assertion that 'one could see she had nothing on underneath it.'

'Was it a large rug?' Havers enquired.

'Quite large,' Sergeant Cudmore said.

'Was it bigger than a fur coat?'

'Yes.'

'But it's a bedcover, isn't it?' Havers said. 'Six foot square. Here – take a look.' With the help of his junior counsel, the QC then stretched the brown and white mottled rug with its garish orange lining across the barristers' bench.

'It's enormous,' Michael Havers said. 'You can see – it's about eight and a half feet by five.'

Havers opened Keith's defence with an address to the jury, complaining bitterly of his opponent's smear tactics against a person who, being accused of no crime, had no chance to speak in her own defence. 'She remains technically anonymous, but the effect of all this is that she has been described as a drug-taking nymphomaniac. How would you [members of the jury] feel if, in another place, witnesses were going into the box and discussing your behaviour, and you could do nothing about it?

'Do you expect me to let that girl go into the witness box? I am not going to allow her to. I am not going to tear that blanket of anonymity aside and let the world laugh of scorn, as it will. This is a girl whose name has not yet been dragged into the mud. If I cannot call her into this court, I propose to call no one who was at that house.'

When the court adjourned for the afternoon. Keith was released on continuance of his £250 bail. Jagger and Fraser again handcuffed together and removed for a second night in custody. An agency photographer took what would become a celebrated picture of Jagger, dishevelled and scruffy, raising his and Fraser's joined arms to shield his face from flash bulbs. Society had got him where it wanted him at last – manacled, in an open tumbril, receiving the curses, boos and catcalls of the mob.

Next morning, it was time for Keith to go into the witness box. An almost audible shudder greeted this least prepossessing defendant, with his fancy clothes and the pale, sickly, wolfish face that seemed living testament to all the depraved goings-on the prosecution had described. The very last thing expected from such an apparently self-incriminating figure was articulateness and candour, and a wit which, several times, left even a cross-examining QC outmanoeuvred.

Michael Havers's first line of questioning was designed to show the jury how little direct control a Rolling Stone had over what went on around him – and how commensurately little responsibility he ought to bear for the behaviour of those in his retinue. This necessitated a brief history of the Stones, from Keith and Mick's first meeting at the age of six to the 'complete lack of privacy, and constant work' which, for all of them, had lasted since 1963.

'Do you need any sort of protection from your fans?' Havers asked.

'Oh yes,' Keith replied. 'I need an army.'

'And why do you need that protection?'

'I've been strangled,' Keith said, touching his neck reminiscently. 'They just get hold of your tie or scarf, and pull . . . My clothes have disappeared,' he went on, grinning apologetically as a rustle of laughter ran around the court.

'And in the course of your travels you have to go to parties and are always meeting people?'

'Yes, I meet *thousands* of people.'

This led neatly to the subject of Acid King David Schneidermann, whom Keith said he had met only twice, briefly, before Acid King David had been invited to Redlands. In any case, he added, the whole idea for a weekend party had been someone else's. Keith himself had only heard on the previous day that it was going ahead. The point was well made that if pop stars did not organize their own parties, they could hardly be expected to know everyone they subsequently found enjoying their hospitality.

At Michael Havers's prompting, Keith gave his account of what now sounded an altogether normal country weekend – the cars arriving late on Saturday, the bacon and egg supper, the next morning's late lie-in (excluding Acid King David's dispensation of LSD) and the afternoon drive, which had ended just before the drug squad's arrival. At that point, Keith said, he had been upstairs, bathing and changing, and had no idea what his guests were doing.

'Do you use incense in your house?'

'Sometimes.'

'Why?'

'Well, I picked up on it from fans who used to send me joss sticks . . . I quite like the smell of them.'

'Is there anything sinister in that?' Havers asked. 'Is it done to conceal the smell of cannabis?'

'No, sir,' Keith said firmly.

He was then shown the briar pipe which police analysis had proved to contain traces of cannabis resin. 'That came from Los Angeles,' he said. 'It was given to me.'

'By whom?'

'An American – a group's road manager.'

'On a trip like that, you could get a lot of stuff . . . a mountain of stuff,' Havers suggested.

'Yeah – always. When I get back to England, my suitcases are full up with rubbish.'

'Did you have any idea that anyone at your house was smoking cannabis that weekend?'

'No, sir.'

'Would you have allowed such a thing to happen?'

'No, sir.'

To counteract the manifestly good impression Keith had made so far, Malcolm Morris began his cross-examination with a well-tried device of British barristers when pitted against their social inferiors – the 'let me see if I've got this right' or 'let us establish if you are wholly or just partially cretinous' approach.

'You heard the opening address to this court by your counsel, did you not?'

'Yes, sir.'

'It was given on your instructions?'

'Yes, sir.'

'He [your counsel] spoke of various things and in the course of that opening speech made it quite clear that your defence was that Schneidermann had been planted in your weekend party as part of a wicked conspiracy by the *News of the World*. Is that part of your defence or not?'

'Yes it is, sir,' Keith replied.

'Is your defence that Schneidermann was planted by the *News of the World* in an attempt to get Mick Jagger convicted of smoking hashish? Is that the suggestion?'

'That is the suggestion,' Keith agreed.

'. . . so, if you are seriously suggesting that this was part of a plot, it is a curious plot in that nothing, in fact, was done to associate Jagger with Indian hemp.'

'He was associated with the whole raid, which is enough, I'm sure,' Keith answered.

'Is this what you are saying – and the jury will want to know – that, because the *News of the World* did not want to pay libel damages to Mick Jagger, it was arranged to have Indian hemp planted in your house?'

'Yes,' Keith said.

'There was, as we know,' Malcolm Morris proceeded, 'a young woman sitting on a settee, wearing only a fur rug. Would you agree that, in the ordinary course of events, you would expect a young woman to be embarrassed if she had nothing on but a fur rug in the presence of eight men, two of whom were hangers-on and another a Moroccan servant?'

'Not at all,' Keith replied.

'You regard that, do you, as quite normal?'

Here, finally, Keith let show a flicker of his contempt for the proceedings.

'We are not old men,' was his retort. 'We're not worried about petty morals.'

Judge Block's summing up, after the lunch recess, began with an irritated reference to the view, expressed four weeks earlier by Dick Taverne MP, that unrestricted reporting of Jagger and Richard's committal proceedings might have created prejudice in the jury's minds. 'That gentleman,' Judge Block observed, 'did not know the quality of a Sussex jury such as you are here now.' Since the quality of a Sussex jury is in general no different from that of a Surrey or Hampshire jury it can only be concluded that the judge was buttering up the jury, as judges very often do, to make it more receptive to his own view of the evidence. The peroration that followed contained several strong indications that Judge Block, in court usher phraseology, was 'summing up for a conviction'.

That much was clear enough in his direction to the jury to 'put out of your minds [i.e. do not in any circumstances overlook] any prejudice you may feel about the way Richard dresses, or his observations about petty morals . . . The issue you have to try is a comparatively simple one. You have to be satisfied that cannabis resin was being smoked in the house when the police went there, and you have to be satisfied that Richard knew of it.

'. . . You must exclude from your mind,' Judge Block continued, 'anything you may have read in the papers about two of the house party either admitting or being convicted of being in possession of certain drugs . . . Finally, I would ask you to disregard the evidence as to the lady who was alleged by the police to have been in some condition of undress, and not let that prejudice your minds in any way.'

With this amazing directive added as an afterthought to the hours of unforgettably lurid detail concerning 'the young lady' which Judge Block had not thought proper to curtail, the jury rose and filed from the courtroom. They were absent just a little more than one hour. At 3:45 p.m., the foreman rose and announced they had reached a unanimous verdict of guilty.

Amid gasps and cries of 'No!' from the girls in the gallery, Mick Jagger and Robert Fraser were put up into the dock and ranged next to Keith for sentencing.

'Keith Richards,' Judge Block began. 'The offence for which you have, very properly, been convicted carries a maximum sentence, imposed by Parliament, of up to ten years.' When the cries of horror from the gallery had abated, he continued:

'That is a view of the seriousness of the offence . . . As it is, you will go to prison for one year. You will also pay £500 towards the costs of the prosecution.'

He turned to Robert Fraser.

'Robert Hugh Fraser – you have pleaded guilty to possessing a highly dangerous and harmful drug . . . You will go to prison for six months. You will also pay £200 towards the costs of the prosecution.'

Lastly, he turned to Mick Jagger.

'Michael Philip Jagger – you have been found guilty of possessing a potentially dangerous and harmful drug . . . You will go to prison for three months. You will pay £200 towards the costs of the prosecution.'

Jagger, as the words hit him, crumpled up and clutched his forehead with his hand. Keith remained, white-faced and stiff-backed, staring in front of him. Robert Fraser blew out his cheeks as if in a blast of icy air. As they left the dock together, amid an uproar of shouts and weeping from the gallery, Jagger dissolved into tears.

News of Judge Block's justice had already reached the crowd outside the court building. As the three were led downstairs, they could already hear chants of 'Shame!' and 'Let them go!'

At the court building's front entrance, a crowd of 600 surged against the big metal gates, struggling for the best view of the two Stones when they were brought out to their prison van. A shout went up as Keith Richard's blue Bentley appeared, carrying Tom Keylock and Marianne Faithfull. Marianne, too, was crying as Keylock ushered her inside for a fifteen-minute meeting with Jagger before he left to begin his sentence.

Half an hour later, while a decoy van fought to get through the spectators outside the rear gate, Jagger, Richard and Fraser were hurried through the front vestibule and into a police squad car. Just outside Chichester, they were transferred to a police van with a seven-man crew. The van then headed for London – or seemed to as far as its passengers could tell. They were, they realized, in the grip of arrangements more inflexibly certain than the best-organized tour schedule.

The first stop was Brixton Prison where, it had been decided, Mick Jagger would serve his sentence well separated from his colleagues in crime. Keith Richard and Robert Fraser, handcuffed together, deduced they were bound for a common destination. Forty minutes later, the van stopped again, at the end of a long, dreary cul-de-sac, before the Gothic main gate of Wormwood Scrubs.

The events of the next twenty-four hours raise the interesting possibility that authority's main purpose in bagging the two Stones was to inflict ritual bathing, delousing and barbering, and then leave them to the mercy of prisoners who would know even better than Judge Leslie Block the proper treatment for prissy and perverted pop stars.

If that was the idea, it failed most miserably. Though Jagger and Richard both underwent full induction as prisoners, exchanging their Carnaby clothes for regulation blue denim overalls and black shoes, no attempt was made to cut their hair or otherwise abuse them. Jagger, at Brixton, was taken to a single cell which – he afterwards said – 'wasn't so much worse than a hotel room in Minnesota'. At 'The Scrubs', as Keith – now prisoner number 7855 – was escorted to his cell, other prisoners shouted out 'Hard luck mate,' threw him cigarettes – and asked him if he wanted any hash.

Directly after the sentences were pronounced, Michael Havers had asked for, and been granted, a certificate of leave for Jagger and Richard to appeal against both their convictions and sentences. The matter was set down for preliminary hearing in the Court of Appeal on the very next day, June 30. Since the full appeal, involving transcripts of the Chichester trail, could not be made ready before the current legal term ended, it was obvious that Jagger and Richard must languish in prison for the next two months or be granted bail. Before going into court next afternoon, Michael Havers was seen by the prosecution counsel, Malcolm Morris, and told that Morris had 'direct instructions' not to oppose his application for bail.

The intervening night had seen demonstrations of protest by Rolling Stones fans that, for once, seemed devoted to a purpose other than simple mayhem. In Piccadilly Circus, 300 teenagers in kaftans and bells held an all-night vigil around the Eros statue. Others, more pertinently, collected in Bouverie Street to shout insults at the *News of the World*. In clubs and discotheques up and down Britain, disc jockeys called for symbolic moments of silence, or played non-stop Stones records. In New York, when the news came through, groups of American hippies mounted angry pickets outside the British Consulate. It was reported that other British pop groups had volunteered to play in a gigantic 'free-the-Stones' concert whose proceeds would be spent on an avalanche of flowers with which to engulf Judge Block. The most spontaneously generous demonstration of professional solidarity came from The Who – a cover version of It's All Over Now and Under My Thumb, recorded in a morning and put out over pirate radio that same afternoon, with a large press announcement that, until Jagger and Richard were released, The Who would do everything possible to keep their work before the public.

Nor was the protest confined to the sphere of pop only. Letters to *The Times* – from playwright John Osborne among others – deplored the harshness of the sentences and the many inconsistencies, to put it no worse, which had marked the trial. A newspaper interview with Christopher Gibbs did something to counteract the rampaging rumour about sex orgies with Mars bars. It carried much weight that this hitherto undisclosed Redlands guest, who swore Keith's party had been 'thoroughly decorous', was an old Etonian and a nephew of the Governor of Rhodesia.

On June 30, Michael Havers QC rose to his feet in the Court of Appeal to request the bail for Mick Jagger and Keith Richard that some inscrutable mechanism within the British establishment had already decided should be given. During the twenty-five-minute hearing, Havers barely needed to develop his argument that Mick Jagger was no drug addict or pusher, that he had verbal permission from a doctor to possess amphetamines, and that insufficient and unfair evidence had been used to convict Keith Richard of allowing his house to be used for cannabis-smoking. Lord Justice Diplock, speaking for his two fellow appeal judges, granted each bail of £5,000, with further sureties totalling £2,000 each, until their full appeal hearing when the new law term opened in September. The court, however, refused Havers's request that Jagger and Richard should be allowed to leave Britain in the meantime, and ordered them to surrender their passports.

Robert Fraser's counsel, William Denny, asked for Fraser to receive bail pending his appeal against sentence. Mr Denny argued that Fraser was no longer a heroin addict and, in addiction, felt 'a sense of grievance' that his case had been tried under the same unnatural spotlight as the two Stones'. His application for bail was refused, but with a proviso that his appeal should be squeezed in before the end of the current law term.

By 4:30 p.m., Mick Jagger was free. He sat alone in the back of Keith's Bentley, smiling wanly at a group of schoolgirls who, somehow, had collected outside Brixton Prison to see Tom Keylock drive him away. At 5:10, the Bentley arrived at Wormwood Scrubs to pick up Keith. Keylock then drove straight to a

Fleet Street pub, the Feathers, where Les Perrin had convened a rush press conference. Both Stones looked weary, crumpled, but impressively composed. Jagger told reporters he had spent some of his time in Brixton 'writing poetry'. Asked how he had been treated, he said, 'Everyone was very kind and helpful.' Keith – who had, at one point, launched into furious kicking of his cell door – confined himself to denying the Stones had ever contemplated a break-up. Jagger drank a vodka and lime, and Keith a whisky and ginger ale, for which the pub landlord refused to accept any payment.

Next morning, Jagger sat in bed once more beside Marianne, with every national newspaper spread round him on the coverlet. Fleet Street had performed a complete volte-face, greeting his liberation with almost audible church bells and cannon fire. Even the Beatles had never drawn so comprehensive a crop of banner headlines and editorial comment. Among the latter was an item whose unlikely source – and still more unlikely author – added all the more weight to words that, with hindsight, fix the precise moment when everyone stopped going barmy.

William Rees-Mogg, until that day, had seemed to have little in common with his great predecessors as editor of *The Times*. He was a man of schoolmasterly mien, slightly bookish and dusty, whose avowed passions were for the classics and Somerset, and who generally stayed remote from mundane editorial matters, like hard news.

William Rees-Mogg was at the furthest possible extreme from Mick Jagger, the Rolling Stones, pop music or teenagers. His instincts, none the less, proved to be those of a courageous as well as deeply moral-minded journalist. On Saturday, July 1, *The Times*'s first leader was given over entirely to the Jagger case. Rees-Mogg had written it himself, headlining it – as perhaps only Rees-Mogg would – with a quotation from William Blake: WHO BREAKS A BUTTERFLY ON A WHEEL.

'. . . Judge Block directed the jury that the approval of a doctor was not a defence in law to the charge of possessing drugs without a prescription, and the jury convicted. Mr Jagger was not charged with complicity in any other drug offence that occurred in the same house. They were separate cases, and no evidence was produced to suggest that he knew that Mr Fraser had heroin tablets or that the vanishing Mr Sneidermann [sic] had cannabis resin. It is indeed no offence to be in the same building or the same company as people possessing or even using drugs, nor could it reasonably be made an offence . . .

'One has to ask, therefore, how it is that this technical offence, divorced as it must be from other people's offences, was thought to deserve the penalty of imprisonment. In the courts at large it is most uncommon for imprisonment to be imposed on first offenders where the drugs are not major drugs of addiction and there is no question of drug traffic. The normal penalty is probation, and the purpose of probation is to encourage the offender to develop his career and to avoid the drug risks in future. It is surprising, therefore, that Judge Block should have decided to sentence Mr Jagger to imprisonment, and particularly surprising as Mr Jagger's is about as mild a drug case as can ever have been brought before the Courts.

'It would be wrong to speculate on the judge's reasons, which we do not know. It is, however, possible to consider the public reaction. There are many people who take a primitive view of the matter. They consider that Mr Jagger has "got what was coming to him". They resent the anarchic quality of the Rolling Stones' performances, dislike their songs, dislike their influence on teenagers and broadly suspect them of decadence.

'As a sociological concern this may be reasonable enough, and at an emotional level it is very understandable, but it has nothing at all to do with the case. One has to ask a different question: has Mr Jagger received the same treatment as he would have received if he had not been a famous figure, with all the criticism and resentment his celebrity has aroused. If a promising undergraduate had come back from a summer visit to Italy with four pep pills in his pocket, would it have been thought right to ruin his career by sending him to prison for three months? Would it also have been thought necessary to display him handcuffed to the public?

'There are cases in which a single figure becomes the focus for public concern about some aspects of public morality. The Stephen Ward case, with its dubious evidence and questionable verdict, was one of them, and that verdict killed Stephen Ward. There are elements of the same emotions in the reactions to this case. If we are going to make any case a symbol of the conflict between the sound traditional values of Britain and the new hedonism, then we must be sure that the sound traditional values include those of tolerance and equity. It should be the particular quality of British justice to ensure that Mr Jagger is treated exactly the same as anyone else, no better and no worse. There must remain a suspicion in this case that Mr Jagger received a more severe sentence than would have been thought proper for any purely anonymous young man.'

In commenting on a case which still had to go to appeal, William Rees-Mogg was technically in contempt of court and, as such, liable to both a heavy fine and imprisonment. That no attempt was made to prosecute, or even admonish, him testifies, not only to the manifest humanity and moral soundness of his editorial but also the new official line that Jagger was now to be let off the hook. The *Sunday Times*, next day, made the same points, and ran the same risk, in a quietly outraged piece by Hugo Young, mentioning the ironic fact that new drug legislation even now before Parliament would transfer the prescribing of hard drugs from private doctors to community treatment centres. Jagger, wrote Hugo Young, had been convicted 'to appease the lust for social revenge'.

That same day, the *News of the World* published a front page editorial, rebutting the 'monstrous' charge that they had planted Acid King David Schneidermann in the Redlands party to kill off Mick Jagger's libel action: 'It was a charge made without a shred of evidence to support it . . . It was a charge made within the privilege of a court of law . . . which denied us the opportunity of answering back at the time . . . These outrageous allegations are of course totally unfounded. We have had no connection whatsoever with Mr Schneidermann directly or indirectly, before, during or after this case.' The paper admitted that it had tipped off the police about Keith's house party and said that the information had come from a reader. The allegations of following and spying on Mick Jagger, and that they had done this to influence the libel, were also totally untrue.

The heavy cash recognizances extracted from Jagger and Richard had presupposed their remaining on bail until at least early September. But on July 4, Michael Havers received news which indicated further amends were being offered for their treatment at Chichester. The Lord Chief Justice, Lord Parker, had personally intervened to bring their two appeal hearings forward to the last day of the present law term, July 31.

That summer's climactic moment of pinching oneself, and finding oneself still awake, had its origins in a twenty-three-year-old television researcher named John Birt, recently recruited to Granada TV's *World In Action* programme, one day to become Director-General of the BBC. A Merseysider by birth and allegiance, Birt had previously felt no special love for the Stones or their music. He none the less shared the outrage of all pop fans at what was now revealed as a concerted attack, through the Stones, by one generation on another. The subject, in Birt's view, was one which should concern a hard-nosed investigative programme like *World In Action*. His executive producer, David Plowright, agreed, and Birt, for his first major TV documentary project, was assigned to set up a half-hour special about drugs, the establishment and Mick Jagger.

Whatever form the programme took, it clearly could not be broadcast until after the hearing of Jagger's and Richard's appeals on July 31. 'Funnily enough,' Birt remembers, 'it never entered our heads that the appeal would be anything but successful. Our whole format was predicated on the idea that Jagger *must* get off.' Birt's confidence remained even after a poll conducted among that larger multitude which derived its views from such papers as the *News of the World*, revealed that 46 per cent felt Mick Jagger had deserved his prison sentence.

The format approved by Birt's editors was hazardously simple – a 'live' television confrontation between Jagger, fresh from the Appeal Court, and members of the establishment which had lately been so intent on crucifying him: a summit-conference, as it were, between the generations in conflict. Birt got in touch with the Stones' office and, after the usual ritual runaround, managed to see Jagger and put the idea to him. Jagger agreed in principle, but contact was then broken while the Stones worked on the new album that Judge Block had all but terminated. At last, in desperation, Birt managed to telephone Jagger at home. Jagger answered the phone himself and, without further prevarication, agreed to be the subject of a *World In Action* special on July 31.

To preside over the encounter, it seemed natural to choose William Rees-Mogg, both for his position as editor of *The Times*, and his personal initiative in restoring moral perspective to the Jagger case. To speak for the Church, Granada approached Dr Mervyn Stockwood, the energetic and outspoken Bishop of Woolwich. To speak for Parliament – in the absence of any incumbent Minister – it procured Lord Stow Hill, who, as Sir

Frank Soskice, had been Home Secretary in the first Wilson Government. Rees-Mogg, a devout Catholic, agreed to take part on condition a member of his faith appeared also. A Jesuit priest, Father Thomas Corbishley, was found to restore the ecumenical balance.

July 31 was yet another day of cloudlessly brilliant weather. At dawn, a queue of girls had already begun to form outside the High Court in Fleet Street, hoping for admittance to the tiny chamber personally presided over by Britain's Lord Chief Justice. The drowsy press buildings echoed to the racket of a portable record player on which someone was playing appropriate Stones songs like Mercy Mercy and It's All Over Now.

When Jagger and Richard arrived, disembarking from the same black Austin Princess limousine, they were cheered into the court precincts like royal champions. 'How does it feel to be free?' somebody shouted at Jagger. 'Lovely,' he shouted back. Wearing the same olive green double-breasted jacket he had put on for his trial, Jagger was then ushered alone into the Lord Chief Justice's court. Keith had contracted a dose of chicken pox, and received permission to wait in a separate room for fear of spreading the infection to his judges.

The mirage-like quality which the day had already assumed made it seem almost natural that the Lord Chief Justice of England, sitting in awesome conclave with two fellow Appeal judges, should appear as mild-mannered, amiable and reasonable as the little local judge had appeared hostile and ill-disposed. 'He was such a nice, kind man,' John Birt remembers. Birt was in court with his Granada TV team, still not altogether certain that *World In Action* would have a programme to put out that night.

Two hours later, as Keith waited offstage, trying hard not to scratch his spots, Lord Chief Justice Parker squashed both his conviction and his sentence. The Appeal Court ruled that Judge Block had 'erred' in his summing-up to the Chichester jury by not emphasizing how flimsy was the evidence that 'Miss X' had been smoking cannabis. All three Appeal judges agreed that, had they tried the case they would have disallowed that whole lurid section of the prosecution's evidence. Keith Richard, therefore, could not possibly be convicted, on the evidence, of 'knowingly permitting' what the prosecution had failed to prove ever happened in the first place.

Still louder gasps of delight greeted Lord Chief Justice Parker's pronouncement on the Jagger case. The court upheld Jagger's conviction, since the amphetamines clearly came within Parliament's definition of unlawful drugs. His prison sentence, however, was quashed, and a one-year conditional discharge substituted. 'That means,' Lord Parker told him, 'you will have to be of good behaviour for twelve months . . . If in that time you do commit another offence, you will not only be punished for that offence but brought back and punished for this one also.'

Jagger bowed his head as the Lord Chief Justice continued: 'You are, whether you like it or not, the idol of a large number of the young in this country. Being in that position, you have very grave responsibilities. If you do come to be punished, it is only natural that those responsibilities should carry higher penalties.'

From the High Court, Jagger was driven to a press conference at Granada TV's headquarters in Golden Square. He arrived in fresh clothes, symbolizing his release from courtroom formality – mauve watered-silk trousers, a cream-coloured smock edged with maroon and green embroidery. With him was Marianne Faithfull, wearing the shortest mini-skirt most of the assembled press had ever seen.

The press conference – filmed by *World In Action* as a prelude to its later, exclusive footage – shows Jagger, flanked by Ian Stewart and Les Perrin, very far from his usual cool and sardonic self. 'He'd been given a lot of Valium beforehand,' Marianne says. 'And he still seemed very scared. You got the feeling he only had to say one word out of place and he'd have been taken straight back to Brixton Prison.'

All questions relating to his drug offence, or drugs in general, have obviously been vetoed in advance by Les Perrin, though Jagger, in his slightly bewildered state, seems willing to answer almost anything. The camera settles on an elderly journalist with sideburns like white ear-muffs. 'Do you think you *do* have a responsibility to the young in this country, as Lord Parker said?' Jagger shakes his shaggy head as if to clear it. 'I've been *given* that responsibility . . . pushed into the limelight. I don't try to impose my views on people. I don't propagate religious views, such as some pop stars do. I don't propagate drug views, such as some pop stars do . . .' 'Do you resent the way you've been treated?' another voice asks. Here, Les Perrin interrupts yet again. 'Look – I'm going to have to cut this. We agreed in advance what was on and what wasn't . . .'

The conference over, Jagger and Marianne, accompanied by John Birt, were put into a white Jaguar with a professional stunt driver behind the wheel, and driven at speed across the Thames to the helicopter port at Battersea. A hired helicopter then lifted them away, down river to the place selected by *World In Action* for Jagger's summit-meeting with the establishment. Birt has two recollections of the journey. One is the shimmering softness of London, spread out below them as they flew eastward. The other is his own acute embarrassment, wedged on the same small seat as Jagger and Marianne when they began to kiss and touch each other passionately.

Their destination, successfully kept secret from all press and television rivals, was a Georgian country house owned by the Lord Lieutenant of Essex, Sir John Ruggles-Brise. Jagger's one stipulation – prompted, no doubt, by recent indoor experiences – was that the debate should take place in the open air. Accordingly, *World in Action* cameras were already set up facing a rustic seat at the end of the conservatory. While the other participants were chauffeured down from London, Mick and Marianne were taken into the house and shown to a bedroom to 'rest'.

'We thought they'd have at least an hour to themselves before we started filming,' John Birt says. 'Then, all of a sudden, I was told Jagger was needed right away. I had to go up and knock on the bedroom door and call him. There was a long silence, when it was very obvious what I was interrupting. Then Jagger's voice said "Okay." '

It looked, in William Rees-Mogg's words, like something Max Beerbohm might have drawn. Certainly, an element of some old-fashioned allegorical cartoon was present in the outdoor scene, the rustic bench, the four distinguished men from politics, journalism and the Church, pooling their collective intellect to communicate with the alien being in their midst. The fact that all four establishment members were hot and crumpled while Jagger, in his open-neck smock, seemed cool and comfortable, only heightened the sense of elderly emissaries, fidgeting before some boy potentate. On a level of pure symbolism – disregarding the fact it had been deliberately set up for the TV cameras – this was Mick Jagger's moment of supreme triumph. The society which had mocked, abused and finally tried to destroy him, now cast itself down before him with all the apologetic reverence due to a misjudged Messiah. The editor, the peer, the bishop and the Jesuit earnestly entreated him to reveal 'what the young people in this country *really* think'.

'Er – Mick,' William Rees-Mogg began with his somewhat pious lisp. 'We know this had been a very difficult day for you . . . Perhaps I could begin by asking you this. You are often taken as a symbol of – ah – rebellion. Do you – ah – feel that society has a great deal in it today that ought to be rebelled against?'

The grainy black and white of the old telerecording is as flattering to Jagger as a Beaton or Bailey lens. His face is calm and simplified to the needs of the occasion, the great lips deflated to a gentle smile, the eyes alert and, somehow, tolerant.

'I didn't think my knowledge was enough to start pontificating on the subject. I didn't ever set myself up as a leader in society. It's society that's pushed one into that position.'

Lord Stow Hill, the former Home Secretary, takes up the questioning.

'In your approach to music – rhythm and so on – what is the way in which you yourself would wish to be understood?'

'For my music,' Jagger replies. 'Just for playing music. That's what I want to do. And, like anyone else, to have as good a time as possible.'

So it continues in the blurred, unreal twilight, the bishop and Jesuit putting their points in turn, and the pop star replying, quietly, lucidly, while a breeze ruffles the curls around his face. Jagger, we realize, has reached a consummation of his talent for speaking with all voices simultaneously. On one level, he seems to be speaking for disaffected youth, of society's 'corruption', of media bias and how the law protects only majorities. Yet he is speaking for the establishment also, in the establishment's own comforting sociological formulae. 'Our parents went through two world wars and a depression. We've had none of that . . . I'm sure you do your best. It may be, for *your* generation . . .' Debating for its own sake clearly becomes more and more enjoyable. 'You've just given a textbook definition of the English Constitution,' he tells Lord Stow Hill. 'It really doesn't work that way at all.'

'. . . But wouldn't you say that some drugs – heroin for example – represent a crime against society?'

'It's a crime against a law,' Jagger says. 'I can't see it's any more a crime against society than jumping out of a window.'

'But surely,' Stow Hill persists, 'a real crime against society ought to be punished to suit the case.'

'People should be punished for crimes,' Jagger says. 'Not for the *fears* of society, which may be groundless.' Game, set and match to the infinitely subtle being who has made himself living proof of his own point.

★

A few weeks later, the *News of the World* published a small paragraph – the kind written by lawyers rather than journalists – announcing that Mick Jagger's libel action against the paper had been dropped. No more was ever heard of Acid King David Schneidermann, alias English, the only person able to prove whether he was, indeed, an LSD wizard, a CIA agent or – as now seems most likely – the purest hallucination of that unreal summer when sunshine, joss sticks and tinkling Eastern bells co-existed so strangely with journalistic grubbiness, official vindictiveness and temporary insanily on the part of the British legal system.

Although Jagger and Richard were free, there could be no doubt as to the overall winner. As on many previous occasions, the *News of the World* had proved what a hopeless task it was for any individual to take on a powerful and unscrupulous Fleet Street paper, however wealthy and well represented they might be, however strong their case might appear. Until now, pop groups and their world had been largely beneath the notice of Fleet Street. The Rolling Stones case revealed what huge fascination as well as hatred such people arouse in the world beyond mere teenagerdom, and also how gratifyingly inept and irresolute they were in rebutting the grossest smears and exaggerations. For twenty years afterwards, rock musicians would allow virtually anything to be printed about them rather than repeat Mick Jagger's mistake. In 1987, when Elton John began proceedings against the *Sun*, which ultimately would win him £1 million in out-of-court damages, the friend who counselled him most urgently to forget the whole thing was Jagger.

With Mick and Keith's chum Robert Fraser, the 1967 judiciary was on surer ground. All the testimonials as to Fraser's character and breeding could not mitigate the seriousness of possessing heroin. His appeal against his six-month sentence was dismissed and he returned to Wormwood Scrubs as prisoner number 7854. With remission, he served four months, working mainly in the prison kitchen. The two liberated Stones felt understandable guilt for having landed their friend so literally in the soup. Both wrote Fraser loving and supportive letters while he was banged up, Keith signing off with his own prisoner number, 'love from 7855'.

Fraser died (of AIDS) in 1986, having never quite recovered from his crushing by the Stones. Fittingly, the art crusader lives on in one of the Sixties' defining images, Richard Hamilton's *Swingeing London*, now owned by London's Tate Gallery and reproduced in dozens of books and countless prints and postcards. Hamilton's painting of a snatched press photograph freezes the moment when Fraser and Jagger were driven off to jail, handcuffed together. Through the open car door, the pop star and the old Etonian cower back, their manacled hands raised to shield their faces from exploding flash bulbs. The era of so-called love and peace was to receive no more bitter salute.

PART THREE

Ten

'Sing this all together – see what happens'

The man with whom Marianne Faithfull began living at the end of 1966 might easily have exchanged his flowered shirts and Cecil Gee jackets for the frock coat and heavy watch-chain of the Victorian paterfamilias. Social revolution might be going on at every level, but it had yet to disturb the age-old idea of male superiority and the role of women as objects for decorative and domestic use. Boy pop stars almost all came from the class whose men still called themselves masters in their own homes. In the aristocracy of new-found wealth and money, each twenty-three-year-old was an encrusted male chauvinist, demanding total female subservience, total fidelity (which need not be reciprocated), and the silently efficient management of meals and servants.

There were times, in their early days together, when Jagger goaded Marianne to such despair, she would simply bolt from their Harley House flat. 'Somehow, I always used to grab up the same things – a five-pound note and a lump of hash. I really did try to run away several times. But Mick would always catch up with me on the stairs and bring me back again.'

As traumatic as the Redlands drug bust was, it had a cementing effect on that early erratic relationship. It allowed Marianne to discover the Jagger whose innate chivalry put her career before his own and tried, in vain, to prevent her reputation from being dragged through the gutter. It allowed her to see how Jagger's outward, disdainful cool masked an inward need for domestic stability and happiness, and how, divorced from his audience and courtiers, he was the most normal and natural of people. She had also discovered, visiting him on that first traumatic evening in Lewes Prison, how instantly and helplessly he could dissolve into tears.

There were those, of course, who whispered that Jagger's real passion was for the social cachet Marianne conferred – that he was chuffed beyond words to be living with the daughter of a real baroness. 'You could see it on Mick's face every time they were at a party together,' Donald Cammell said. 'It was pure possession. "Look what I've got, isn't it fantastic!"'

The end of the drug case was the start of a new life together, in the house that Jagger had eventually chosen. Deciding he could not bury himself in the country like Keith, Bill and Charlie, he had opted, instead, for one of Chelsea's most desirable locations, paying £40,000 for number 48 Cheyne Walk, by the Thames near Albert Bridge. The house was of the tall, narrow, asymmetrically elegant Queen Anne type, modestly squeezed in along the 'Walk's' many more showy and forbidding residences.

Nicholas, Marianne's three-year-old son by John Dunbar, would live with them at Cheyne Walk, Jagger insisted. He had, from the beginning, shown a fatherly fondness for Nicholas, and was determined to give the little boy as stable and secure a home as possible. 'Mick always thought it was terrible that John Lennon would never let Cynthia have a nanny for their son, Julian,' Marianne says. 'In fact, he could do everything for Nicholas that a nanny could – but he still insisted we had to have one. He interviewed all the applications himself. You'd have thought he'd been dealing with servants all his life.'

Christopher Gibbs designed the interior of the house and

supplied tasteful – and very costly – antique furniture from his Chelsea shop. Marianne made additional purchases, sometimes on a scale more suited to her Sacher Masoch ancestors' salons in Vienna. For one sumptuous crystal chandelier she paid £6,000 – a sum which Jagger, under normal circumstances, would have parted with only in direst agony. 'Look at that!' he kept saying to their first visitors, staring upwards. 'Six thousand quid for a fuckin' *light*!'

It was only when they flew into Heathrow airport together from Ireland, and were unable to find a taxi-driver in the entire rank willing to drive them to Chelsea, that Marianne realized the extent of their joint notoriety. Though the establishment might have pardoned Jagger his drug offence, the public at large continued to thrill with voyeuristic relish at stories of sex orgies and misplaced Mars bars. For Marianne, the chaste creature who had sung As Tears Go By and made charity appeals on Radio Caroline, living out of wedlock with the infamous Jagger was a fall from grace. 'I know that, even to this day, people in Britain bear me a grudge. They think I let them down in some way – that they put their trust in me, and I betrayed them.'

Notorious they might be – but fashionable, too, in a way that Jagger on his own could never quite become. 'Mick prided himself on being so cool, but he realized he'd got nothing on the *real* upper class for coolness,' Marianne says. 'The cool they had was centuries old. They were the most restful people to be with because nothing we did ever seemed to shock them. Especially the older ones, like Tom Driberg or Diana Cooper. Everything we were doing they'd seen before, in the Twenties. "Cocaine!" they'd say. "My dear, I was at dinner parties in the Twenties when every silver salt cellar was *full* of cocaine!"'

By far the most revealing portrait of Mick and Marianne together at Cheyne Walk is a profile written for the *Sunday Telegraph* magazine by Gina Richardson, a gifted young journalist who died tragically soon afterwards in a road accident. She describes the elegant house shut in at midday by heavy drapes; the carpet, tapestries and smouldering joss sticks, and the two central figures whose doll-like smallness give them 'the air of children left in charge while grown-ups are away'. She confesses to finding Jagger physically mesmeric, but feels the effect is rather spoiled by his habit of slopping round the house in slip-on mules, 'like a housewife'.

From Richardson we learn that Marianne has taken Mick's cultural education in hand, with visits to the theatre, opera and, especially, the ballet. He was always saying how much he wished he could have been Nureyev. The most lasting impression of all was produced by the Royal Ballet's *Paradise Lost*, in which the principal dancers appeared through an outsize pair of lips, uncannily like Jagger's own. 'Mick thought the set, by Kenneth Macmillan, was absolutely fantastic,' Marianne says. 'It was like seeing himself there on the stage.' Almost the same design would turn up, five years later, as the logo of the Rolling Stones' own record label.

He had always been a glutton for books. Nowadays, in the prevailing fashion, his reading tended towards the philosophical, the spiritual and mystical. He would send regular orders to his friend Miles at the Indica Bookshop, for such required underground classics as *The Secret of the Golden Bough* or Charles Henry Fort's *Book of the Damned*. He was particularly interested, Miles remembers, in books about fairies, goblins and elves. Like every other pop celebrity that summer, he and Marianne based their whole lives on astrological data, and used the Chinese *I Ching Book of Changes* to make even quite mundane decisions, casting the hexagram for reference points within the volume which – its hippy devotees said raptly – had baffled even the intelligence of Confucius.

Both of them were swept up in the Beatles' brief flirtation with Transcendental Meditation and its founding guru, the Maharishi Mahesh Yogi. On August bank holiday weekend,

1967, Mick and Marianne joined the Beatles' famous pilgrimage with the Maharishi to undergo initiation at a teacher training college in Bangor, North Wales. They did so against the advice of better informed underground figures like Miles, who had heard from friends in India that the Maharishi might be a little less than divine. The weekend was cut short, however. On bank holiday Monday, news came that the Beatles' manager, Brian Epstein, had been found dead of a barbiturates overdose in London.

Britain's two pre-eminent pop groups, though still rivals in public were closer friends than ever in private. Hippydom had much to do with it: in kaftans and beads, the Beatles seemed no longer such naive provincials, the Stones no longer such metropolitan sophisticates. Now they were brothers, with a common enemy. The viciousness with which Mick and Keith had been prosecuted was a portent of times when even Beatles would lose their talismanic charm and be busted like anybody else. The Beatles and Brian Epstein had joined Graham Greene, John Osborne, David Hockney and other creative heavyweights in writing to *The Times*, calling for the legalisation of marijuana and, by implication, protesting against the two Stones' punishment.

Ferocious Top Twenty competitors as the Beatles and Stones remained, they nowadays even helped one another secretly in the record-studio. Mick had been present with Marianne at the indoor carnival that culminated in John Lennon's *Sgt. Pepper* masterpiece, A Day In the Life, and had joined in the background chorus on All You Need Is Love. In August, Lennon and McCartney lent their voices anonymously to We Love You, the Stones single whose title was Mick and Keith's ironic afterword to Chief Inspector Gordon Dineley, Malcolm Morris QC, Judge Block and the *News of the World*.

The Beatles' growing discontent with Brian Epstein had, to a large extent, stemmed from the seemingly more effective performance of the Stones' manager, Allen Klein. In 1965, indeed,

Paul McCartney had proposed employing Klein in a consultative capacity, to maul EMI Records on the Beatles' behalf as he had mauled Decca for the Stones. Though Brian Epstein successfully fought off that scheme, he was never able fully to recapture his protégés' confidence. They had heard too many stories from Mick Jagger about the miracles Klein could do.

For a brief time after Epstein's death, serious discussions took place between the Beatles and Stones about some kind of joint investment in a studio and management office, both to be run by the Beatles' aide, Peter Brown. The latter idea, for some reason, caused Klein acute heartburn, and he flew to London instantly to warn Brown off. On the same visit, he made yet another clumsy lunge at his true heart's desire, turning to Brian Epstein's brother Clive and growling, 'How much d'ya want for the Beatles?'

Merger discussions went as far as finding a site for the prospective studio – a disused brewery in Camden Town, next to Regent's Park Canal. The Beatles, abetted by their electronics wizard 'Magic' Alex Mardas, had all kinds of airy-fairy plans. 'We'll need a hotel as well,' Paul McCartney said. '. . . So that the groups will have somewhere to stay when they're recording. And we'll build a heliport, so that foreign groups can land at Heathrow and be brought straight here . . .' When practical Jagger asked what it would all cost, John Lennon looked at him in surprise. 'Oh – *we* won't pay for it,' he said. 'We'll get someone else to pay for it . . . Like that computer,' he said, turning to McCartney. 'Whatever *did* happen to that computer they gave us?'

'I think it's still in Ringo's garage,' McCartney said vaguely.

For Jagger, this entente with the Beatles was not without ulterior purpose. His conversion to flower power made him hanker to turn the Rolling Stones into a psychedelic band such as the Beatles had effortlessly become. The Stones' long delay in finishing their album in progress stemmed mainly from Jagger's insistence that it must touch all the same mystical chords as *Sgt. Pepper*.

It was an obsession which led the Stones rapidly to their artistic nadir. We Love You is a single that loses all ironic point in its feeble attempt to echo the Beatles' summer anthem All You Need Is Love. Even the cell-door that slams midway in the song seems like a direct crib from the coffin lid crashing down on the final chord of A Day In the Life.

To promote their new single, the Stones borrowed another device pioneered by the Beatles – a short film sequence whose screening on BBC-TV's *Top of the Pops* show saved the musicians themselves the bother of appearing. The film employed even heavier-handed irony, featuring Mick Jagger as the persecuted Oscar Wilde, with Marianne as Lord Alfred Douglas and Keith Richard as a highly unlikely Marquess of Queensberry. Predictably, *Top of the Pops* refused to screen it.

To be fair, no record album ever has suffered the handicap of having its three main musicians variously on trial and in prison, nor involved simultaneous internecine strife between musicians and manager, nor had to contend with the thousand-and-one incidental conflicts and vexations which beset the Stones during their ten-month labour to produce music expressing love, peace and flower-garlanded happiness. That any finished album at all emerged seems miraculous. As with an amateur dramatic production in which actors forget their lines, the scenery falls down and the producer has a heart attack, one must try to focus on the positive aspects.

The Stones themselves to this day regard *Their Satanic Majesties Request* as the lowest of low points in their career. 'It was one of the three times we came really close to splitting up,' Bill Wyman says. Though Keith likes the album better than he once did, it still mainly evokes indecision, compromise and almost terminal boredom. 'It ended up as a real patchwork. Half of it was "Let's give people what we think they want." The other half was "Let's get out of here as quickly as possible."'

Sgt. Pepper was the all-powerful, ultimately suffocating influence. The Beatles had covered their retreat from concert performance with a studio show whose myriad technical effects only heightened the atmosphere of live circus or vaudeville. The Stones' – at least Mick Jagger's – intention was the same, touched with some native belligerence, of course, in place of Beatle whimsy, but having no greater overall ambition than to muscle in on their friends' enchanted island.

So Mick and Keith, when they were not in court or detained at Her Majesty's pleasure, cudgelled their brains for incandescent imagery and riffs that would have the mesmeric power of Hindu mantras; with half an eye still lingering on Maharishi Mahesh Yogi, Mick Jagger set about developing a vocal style as tuneless as if he had a clothes peg attached to his nose. And when inspiration failed – which it did, almost continuously – there was always the same recourse to divine help. They turned the stereo needle back to A Day In the Life, Within You Without You or Lucy in the Sky With Diamonds.

By early July, when Jagger and Richard were on bail pending appeal and Brian Jones had begun undergoing residential psychiatric treatment, scarcely anything on the – still untitled – album was in a satisfactory finished state. The Beatles, for all their carte blanche at Abbey Road studios, worked in harness with a producer, George Martin, whose musicianship they still respected as a formative and disciplining force. Gifted engineer as Glyn Johns was, he remained, in the Stones' eyes, little more than a knob-twiddling functionary. Johns would frequently arrive at Olympic Studios no more certain than the girls on the doorstep that the session would take place as scheduled.

The delays were not wholly due to outside influences. Glyn Johns could see through his control-room window how deliberate the Stones' vacillation and tinkering often was, and what a combustible effect it had on Glyn's companion at the control-desk. To external pressures, the Stones added their own barely concealed wish to do it badly, and thus defy, provoke and alienate their manger, Andrew Loog Oldham.

The year-long coolness between Oldham and the Stones had intensified in the era of drug busts which Oldham privately considered merely stupid and time-wasting. His distance from Mick and Keith in their legal ordeal – and the growing resentment all the Stones felt against him – made all the more galling Oldham's appearance at Olympic Studios, early in 1967, ready to work his Svengali magic on behalf of his boys yet again.

His boys showed their unwillingness to be moulded by keeping him waiting at the studio for hours, sometimes days at a time. 'They like to make out that they wound me up by going in and playing nothing but the blues, and playing terribly,' Oldham says now. 'But I didn't give a stuff about the blues so how would I know? I put up with being messed around for about seven weeks, then one day I decided I'd had enough and just left. "From here on," I told them, "you can deal directly with Allen."' Thus did Andrew Loog Oldham let go of the greatest money-making machine rock would ever see.

Further time away from the studio was spent in planning an album-sleeve which, Jagger insisted, must be even more elaborate and costly than *Sgt. Pepper's*. Michael Cooper – who had photographed the Beatles in Peter Blake's pop art hall of fame – was commissioned to surpass himself with a portrait showing the Stones as medieval troubadours, kneeling around Jagger dressed in starred robes and a conical wizard's cap. The Stones helped Cooper build his studio set and carry in the baskets of flowers and fruit he had ordered as props. More time passed while Michael Cooper photographed Jagger in his wizard robes, sitting alone, hugging his knees, on a bed of crushed silver foil.

Cooper's photograph was then processed into an opaque plastic square which the finished album-sleeve had stuck to it like a table place-mat: the Stones in multi-coloured 3D, against a background of mountains, planets and minaret-spires, banked up with blurry patterns, flowers and fruit.

As autumn wore on, and a December release-date became inevitable, they at last agreed on a title: *The Rolling Stones' Cosmic Christmas*. Jagger then found a better idea inside the front cover of the passport he had so recently almost forfeited. Those large, old-fashioned passports used to announce: 'Her Britannic Majesty's Principal Secretary of State for Foreign Affairs Requests and Requires' that the bearer be allowed passage without let or hindrance. Jagger's title – touched by lingering anti-establishment rancour – was *Her Satanic Majesty Requests and Requires*. When Decca refused to sanction so blatant a slur on the Queen, the line was altered to *Their Satanic Majesties Request*, giving the far more appropriate sense of being formally invited to some diabolical garden fête.

On October 30, Brian Jones appeared for trial before Inner London Sessions on the drugs charge that had hung over him since the previous June. He arrived in his silver Rolls, dressed with almost excessive formality in a pinstripe suit, white shirt and spotted tie. But the tie was pulled too tight, as if in desperation at his own mirror-image that morning.

Brian's willingness to plead guilty to cannabis-possession had persuaded the police to offer no evidence concerning the cocaine and methedrine found at his flat. He further admitted responsibility for any cannabis smoked earlier by his party guests, thereby disposing of the flimsy possession charge against his companion in the dock, Prince Stanislas Klossowski de Rola. Stash was immediately discharged with a paltry award of 75 guineas towards his legal costs.

In Brian's case, all his counsel, James Comyn QC, could do was plead for mercy, offering the mitigating circumstances that Brian had never taken hard drugs, apart from LSD, and had vowed he would never touch cannabis again. His psychiatrist, Dr Leonard Henry, was called to testify to Brian's disturbed mental state at the time of his arrest, and to support Comyn's plea that he shouldn't be sent to prison. 'It would completely destroy his mental health,' Dr Henry said. 'He would go into a psychotic depression . . . he might even attempt to injure himself . . .'

Brian's performance in the witness box seemed only to corroborate James Comyn's description of 'a young man with a brilliant future . . . who very much wants to go on with his composing.'

'Is it your intention to have nothing more to do with drugs?' Comyn asked him.

'That is precisely my intention,' Brian answered, almost in a whisper. 'They've only brought trouble and disrupted my career. I hope this will be an example to anyone who's tempted to try.'

None of this deterred the court Chairman, Mr R.E. Seaton, from his resolve to combat what he called 'a growing canker in this country at the moment'. After a ninety-minute adjournment, Brian was sentenced to concurrent prison terms of nine months and three months, and ordered to pay £262 in costs. As a tumult broke out from the girls in the public gallery, James Comyn gave notice of appeal and asked whether, in the meantime, Brian could have bail. 'No,' Mr Seaton replied.

The silver Rolls-Royce remained where he had parked it as Brian was brought out, loaded into a grey van with the day's other prison fodder and driven away to begin his term at Wormwood Scrubs.

For him, there would be no night vigil by hippies around Eros – no public protest at all, barring the slight scuffle which occurred later that day in the King's Road between police and a group of impromptu demonstrators, including Mick Jagger's younger brother, Chris. The prison staff, deprived for their earlier quarry, were jubilant at finding another 'bloody longhair' in their midst, and began loudly discussing how Brian's gold thatch would soon be planed to the scalp. The other prisoners, thinking him homosexual, remained coldly hostile. That night, under his rough prison blanket, he must have known all the horrors of total abandonment.

His psychiatrist contacted the Wormwood Scrubs medical officer and, at least, succeeded in excusing him the regulation prison haircut. Next day, the doctor appeared with James Comyn before a High Court judge in chambers to plead for Brian to receive bail on medical grounds. It was granted, for a surety of £750 and on condition that Brian agreed to undergo the independent examination of a psychiatrist appointed by the court. An hour later, the Wormwood Scrubs screws handed Brian his crumpled pinstripe suit and told him he was free to go.

At this point, six months after his brief celebrity as pop music's cleansing fire, the magisterial and facetious voice of Judge Leslie Block was heard again in the land. Speaking at the annual dinner of the Horsham Ploughing and Agricultural Society, Judge Block amused his rural audience by a punning reference to Brutus's outburst against the mob in Julius Caesar, 'You blocks, you stones, you worse than senseless things . . . We did our best, your countrymen, I and my fellow magistrates, to cut these Stones down to size,' Judge Block continued. 'But it was not to be. The Court of Criminal Appeal let them roll free . . .'

Private function as the dinner was, a senior magistrate should have known better than to make jokes about past victims of his judgment, especially now that another Rolling Stone was on bail pending appeal against a prison sentence. A Labour MP, William Wilson, announced he was referring the matter to the Lord Chancellor. Les Perrin, the Stones' publicist – who had picked up Judge Block's speech from a Sussex local paper – issued a press release that was more like a protest pamphlet. 'Is this the kind of justice Britain expects? Is this man typical of those who hold the title, the high and esteemed office to try and sentence people? How can the public believe, in the light of this utterance by Judge Block, that the Rolling Stones can get an unbiased hearing? His statement smacks of pre-judgement – a getting-together to "cut the Stones down to size". It is a pity he did not observe the ethics of sub judice to Mr Jagger, Mr Richard and Mr Jones by remaining silent.'

On December 12, the finished new album, with its Delft blue and white border and Technicolour plastic griddle, finally went on sale in the British and American shops. The long interval since *Between the Buttons*, and the garish events of the past summer, had created the largest-ever public for a Rolling Stones LP. Advance orders in the US alone totalled almost $2,000,000. Probably no pop record, before or since, was so eagerly awaited, or so stunning a disappointment. All but the most besotted Stones fans recognized *Their Satanic Majesties* for what it was – an attempt to impersonate *Sgt. Pepper*, lacking all the qualities of the Beatles' master work and simultaneously reflecting all the delay, conflict and compromise which had bedevilled it.

The Beatles had used their free run of Abbey Road studios to create a song cycle as rounded as a symphony, yet with all the intimacy of a puppet or Punch and Judy show. The best the Stones could do in reply was a rather lame singalong chant (Sing This All Together – See What Happens), opening and closing side one in a cacophony of massed bells, rattles and gongs. Where the Beatles had used comic sound effects to express the joy of playing on top form, the Stones used them merely as infilling for many obvious, yawning gaps. So, interspersed at random, there were excerpts from a street market, a striptease club, some giggling, snoring, a voice saying – rather too audibly – 'Where's that joint?'

One song only, She's a Rainbow, found Jagger and Richard on form in the brusquely wistful manner of Ruby Tuesday or Lady Jane. The rest, like the cover, was a blur from which the real Stones emerged in only wavering glimpses – Keith's throaty guitar, for instance, on Bill Wyman's nervous debut composition, In Another Land. Here and there, too, were flashes of the virtuosity still able to ignite in Brian Jones. Though Brian, when coherent, had bitterly opposed the psychedelic approach, it was his Moroccan drums and percussion which gave the album whatever mysticism can be felt in it. Brian also played Mellotron on 2,000 Light Years From Home, the song written by Jagger during his night in Brixton Prison – a non-starter, according to Glyn Johns, until Brian sat down and improvised its eerie electronic descant.

The release date of *Their Satanic Majesties* happened also to be the day Brian's case came before Lord Chief Justice Parker in the Court of Criminal Appeal. Here, in addition to his two regular psychiatrists' testimony, the judges considered a file prepared on Brian by the court-appointed psychiatric expert, Dr Walter Neustatter. This referred to Brian's 'extremely precarious state of emotional adjustment' and 'fragile grasp of reality', arising from sexual anxieties which, in Dr Neustatter's opinion, verged on an Oedipus complex. The doctor had been struck, however, by Brian's considerable personal resources and 'capacity for insight to contain his anxiety'. Dr Neustratter confirmed Dr Henry's view, that imprisonment would drive him to a complete mental breakdown, possibly even to suicide.

Once again, the Lord Chief Justice showed a degree of mercy which smaller judges had not. Brian's nine-month prison sentence was set aside: he was instead fined £1,000 and put on probation for three years. A further proviso was that he should continue receiving psychiatric treatment.

One other Stone, Mick Jagger, was in court to hear Lord Parker's verdict. Afterwards, Brian paused only long enough to mumble to reporters, 'I want to be left alone to get on with my life,' before disappearing into the back of his silver Rolls. The darkened rear window showed a daguerreotype of anguish, its face buried in its frilly-cuffed hands.

Brian celebrated his release with an orgy of drink and pills that, within two days, put him back into hospital again. He had collapsed at Courtfield Road after going out to a club and playing double bass onstage with the resident band. As he slapped at the bass, he also began kicking it, softly at first but with greater and greater ferocity until he'd splintered it to matchwood. Even after the bass was destroyed, Brian continued to play it, his fingers shaping, chords in the air, his face inclined earnestly down towards notes only he could hear.

It was a change as sudden, as chemically mysterious, as sunlight turning rancid. At one moment, it seemed, all the young of America and Europe were holding out flowers and making signs of peace. At the next, they had taken to the streets and were smashing windows and wrenching up paving stones. Instead of beads and kaftans, all at once, there were badges, slogans and military fatigues; instead of gurus, angry-faced student activists; instead of 'happenings' and 'love-ins', ferocious street battles for which many a one time beautiful person had thoughtfully forearmed himself or herself with a knitting needle to jab police horses in the belly or testicles.

It was a wave seemingly from nowhere that broke, almost completely, on the year 1968: beginning with student riots in Paris that spring, continuing through the summer in Berlin, Amsterdam, London, Washington, Detroit, Los Angeles – riots, burnings, marches and demos, enacted against the shadowy subplots of Vietnam and Czechoslovakia, by chanting, angry battalions of the young. It was a revolution whose motives no one fully understood, least of all its participants; whose leaders enjoyed only the briefest heyday; whose armies had no sooner mustered than they dispersed to fresh amusements. It was a cloud of irritant pollen soon blown away, all but for one or two fatal seeds which, planted in certain minds, would become the means of holding the next decade to ransom. The German Baader-Meinhof, the Italian Red Brigades, the Provisional IRA – all terrorism carried on in shoulder-length hair and patched blue denim traces a common lineage back to this splitting open of the Age of Aquarius.

The uprising, like all others, needed anthems. And for once, the chief anthem-givers were found wanting. 'You say you want a revolution,' wrote John Lennon. '. . . Well, you can count me out.' He who was the new, angry order's chief hope preferred to make his protest by spending a week publicly in bed beside his Japanese consort, Yoko Ono. The rest of pop still sang about San Francisco and flowers. There was only one source where the elixir of anarchy – background battle-music, a soundtrack for eddying tear gas – might conceivably be found.

Oddly enough it was not Keith but Bill Wyman who first picked out the restoring riff on a rehearsal-room piano while waiting for the others to arrive. 'Brian and Charlie came in next. I played them this riff and we messed around with it for about twenty minutes. When Mick and Keith walked in, they both said "Hey – what's that? Sounds good." Mick went away and wrote a great lyric for it and we recorded it straight off.'

The result was Jumpin' Jack Flash, undisputedly the Stones' best performance on record, a two-minute masterpiece whose malign energy lives on in it like some sexual poltergeist. If Jagger and Richard ever received divine guidance, it was here in their abandonment of woolly psychedelics to return to unashamed, two-fisted rock. As partners, they had never – have never since – worked better. Jagger, at last, had written the proper litany for Keith's chord-shapes, a Grimms' fairy tale ('I was raised by a toothless, bearded hag . . .'), each verse a small nightmare, dissolving its bathetically sardonic refrain. The guitar, likewise, matched Jagger's body almost visibly, its insolent bass his jumps and struts, its tinkling treble the drawn-out lips grimacing 'It's a-a-a-aw right . . .' He has never come clearer than in the sound of that half-evil, half-playful, spring-heeled silhouette.

On May 12, 1968, the *New Musical Express* Poll-Winners' Concert at Wembley Empire Pool featured one unscheduled attraction. The Rolling Stones walked onstage and without preamble launched into their first public performance of Jumpin'

Jack Flash. Even on that audience primed to hysteria, its effect was an instantaneous jolt let in through one collective vein: before the intro chords had finished, thousands were on their feet, stamping and strutting like the voodoo-possessed.

With the single, on May 24, came a promotional film sequence like none seen before in pop or rock. The Stones, in robes that could have belonged equally to hippy mandarins or a wizards' coven, their eyes elongated by gold warpaint, performed at levitating camera angles, as remote from their own actions as Inca priests brooding over temple rites. Jagger was a wraith conjured up between them, an enormous head and still more enormous mouth, bowing and leering 'It's a-a-a-aw right . . .' like a pageboy at the very entrance to Purgatory.

The wild response to their *NME* concert appearance, and the speed with which Jumpin' Jack Flash flew up the British and American charts, removed any last notion among the Stones that their future lay in elaborately crafted studio albums. After a two-year layoff, the concert stage once more exerted its old, irresistible magnetism. Immersed as they were in a new album, with a new producer, the Stones – that is, the four fully functioning Stones – agreed they must go out on tour again.

The road, however, was not as open as it had formerly been – especially not the gold-earning trans-America road. Two years beset by hippies, drop-outs, draft-dodgers and associated unpatriotic evils had reduced the American establishment to the fearful belligerence of an Indian-encircled waggon train. No one with a conviction for possessing drugs – or, as US Immigration phrased it, 'a crime of moral turpitude' – was permitted even the shortest sojourn on American soil. The previous September, when Mick and Keith had flown to New York to oversee the *Satanic Majesties* album sleeve, they had been stopped at Kennedy airport, questioned at length and permitted only temporary entry pending a full official review of their prosecution in England.

On May 21, the still-unscheduled '68 American tour was

wiped out of existence. Les Perrin, the Stones' publicist, answered his phone at home in Sutton to hear a familiar lisping voice say, 'Les – they're coming in through the window.' Brian Jones was being busted again.

The Gay Hussar, in Greek Street, Soho, is a small, scarlet-painted Hungarian restaurant whose wild cherry soup, cold pike and red cabbage are, for some reason, particularly favoured by politicians, authors and newspaper editors. Among the lunchtime throng in its more fashionable downstairs, several times in 1968, could be espied a pair ill-matched even for those hallucinogenic times. One was Tom Driberg, MP for Barking, Essex, and noted radical journalist. The other – but for his expansive consumption of Gay Hussar dishes, inconspicuous almost to vanishing point – was Mick Jagger.

Since meeting Jagger socially a year or so earlier, Driberg had, twice at least, proved himself a powerful ally. It was he who first raised in Parliament the deplorable handcuffs episode at Jagger's and Robert Fraser's trial. He also had signed the famous *Times* letter, along with Graham Greene and the Beatles, calling for legalization of soft drugs, despite its possible impact on his majority among the Essex voters.

Much of Driberg's interest in Mick Jagger was that of an elderly homosexual, secretly addicted to the juvenile 'rough trade'. But much was a genuine desire to understand, and perhaps find benefit in, a power which the older man was too good a journalist not to find awesome. Never in Driberg's long career among influential people had he seen influence so systematically wasted. These Gay Hussar meetings were an attempt to persuade Jagger to put his power and influence to use through the medium of conventional politics.

The thought of standing for Parliament was one which had long attracted Jagger – and would do so intermittently for some years to come. At Driberg's prompting, he would discuss it seriously, with his usual articulateness, flattered by the MP's interest in him though aware – as always – where that interest began. But even Tom Driberg, with all his oratorical skill, and bottles of Hungarian Bull's Blood, could not extract from Mick Jagger even an undertaking to read the Labour Party manifesto.

Jagger's was not a unique malady. The same uneasy feeling had visited other pop stars in the top echelon – that fame and wealth and idolizing could become a form of deprivation; that, meanwhile, important things were passing them by. The Beatles had said as much: their years of touring had been like years in prison. To them, a convict's bread and water seemed hardly more monotonous than their own unending surfeit, the ritual extravagance and ritualistic wastefulness that reduced a superstar millionaire's habitat to the squalor of a cell with neither light nor air.

None of the other Stones faced this problem of intellectual unfulfilment. Charlie and Bill seemed quite happy to fill up the long intervals between album-sessions with hobbies like photography or collecting antique silver. Even Brian, in his quieter periods, carried on boyhood pastimes like locomotive-spotting and collecting data on types of London bus. Two double-deckers he had bought were already housed in a northern transport museum; as his mental confusion increased, so did a compulsion to buy further vintage buses and charabancs. Shirley Arnold at the Stones' office frequently had to deal with the indignant vendor of yet another bus which Brian had bought when drunk or stoned and had then totally forgotten.

As for Keith, it seemed he needed nothing outside his existence as prototype of a rock star. In the same way that Keith onstage had inspired a whole era of guitarists to copy his wolfish silhouette, so his private lifestyle had become the model for an entirely new human species. It was an existence characterized, above all, by gigantic inertia – by hours spent in rooms devoid of light and stewn with album sleeves, liquor bottles and cigarette ends; by days, and most nights, passed in the tenacious pursuit of doing nothing but lying prone on a couch, near a lamp draped with a Batik scarf, drinking, smoking and 'toking', listening to thunderous hi-fi and tinkering with an acoustic guitar.

Keith now lived with Anita Pallenberg, mostly at Redlands, the Sussex cottage whose half-timbered exterior still gave no hint of the orgiastic world within. From time to time, local people would glimpse the wrecked-looking country squire and his grimly beautiful blonde, driving in the 'Blue Lena' through West Wittering or, on rare occasions, coming out of neighbourhood shops. A villager who saw them often remembers the extraordinary blackness around Keith's eyes, even before he took to wearing mascara, and how he always seemed to smoke cigarettes twice as long as normal. Lurid tales circulated about what went on behind the seven-foot boundary wall Keith had recently obtained planning consent to build – how he would zoom around his lake in a miniature hovercraft, or hunt water rats with a shotgun, accompanied by his giant deerhound, Syphilis.

Though Jagger could live the same incubated rock star life for weeks at a time, quite happily, he continued to feel disturbing impulses – in tune with the new mood of student militancy – that he should be doing something more with his vast reputation than just making another album. What exactly he should be doing, though, continued problematical. The avenue of conventional politics, as suggested by Tom Driberg, involved dedication and self-denial that were clearly unthinkable. Far more attractive was the idea of total revolution, a concept grown so fashionable, it could be discussed even by twenty-five-year-old millionaires, sipping wine or tequila in their Queen Anne town houses. Thus far among would-be rock star revolutionaries, only one had put forward anything like a plan for effecting social change. John Lennon suggested putting LSD into the House of Commons water-supply, to see what good might come from freaking out the whole of parliament.

The Beatles, to their eternal credit, were making one gigantic, ill-starred effort to carry through the revolutionary precepts of hippydom. Their Apple organization, founded in the summer of 1968, was an attempt to use their collective millions to help young people in every branch of the creative arts. Apple, in Paul McCartney's phrase, would be 'a kind of Western Communism' – a business without greed, run only for mutual stimulation and enjoyment, fuelled by the amity and open-heartedness that was the prerogative of everyone under thirty.

Philanthropy such as the Beatles were now splashing forth, over youthful musicians, writers, film-makers, poets and Punch and Judy men, had no appeal for the calculating and practical head Stone. Marianne Faithfull remembers that when the ex-Animal Chas Chandler first brought Jimi Hendrix from New York to London, he approached Jagger as a possible co-sponsor, and Jagger 'simply turned and ran'. Hendrix's subsequent rise to fame had, if anything, deepened Jagger's disinterest in helping new recording talent. He seemed jealous of Hendrix, even suspecting him of trying to steal Marianne from him late one night at a West End club.

Since the break with Andrew Loog Oldham in October, 1967, the Stones' management office had been in Maddox Street, close to Piccadilly. A small, top-floor suite, formerly maids' quarters in a Georgian town house, it was far from the opulence with which the Beatles had surrounded their new business family. It had been the best the Stones' staff could do after weeks of being turned down by landlords all over the West End. They got Maddox Street only by luck, through a friend of a friend, by pretending it was to house a music publishing company, and by scrupulous avoidance, at all times, of the phrase 'Rolling Stones'.

To run the Maddox Street office, Mick Jagger approached Jo Bergman, the American girl who had worked for Brian Epstein in the Beatles' fan club and, later, as Marianne's assistant and companion. Petite and cosy, with an air of high-powered calm,

Jo was to assume most managerial functions for the Stones in Europe, presiding over a tiny staff whose mainstay continued to be their old fan club secretary, Shirley Arnold.

Shirley remembers with what keenness Jagger took on his new role of employer and businessman. 'He loved coming in for boardroom meetings with lawyers and accountants, or when Allen Klein was in town.' At Maddox Street there would be none of the slackness and promiscuity which characterized the Beatles' Apple workforce. 'Mick was always utterly meticulous,' Jo Bergman says. 'He liked to know everyone was doing things – for him, of course – with total efficiency.' When, on rare occasions, his eye alighted on a secretary for reasons other than stenographic, the ensuing business was conducted as discreetly as a Bourbon king with a scullery-maid. Only the girl's flushed face and half-unhinged false eyelashes would give the game away.

To Maddox Street, along with the equally apportioned Rolling Stones fan mail and hate mail, were diverted the frequent ivory-white envelopes, hand-delivered from hotels like the Connaught or Dorchester, and containing fulsome appeals to Mick Jagger to read the enclosed synopsis, treatment or full shooting script. It was a fact tantalizing to film producers on both sides of the Atlantic that, in four years as a nonpareil crowd-puller, and despite embodying female fantasy at least as potently as Rudolf Valentino, Jagger still had not starred in a feature film.

The grandiose five-picture schedule announced by Allen Klein had by now dwindled to a faintly recurring rumour among music journalists that they might still do something with the script of *Only Lovers Left Alive*. Klein, meanwhile, blocked all outside offers, insisting that his original plan would still be carried through. There had, besides, been a little too much real life drama lately for the Stones to want to manufacture any before the camera.

It was natural that a spirit as flirtatious and procrastinating as Jagger's should enjoy the wooing of film moguls, the expensive lunches, the agreement in principle to play ambitiously unlikely roles, the enthusiasm to read scripts which, as a rule, he would close after the second or third page. Lately, however, in his restlessness and wish to extend himself, he had given the whole question of movie acting concentrated thought. It weighed with his competitive nature that Marianne was following up her pop success with a career on the legitimate stage and in films. She had appeared in Chekov's *Three Sisters* at Chichester Festival Theatre, to unanimous critical acclaim, and was now to star in a new Roger Vadim film, *Girl on a Motorcycle*.

Towards the summer's end, Jagger did finally succeed both in finishing a script and liking it. The film was to be called *Performance*. Its writer and putative co-director was Donald Cammell, the Stones' old painter friend from Paris. It told the story of a young English gangster, on the run from members of his own mob, and his encounter with an eccentric and reclusive pop star. Jagger, after practically no hesitation, agreed to play the pop star, Turner. The theme music was to be written by Jagger and Richard and played as a soundtrack by the Rolling Stones. Largely on this basis, Cammell was able to raise £1.8 million in financing from the Warner Brothers Corporation. To Warner Brothers it seemed a safe enough investment. They presumed they were getting a happy, zany pop music picture like the Beatles' *A Hard Day's Night*.

Marianne was considered for the part of Turner's girlfriend before it finally went to Anita Pallenberg. The choice was obvious – and, in any case, the film's winter shooting schedule would have been impossible for Marianne. That summer, she had discovered she was going to have Mick Jagger's baby.

This time, the raid on Brian took place at 7:30 in the morning. He had moved from Courtfield Road and was living temporarily in a rented flat at Royal Avenue House, a King's Road mansion block. Awakened by thunderous knocking and pealing on the front door bell, he took one look through the security spy-hole, then dived for the telephone. His panic-stricken words to Les Perrin – 'They're coming in through the window, Les' – were not far short of the truth. A policeman was actually climbing into the flat via its interior rubbish-chute.

When Jo Bergman reached Royal Avenue House, shortly before 9 a.m., a smiling policeman let her into the flat. Three more hefty officers stood over Brian, in his skimpy kimono, showing him a lump of cannabis which one of them had taken from inside a ball of brown wool in the living-room bureau. Brian's reaction was one of the incredulous dismay. 'Oh – *no*,' he moaned. 'This can't happen again, just when we're getting on our feet.'

Later that same day, May 21, Brian went to Great Marlborough Street Magistrates' Court, charged with possessing 44 grains of cannabis resin. He was released on £2,000 bail pending trial, once again, before Inner London Sessions. He also faced punishment for breach of the probation order placed on him by the Court of Criminal Appeal.

He spent that night in the care of Allen Klein's nephew, Ronnie Schneider, sleeping in Schneider's room at the London Hilton. 'The hotel didn't want to take him,' Schneider says. 'I told them that if they wanted to throw Brian out, they'd have to throw me out, too. He went to sleep in the spare bed, crying and holding my hand. Next morning, we had a big meeting with the lawyers on Brian's case. Brian kept coming up behind me and kissing the back of my head. He told me I'd saved his life.'

The second bust plunged Brian back to zero, cruelly, at the very point when his efforts to rebuild himself as a person and a musician seemed to be paying off. True to his Appeal Court undertaking, he had kept clear of drugs; he had left his psychiatrist's care and was now obliged only to make the statutory regular visits to his probation officer.

In the studio, too, he had revived, feeling a surge of optimism in the Stones' return to their r & b roots and in the obvious quality of their new producer, Jimmy Miller. Leaving his Mellotron and flute and Moroccan pipes, he had gone back to playing bottleneck blues guitar with an impassioned elegance already defining several tracks for the album that would become *Beggars' Banquet.* The sessions were being filmed by the French director Jean-Luc Godard as part of a polemical drama-documentary about glamour and violence in the Sixties. With Jean-Luc Godard at Olympic Studios, and cameras turning over every night, it was natural that Anita Pallenberg should frequently drop by – but even that had not seemed to shake Brian's composure. He had assured several people vehemently, 'I'm not interested in Anita any more.'

Now, once more, he was the piteous, impossible Brian of four months ago, whose only defence against the horrors crowding in on him was Scotch and pills and snatching up the telephone. 'Whenever the phone went at 2 a.m., I'd always know who it was,' Jo Bergman says. 'He'd spend perhaps an hour talking to me about some tiny thing that was on his mind. As soon as he'd rung off, he'd ring straight back and talk for another hour about the same tiny thing. Then he'd ring back *again*, horror-struck to think he'd woken me up. Next morning, I'd discover I was one of half a dozen people Brian had been ringing up through the night.'

Les Perrin's wife Janey was someone else Brian turned to constantly, for reassurance, a sympathetic ear, or just human company. 'He'd ring me about *anything*,' Janey Perrin says. 'He'd ring to say he'd got a toothache . . . a headache . . . that he couldn't turn the tap off in the kitchen. Once, he sent me an eighty-six-word telegram. Another time, he rang me from the Dorchester and said he was going to commit suicide. I was so exasperated, I said, "All right, Brian – go into the bathroom and do it, so as not to make a mess." That brought him round a bit. Another time, he swore while he was talking to me. He rang back almost in tears, to think I'd heard him use a foul word. In the end when he rang up, he wouldn't say, "It's Brian." He'd say, "This is your other son."'

What chiefly terrified Brian between May and September, when his case came to court, was that the other Stones might secretly be planning to go on tour without him – perhaps even with a new guitarist in his place. In August, the British music press reported that Eric Clapton had been asked to join the Stones when his supergroup, Cream, disbanded at Christmas. It was a constant theme of Brian's late-night telephone calls to anyone who would listen: how his drug bust had given *them* the perfect excuse to get rid of him. At times, the Chelsea police seemed only walk-on players in that longer-term conspiracy by so-called friends to steal his stardom first, then his woman, and finally to eject him from the band he had created.

In fact, despite their exasperation with Brian, and their severely limited capacity for unselfish action, Mick and Keith both genuinely sympathized with him in this new, undeserved crisis, and made intermittent efforts to show him moral support. For all they knew, indeed, Brian's busting could presage renewed police attacks on either or both of them. Their sympathy was, perhaps, too sudden for Brian to recognize it as such. Spanish Tony Sanchez remembers a summer day at Redlands when Mick Jagger took Brian into the house for a serious talk about his approaching trial. Shortly afterwards, Brian rushed through the open French windows, shouting, 'I'll kill myself' and jumped straight into Keith's water-filled moat. Jagger plunged in to rescue him before realizing that the water was only four feet deep. The two staggered out together, Brian laughing hysterically, Jagger enraged at the ruination of his new velvet trousers.

One sensible decision reached by the others on Brian's behalf was that, until his reappearance before Inner London Sessions, he had better be as far as possible from the Chelsea police, his dangerous social circle of junkies and the pressmen who would now be dogging his every move. One of his casual girlfriends, Linda Keith, had recently attempted suicide at his flat; two more were visiting him in hospital, often at the same time. There were also insistent demands from the mother of his elder son called Julian for money to buy the lad a toy typewriter.

It was Keith Richard's well-intentioned idea that Brian should live at Redlands with Suki Poitier, under the care of Keith's own chauffeur, Tom Keylock. There he remained from July to late September, apparently content to be surrounded by reminders of Anita. There the others would meet and try to rehearse, although Brian had lost the will for anything beyond his own desultory, and somehow secretive, accoustic strumming. He managed to keep off drugs but compensated by drinking more heavily than ever. One Sunday, when Mick and Marianne had driven down to see him, he flew into a drunken fury, lunged at Mick with his fists, then threatened him with a carving knife. Marianne remembers his panting, bloated face – the face which, to Jo Bergman, only too clearly denoted its astrological sign. 'He was a double Pisces. His face really did seem to be turning back to water.'

The breach seemed healed on September 24, when Mick and Keith both attended Inner London Sessions to see Brian treated with wholly unlooked-for clemency. The jury found him guilty of possessing cannabis. But the Chairman, Reginald Seaton, decided it had been 'a lapse' from previous sincere efforts to stay straight. Brian was fined £50 with £100 costs. Afterwards, Mick and Keith posed for photographs with him, their arms round his shoulders: two decolleté young gods of 1968, flanking someone who might have been an older, unwell relative.

From time to time, in his miasmic anxiety and depression, Brian would remember his plan to return to Morocco and record the ethnic music that had so excited him there – in particular, the wonderful Joujouka pipers in the foothills of the Rif. Even that bright memory seemed stained by the thought of how friends had betrayed him. To return to Morocco meant returning to the day when he had lost Anita; when he had returned from the Djemaa el Fna to find her and Keith and Tom Keylock and the Bentley all gone.

His first trip back to Tangier, with Suki Poitier and Christopher Gibbs, brought on an almost eerie repetition of the last night he and Anita had ever spent together. 'I suddenly got this call from Brian to go down to their room,' Gibbs says. 'Suki was lying on the floor, unconscious. Brian had clearly given her the most terrible beating-up. "Can you call an ambulance, man?" he said. It was entirely in the nature of things to Brian that someone else called the ambulance to take the girl he'd beaten up to hospital. "No, Brian," I said. "You call an ambulance – and *quickly*." It was obvious that simply hadn't occurred to him.'

In the spring of 1968, he persuaded Glyn Johns to join him on an expedition to record the G'naou, a troupe who performed on steel drums and outsize metal castanets. Brian's idea was to show the link between African and American black music by taking the G'naou tapes to New York and overdubbing layers of jazz or soul. In the event, he was too drunk, or stoned, even to hear the G'naou troupe properly. Glyn Johns grew understandably bored, and the taping was a fiasco.

In October, accompanied by the long-suffering Suki and a sound engineer named George Chkiantz, Brian returned to Tangier, determined to record the Jajouka in their pre-Roman Rites of Pan festival. Brion Gysin met them at Tangier with his Moroccan partner, Hamri, and drove them up to the village that nestles in an eyrie so acoustically perfect, one can hear a dog barking on an adjacent mountain, and the waves breaking on rocks half a dozen miles below.

For almost two days and nights, Brian squatted there with Suki, smoking *kif*, apparently entranced by the soft, incessant pipe melody that – owing to the Jajouka's ability to blow out while inhaling – seems not to pause even for breath. Only a few Europeans had been to the village before; fewer still had seen this private version of the Pan rites, with children dancing, like figures from a cave mural, in brazen, unearthly light. At 4 a.m., the party bedded down in a communal hut: by noon, the festival had begun again.

Towards evening, Brion Gysin remembers, two of the musicians put down their instruments and rose to begin preparations for the meal the visitors had been asked to share. A moment later, they walked past Brian and Suki, carrying a snow-white goat. As Brian looked at the goat, with its bewildered, pale-fringed eyes, a strangled noise came from him: he said in a whisper, 'That's *me*.' Suki and Brion Gysin smiled, agreeing there was some resemblance. But Brian did not smile. He continued to watch, fascinated, and to whisper, 'That's *me*,' as the two men carried the white goat into the shadow of a lean-to, and one of them drew out a long-bladed knife.

Eleven

'There's just no room for a street-fighting man . . .'

The few close friends who knew about Marianne's pregnancy were surprised to see with what unaffected pleasure Mick looked forward to fatherhood. It was one further paradox in a character so narcissistically self-absorbed that he loved small children and enjoyed taking care of them; to a child he always granted an intimacy withheld from his closest adult friends. His happiest hours with Marianne came when he forsook his court to go off for a day in the country with just her and her three-year-old son, Nicholas. With Nicholas, he was less surrogate father than elder brother. He would play with the little boy for hours, pushing him high on swings or whirling him round by the arms in some empty Berkshire meadow.

Jagger desperately wanted this first child of his own: he also wanted Marianne to become his wife as soon as John Dunbar would divorce her. Marianne had always demurred before, afraid of such a commitment a second time – a little wary, too, of acquiring so voluble a mother-in-law. 'Somehow,' she says, 'I always felt there couldn't be *another* Mrs Jagger.' Even so, she felt her resolve weakening. For, since his discovery that she was carrying his child, he had treated her with almost maternal tenderness.

Jagger's support was doubly needful when the story got into the papers, as it soon did. In pre-feminist 1968, there were few social stigmas worse than that of being an unmarried mother even if you were not already notorious as a shameless wearer of fur rugs and abuser of Mars bars. Marianne's pregnancy, indeed, did far more than pillory her with further lipsmacking banner headlines. It touched off a whole crusade against the Sixties' 'Permissive Society', with its flattened sexual and moral boundaries, by attention-seeking media figures, politicians and clergy. What should have been the most private matter to Jagger and Marianne became the stuff of speeches and parish newsletters throughout the land. The Archbishop of Canterbury himself spared a moment in his pulpit to ask for intercessionary prayers on Marianne's behalf. Loud criticism also emanated from Mrs Mary Whitehouse, a northern schoolteacher and self-appointed spokeswoman for Britain's silent moral majority. Once again as chivalrous knight errant, Jagger agreed to defend Marianne and debate morality with Mrs Whitehouse on a special edition of the David Frost television show.

'The fact of the matter . . .' Mrs Whitehouse said, looking at Jagger through flyaway-rim spectacles and smiling her bright, metallic smile, '. . . is that if you're a Christian or a person with faith, and you make that vow, when difficulties come, you have this basic thing you've accepted. You find your way through the difficulties.'

'*Your* Church accepts divorce,' Jagger replied. 'It may even accept abortion – am I right or wrong? I don't see how you can talk about this bond which is inseparable when the Christian Church itself accepts divorce . . .' It was, of course, beyond his power to confess that he wanted to marry the girl, but couldn't.

Marianne's son, Nicholas, was playing in the Cheyne Walk music room – a small garden house, smelling strongly of cats – the day Jagger sat down with Keith to try to articulate his thoughts about the revolution he so fervently half wanted to join. 'Everywhere I hear the sound of marching, charging feet, boy,' he sang, against Keith's beating-to-quarters guitar riff. 'Summer's here and the time is right for fighting in the street, boy . . .'

To his credit, he had tried the real thing, linking arms with the anti-Vietnam War demonstrators outside the American Embassy on the day when Lady Bracknell's prophecy came true of 'acts of violence in Grosvenor Square'. The press soon spotted Jagger and chased him from the scene, well before police horses started falling down. Today, looking from his summer house to his Queen Anne mansion, he realized where his true allegiance must lie. The insolent battle cry trailed off into indecision; the passion curdled into even colder feet than Lennon's. '. . . but what can a poor boy do, 'cept to sing in a rock 'n' roll band . . .'

Chaos was far more effectively present, had he realized it, in another new song, whose recording had been observed in its entirety by Jean-Luc Godard's documentary film crew. Godard subsequently dropped the title he had meant to give his film, *One Plus One*, and instead gave it the song's name, Sympathy for the Devil.

Even before Jumpin' Jack Flash, there were those eager to connect the Stones' music with a darker, more deliberate paganism. They had acquired a fervent fan, and a slightly unsettling friend, in Kenneth Anger, film-maker, connoisseur of the occult and disciple of Britain's most notorious black magician, Aleister Crowley. To Kenneth Anger, the Stones in their concerts showed the power to invoke forces not invoked since Crowley, 'The Great Beast,' had gone to his sacrilegious grave. Mick Jagger, in Anger's ravished eyes, was no less than a latter-day Lucifer, with Keith as his attendant devil, Beelzebub. So he wanted to cast them in his intended masterpiece, a screen version of the black magic epic *Lucifer Rising*.

There was also Anita Pallenberg, whose knowledge of the black arts was rumoured to be extensive, and whose influence over and around the chief Stones had aroused suspicion that she was actually a witch. Spanish Tony Sanchez, Keith's intermittent chauffeur-bodyguard, claims to have seen the collection of human relics allegedly used in spells against those who had incurred Anita's displeasure.

At Anita's prompting, Keith himself had grown fascinated by black magic and witchcraft and convinced – as many others had been – that Kenneth Anger possessed the powers of a Magus, or sorcerer. At one point, Keith and Anita even contemplated a pagan marriage ceremony, with Anger officiating: they were deterred – according to Spanish Tony – by an unmistakable warning from 'the other side' not to meddle in realms they did not understand.

Jagger, too, flirted briefly with black magic, as an extension of his interest in mysticism and fairies. Flattered, above all, by his transmogrification to Lucifier, he offered to compose theme music on his new Moog synthesizer for Kenneth Anger's film *Invocation of my Demon Brother*. His experiments with the black arts, however, did not proceed one step further than was quite prudent. For something like a year afterwards he, very noticeably, wore a large wooden crucifix.

It was not Kenneth Anger, but the eclectically read Marianne, who gave Jagger his reference-point for a song in which Satan would make an actual, named appearance. Marianne had just read Mikhail Bulgakov's *The Master and Margarita*, a surrealist Russian novel of the 1930s, in which Satan pays a visit to contemporary Moscow to survey the effects of the Revolution. Bulgakov's is the smooth-talking Satan later epitomized by George Sanders: a figure in immaculate evening dress, with a long cigarette-holder, bowing low and purring, 'Permit me to introduce myself . . .'

The phrase launched Jagger into a lyric of daring bad taste: a soliloquy by just such an urbane and ingratiating Mephistopheles, looking back over his interventions in human affairs, from Christ's Crucifixion through the Russian Revolution to Hitler's blitzkrieg and the Kennedy assassination. A similar irresistible impulse in the studio wrenched the song away from its original, rather folksy arrangement, into a bongo-spattered samba beat that seemed to find a groove more compulsive than any blues. As Jagger moved through his Devil's apology, overweening politeness rising to the glottal roar of a punk samurai, an impromptu chorus, 'Woo-woo, woo-woo,' broke out among Anita Pallenberg and her friends in the control-room. Played back, it seemed indivisible from the song: a soundtrack from a coven of sarcastic witches.

Christopher Gibbs had suggested naming the new album *Beggars' Banquet* in accord with the prevailing atmosphere of wizards, hobgoblins and devilish paradox. A final mix was ready in time to be played at Mick Jagger's twenty-sixth birthday party, at Spanish Tony's Vesuvio Club, on July 26. The guests included John Lennon, Paul McCartney and other pop notables whose opinion Jagger particularly valued. Their acclaim was instant and unanimous. At the first wild bongo beat of Sympathy for the Devil, almost the whole company surged on to the floor to dance the whole album through. For Jagger, it was a night of triumph, marred only slightly when Paul McCartney gave the club disc jockey the Beatles' new single to play, and everyone went wild a second time, listening to Hey, Jude.

In *Beggars' Banquet*, the Stones had produced an album whose simplicity and minimal elegance seemed more marvellous, recalling the washy jingle-jangle of *Their Satanic Majesties*: an album whose daring, often dangerous, themes are hidden within the forthright, artless styles of blues or country music. Exhortations to riot, blaspheme or fornicate are conveyed by no more than the lilt of a hillbilly piano. Complex evils come hidden among plainly strummed acoustic guitars. It is a work which shows the Stones simultaneously pushing into territory never charted by pop, and rediscovering the spirit of Eel Pie Island. The most arresting minor track – more so than the melancholy No Expectations or the semi-pornograpahic Stray Cat Blues – is Jagger's devout treatment of Prodigal Son, a gospel classic written by the Reverend Robert Wilkins forty years before. Even on unfamiliar and risky ground, everything went right. Salt of the Earth, a song for 'the hard-working people', makes a rather better showing nowadays than that deluded anthem, All You Need Is Love.

The original *Beggars' Banquet* sleeve, art directed jointly by Jagger and Richard, was to have depicted, simply, a lavatory-wall, shot from just above pedestal-height, with song titles and studio credits scrawled as graffiti around its pipes, toilet-roll holder and evil-looking cistern, among examples of invatorial philosophy such as 'God rolls his own' and 'Wot! No paper!' Not surprisingly, both Decca and the Stones' American label, London, rejected the design. The Stones refused to consider any alternative. The release-date, August 24, was moved back into September.

Street Fighting Man had, meanwhile, been launched on an American summer already rent by assassination and race-riots – only days, indeed, after Mayor Daley's Chicago police had systematically beaten up innocent delegates at the Democratic Party Convention. Street Fighting Man was denounced as plain incitement to further violence and banned by every radio station in the Chicago area, together with dozens more across the country.

The battle with Decca over the lavatory-wall sleeve deteriorated into a public slanging-match between Jagger and Sir Edward Lewis. Decca's Chairman was quoted as calling the sleeve 'silly' and 'offensive'. Jagger retorted that Decca had seen nothing offensive in issuing a Tom Jones album (*A-Tomic Jones*) with a cover showing an A-bomb's mushroom cloud. Next, he challenged Decca to issue the sleeve in a plain brown paper wrapper marked 'Unfit for Children'. Sir Edward did not rise to the challenge. The release-date was moved back again, to sometime in October.

While the Stones battled with Decca, their managers, past and present, battled with each other in a wild fandango of changing partners and rebounding writs.

For more than two years, Eric Easton had been trying to obtain legal redress for his ousting from the Stones' co-management by Andrew Loog Oldham in cahoots with Allen Klein. Easton was suing Oldham for breach of contract, and suing Klein for having engineered that breach. Proceedings had been delayed initially by Oldham's nimbleness in avoiding service of the legal papers, and subsequently by Allen Klein's will o' the wisp appearances in London and equally sudden disappearances back to New York.

In November, 1967, Easton finally succeeded in bringing Oldham before a High Court judge. It was a bizarre occasion, of which the undoubted highlight was an attempt by each ex-partner to have the other jailed for contempt. The result was an order from Mr Justice Buckley, freezing some two million dollars in Rolling Stones royalties until Easton's claim against Oldham and Klein was resolved.

By this time, of course, Oldham was no longer acting directly as the Stones' manager – was, indeed, on hostile terms with them following his walkout during the non-making of *Their Satanic Majesties*. After the Oldham-Easton High Court battle, the Stones took the opportunity to repudiate the original agreement made with their co-managers. They claimed it had been signed by only one of them – Brian Jones – and was legally invalid, anyway, since Brian had been under the age of twenty-one.

By this time, too, Oldham and Klein were no longer the cosy, conspiratorial duo which had cut up Eric Easton. The matter at issue was the $1.25 million in advance royalties which Klein had wrung from Decca in 1966 and which – Oldham then assumed – had been paid into his and the Stones' joint publishing company, Nanker Phelge Music Ltd. Instead, he discovered, the money had been placed with something called Nanker Phelge *USA*, an entirely separate company formed by Klein a week after the Decca deal, with himself as president and sole shareholder.

Oldham's response – though he was still linked to Klein in the Eric Easton case – was to file suit against him in America, claiming that Nanker Phelge USA had been used as 'a vehicle for the diversion of assets and income' from Oldham, the Rolling Stones and Nanker Phelge UK Ltd to Allen Klein 'for his own personal use and benefit'.

The suit was worth $1.5 million, and it quickly became bogged down in the litigious everglades that were Klein's natural habitat. Klein's contention was that, since his company had done the Decca deal, his company would naturally have received the proceeds; and that, since the Stones were guaranteed their royalty payments spread over a twenty-year period, the name he chose to call the handling company was irrelevant. In any case, once filed, the Oldham lawsuit had to take its place in a queue of some fifty other legal disputes involving Klein.

The Oldham-Klein case dragged on for most of 1968 – a year in which Klein waxed still greater in New York, first by acquiring the nearly defunct Cameo-Parkway record label, then by raising its shares to many times their value with rumours of acquisitions and takeovers. In the event, Cameo-Parkway's only acquisition was the firm of Allen Klein and Company (whose listed assets, oddly enough, included General Motors shares to the precise value of $1.25 million).

In October 1968, Allen Klein approached Andrew Loog Oldham with a deal. He would buy off Oldham's lawsuit, plus all his residual interests in the Rolling Stones, for one million dollars, to be paid on the instalment-plan. It was, as he well knew, an offer Oldham could not refuse.

That left only the unfortunate Eric Easton, still trying to obtain satisfaction by conventional legal means from a portly man in New York whose far more important pursuers now included the US Securities and Exchange Commission, and from a blond young man in London whose overwrought emotional state now led him to spend his weekends in the therapeutic care of nuns. On Monday morning, the nuns would unlock the door, and Andrew Loog Oldham would return to his life as a boy tycoon.

Oldham kept on with his Immediate label, turning his attention to a 'Mod' group, the Small Faces, and their gravel-voiced boy lead singer Steve Marriott, whose insecurity and neuroticism made him a worthy successor to Brian Jones. 'To get Steve to go onstage and entertain, you had to entertain him all the time. So, before we checked out of some grand hotel, we'd saw through the legs of the bed and the chairs in our suite so that the next people to use them would go crashing to the floor.'

In 1970, Oldham moved to New York, leaving behind a wife, Sheila, and a son, Sean, named after his friend, the theatre designer Sean Kenny. In 1974, he married a Colombian model and film star named Esther Farfan. The couple divided their life between Bogotá and New York, where Oldham teamed up again with Allen Klein, remixing tracks on Klein's old Cameo-Parkway label. Oldham himself by now owed large sums in back income tax and kept the authorities at bay mainly thanks to generous loans from Klein. No doubt he had ample time to rue his earlier unkind comments about Klein's taste in knitwear.

The Warner Brothers executive who had visualized *Performance* as a film on the lines of *A Hard Day's Night* would doubtless have been spellbound by the early scene in which James Fox as Chas, the young Cockney hoodlum, ritualistically pours acid over the Rolls-Royce of a hostile barrister, then shaves the head of a bound and gagged chauffeur, whistling a cheerful barber's shop air. The scene in which Chas's gang boss, a bald, hairy-chested brute, given to sententious utterances about 'Old England', huddles in his vest under a pink satin counterpane while his half-naked catamite preens himself nearby, might also have given warning that the film starring Mick Jagger was something other than all-round family entertainment.

When Jagger came on set, early in October, Donald Cammell's production team was ensconced in the cavernous Mayfair house that was to be the home of the reclusive pop idol, Turner. With Christopher Gibbs as set-designer, the house quickly assumed the appearance of a Rolling Stone habitation: vampire-dark, hung with exotic drapes and, in certain visible places, none too clean. Here, hiding out from his gang boss, Chas was to undergo initiation into drugs, wigs and other weirdness by Turner and two female companions.

The requirements of playing Turner had caused Jagger to agonize at length over whether it might not do his real life pop image irreparable harm. For most of the picture, Turner had to wear full female make-up, lipstick, powder and rouge. At the climax of the magic mushroom trip administered to Chas, Turner underwent transformation from pop star to underworld gangster, with his hair slicked back like a Fifties Teddy boy.

But most of all, Jagger worried that the character developed in Donald Cammell's script – the morose and playful, pretentiously bookish superstar hermit – bore not the slightest resemblance to himself. Long discussions with Cammell and the film's director, Nicholas Roeg, could not find a coalescence of Turner and Mick Jagger that would hold up for a minute before the cameras. Then, as always, his mimic's gift came to his rescue. The Turner he chose to play was an amalgam of two close acquaintances. In appearance, black-clad and brooding, festooned with outsize silver belts and baubles, Mick turned into Keith Richard. In voice and mannerisms, he turned himself almost uncannily into Brian Jones.

As Turner's girlfriend, Anita Pallenberg, at least, was perfectly cast. Everyone who knew her recognized the rangy blonde, dressed only in a marmalade-coloured fur, teasing the bewildered Chas with her green eyes and long, golden legs. Her role in the strange house, impermanent, indifferent, laughingly malevolent, corresponded exactly to her role within the Stones. Her part in disorienting the painfully straight young gangster chiefly lay in confusing him – as she had apparently confused Brian – about his sexual identity. At one point in Chas's ordeal, Anita holds a mirror up to his face, reflecting it above her own bare breast. The scene was to have a lasting effect on James Fox, and make more than one bystander remember the old whispers about Anita's supposed power as a sorceress.

It began as a joke between Mick and Keith that Donald Cammell's script required Turner and his girlfriend to make lingering love, together with an androgynous French girl, in the star's huge carved and canopied antique bed. After shooting had begun, however, Cammell realized that Keith was deeply uneasy about Anita's role as Mick's lover and, in particular, their simulation of sex together for the camera. 'And, of course, Anita didn't help his insecurity,' Cammell remembered. 'She seemed to be teasing Keith about wanting Mick, the way she'd teased Brian about wanting Keith. While we were shooting at Lowndes Square, Keith hardly ever came near the house. He'd sit outside in his car and send in messages.'

In the event, their screen encounter brought a resolution of the love-hate feeling which had so long smouldered between Anita and Mick. As the cameras turned, under a perfect alibi of fiction, the two began to make love in earnest. In its final, much-edited version, the film shows little more than Anita's lips nibbling Jagger's huge ones, and a cinematically fashionable tumble and twist of limbs. However, the off-cuts were illicitly spliced together into a separate short feature which, a few months later, won a prize at a festival of blue movies in Amsterdam.

Keith knew what had happened, though – like Brian before him – he somehow could not bring himself to accuse Anita outright. His retaliation was endlessly to postpone working with Mick on the single Jagger-Richard song required for the film – a song sung to Chas by Turner, transformed to a hallucinogenic gang boss. 'Keith just *refused* to get down to it,' Cammell said. 'I kept asking Mick "Where's the goddammed song?" Mick kept saying "It's okay, it'll be ready" but he knew very well what Keith was doing, and why.'

Finally, near desperation, Cammell himself sat down with Jagger to write a song they called Memo From Turner. When the Stones met to record it, Keith's antagonism remained all-pervading. 'With Keith against it in the studio, the song sounded just awful – still and lifeless,' Donald Cammell remembered. 'But without the song, we couldn't end the picture. Keith knew he had the power to sabotage the whole thing.

'In the end, I got Mick alone. I took him into a pub in Berwick Street and said, "Mick, for God's sake, what about the *song*?" Standing there at the bar, he suddenly burst into tears. It was a thing he could always do for maximum effect – just like John Gielgud. "I'm sorry," he said. "I blew it." It was then that I realized he'd decided to get the song finished. From then on, after all that indecisiveness, the decisions were made like *lightning*.'

Memo From Turner was re-recorded by Jagger with a studio full of high-powered session musicians, including Stevie Winwood and Jim Capaldi. This left *Performance* devoid of any Stones music, since its musical director, Jack Nitzsche, used American session men – notably slide guitarist Lowell George – to play over the film's opening and closing credits.

While Jagger worked on *Performance*, Marianne spent much of her time in Ireland, at a house in County Galway, rented from Molly Cusack Smith, Master of the local hunt, the Galway Blazers. It was a setting chosen to afford maximum peace and tranquillity during the middle and late phase of Marianne's pregnancy. She was determined to take every care, remembering how casual she had been while carrying Nicholas, and because her doctor had warned there might be complications. She thus remained unaware of the drama between Mick, Keith and Anita, engrossed by happy thoughts of what a father Mick would make. They both wanted a girl and had already chosen a name for her – Carena.

In the seventh month of pregnancy, despite all her care, Marianne lost the baby on which she and Jagger had pinned inordinate hope. Such things are never other than devastating. Like any other young couple, they cried out the cruel disappointment in each other's arms: two child-like figures, in that grown-up house, between whom the bond of love and sympathy could never be so strong again.

On December 5, *Beggars' Banquet* was released, four months late, clad in a tasteful buff-coloured sleeve adorned only with the title, the artists' name and 'R.S.V.P.'. The fight over the lavatory-wall sleeve had gone on well into October, with Decca continually postponing release dates until it seemed the Stones might not release an album at all in 1968. The result was inevitable: while the critics and public went wild about *Beggars' Banquet*, the Stones themselves were only bored by it.

Their attitude was made plain in the album's launch-party – a mock-ceremonial banquet at the Queensgate Hotel, attended by dignitaries such as the future British ambassador in Washington, Lord Harlech, and concluding in a custard-pie fight. Lord Harlech evidently enjoyed the pie-throwing. So did Les Perrin, whom one cameraman snapped, towering above the fray, oozing missile in hand, his usual decorum quite forgotten. Another lens caught Brian Jones slamming a pie into Mick Jagger's face, with what, bystanders agreed, seemed somewhat excessive force.

The mood of sarcastic bonhomie continued in a Christmas special Jagger had undertaken to do for BBC television – the famous *Rolling Stones Rock and Roll Circus*. Recorded over two days, December 11 and 12, at the old *Ready, Steady, Go* studios in Wembley, it featured the Stones in live performance with superstar friends such as John Lennon, Eric Clapton, The Who and Jethro Tull as supporting acts, interspersed with jugglers, lion-tamers and clowns. A certain similarity might have been detected to *Magical Mystery Tour*, the Beatles' TV special shown almost exactly a year previously, save that where the Beatles had sadly flopped, Mick Jagger was determined to have a hit.

During forty-eight hours of almost continuous filming, the *Rock and Roll Circus* presented its carnival-hatted and decibel-drowned big-top audience with many remarkable sights. There was John Lennon, dressed as a be-ruffed and stockinged juggler, accompanied by Yoko Ono in the black vestments of a witch. There was the blues musician Taj Mahal, in bewildering propinquity with the concert pianist Julius Katchen, the black fashion model Donyale Luna and the Merry Prankster Ken Kesey. There was the unprecedented novelty of seeing John Lennon play his song Yer Blues with an ad hoc group comprising Eric Clapton on lead guitar, Keith Richard on bass and Mitch Mitchell, from the Jimi Hendrix Experience, on drums, while Yoko crouched nearby, enveloped in a black bag. There was the more predictable surprise, during The Who's performance, when water spurted from Keith Moon's drums. There were the varied sideshow astonishments of seeing Mick Jagger dressed as a ring-master, posing with a tiger; Keith Richard as a vampire-faced, moustachioed stage-door Johnny; Brian Jones in a top hat sprouting satyr horns – a lecherously colourful figure, divorced from the small, defeated voice which gasped out his only line of dialogue: 'Here come the clowns.'

There was, finally, the Stones' own contribution, begun so far into the second night that most of the audience had gone home: a transfixing performance which ranged from old r & b favourites like Route 66 to a Jumpin' Jack Flash set about by lights which could actually damage eyesight, and, climactically, *six* takes of Sympathy For the Devil, with Jagger wrenching off his red T-shirt to reveal Satan daubed on his chest. The superstar cast then joined the stupefied audience to sing Salt of the Earth from a prompt-board, swaying from side to side.

Rock and Roll Circus was not televised that Christmas – nor ever. The veto was Mick Jagger's. He liked the film but not the way he himself looked in it, and he felt that the Stones had been upstaged by The Who.

On December 18, an apparently reconciled Mick and Keith took a ship for Rio de Janeiro, accompanied by Anita, Marianne and three-year-old Nicholas. They were to spend a month travelling through Latin America, reportedly enlarging their knowledge of magic by hobnobbing with headhunters and pygmies in the Amazonian rain forests. 'We are very serious about this trip,' Keith told the *Sunday Express*, 'We are hoping to see a magician who practises both black and white magic. He has a very long and difficult name which we can't pronounce – we just call him "Banana" for short.'

It was in fact to be a perfectly normal holiday. Mick had suggested Majorca before Marianne reminded him he was now a millionaire. To Keith, the most restful part was the sea voyage from Lisbon to Rio, among middle-aged people who drank pink gin, dressed for dinner each night and regarded the Jagger-Richard party as some sort of mysterious addition to the ship's entertainment programme. 'We used to see the same couple in the bar, who kept saying to us, "Who *are* you? What's it all about? Come on, give us a clue. Just give us a glimmer." That's when Mick and I started to call ourselves. The Glimmer Twins.'

Nicholas Dunbar remembers the holiday chiefly for the time he spent with his mother and Mick, living in a simple hut at the edge of a long, white beach. Every day, Mick would take him off to play or paddle, all the time gently helping him over the hurdles from babyhood to boyhood, showing him how to undo his own buttons to pee. 'I remember his voice saying, "Mind your feet on the sharp stones. Put on your sandals."'

Their only experience with magic occurred by accident, when they blundered into a celebration of macumba – voodoo rites which no outsiders were permitted to see. 'I remember when you and Mick got stoned,' Nicholas would say to Marianne in later life. 'I mean – I remember when those people started throwing stones at you.'

Back in London, at one of the parties that still happened every night, Miles, from the Indica Bookshop, caught a glimpse of his old Cheltenham friend, Brian Jones. There was the usual frock-coated finery, the gorget and flowered cravat, the wide-brimmed hat pressing his gold fringe down around his eyes and cheeks. There was the usual girl companion, blonde like himself – or like someone he both longed and dreaded to forget. In the midst of the party, Brian and the girl had both nodded off to sleep, their big hats and weary child faces together, amid the dancers and noise, innocent as babes in the wood.

Late one afternoon in January, 1969, John Lennon and Yoko Ono slipped furtively from a white Rolls-Royce, into the foyer of the Dorchester Hotel. The couple were by now almost indistinguishable, save for John's beard and Yoko Ono's air of continually propelling him forward. Five minutes later, in a bedroom overlooking Hyde Park, they finally came face to face with Allen Klein.

For Klein, it was an emotional moment. His desire for the Beatles, undiminished after four years, had seemed no closer to fulfilment in the eighteen months since Brian Epstein's death, notwithstanding the managerial chaos which Epstein had bequeathed: Klein had merely been one entrepreneur among many, watching the Beatles' Apple venture slide into disaster, and longing to apply drastic remedies. He had seen John Lennon with Yoko at the Stones' *Rock and Roll Circus* and, recognizing his isolation from the other Beatles, had bombarded Lennon's mansion with telephone calls, all to no avail. Then, in January 1969, Lennon had confessed to *Rolling Stone* magazine that, if Apple went on losing money at its present rate, he would be 'broke in six months'. Allen Klein's moment had come.

This short meeting with John and Yoko at the Dorchester

was, despite his own nerves, a virtuoso Klein performance. At its conclusion, Yoko sat down and, at John's dictation, typed a note to Sir Joseph Lockwood, Chairman of EMI: 'Dear Sir Joe – from now on, Allen Klein handles all my stuff.'

George Harrison and Ringo Starr met Klein a few days later, and were similarly impressed. His offer seemed irresistibly sensible. He would go into Apple and clear out the spongers and spendthrifts. He would then make them richer than even they, the Beatles, had ever dreamed, by gaining them control of the companies Brian Epstein had set up around them, and by renegotiating their royalty rate with EMI. George and Ringo, too, liked Klein's blunt manner and his picturesque fiscal imagery. 'Ya shouldn't even have to *think* about money,' he told them. 'You should be able to say "F.Y.M. – Fuck you, Money!" '

Paul McCartney, however, no longer saw Allen Klein as the Beatles' only possible saviour. McCartney never liked rough diamonds; he had, moreover, almost persuaded the others to hire his prospective father-in-law, the New York lawyer Lee Eastman, to take over Apple and fight the two boardroom battles they now faced. McCartney attended only one meeting with Klein, and walked out soon after it had begun. This, apparently, mortified Klein almost to the extent of abandoning his dream. 'It was an ego thing,' his nephew, Ronnie Schneider, says. 'He wanted all *four* of them to like him. I told him that was crazy. "What the hell!" I said. "It's a majority decision." '

McCartney's dislike, and the Eastman family's contempt, merely stiffened the others' resolve to bring in Klein as their manager. It was in vain even for Lee Eastman to point out how low Klein's reputation stood in New York as a result of the Cameo-Parkway affair, and that he now faced prosecution from the US Internal Revenue Service on ten counts of failing to file income tax returns.

As with the Stones in 1966, Klein had offered his 'Let me show you what I can do before I take a cent of your money' ploy.

He would work unofficially, in 'co-operation' with the Eastmans, looking into Apple's financial plight while they dealt with boardroom strategy, but taking no percentage until *all* the Beatles were ready to put their trust in him.

The news brought a curious response from Mick Jagger, who had recommended Klein to the Beatles so many times over the years, but who was now heard to tell John Lennon on the telephone: 'You're making the biggest mistake of your life.'

Jagger had returned from South America with a deep tan that faded almost as quickly as his pleasure in the unpretentious life. Plans were now under way to re-shoot *Rock and Roll Circus* in circumstances guaranteeing that the Stones would not be upstaged again. The circus-ring this time was to be the Colosseum in Rome. Ronnie Schneider, at Klein's office, had actually booked the immortal ruin as backdrop for Mick's second take. 'I went to Michael Lindsay-Hogg [the director] and told him "Okay, you got the Colosseum." But he said he wouldn't know what to shoot there.'

Problems were reported, too, from the Warner Brothers Corporation, whose executives had now seen *Performance* and realized it was no happy-go-lucky pop farce. At an early screening, the wife of one WB man was so overcome with nausea, she actually vomited. Despite angry representations, that included a telegram jointly from Donald Cammell and Jagger, Warner Brothers refused to consider releasing *Performance* until it had been extensively cut and re-edited.

Early in 1969, Jagger was offered a second film – a starring role this time, and one so bizarrely out of character, he could not help be both flattered and challenged. He agreed to play Ned Kelly, in a film about the nineteenth-century Australian bandit and folk hero. The director was to be Tony Richardson, whose Woodfall Film company had made, among other things, the excellent *Charge of the Light Brigade*. As an extra inducement, Marianne Faithfull was given the supporting part of Kelly's girlfriend. Shooting was to begin in Australia, the following July.

The necessity of planning the year ahead – and, in particular, the American tour that was becoming ever more crucial – raised yet again a problem Jagger, no less than the other Stones, had long shrunk from facing. By May 1969, the decision could no longer be postponed. Some way would have to be found of dumping Brian Jones.

It was not, even now, a decision taken lightly. All Brian's hopelessness over the past three years could not cancel out the bonds of their early friendship – the realization that, without Brian, none of them might be where they were today. Even last year, confident of what seemed a bottomless income, the Stones could afford to keep on carrying Brian. This year, in an atmosphere of worsening financial anxiety, they couldn't afford *not* to jettison him.

With two drug busts on his record, Brian hadn't a hope of getting the work permit necessary for a major American tour. The fact that he had appealed successfully against this second conviction – on January 13 – was not likely to soften the hearts of US Immigration officials.

Brian was living out of London now, in surroundings as far removed as they possibly could have been from any of his metropolitan harems. In November 1968, he had paid £38,000 for Cotchford Farm near Harefield, Essex, former home of A. A. Milne, the creator of Winnie-the-Pooh. Since Milne's death in 1956, the property had been maintained as a semi-public national monument, its grounds dotted with shrines to the immortal 'bear of very little brain', his owner Christopher Robin and their friends Piglet, Eeyore and Rabbit. Brian's journey through the Sixties, from Cheltenham to Windsor, Chelsea and Morocco could hardly have ended in a more unlikely final resting place: the House at Pooh Corner.

Jagger had special reason to feel a resurgence of sympathy for Brian. Since Brain's departure from Chelsea, the local police had been obliged to find an alternative Stone to harass and pursue. Recently, as Jagger was riding along the King's Road with his new young chauffeur, Alan Dunn, a patrol car had flagged down his Rolls, and two officers had demanded to search both Jagger and the car. Jagger had refused, ordering Dunn to lock the car and then telephone for his solicitor to come straight there.

On May 28 – the day his film role as Ned Kelly was announced – Jagger opened the door at Cheyne Walk to behold the very CID man who had last busted Brian, accompanied by half a dozen other officers. 'I didn't get the chance to say anything,' Jagger commented later. 'One of them stuck his foot in the door and the rest came barging in. They put me in the dining room while they searched the place.' Within a few minutes, the squad had unearthed a small wooden box containing approximately one quarter-ounce of cannabis.

Jagger and Marianne were taken to Chelsea police station and charged under the usual act. Next day, they appeared together at Great Marlborough Street Court, to plead not guilty to possessing cannabis. The magistrate adjourned the case until June 23, remanding each on £50 bail.

Finding himself in Brian Jones's place as the Chelsea drug squad's favourite target was a salutary lesson to Jagger that Brian's catastrophes had not all been self-induced. Though Brian must be sacked if the Stones were to survive, Jagger now agreed it must be on terms as tactful and generous as possible. The offer, worked out in consultation with Allen Klein, was that Brian be asked to leave primarily to allow the Stones to go on tour in America. As far as the press and the fans were concerned, it would be only a temporary absence, to allow him to work on solo projects like his *Jajouka* album. As well as his royalty share from past Stones albums, a settlement of £100,000 would acknowledge the Stones' debt to his musicianship and personality.

Tact and consideration were evident in the method chosen by Jagger to prepare Brian for the approaching shock. He and

Keith separately got in touch with Alexis Korner, the Stones' – especially Brian's – old blues mentor. 'Mick and Keith told me Brian was sick and they were worried about him,' Korner remembered. 'Because he wouldn't talk to them, or didn't trust them, they asked me if I'd go down to his place and see him.' Remembering the boy who had parachute-rolled through the kitchen window at Moscow Road – his neat Italian suit, and 'beautiful mixture of good manners and rudeness' – Korner agreed to try to do what he could.

Twelve

'He hath awakened from the dream of life'

Mary Hallett knew Cotchford Farm better than did either of its two famous owners, the author and the pop star. She was born there, in the great, secure age when Sussex was a remote county, and the sixteenth-century house served merely as adjunct to hard-working land, shared by two farm labourers and their large Edwardian families. Mary was one of eight children who helped their father with the haymaking and milking, and rescued lambs from winter snowdrifts before the crows could peck out their eyes.

When A. A. Milne owned Cotchford in the Twenties, Mary Hallett lived still only a few minutes' walk away. She remembered the author's shiny motor car, and the celebrity enjoyed by Milne's small son, on whom Christopher Robin had been modelled. 'He *was* a dear little chap – but he was a mischief, too. He used to like my brother, who worked at the stables, to shut him up inside the horses' feed-bins.'

Forty years later, after her birthplace had changed from labourer's cottage to rich man's country mansion, with trim lawns, topiary bushes – even a swimming pool – Mary Hallett got to know Cotchford Farm all over again. Its present owner, an American named Taylor, needed help in the house because his wife had fallen ill. It was arranged that Mary should go in every day for the Taylors to clean and keep house.

The news that the Taylors were moving from Cotchford, in November, 1968, and that it had been bought by a Rolling Stone, who intended to live there permanently, caused Mrs Hallett understandable dismay. Though not specially prejudiced against the Rolling Stones – being of a generation unable to tell one pop group from another – she had read and heard enough about such people to know she probably would not get on with them. At the new owner's request, however, she agreed to continue coming in on a trial basis. So, with many misgivings, she made the acquaintance of Brian Jones.

It was an experience which caused her to revise her idea of pop musicians as drunken louts. 'You couldn't have wished for a nicer, more polite boy. In all the months I worked for him, he was kindness itself to me. And always so well mannered. With Brian, it was never "I want . . ." or "Do this . . ." It was always "Please, Mrs Hallett, would you mind . . ."

'Nobody could have been more generous. After I'd started working for him, he discovered I wasn't on the telephone. Straight away, he had a phone installed for me – and the bill was always paid. Whenever it rang, I'd always half expect to hear Brain's voice. "Oh, Mrs Hallett . . ." he'd say, so woebegone. "I *can't* get this fire started. *Do* you think you could come over?"

'It was a pleasure to work for him – he was so appreciative of every little thing. We had a long talk together one day while I was cleaning and he was sitting at the kitchen table. I'd seen him reading this big, old-fashioned family Bible, like the one we used to have when I was a girl. I discovered he knew his Bible very well – better than I did. I always had the feeling he was a very lonely boy. After I'd been out shopping, I often used to come home and find Brian sitting and waiting for me on my front door step.'

*

It was at Cotchford Farm that Brian Jones, one evening late in May, finally ceased to be a Rolling Stone. Mick Jagger and Keith Richard drove down together from London to do the job they had postponed for more than a year, accompanied – as a further instrument of clemency – by Charlie Watts. Even Charlie, kind-hearted as he was, realized there was no other way.

The moment was not as traumatic as everyone had expected. Mick and Keith pretended not to be firing Brian for ever; he, in turn, pretended he was glad to go. They agreed the press should be told he was leaving voluntarily, because of musical differences with the others. Brian undertook to say nothing of the matter until Mick and Keith could find someone to replace him. The four broke up on friendly terms. Then Brian went into his kitchen, laid his head on the scrubbed wooden table, and wept.

Despite his promise of secrecy, he could not resist telephoning the Stones office next day and confiding in his great ally, Jo Bergman. 'He said, "You will go on doing things for me, won't you, even when I'm not in the Stones?" I said, "Oh, of *course*, Brian, for goodness' sake . . ."' Peter Jones, the music journalist, met him in London that same week, wearing a look that was half-shamefaced, half-triumphant, as if he had done something very silly but couldn't help feeling pleased.

Alexis Korner, on visits to Cotchford, found Brian excited by the challenge of starting again in what was, after all, the prevailing fashion among top musicians. Eric Clapton had disbanded the hugely successful Cream, to link up with Stevie Winwood, from Traffic, in the experimental heavy metal group Blind Faith. Graham Nash had left the Hollies, uniting with Steven Stills of Buffalo Springfield and Dave Crosby of the Byrds, to form Crosby, Stills and Nash. With Brian's reputation and his circle of virtuoso friends like Lennon, Townshend and Hendrix – so Korner reasoned – he would not be without a band for long.

He was talking already about starting a pure blues outfit, on the model of Korner's Blues Incorporated but with the cutting-edge of new American groups like the Allmann Brothers and Creedence Clearwater Revival. It was the time of Creedence's first great 'swamp-rock' hit, Proud Mary. John Fogarty's voice, rasping against the lazy paddle-wheel beat, echoed repeatedly through Cotchford Farm as Brian poured out his plans to Alexis Korner. 'He was excited in a vague way,' Korner remembered later. 'He'd start to talk, then he'd stop and put on another Creedence record, slurring the needle across it. Then he'd have a different idea. He and I would form a new band together and take it on the road. At that point, I had to say, "Now, hold *on*, Brian . . ."'

On his first trip down to Cotchford to pave the way for Mick and Keith, Korner had been shocked by the change in Brain's appearance – by his haggard face, his developing paunch, in particular his complexion, bloated white and glistening, 'like old, cold fat'.

He had greatly improved since then, helped by the country air, the constant, restful quiet and, not a little, by Cotchford Farm's powerful association with a tranquil, secure world of childhood. Knowing the Winnie-the-Pooh stories almost by heart as he did, it gave him special delight to show Alexis the statue of Christopher Robin in the garden, the sundial – under which Milne's original manuscripts are reputedly buried – and the bridge over the little stream where Pooh and Christopher Robin invented their Poohsticks game. He felt proud to be the guardian of such a shrine, as if the money he paid for the house had brought him an extra gift of responsibility and trust.

He had managed to stay off drugs, he told Alexis – was, indeed, so terrified of being busted again that he would not allow so much as a joint to be rolled under his roof. He was drinking less, too, forsaking whisky and brandy for beer and white wine. But for his asthma – the recurrent problem that caused him to keep a small inhaler always with him in summer time – he could be believed when he said he hadn't felt so good in years.

He was insistent that Alexis should spend regular weekends at Cotchford with his wife, Bobbie, and their daughter, Sappho. The Korners both remembered Brian's excitement, one weekend, at having persuaded his parents to come from Cheltenham soon and stay a whole week. 'He wanted to show them he lived in a *real* house,' Alexis Korner said. 'That seemed important – proving to his father that his music had brought him to a quite conventional end.'

Happily excited as he was, there still remained fears and anxieties that Brian would confide to Alexis as they sat in the ingle-nooked living room or – as summer drew on – outside, next to the swimming pool.

Chief among his anxieties was a gnawing suspicion that Mick and Keith's clemency might be no more than some elaborate game; that, having persuaded him to leave the Stones, they might now be plotting to renege on the terms of the agreement. The promised £100,000 had not yet been paid. Brian needed money, both to support his superstar lifestyle and to maintain so large and extensive a property.

To renovate the farmhouse he had employed a builder named Frank Thorogood, a schoolfriend of Tom Keylock whom Keylock had first brought in to do extensive work for Keith Richards at Redlands. On top of the £32,000 Brian had paid for Cotchford Farm, he was committed to £10,000-worth of improvements by Thorogood and a four-man gang hired in Chichester. The work ranged from restoring antique beams in the kitchen and making a new stone floors upstairs, to draining and levelling a large field behind the house.

Unofficially, Frank Thorogood's job was to keep an eye on Brian during Tom Keylock's frequent absences on service for the other Stones. Keylock gave him the power to draw money from the Stones' London office to pay incidental expenses. He even moved in to Cotchford Farm, living through the week in a flatlet above the garage and returning to his wife and family at weekends.

Brian's soft-heartedness and need of friends made not only Thorogood, but also the most temporary workmen free of his home, his food and wine. Mary Hallett, his housekeeper, remembered that Thorogood spent much of the time sitting around the house with Brian, sunning himself in the garden or swimming in the pool.

Sometimes even Brian would complain to Alexis about Frank Thorogood. Then his mood would change again: he would put on Proud Mary, and talk further about blues bands yet unformed. The Korners would leave him in his Winnie-the-Pooh garden, stretched out along the diving board of his bright blue swimming-pool, staring up into a sky almost as blue as it used to be in Morocco.

Mick Taylor was eight years old when he saw his first guitar. His parents – themselves young enough to be rock 'n' roll fans – had taken him to a Bill Haley concert at the Golders Green Hippodrome. Between the baby-faced small boy and the glinting, amber silhouette on Haley's chest there passed a charge which was to give the boy's life thereafter a wonderful simplicity. All he thought of was getting a guitar, learning to play it, then playing it better and better. By the age of twelve, he was sought after by every amateur group in Hatfield, Hertfordshire, the drab aero-engineering suburb where his father worked as a fitter for de Havilland Ltd.

Shy and quiet as he usually was, the guitar gave Mick Taylor nerve enough for anything. At fourteen, he went to see a concert by John Mayall's Bluesbreakers, featuring Eric Clapton, in nearby Welwyn Garden City. He talked his way backstage, only to find that Eric Clapton hadn't turned up that night. The fourteen-year-old schoolboy persuaded John Mayall to let him play lead guitar in Eric Clapton's place.

He was still only seventeen when John Mayall asked him to become the Bluesbreakers' lead guitarist as a replacement for yet another graduate from that seminary of British rock. Peter Green, who had succeeded Clapton, was now leaving, with bass-player John McVie, to form Fleetwood Mac. One day, Mick Taylor was at school in Hatfield. The next, he was on the road as star instrumentalist in Britain's best, as well as busiest, pure blues band.

He remained with John Mayall for four years, playing almost every night, refining his technique and also strengthening his nerves under the autocratic leader who would train up such brilliant pupils only for so long as they threatened no direct rivalry to himself. 'John was a great eccentric,' Taylor says. 'He'd lived in a tree once – somewhere near Manchester. He collected erotica and wore all his harmonicas on a belt round his waist. And every conversation you had with him, he'd record on a tiny little tape.'

In May 1969, when John Mayall announced yet another reshuffle of the Bluesbreakers, Mick Taylor realized he had become too good for Mayall's peace of mind, and had better find employment elsewhere. Then, one night, John Mayall rang him up in Paddington and asked if he fancied becoming lead guitarist in the Rolling Stones. Mick Jagger had asked Mayall, along with many other people, to nominate a successor to Brian Jones. Mayall had recommended his ex-pupil as the best young virtuoso in contemporary rock. It was arranged that Taylor should meet the Stones at Olympic Studios, during sessions for the album that would become *Let It Bleed*.

He went along, very nervous, thinking the Stones needed someone only for temporary session work. 'I'd never met any of them before. The only one I'd ever seen was Mick Jagger, sprinting down the King's Road one day with a pack of photographers after him.

'I met their producer, Jimmy Miller, first. Then the Stones themselves started drifting in. Keith, I remember, arrived about three hours late. It was all very easy and friendly. The track they were working on was Live With Me. I gave them a riff – it seemed to work in well. I still thought I was being auditioned to play just on the one album. It wasn't until the end of the session that I realized they were asking me to join them.'

The deal offered by Jagger was not instant full membership. Mick Taylor would join the Stones initially as an employee, for a salary of £150 per week. Only if things proved satisfactory would he receive a share of their concert fees and record royalties.

On June 9, Les Perrin's office was finally allowed to give the prearranged story to the press that Brian Jones had 'resigned' from the Rolling Stones because of disagreements over musical policy. His replacement would be a twenty-year-old unknown whom first newspaper pictures revealed to be so angelically boyish, with his round, clear face and thick, wavy hair, there was even some speculation that the Stones might be turning into middle-aged pederasts. It was further noted of this apparently willing sacrifice to decadence incarnate that he neither drank nor smoked, and was into macrobiotic food.

To reporters who reached him on the telephone at Cotchford, Brian dutifully gave the same story of a regretful decision to quit the Stones 'because I no longer see eye to eye with the others over the discs we are cutting . . . I have a desire to play my own brand of music . . . We have agreed that an amicable termination of our relationship is the only answer.'

The plan to induct Mick Taylor into the Stones slowly, by way of album-sessions, was thrown suddenly into reverse, however, when Mick Jagger accepted an invitation from Eric Clapton to the debut performance of his new supergroup, Blind Faith. The concert took place in Hyde Park and – extraordinary innovation! – was free of charge to its audience. The result exceeded all expectations. A crowd of 150,000 carpeted the greensward, from Marble Arch back to the Serpentine. They could hear the metal thunder, that afternoon, in boroughs as distant as Fulham and Notting Hill.

Jagger was astonished by the size – and benevolent spirit – of the Blind Faith audience. Being Jagger, too, he could not help but wonder how much larger an impromptu audience he himself might be capable of attracting. There and then, with Keith, he sought out a representative of the concert organizers, Blackhill Enterprises, and offered to appear at a similar event with the Stones, on the very earliest date it could be arranged. Within hours, an announcement went forth which seemed to confirm this new mood of generosity among rock stars. The Rolling Stones, with their new guitarist Mick Taylor, would give a free concert in Hyde Park on Saturday, July 5.

They never intended it to inaugurate the era after Brian. Jagger had even rung Shirley Arnold at the Stones' office, and asked her to try to persuade Brian to come.

Her name was Helen Spittal – though, in the ordinary course of events, no one would have bothered to ask it. Her face was pointed and pale, her hair regulation madonna-length; round her neck, in the same state of readiness as a gunslinger's Colt 45, she carried a cheap Instamatic camera. She was sixteen years old and, despite the fierce-elbowing competition all around her, was recognizably Brian Jones's greatest fan.

She had begun as merely a Stones fan, willing to get up at 5 a.m. and walk from her parents' home in Hampton across to Barnes, in the faint hope of seeing the Stones emerge from Olympic Studios after recording all night. Albums full of Instamatic prints, taken in bad light, showed the invariable friendliness of these encounters – mostly with Mick Jagger. 'I never used to see Brian at Olympic that much. Once when he was there, he came across and blew me up for being out so early in the morning by myself, and worrying my parents.'

To Helen, Brian was never other than friendly, considerate – in a strange way, even fatherly. He would usually chide her for being out so early, or so late, and for neglecting her school work. With this, his greatest idolator, he, paradoxically, lost all pretence, posing for her Instamatic camera with a resigned and hangdog, 'God I look awful' grin. In one blurred London street shot, taken by someone else, the little girl he cuddles close to him could be his daughter or niece. His reputation as a sexual buccaneer is something which, to this day, Helen Spittal finds hard to accept.

Knowing Brian's fondness for Helen, and vaguely perceiving her beneficial effect on him, the Stones' office gave her privileges allowed no other fan. Tom Keylock would tell her when they were next recording at Olympic. Shirley Arnold would relay her messages to Brian, and his back to her.

'He'd often said he'd invite me down to Sussex, to see Cotchford Farm. A few days after he'd left the Stones, I got a message from Shirley that Brian wanted me to ring him. While we were talking, he suddenly asked me if I'd like to go down there and spend the day.'

Every minute of that day remains vivid in Helen's mind. She went by train to Haywards Heath, telephoned Brain from the station, and he sent a local mini-cab to collect her. She arrived at Cotchford Farm in dazzling sunshine. Brian was waiting for her in the driveway, with his two dogs. He wore the striped matelot shirt she always pictured him in, with red and black striped trousers and an old, scuffed pair of canvas shoes.

Even Helen's uncritical eye could not help but notice his poor physical state – in particular, the sagging paunch under his shirt. Brian himself was painfully conscious of this. Walking with her round the garden, proudly pointing out the sundial and Christopher Robin statue, he agreed to be photographed only on condition the prints never left her private album.

Inside the house she made the acquaintance of Anna Wohlin, a twenty-three-year-old Swede who had moved in with Brian only three weeks previously. Anna had been visiting London regularly since 1962 and had become a fringe member of the Stones' circle, chumming up also with Jimi Hendrix, Rod Stewart and the Yardbirds. Brian had known her vaguely for some months, but had only taken a serious interest in her early in 1969 as his affair with Suki Poitier began to wane. He had in fact bought Cotchford Farm with the intention of living there with Suki. But their relationship was founded less on passion than friendship and mutual commiseration for the loss of Tara Browne. Besides, Suki was a city girl who became uneasy if she ventured more than a couple of miles from Chelsea's King's Road.

To Helen Spittal, the young Swede seemed like yet another stand-in for Anita Pallenberg with her rangy figure, pale blonde hair and huge, star-lashed eyes. Anna herself would maintain that, on the contrary, Brian had fallen in love with her as a person in her own right, that their relationship had brought him happiness and emotional stability, and that they planned to marry and start a family.

Certainly, the household at Cotchford seemed cosy and happy enough. Brian got on well with his housekeeper, Mrs Hallett, and his gardener, Mick. Always fond of animals, he had acquired an Afghan hound named Luther, a cocker spaniel named Emily and three spaniel puppies. One day, while out driving with Anna, he saw an injured cat lying in the road after having been hit by another driver. Brian tenderly scooped up the cat, drove it to the nearest vet and paid for it to be nursed back to health.

A trusting, home-loving young woman, Anna cooked Brian's meals, pandered to his every whim and made herself scarce whenever his rock star friends drove down from London to visit him. One she specially remembered was John Lennon, himself still unwillingly shackled to a supergroup, who urged Brian to get out of the Stones and repeated his terse advice, 'Don't weaken', many times subsequently over the telephone.

The only blot on the landscape seemed to be the builder Frank Thorogood, who seemed to have an almost mesmeric hold over Brian. Thorogood regarded himself as one of the family, eating dinner with Brian and Anna every night, ordering groceries for his building crew on Brian's account, inviting them to help themselves to fresh vegetables from the farm's kitchen garden. According to Anna, Thorogood even made a clumsy attempt to seduce her. Nor was the costly restoration work proving to be of high quality. One day as Anna stood in the kitchen, a newly installed ceiling beam came crashing down, missing her only by a few inches.

Since Helen Spittal clearly offered no threat, Anna welcomed her in a friendly way and the two became good friends as the day progressed. Anna told Helen that Brian was now completely off drugs and was terrified when any of his visitors – like Keith – brought them into the house. When Anna had moved in, she said, Brian had gone through her luggage and even her toilet things to make sure they did not contain even mildly illegal substances.

For most of the afternoon, the three sat beside the swimming pool, drinking wine and talking while Frank Thorogood moved around in the distance on what seemed to Helen to be somewhat desultory building work. She asked whether Brian was going to the Stones' free concert in Hyde Park, two Saturdays from now. He said he didn't think so. 'The way the Stones feel about me now,' he added, 'I'd probably be the only one they charged to go in.'

He talked a lot about Creedence Clearwater Revival, saying *that* was the kind of music he wanted to play from now on. He insisted on taking Helen into the house to hear Proud Mary on the stereo system he kept in his bedroom. While it was playing, she remembers, Brian looked out of the window and saw Frank Thorogood in the garden. 'He suddenly went all strange. He said something like "That man's not doing what he's *supposed* to be doing . . ."'

Later, Helen sat downstairs on Brian's lime green velvet sofa while he talked about his plans for a new group and meditatively strummed a Gibson Firebird guitar. 'He was asking me about my exams at school. I told him I'd got an English exam the very next day. He got quite annoyed – he told me I ought to be at home, revising for it. Then he insisted I ring my parents, to let them know I was all right.'

In the evening, the girls watched *Top of the Pops* on television. Anna cooked a chicken for dinner, which was served in the dining room. Brian didn't eat, but wandered back and forth, under the low beams, drinking from the bottle of red wine in his hand. He kept saying how much he loved being at Cotchford – how when he died, he wanted to be buried there.

Wednesday, July 2, was an uneventful day at Cotchford Farm – hot, sunny and quiet but for the coo of doves and the drone of bees. It was a day on which the high pollen count brought suffering to asthma and hay-fever victims all over Britain. As she worked around the house, Mary Hallett could hear Brian wheezing in distress and the frequent hiss of the decongestant inhaler which, in this long hot spell, he had seldom let out of his sight.

Midway through the afternoon, Mrs Hallett remembered, Brian took a phone call which made him forget his asthma and put him in a state of euphoria. 'He came running up to me and said, "My money's coming through from America at last! Everything's going to be all right!"'

Frank Thorogood, as usual, had three or four of his workmen dispersed around the grounds. At about 6 p.m., the crew drove away and Thorogood retired to his pied-à-terre above the garage, where he was to spend the evening with a young woman named Janet Lawson. Anna Wohlin would later remember Brian's annoyance that Thorogood was using the flatlet 'like a hotel'.

Brian and Anna spent the early part of the evening drinking and watching Rowan and Martin's *Laugh-In* show on television. Brian still fulminated against Thorogood, threatening to have the Stones' office stop all further payments to the builder. But at about 10:30 p.m., his mood suddenly changed. He walked over to the garage flatlet and asked Thorogood and Janet Lawson to join Anna and him for a drink beside the swimming pool. Thorogood would later testify that Brian already seemed fairly drunk, that his gait was unsteady and his speech slurred.

Thorogood and his lady friend made their way to the rustic bench at the pool's shallow end where Brian and Anna were already seated with bottles of brandy, whisky and vodka. Two spotlights, which Thorogood's men had just installed, shone down on the blue-tiled, motionless water.

The four between them almost finished the brandy and vodka and drank about half the bottle of whisky. From time to time Brian would swallow a black pill, a legally prescribed downer such as he always took at night to calm his nerves and fears and ease him towards sleep on the mingling streams of music and alcohol.

But tonight, the downers seemed to have lost their usual calming effect. Still in a state of euphoria that he was to be paid off from the Stones at last, Brian found it increasingly difficult to sit still. At around midnight, he stood up and announced he was going in for a swim. Janet Lawson – who, ironically, happened to be a trained nurse – told him he shouldn't go into the water after drinking so much. Anna, too, protested, saying she was tired and wanted to go to bed. Brian took no notice of them and went into the house to change. When he reappeared in his swimming trunks, Thorogood, the minder he did not know he had, offered to go into the water with him.

Thorogood, as he would later admit, was also very drunk, but managed to play the part of rock star's faithful pal, helping Brian to mount the springboard over the ten-foot deep end. Hitting the water was hardly a shock, since Brian had turned the thermostat up to eighty degrees. Both men as they swam seemed 'sluggish' to Janet Lawson, she would later say, but they seemed to be feeling no serious ill-effects.

Anna also agreed to swim but quickly came out, complaining that she was cold, and went into the house to change. Janet, who

Introducing Mick Taylor, June 1969. *(Hulton Getty)*

The Sympathy for the Devil session, minus witches. *(Hulton Getty)*

Top left: Fancy dress for the never-to-be-released Rolling Stones Rock 'n' Roll Circus. *(Rex Features)*

Left: Bianca watches her marriage end on her wedding day. *(Rex Features)*

Above: Brian's funeral, July 1969. *(Hulton Getty)*

Darkness closes in on Altamont. *(Robert Altman/Retna Limited, USA)*

Trying to hide the Lips in leylandii in the early days with Jerry.
(Laslo Veres/Hulton Getty)

The Glimmer Twins with Keith's son, 1973. *(Michael Putland/Retna)*

Above: Ronnie and the first Mrs Wood, 1979.

Right: Jagger, Wyman and Paul McCartney, 1978. *(Michael Putland/Retna)*

Bill Wyman and Mandy Smith. 'I'm like a kid with a new toy.' *(Retna)*

Voodoo Lounge, 1995. *(Rikken/Sunshine/Retna)*

The last of the old line-up. *(Rex Features)*

Keith discovers bad hair, 1999. *(Sam Wix/Retna)*

Mick and grown-up Jade party together. *(Richard Young/Rex Features)*

Mick, Jerry and daughter Elizabeth. *(Rex Features)*

Wembley, 1999. 'All other rock stars are still only his apprentices.'
(Howard Denner/Retna)

could not swim herself and was bored with watching, followed Anna inside. A few moments later, as he would later testify, Thorogood emerged from the pool and walked towards the house in search of cigarettes.

As Thorogood appeared at the back door, he met Janet on her way outside again. He later remembered that, as he reached the living room, the telephone began to ring. Anna came running downstairs, calling out that it was for her. At that moment, they both heard Janet shout for help.

The builder and the Swedish girl rushed out to the pool. The spotlights showed Brian at the deep end, lying face down at the bottom, his golden hair floating around him like a spread fan.

Shirley Arnold's parents in South London had just acquired their very first telephone. It rang for the first time sometime after midnight on July 3. Shirley herself picked up the receiver.

'It was Tom Keylock's wife. She said something like, "Brian went into the swimming pool but he didn't come out again." I thought she meant he'd wandered off into the woods or something, and they couldn't find him. Even when I put down the receiver, I still thought she was saying Brian had got lost.

'I rang her back a few moments later and said "Have they found him?" "No," she said. "You don't understand. He's dead."'

Thorogood had initially tried to contact Tom Keylock, but had found Keylock neither at home nor with his alternative masters. Earlier in the day, he had driven down from London to West Wittering to pick up two guitars which Keith Richard needed for that night's recording session. Though the journey took Keylock quite close to Cotchford Farm, he saw no reason to call in there. Since the Stones' session would not begin until very late, Keylock took his time on the journey, stopping to have a meal at a place he can remember now only as 'some sort of country club'.

By the time he reached Olympic Studios with Keith's two guitars, the Stones had been contacted, and were sitting round in an incredulous daze. 'We think Brian's dead,' Mick Jagger told him.

Keylock and Les Perrin arrived at Cotchford Farm together, shortly after 3.30 a.m. They found the garden overrun with police. Brian's body had already been removed. At the poolside there remained only the towel on which, apparently, his companions had rested his head while trying to revive him.

The size of the police contingent, and their overtly sceptical attitude, clearly indicated suspicion that drugs were involved somewhere. As Les Perrin walked round the pool-edge, he spotted Brian's asthma-inhaler lying on the grass. 'Very clever, Mr Perrin,' was the sarcastic reply of the officer to whom he pointed this out. 'You're working like a good PR man. What did you do – drop it down your trouser-leg?'

Keylock, meanwhile, drove off to collect Frank Thorogood from East Grinstead police station and hear the builder's account of how Brian Jones had died. Thorogood said he had made three attempts to reach Brian before getting a grip on his hair strong enough to raise him to the surface. Thorogood and Anna Wohlin had together lifted him from the pool, and Janet Lawson, with her nurse's training, had attempted artificial respiration, pumping water from Brian's mouth and massaging his chest. When this had no effect, Anna had tried the 'kiss of life' method. At one point as she knelt over him, she had felt Brian's hand grip hers. There was no other movement.

The story broke in that morning's *Daily Mirror* – a brief stop press item, under a '3:30 a.m., latest' sticker, by Les Perrin's old Fleet Street crony, Don Short. London's two evening papers, the *News* and *Standard*, confirmed it at midday in identical one-inch banner headlines, BRIAN JONES DEAD IN POOL TRAGEDY.

It was a story to delight the simplistic heart of every

mass-circulation feature writer. The following day's *Mail*, *Mirror*, *Express* and *Sketch*, in addition to front-page follow-ups on Brian's death, all carried lengthy inside spreads, chronicling his boyhood in Cheltenham, his rise to fame as a Stone, his illegitimate children, his drug busts, the bizarre coincidence of his having died at the House at Pooh Corner. The *Express* story took its headline from Alexis Korner's assertion that, since Brian split from the Stones, 'he had never been happier'. The *Mail* ended by quoting portentously from Winnie-the-Pooh's search for his hidden treasure trove. '"That's funny – I know I had a jar of honey there . . ." Brian Jones had the honey, labelled for all to see. But when he reached for it, it never seemed to be there . . .'

Of the many pop celebrities asked to comment on Brian's death, only two managed anything memorable. George Harrison said, 'I don't think he had enough love or understanding.' Pete Townshend of The Who, with somewhat greater insight, said, 'It's a normal day for Brain . . . like, he died every day, you know.'

The Stones themselves, taxed with that perennial news-hound's question, 'How do you feel?', could only mumble that they felt devastated, and try to carry on with the day's business, an appearance on BBC-TV's *Top of the Pops* show to launch their new single, Honky Tonk Women.

Afterwards, all of them drifted back to the Maddox Street office as if reluctant to lose the solace of being together. 'They were all in a terrible state,' Shirley Arnold says. 'Charlie was crying. Mick kept wandering to and fro and tripping over a dog's bowl that was on the floor.' Shirley herself had spoken to Brian by telephone on the day of his death, and had afterwards written him a long letter saying she'd always do anything she could to help him. Mick Taylor – who had never met Brian – could only sit there, inwardly noting 'a sense of inevitability, as if everyone had been half-expecting it to happen.'

The immediate question was whether they should go ahead

with the Hyde Park free concert in two days' time. Jagger said it was too late to cancel an event on which thousands were depending – and for which he, personally, had already accepted some considerable inconvenience. The day after the concert, he was due to fly to Australia to start work on *Ned Kelly*. The film's producers, in a state of agitation since Jagger's cannabis bust, had only just learned that his bail from Great Marlborough Street Court would allow him to travel abroad. They now feared that the free concert on July 5 would give him an excuse not to be on set, as promised, on July 9. They had even hinted that, if he sang in Hyde Park on Saturday and didn't appear in Australia the following Monday, they'd sue him.

It was Charlie Watts, sitting dejectedly in his corner, who first mumbled the notion that would save the fans' treat and also not waste the special souvenir number of the *Evening Standard* already in preparation, the six Granada TV crews already in transit, the stage outfit already chosen by Jagger at the Mr Fish boutique, and the expenditure already incurred from hiring such disparate items as potted palm trees, African tribal dancers and a military armoured personnel-carrier.

'Couldn't we do it as . . . sort of a memorial to Brian?'

Cavalry officers from Knightsbridge Barracks, cantering in pairs round the outer sand track, were not, as usual, Hyde Park's earliest visitors that summer Saturday morning. As the sun climbed over feathery horse chestnut trees and the dew glittered dry on new-cut grass, a few figures had already begun to stir in the encampment of sleeping-bags, strewn for several hundred yards all around a flimsy, low-lying wooden stage. Cavalry officers trotted on with averted eyes. Ducks, coots and black-faced Canada geese swooped in from their island colony and massed along the Serpentine edge, as if sensing better than usual pickings today.

By mid-morning, every quarter of Swinging London had registered a noticeable drop in population. The Portobello Road antique fair, the boutiques and hypermarkets along Kensington High Street, the pubs of Chelsea, Fulham and Bayswater, all seemed unaccountably quiet. For the present, only taxi-drivers knew where the Saturday crowd had gone. Taxi-drivers, spinning along Bayswater Road, had seen what appeared, by midday, to be a great rug of semi-clad humanity stretching from Speaker's Corner to the Serpentine.

The six Granada TV film crews were also at work early, filming the first awakening of those who had slept in the park overnight to ensure favourable vantage points, and the diverse activities with which they beguiled the hours before the first warm-up band took the stage. Since Hyde Park numbers among its amenities a substantial police station with adjacent dog-kennels, those activities were of the most bucolic, innocent nature. Wild-haired, bare-midriffed figures of both sexes could be seen sitting in deckchairs, blowing soap bubbles, rowing in skiffs on the Serpentine, feeding the ducks or strolling along the paths in an intensifying heat haze. If love had perforce been confined to damp groundsheets in the pre-dawn hours, the peace was unquestionable. It would be estimated by police surveillance helicopters and other, unseen, crowd-monitoring devices that something like quarter of a million people were in Hyde Park, waiting for the Rolling Stones and, meanwhile, doing no damage whatever.

Random interviews conducted by Granada among the 250,000 showed what a fund of goodwill had been created by the Stones' gesture '. . . They make you feel you can have a good time and not worry . . .' 'They're not like the Beatles, spending seven days in bed . . .'

Another camera alighted on Tom Keylock, in pebble lenses and cherry-red cardigan, briefing the auxiliary stewards hired to protect the stage and its environs during the Stones' performance. The stewards were Hell's Angels, English imitators of California's motorcycle terrorist-gangs, uniformed in black leather, chin-strapped Nazi helmets, spiked belts and steel-toed boots, their backs metal-studded with ceremonial names such as 'Rocky X', 'Wild Child' and 'Wild Little Willie'. Keylock's instructions – not fully audible – concerned the handling of that sworn Angel foe, the ''ippy'.

The addition of hard rock to already combustible elements, hot sun, melting ice cream, sweltered hot-dog onions, shirt-sleeved policemen and scowling Hell's Angels, could not discompose the prevailing atmosphere and conventions of an English garden fête. It was a mood perfectly expressed by the day's compere, Sam Cutler, who spoke to the crowd like some hippy vicar, exhorting everyone to be cool and polite to each other, interspersing performances by King Crimson, Screw, the Battered Ornaments and Alexis Korner's New Church band, with advice concerning cramp and heat stroke, appeals to respect the trees, and the names of lost children awaiting their parents at the Serpentine boat-house.

The very Hell's Angels – as their blank suburban faces and freshly shampooed hair might have indicated – bore as much similarity to their Californian cousins at tapioca does to paraquat. At one point, the stage-front press enclosure became over-full of supernumerary females – among them Suzy Creamcheese and Jagger's soon-to-be inamorata, Marsha Hunt, fetchingly outfitted in white buckskin. 'Clear 'em out,' the chief Angel, 'Wild Child', ordered a swastika-capped lieutenant. 'Do you want me to use *force* or something?' the swastika-cap queried nervously.

Yet another camera crew was in position to film Mick Jagger emerging from 48 Cheyne Walk and then join him in the limousine, with Marianne and Nicholas, as they drove a roundabout way from Chelsea to Mayfair and up a deserted back-double to the east of Hyde Park Corner. Jagger wore an apricot blouse split to the waist, and seemed excited in the way schoolboys are before a sports day or swimming gala. 'Fantastic day, innit? Yeah . . . what, Nicholas? Is Charlie going to wave to you, Nicholas?'

The other Stones had made their separate ways to a first base rendezvous, not at the obvious Park Lane Hilton Hotel but at its much less smart neighbour, the Londonderry. From their tenth-floor suite, they could see the outer perimeter of their audience and hear the vague thunder echoing over the treetops. Among the party was Allen Klein, apparently still persona grata, perched on his hands on a gimcrack table-top wearing – as always on such occasions – an expression of almost child-like wonderment.

Shortly before 3 p.m. from the direction of Speakers' Corner, a military armoured personnel-carrier, such as had recently come into use in earnest in Northern Ireland, could be seen, moving through the half-naked crowd and flattened deckchairs as cautiously as if this were the Belfast Falls Road. Inside, sprawled on mattresses, were the five Stones and their two official photographers, Michael Cooper and Spanish Tony Sanchez. On the day they needed it least, the Stones' pre-performance security had never been better.

From the armoured personnel-carrier they were decanted into a caravan trailer behind the stage, though still in full view of several hundred fans whom the Hell's Angels had given up trying to intimidate. From time to time, Charlie Watt's arm would appear from a window to pass out an apple or orange from the plentiful supplies within. The stage, meanwhile, had been cleared of all inferior equipment and personages, furnished with the Stones' own giant amplifiers and embellished with a huge blow-up colour photograph of Brian Jones. Tom Keylock and his helpers set down several brown cardboard boxes, from which one telltale white butterfly floated free. Those near the stage-front, versed in such portents, saw its palm-leafy wings suddenly infiltrated by celebrities and their unreprovable children.

Whatever the 250,000 people in Hyde Park expected of Mick Jagger that afternoon, none could have expected him to take the stage in lipstick, rouge and eye-shadow, and wearing a white, frilly garment which, for all the white vest and bell-bottoms visible beneath, still resembled nothing so much as a little girl's party dress. Round his neck was a tight, brass-studded leather collar. On the place where his bust ought to have been there hung a stout wooden crucifix, as if his experiments with the occult had left him still not quite easy in his mind.

Folding his hands in an Eastern sign of *namaste*, then blowing kisses from his fingertips, he greeted the quarter of a million in that now familiar drawl, lodged indeterminately between Dartford and Memphis.

'We're gonna have a good time – awright?'

As the sound of agreement washed back like a slow wave, out to the distant archipelago of Kensington and Knightsbridge, Jagger brought his face close to the microphone, flipping back his chin-length wings of hair.

'Now listen . . . cool it for a minute. I really would like to say something about Brian . . . about how we feel about him just goin' when we didn't expect it . . .'

From behind his back, like a little girl revealing a surprise present, Jagger took a small calf-bound book. Holding it up in both hands, tossing back his hair once more, he began to read what perhaps half a dozen among his quarter of a million listeners recognized as a stanza from Shelley's *Adonais*.

> Peace, peace! He is not dead, he doth not sleep –
> He hath awakened from the dream of life –
> 'Tis we who, lost in stormy visions, keep
> With phantoms an unprofitable strife,
> And in mad trance strike with our spirit's knife.
> Invulnerable nothings! We decay
> Like corpses in a charnel. Fear and grief
> Convulse us and consume us day by day
> And cold hopes swarm like worms within our living clay.

Out over the huge, restive expanse, the whole of Stanza 39

echoed in a voice as empty of artifice as it could remember to be and as close to public sincerity as it knew how. Jagger's frills billowed gently in the breeze as he turned to a new page, marked by his finger, and Stanza 39 segued into Stanza 52:

> The One remains, the many change and pass.
> Heaven's light forever shines, earth's shadows fly.
> Time, like a dome of many-coloured glass
> Stains the white radiance of Eternity
> Until Death tramples it to fragments – Die!
> If thou would be that which thou doest seek.

As Shelley's words died away into deep silence, Tom Keylock and his helpers picked up the cardboard boxes and shook them outward, releasing several hundred white butterflies. It was afterwards claimed that most of the butterflies had been killed by confinement without an adequate air-supply. Enough survived to crowd the air above the crowded grass – and, later, to devastate gardens and allotments for several square miles around.

The tribute to Brian had been grand, even gracious – but it was over. The last white butterfly unclipped the microphone. On the first chord of Honky Tonk Women, Jagger's frilly wings jack-nifed into their own special kind of flight.

For Mick Taylor, the next hour passed in a blur of heat and faces and bodies and their manifold odours; of noise both stupendously near and unreally distant, like sea-echoes in the ear of a shell. 'I'm always asked if I was nervous, coming out to play with the Stones for the first time in front of 250,000 people. The honest answer is, I don't know. I can't remember. It was all over too quickly.'

Granada film crews, shooting from the stage-front pit and from the crowded plantation in the wings, preserved for posterity what is, possibly, the Stones' worst musical performance ever. They had not played together publicly for more than a year and, what with the trauma over Brian, had managed only one brief limbering-up session in the basement of the Beatles' Apple house. It was, in short, one of those times when Keith Richard walked onstage looking as if he had just got out of bed, and when half, if not more, of every chord he played seemed still resolutely drugged to the eyeballs.

Within the clumsy, ramshackle playing, visible only to a few thousand on the grass, and a few dozen more on the branches of surrounding trees, Mick Jagger gave a performance which galvanized even those nearly comatose with sun and grass and patchouli oil. At one astonishing moment, he dropped to his knees and spread his hair forward over a hand-mike supported between his thighs, closing his lips over the bulbous head. There in broad daylight, before 250,000 people, Mick Jagger seemed to be sucking himself off.

On Monday July 7, as Jagger flew off to Australia and the last of the rubbish was being cleared from Hyde Park, the inquest on Brian Jones took place at East Grinstead coroner's court. In the front row sat his father, the stiffly correct aeronautical engineer from Cheltenham. A distraught Anna Wohlin was escorted into the building by Frank Thorogood.

Anna, Thorogood and his female friend Janet Lawson each told their story of the midnight swim at Cotchford Farm and explained their reason for leaving the poolside only minutes before Brian had drowned. Each relived the shock and panic as Thorogood hauled Brian from the warm, blue water, and the attempt to revive him which, despite the participation of Lawson the trained nurse, quickly proved to be hopeless.

Dr Albert Sachs, consultant pathologist at the Queen Victoria Hospital, East Grinstead, gave the results of the post-mortem which had shown Brian's liver to be twice normal size and in 'an advanced state of fatty degeneration'. His heart also was distended far beyond normal proportions. Blood and urine tests had revealed a high alcohol content and 'an amphetamine substance', although there was no trace of barbiturates. The cause of death was drowning, 'associated with alcohol, drugs and severe liver failure'.

It was less than two years since another famous young Brian, the Beatles' manager Brian Epstein, had died on another idyllically warm summer's night from a similar lethal cocktail of stimulants and booze. As with Epstein, the instant public reaction was to assume Brian Jones had committed suicide. Certainly, there was enough circumstantial evidence for the inquest to glance at this possibility. He had just been fired from the band he had created, after years of increasing impotence and alienation within it. He was normally a strong swimmer who ought to have been able to keep afloat in heated water whatever his intake of drink and pills. But Lewis Jones took the stand to rebut firmly any idea that his son had been a prey to depression in the weeks before his death. Lewis testified that, when they had stayed with him in mid-May, Brian seemed happier than they had seen him in years.

The only clue seemed to lie in the asthma Brian had had since childhood. Anna Wohlin said he had often needed his inhaler to help him breathe while he was in the pool. But she claimed that during her six weeks at Cotchford Farm she had never seen him suffer a bad attack. Lewis Jones said Brian had been acutely asthmatic as a small boy, but that he 'seemed to have grown out of it'. Only his housekeeper, Mrs Hallet – who was not called to give evidence – seems to have heard the wheezing fit that came over him on the morning of his last day alive. The verdict of the coroner, Dr Angus Sommerville, was death by misadventure.

Brian's funeral took place on July 10 at the parish church only a few steps away from his parents' home where he had once sung in the choir. The face of Lewis Jones seemed carved in granite as he steered his wife, Louisa, through a nightmare scrimmage of fans, photographers and enormous floral tributes of the type usually associated with dead Mafiosi. Behind Brain's parents walked his younger sister, Barbara, the officiating clergy Canon Hugh Hopkins, Tom Keylock and Suki Poitier. Then came Bill Wyman, Charlie Watts, Spanish Tony Sanchez, Les Perrin and Linda Lawrence, that most persistent among Brian's former girl-friends, carrying one of the two illegitimate sons he had mischievously named Julian.

In his sermon Canon Hopkins attacked the godlessness and materialism of a world that had put a goldenly talented boy into a wooden box aged only twenty-six. He also asked the congregation to pray for Marianne Faithfull, another Sixties child currently at death's door on the other side of the world. To sum up Brian there was not much the canon could say, knowing little of the good qualities that lay behind the ruthless ambition and self-destructive devilment. He could only attempt to comfort stone-faced Lewis Jones with an epitaph jointly culled from the New Testament parable of the prodigal son and the telegram which a beleaguered Rolling Stone had sent his parents a year earlier. 'This, my son, was lost and is found again . . . Please don't judge me too harshly . . .'

One memory of their prodigal son's last days would always remain with Lewis and Louisa Jones. It was of a moment during their visit to Cotchford Farm in May, 1969. Brian was rummaging through a kitchen drawer when he came across a photograph that almost seemed to paralyse him. Lewis remembered how he stared at the face in it – at her straw-blonde hair and double-daring smile – and murmured softly to himself, 'Anita . . . Anita . . .'

Over the next three decades, Brian's death would create one of rock's most lasting legends. He was in every way the perfect victim of his milieu, brilliant, wicked, charming and hopeless, the pattern that in future months would also send Jimi Hendrix and Jim Morrison prematurely into their coffins. Even to modern Stones fans not yet born when he died and unaware of his presence on their early records, Brian's reproachful drowned ghost still floats above the band every time they take the stage.

The legend is that Brian did not die by accident or misadventure but was murdered or inadvertently killed by someone connected with the Stones, and that the facts were covered up afterwards to protect the band. Thirty years on, fresh revelations and 'confessions' from those involved would still be capable of sparking newspaper headlines and extensive reviews of the mystery all over again. Brian Jones was to become rock's equivalent of John F. Kennedy.

Certainly, in the immediate aftermath of his death some events took place that even then Keith Richard admitted, were 'very weird'. Mary Hallett, Brian's housekeeper, who lived nearby, remembered a flurry of comings and goings at Cotchford Farm by vehicles that belonged neither to his family nor the police. A number of bonfires were lit in the grounds, though this was nowhere near the season for burning leaves. 'I didn't like to go and see what was going on,' Mrs Hallett remembered. 'But a man who worked in the garden told me someone was out there burning Brian's clothes.'

Brian had been virtually broke, with debts of almost £200,000. His estate was valued at £33,784, a sum largely realized by the sale of Cotchford Farm. The promised pay-off from the Stones of £100,000, which so elated him on the day of his death, would have settled no more than half his debts. Some believe his home may have been plundered of its more desirable contents before they could be included in his estate. According to Shirley Arnold, his parents received suspiciously few of his possessions after his death. 'I went down to see Mr and Mrs Jones in Cheltenham a few weeks later. Everything they'd been sent from Cotchford was spread out in their garage. They didn't have all of Brian's guitars, or his Mellotron.'

The murder theory would bubble back to the surface every five years or so. Two former Stones insiders whom I interviewed for the first edition of this book told me unequivocally that Brian was murdered, but that they were too frightened to say any more. Both asked me not to quote them directly or give their names. In 1983, a former friend of Brian's named Nicholas Fitzgerald came forward with new 'evidence' which, if true, would significantly have altered the coroner's view. At the inquest it was said that police and emergency services arrived at Cotchford Farm only fifteen minutes after Brian was found floating in his pool. Fitzgerald, however, suggested that as much as two hours might have elapsed before help came – a period in which Brian was left to expire while unnamed guilty ones made their escape.

The death of the builder Frank Thorogood in 1995 gave the mystery a fresh twist. Tom Keylock, the Stones' former driver and fixer, claimed Thorogood had confessed to him on his deathbed that he was responsible for Brian's death. Angered by Brian's threats not to pay him, he had apparently waited for the two women to leave the poolside, then, in a moment of drunken vengefulness, had pushed Brain's head underwater and held it there. This in turn flushed out Anna Wohlin, Brian's former girlfriend, who had subsequently returned to Sweden and married. Anna unequivocally named Thorogood as Brian's 'murderer', claiming that the builder had become angry after some horseplay in the water between the two men. She said that as his woman friend Janet Lawson raised the alarm, Thorogood had been in the farmhouse kitchen, impassively lighting a cigarette as if aware Brian was already past help. Likewise, when a hysterical Anna tried to raise Brian from the bottom of the pool, Thorogood had been curiously slow to jump in and help her.

Anna claimed to have been the centre of an elaborate cover-up by the Stones' minders and PR man to protect them from yet further damaging involvement with the law. In the days immediately following Brian's death she said she had been kept under wraps (chaperoned by Bill Wyman and his Swedish girlfriend Astrid) to stop the press from getting to her. Les Perrin, the

Stones' press officer, by her account, was a cold, threatening figure who alternately tried to browbeat and frighten her out of ever talking to the media. She also claimed to have been pregnant with Brian's child, though not realizing it until after his death and soon suffering a miscarriage in her grief.

An alternative account, from a supposed witness identified only as 'Marty', has Brian inviting several of Thorogood's building crew over for drinks at the poolside. According to 'Marty', Brian deliberately taunted the men with his wealth and fame until they were almost ready to lynch him there on dry land. Instead, they all went into the water, and Brian became the victim of drunkenly brutal horseplay that went too far.

His most faithful friend turned out to be his teenage fan, Helen Spittal. Just as she'd promised, the last photographs Helen took of him – on the day he said he hoped he would die at Cotchford – remained in her private album forever.

Thirteen

'We're gonna kiss you goodbye'

On July 8, 1969, while Mick Jagger slept away his jet lag in a Sydney hotel suite, Marianne Faithfull slipped out of their bed and across the twilit room to the dressing-table mirror. What she saw reflected there gave her the final impetus to end her life. She picked up the telephone, dialled room service and asked for a cup of hot chocolate. Then she took a bottle of 150 Tuinal sleeping pills and began methodically swallowing them, forcing each mouthful down with sips of chocolate. Having taken enough barbiturates to kill three people, the girl from the Renoir painting that had become a nightmare by Bruegel, settled down beside her still slumbering rock-star lover and waited for death.

The experience of almost dying is one that Marianne – like others accidentally recalled to life – can describe in vivid, almost nostalgic detail.

'I remember finding myself in this big, grey, still place where there was no climate at all – no wind or cold or sun, no weather of any kind. And Brian Jones was there. I remember talking to Brian, who was *terribly* pleased to see me. He said he'd woken up cold and frightened, not knowing where he was. He'd been looking and looking for a familiar face. "Oh, I'm so glad—" he kept saying. "I'm so glad that you're here."

'We started walking along together through this great big, weatherless place, Brian and I – not so much walking as jogging with long, slow strides. Brian was talking in just the way Brian would, hopeless but funny as well. "Hey man – what a drag . . . Woke up this morning, reached out for the pill bottle and realized I was dead . . ."

'We jogged along like this, right up to a place where the land stopped – like the edge of a plane. Brian turned to me and said, "I've got to go on from here alone." Then, far away behind me, I could hear three voices calling to me. One was my mother's. One was Nicholas's. And the other was Mick's.'

Jagger had awoken, found Marianne unconscious and called help in the nick of time, not only to save her life but also prevent the brain damage that so massive an overdose could have caused. Of all sad mementoes to the Rolling Stones saga, none is more harrowing than the picture an Australian photographer snatched as Marianne was brought out of the hotel on a stretcher. The face under the rough blanket could be some dead child's, preserved in a Victorian locket.

She remained in a coma for six days. For most of the time Jagger stayed at her bedside – at this moment, ironically, more her protector than he had ever been. When a British journalist bluffed his way into St Stephen's hospital and actually got into Marianne's room, Jagger had to be restrained by Les Perrin from physical assault. 'I'll get him . . .' he kept babbling to Perrin. 'I'll *get* him.'

The despair that had engulfed her was not wholly Marianne's own. For six weeks, up to Brian's death and the Hyde Park concert, she had been playing Ophelia in *Hamlet* at the Royal Court Theatre. 'I'd willed myself into a suicidal state of mind, quite apart from what was going on around me. And I'd cut my hair very short. All the business about Brian and Ophelia seemed to get mixed up in my mind. When I woke up in that hotel suite and looked into the mirror, I thought it was Brian's face looking back at me.'

She tried to explain it to Jagger after she had returned to consciousness and found him beside her, holding her hand. What she could not explain – nor he begin to comprehend – was that dying, after Ophelia's and Brian Jones's fashion, seemed the only remedy for living with Mick.

Marianne convalesced in Sydney throughout the two months that Jagger spent in Australia, trying to portray the country's principal folk hero on film while simultaneously making plans to save the Rolling Stones from imminent financial catastrophe.

It was already clear that *Ned Kelly* was an ill-omened project, conceived on free-spending Sixties euphoria and nurtured largely by the publicity around its star. Jagger did his best with the role, working at his Irish accent and bush-ranger's scowl, completely in the dark – as all film actors are – about the shape or quality of the finished picture. The production was hampered by the outrage of many Australians at seeing their nation's Robin Hood portrayed – as some put it – by 'a limey pantie-waist'. There were even threats from a present-day outlaw gang to kidnap Jagger and cut off his hair. Out at the location, conditions were often chaotic, with Jagger protesting to Tony Richardson about the awful script and Marianne's understudy, Diane Craig, forced to go before the camera without having learned her lines. In one scene a prop pistol exploded, badly gashing Jagger's left hand. When he visited Marianne in hospital he pretended the bandage was part of his Ned Kelly costume.

In September, after filming had ended, they flew to Indonesia together for a holiday intended to repair the ravages of the summer. It worked – as long as they were left alone together. Back in London, Jagger was plunged into fresh preoccupations. And Marianne found her predicament to be as desperate as ever.

Once again, her warmly and chaotically passionate nature found itself trapped into the congealing gold of a public image as hard and bland and all-protecting as if Jagger's personality truly were encased in amber. 'The worst thing of all about being with

Mick was this rule he laid down that you must *never* show emotion, in case people realized you weren't cool. Over the months, everything used to get bottled up inside me. I remember, on one of those holidays with everyone in Morocco, being in the middle of the Atlas Mountains and suddenly just bursting into tears.'

In three years, inevitably, their mutual physical attraction had dwindled. Marianne could resign herself to the fact that, when Jagger lay beside her in their Moroccan-draped four-poster at Cheyne Walk, it was usually just to pore over the latest book she'd got him to read. She could resign herself to the knowledge that, as his desire for her decreased, he more and more frequently exercised the droit de seigneur he held over half the women of the Western world. 'Mick's other affairs *did* bother me. But that wasn't as bad as the feeling of being pinned against the wall by the whole superstar thing. I sometimes think it might have helped if there had been more drink around instead of just dope. If Mick and I had got drunk together a few times, we might have stood a chance.'

He could still be an artfully persuasive lover, wooing her back from fury or estrangement with gifts and flowers. One of Marianne's minor grievances was his attitude to money. To keep up the Cheyne Walk house – as a woman *must* keep house for her lord and master – he allowed her only £25 a week. Yet he had bought a country cottage for her mother, Baroness Erisso. And he was always kind and generous to her son, Nicholas.

The disintegration of their love was reflected by the country house they had planned to live in together, in those far off days, eighteen months ago, when Jagger's greatest joy seemed to be whirling Nicholas round by the arms or pushing his swing higher and higher towards the sun.

Christopher Gibbs, the antique dealer, had been commissioned to find a property no whit less grand then Bill Wyman's new Suffolk mansion, Gedding Hall. 'The whole process took an *extremely* long time,' Gibbs says. 'As Mick, Marianne and I were setting off to look at a house I'd found, Marianne would say, "Let's have lunch in Henley on the way." "But Marianne," I'd say, "Henley isn't on the way. We're going to Shropshire." "But it *could* be on the way," she'd say. The result was that a two-hour journey would take six or seven hours.'

Gibbs's most promising find was Stargroves, a mock-Gothic folly, near Newbury, Berkshire, which had belonged to the eccentric Sir Henry Cardon and was now on the market for the extremely small sum of £20,000. 'Mick and Marianne drove down to look at it in pitch darkness, with a great carload of people that included the author Terry Southern. Anyway, dark or not, the *chemistry* was right.'

Elaborate plans were put in hand for the restoration of Stargroves, both inside and out. An elderly groundsman, acquired with the property, shuffled round with Marianne, listening dazedly to her schemes for making mazes and medieval herb gardens. Jagger, however, seemed to lose interest in the place almost as soon as he'd bought it.

For him, too, this was a time of great depression and anxiety. Even his talent for shutting out unpleasantness could not blind him to the high level of Marianne's drug-intake. Nor could his famous 'cool' restrain him from furious anger when her *grande dame* carelessness with hash or pills opened up the road to Brixton Prison all over again. Already, thanks to Marianne, one bust for marijuana hung over their heads, jeopardizing the whole strategy Jagger had worked out to save the Stones from ruin. Worst of all, the hash and speed and coke had begun to affect Marianne's looks. The lovely, misty face had grown haggard, the great, liquid eyes vague and foggy, the voice hoarse with fag smoke. To someone who measured life in looks and profit, it must have hurt to see such a prize become such a liability.

Matters were only made worse by the arrival of Keith Richard and Anita Pallenberg to live at number 3 Cheyne Walk, only a couple of hundred yards to the east. The move had been intended to facilitate Mick and Keith's songwriting partnership as well as to liberate Anita from the restraints of country life. For £50,000, the undead king and queen of rock acquired the Queen Anne residence of a former Tory government minister, Anthony Nutting. They moved in in August, 1969, the month that Anita gave birth to their first son, Marlon.

Marlon Richard opened his eyes to eighteenth-century wood-panelled rooms, transformed by Anita into replicas of Moroccan hashish-dens, their elegantly wrought ceilings supporting beaten metal lamps inlaid with fake rubies and emeralds. The second-floor drawing room, where Tory ladies had once sipped tea, was now devoted to tripping – or, possibly, more exotic rites – before an altar formed by the fireplace and two giant candlesticks. From the ceiling hung a ball of multi-faceted mirror glass that could be made to turn slowly, drenching the walls and moulded cornices, and whatever figures lay below, in wriggling patterns of coloured light.

Keith and Anita, in their secret black and midnight hours, had long since ridden the speedball rollercoaster to the seeming shelter and level-headedness of pure heroin. Like all before them, they had no thought of becoming addicts. 'Heroin is like a slow process of seduction,' Keith says. 'You try it, and you stop. You find you don't feel any worse than after a dose of flu. You say "Hey – they've been lying to me. I'm not hooked!" That's when you *are* hooked. Your body needs it and you'll do anything to get it.'

Keith and Anita were the last encouragement Marianne needed to throw caution to the winds. By late 1969 she, too, had begun taking heroin, believing she could stop whenever she chose. 'People always assume I was already a junkie when I was with Mick – but I wasn't. At that stage it was still an experiment. I went into it with my eyes wide open.'

*

The end of the decade, looming unreally beyond September, added fresh urgency to the manoeuvre that Mick Jagger had long been secretly plotting and preparing. It was a manoeuvre compared with which Sinbad's unseating of the Old Man of the Sea from his back seemed relatively straightforward. The Rolling Stones wanted to break away from Allen Klein.

Klein, in 1966, had promised he could earn them greater sums than pop stars had ever earned before. That promise Klein indubitably had kept. At an initial rough estimate by Mick Jagger's parallel accounting system, something between ten and seventeen million dollars in record royalties and tour grosses had been collected by Klein's company on the Stones' behalf. But the money wasn't in their bank accounts. What they had received – a trifling million or two – they had spent in the blithe Sixties' belief that there was plenty more where that came from. Between them, they had frittered away fortunes, but that was not the worst part: they also had spent as if each pound and dollar wholly belonged to them. By mid-1969, the day of reckoning was at hand for careless living right back to 1966. The British tax authorities had begun taking an active interest in their affairs.

The appointment of Prince Rupert Loewenstein as Mick Jagger's personal financial adviser eighteen months previously, further underscored Jagger's mood of disenchantment with Klein. Loewenstein it was who gave the party at which Jagger first wore his Hyde Park dolly dress; in subsequent conversation he had proved himself a man of business infinitely more to Jagger's socially conscious taste than an uncouth accountant from New Jersey. Prince Rupert was an authentic sprig of Austrian royalty whose Savile Row suit, but for history's accident, might have been a gold-braided uniform and his pince-nez a haughty Hapsburg monocle. History having decreed that Prince Rupert should manage empires rather than possess them, he had wisely developed certain useful plebeian attributes, principally a voice with the swift, calculating click of an abacus, and eyes in which visions of imperial glory had been replaced by the less subtle colours of a Las Vegas fruit machine.

Prince Rupert Loewenstein waited in the wings to become the Stones' business manager as soon as Klein could be persuaded to pay over their money and terminate his management contract. The moment for such a change could hardly have been less opportune. In a few months – mid-1970 to be exact – the Stones would reach the end of their contract with Decca Records. Since, as was well known, they would rather commit hara-kiri than re-sign with Decca, there was bound to be spectacular competition among other record companies to acquire them. Klein, on visits to London, was already to be heard boasting about the deal he intended to do. At the same time, Prince Rupert looked into the possibilities offered by the anti-Klein methods of courtly correspondence and mandarin politeness.

Klein in normal circumstances would bitterly have resented – and taken rapid steps to counteract – any such subtle erosion of his power. But Klein was deeply preoccupied elsewhere. Since the previous May, his attention had been concentrated on four individuals who, even at this point of dissolution, managed yet again to throw the Stones into eclipse. Three of the four Beatles had now accepted Klein as their manager, allowing him to move into the Apple house and begin his great work of recouping their mislaid millions. All summer the British press had teemed with stories of the carnage wrought by Klein among Apple's defenceless hippies, and of his boardroom skirmishes with Beatle stakeholders like EMI, Sir Lew Grade and the Triumph Investment Trust. Few of these stories even mentioned that Klein managed the Rolling Stones also. The exception was the *Sunday Times*, whose formidable Insight team compiled a lengthy examination of Klein's business methods based on his relationship with Andrew Oldham, Eric Easton and the $1.25 million Decca advance. 'The Toughest Wheeler Dealer in the Pop Jungle', as Insight dubbed him, issued a writ for libel forthwith.

The Stones might want no further part of Klein. But they still bitterly resented his treating them as also-rans to the Beatles. By August, relations between Klein and them were, to put it mildly, distant. When Keith Richard exchanged contracts for 3 Cheyne Walk, he needed £20,000 to make up the purchase price. Tom Keylock was sent to see Klein in New York with instructions not to come back without the money. 'I just kept on walking until I was in Allen's office,' Keylock says. 'He was so amazed I'd managed to get to him, he agreed to give me the money for Keith.'

That was the problem Jagger had been pondering in Australia while mouthing his awful *Ned Kelly* lines. The only way the Stones could put themselves in the black again was to undertake the American tour they had been discussing, and postponing, since mid-1968. Mick, Keith, Bill and Charlie were all agreed that they had to get back on the road again, and they had to do it independently of Klein. However, it was vital not to provoke an open rift with Klein. Once any legal proceedings began, Klein would be able to freeze all their funds pending a court decision that might take years.

Jagger's solution was to approach Ronnie Schneider, Klein's nephew and principal adjutant in the bloody reorganization at Apple. Schneider had always been fraternally fond of the Stones, particularly Brian and Keith; he also had become disaffected by his uncle's apparent emotional fixation on the Beatles, and was looking for a chance to break into solo management. Klein, still deep in Beatle boardroom conflict, consented to let Schneider handle the Stones' tour, provided he did so from the Klein office. When this proved unworkable – as it did almost immediately – arrangements were too far forward to cancel. Ronnie Schneider was in charge of the Rolling Stones.

The news that the Stones were to tour again caused a momentary diversion from Fleet Street's running saga of the Beatles, Apple and Allen Klein. One radio interviewer even asked George Harrison why he thought Jagger and Co. were going back on the road again. 'I think they need the money,' was George's spot-on reply. '. . . and that new guitarist of theirs is fantastic.' Keith Richard, too, spoke of the new dimension and subtlety Mick Taylor had brought to the band. 'It's taken a bit of time to weave him in but the band's really together now. We're really looking forward to getting back out there . . .'

In fact, all of them were jittery at the prospect of returning to a milieu barely recognizable as the one in which their reputation had been made. When they had last toured, in 1967, it was still basically as a pop group, obliged to do little more than fill a theatre with screams. These past two years had seen the evolution of pop into rock – a simple excess of sound and spirits into a culture: a *consciousness*. Rock was not only a thousand watts louder; it was also a thousand times more serious. Seriousness devolved equally on the bands (not groups any more), playing songs as grandiose and difficult to halt as ocean liners, and on the audiences, listening with an intentness that implied almost comparable virtuosity. Few enough ex-pop groups had dared chance their arm in the new rock world. The Beatles themselves would ultimately perish, not so much from the financial coils enmeshing them as from fear that if they played in public again – as Paul McCartney wanted – people might actually listen to them.

The Stones were already figureheads of the new culture, thanks to a young American entrepreneur named Jann Wenner who had adored them from the beginning. In 1968, Wenner launched the first-ever intelligent rock paper from the hippy capital of San Francisco and gave it the name *Rolling Stone*. As well as an inspired editor, Wenner was a determined socialite who mingled on equal terms with the stars his paper covered. He soon got to know Jagger and even persuaded him to help finance a short-lived British edition of *Rolling Stone*. Wenner's encouragement and promise of support was crucial in persuading the Stones to cross the Atlantic once again.

Since putting on a rock tour in 1969 was a process understood by no one in the Stones' employment, Jagger sought help from his old friends The Who, already expert travellers in the modern manner. The Who lent the Stones their road manager, Peter Rudge, who had begun his career booking pop groups for the Cambridge May balls. Rudge's brief from Jagger – inspired by past dissatisfaction with American promoters – was to assemble a road show that would be completely self-contained. The Stones would travel with their own maintenance, publicity and security staff and their own compere, Sam Cutler. Removing the last perquisite of local promoters, they would even book their own supporting acts. Their choice for this first tour was the husband and wife duo, Ike and Tina Turner, and their old blues idol, B. B. King. Keith reacted strongly to suggestions that their supporting acts might overshadow the main attraction. 'I *want* a strong opening act,' he insisted. 'If they're good, it's going to make me work that much harder.'

The crucial factor, as everyone knew, would be Jagger's own performance. In a world where the long-haired rock star had grown commonplace, a head-tossing cliché, how could Jagger re-create his old, unchallengeable spectacle and shock? He pondered the matter at length, with frequent reference to an earlier figure whose leaps could bring the heart of an audience into its mouth. At one point, he called Jo Bergman and said, 'Find me a Diaghilev.'

Any idea that the Stones had lost power as a concert attraction was dismissed by the instant reaction of promoters across America. Ronnie Schneider, in London, was inundated with transatlantic calls, offering them virtually any price or guarantee they cared to name. For a concert relayed on closed-circuit TV in the current style of world-title prize fights, one showman was prepared to pay four million dollars. Schneider, for all his excitability, was prudent enough to divide the itinerary between established promoters and top prestige venues like the Los Angeles Forum and New York's Madison Square Garden. The advances that rolled in gave the tour its sorely needed financial float – especially since Ronnie Schneider ordered the cheques to be made out, not to its overall booking agency, William Morris Inc., but to the Stones' own ad hoc company, Stone Tours.

America's ears were simultaneously to be assaulted by no less than three new Rolling Stones albums. The first was a collection of golden oldies entitled *Through The Past Darkly* and dedicated to Brian Jones – whose presence, indeed, permeated every track. Then there was a fourteen-cut promotional disc, issued to 200 radio stations in the hope of its being broadcast complete as a history of the Stones from Route 66 to Love In Vain, a sneak preview track from their new album *Let It Bleed*.

Let It Bleed, now in final mixing stage, was scheduled for release in early December, when the tour would be reaching its climax. Just how large a climax, no one, of course, imagined – nor how horribly apt an album title could prove to be.

'Are you,' a laconic woman journalist asks Mick Jagger, 'any more *satisfied* now than when you last came over here?'

The question is so uncharacteristically witty for an American press conference that even Jagger deigns to show a flicker of amusement.

'D'you mean financially?' he banters, craning to see her in the media crush. 'Sexually? Philosophically?'

'Financially and philosophically satisfied.'

The place is New York's chic Rainbow Room, perched on the 30th floor of Rockefeller Center. The date is November 25, two days before the Stones' appearance at Madison Square Garden. The mood is euphoric – an upswing nothing now can spoil. Around the white-suited Jagger, camera shutters snap and buzz. Protective arms endlessly reposition the microphone into which, smiling broadly, he delivers a slightly more expansive non-reply than usual.

'Financially . . . just sa'isfied. Sexually sa'isfied . . . y'know. Philosophically . . . tryin' . . .'

'Don't expect them to scream,' someone whispered as a last warning to Jagger before he went onstage at Los Angeles Forum on November 7. And certainly, the 18,000-strong audience, traversed by Zeppelin searchlight-beams, bore out in their murmurous restraint everything the Stones had heard about the bromide effect of 'serious' rock.

It lasted until the searchlights cut off, plunging the miniature universe into a more dizzying dark, and a voice of giant, unapologetic Englishness said, ''Ere they are, ladies and gentlemen, after three years . . . the greatest rock 'n' roll band in the world . . .' Before Sam Cutler could say 'Rolling Stones', the entire darkness was on its feet, screaming to the full force of its lungs.

On a stage drenched with psychedelia's painful blue-white light – discovered there, somehow, in mid-leap – was a figure whom no Diaghilev had dressed in its gamine black off-the-shoulder jersey and split-flared gaucho trousers, pinched together by a broad, heavily studded belt. Round its bare neck with a knee-length scarf, of the type that throttled Isadora Duncan. On its head was a red, white and blue striped top hat. Attentiveness and Woodstock dignity melted against a voice so hardly on key, it seemed not quite human, bawling out the fable to its sub-human genesis:

'Aah was bawn in a cross-fire hurri-caayne . . .'

Keith Richard, in spangled orange and earrings, a gipsy dipped in ketchup, played an almost indecent-looking see-through guitar. Charlie Watts at his drums seemed to have changed clothes at the last minute with an ordinary construction worker. Bill Wyman was in one-piece Faustian red. Only Mick Taylor conformed to West Coast type with his shoulder-length hair and leg-of-mutton smock sleeves, his virginal face angled sideways, as he followed his own playing, solemn as some thinking girl in a novel by George Eliot.

They were, in short, outlandishly different and triumphantly unreformed. Playing their old songs, about London dolly birds, or their new ones, about Hitler and Satan and riot and rape, the same vicious power was still there, plunging and re-plunging into its listeners' minds like a mainliner's needle or a vampire's fangs. For, in that time of rampaging pretentiousness, it seemed as miraculous that they bothered to play the old songs as that they dared to play the new.

For most of the large number of serious rock critics present, Mick Jagger's new range of theatrics caused as much discomfort as a hand straying to their collective knee. The moment in Jumpin' Jack Flash when he took off his studded belt and whipped the stage with it was considered a detail too fraught with innuendo for most even to mention. For the *New York Times*'s Albert Goldman the conclusive moment came in Street Fighting Man, when the Forum audience stood up and beat time with upraised arms and clenched fists.

'Ja wohl!' wrote Albert Goldman. 'Mein friends, dot's right! Dot good old rock 'n' roll could warm the cockles of a storm trooper's heart. OK – they don't give you a torch and an armband, like in the *real* old days, and send you down the Rhine to swing with the summer solstice. But you can still squeeze in hip by haunch with thousands of good *kamerads*; still fatten ears, eyes and soul on the Leader; still plotz out while he socks it to you in stop time, and best of all, boys and girls, you can get your rocks off, no, with that good old arm action that means . . . well, you know what it means.

'No question about it, Der Führer would have been gassed out of his kugel by the scene at the Forum . . .'

Even Albert Goldman could not deny that just the warm-up acts in the Stones '69 tour were outstanding entertainment value – first B. B. King in his grey flannel suit, bending elegant notes on his guitar, Lucille; then Ike and Tina Turner, a laconic guitarist standing by, while his half-naked princess wife teased a hand microphone into an erect phallus, fondling it with bejewelled fingers, flicking it with her tongue as she murmured and gurgled an act of fellatio, communicable to thousands. Of all the influences on Mick Jagger's stagecraft, none was to be so great as Tina Turner. He would stand each night and watch her, his body absorbing her mannerisms like data being fed into a computer.

Two sell-out shows at the Forum grossed $260,000, breaking the Beatles' record for a single night's concert-earnings – as well as roughly quintupling the Beatles' share of the box-office receipts. At San Diego two nights later, the sports arena was stormed by 2,000 fans who had been unable to buy tickets. Forty-six were charged with offences ranging from drug-possession to throwing rocks at cars.

A new hazard of touring was the plethora of political groups, weaned from love and peace to more strident protest, and anxious to acquire the huge rock audience as a target for their propaganda. The Black Panthers in particular dogged the Stones' tour, because black musicians were involved and because Jagger himself, in his revolutionary phase, had several times intimated sympathy for the black militants. In Oakland, the Panthers demanded that Jagger formally announce his allegiance; when he did not, death threats were issued. 'I went backstage,' Ronnie Schneider says, 'and Ike Turner shouted to me, "Hey Ron – if you're worried about the Panthers, come stand with us." All of their bodyguards – and Ike and Tina, too – were carrying guns.'

As tour manager, Schneider had been enjoying himself since he had been able to shout down the telephone at Bill Graham: 'Frankly, Bill – what have you ever really *done*?' Admittedly, all Graham had done was run the San Francisco Mime Troupe, organize Bob Dylan's 1964 American tour, turn the Fillmore West into rock's premier auditorium and, through his association with Jefferson Airplane and the Grateful Dead, become the most powerful – as well as most respected – rock music promoter in

California. He was, none the less, running only some of the Stones shows and obliged to liaise with Ronnie Schneider about matters he was accustomed to decide for himself. Disputes between the two grew ever more fierce until at Oakland, in a fight over who should and should not stand on the stage, Schneider hit Graham with his briefcase.

The tour had reached Dallas when some news came in from London which sent Mick Jagger's courtiers into an agonized huddle outside his motel room door. British newspapers were reporting that Marianne Faithfull had left London for Rome in the company of Anita Pallenberg's one-time boyfriend, Mario Schifano. Questioned by reporters, Marianne had made it clear she was leaving Jagger for Schifano, whom she described as her 'Prince Charming'.

Jagger was, as predicted, furious. Though he himself had been having a semi-public affair – with American actress Marsha Hunt – it seems never to have occurred to him that Marianne would do the same. To be cuckolded thus, in the very spotlight, dealt his pride a terrible blow. Out there, under the Zeppelin beams, they would know all about it. They would know there was a better lover in the world than Mick Jagger. Still, the image made its inexorable demands. He must rouge and powder himself, tie on his Isadora scarf, tip his Uncle Sam topper and leap forth like Nijinsky with his mock-Dixie yell of 'Hi y'all . . .'

Consolation came in the madness of the road, the whirl of limo travel, wrapped in his silver cloak, the harem attentiveness of girls for whom sleeping with rock stars had become practically a vocation. The Stones, by divine right, could avail themselves of such famous groupies as Miss Mercy, Susie Suck or, most memorably, the Plaster Casters, a duo who made commemorative plaster casts of their conquests' erect penises. Despite the challenge implicit in rival plaster casts, there was still no doubt as to the groupies' ultimate objective. The story is told of a particular girl who, upon emerging from each night's exertions with this or that rock legend, always made the same comment: 'He was great – but he wasn't Mick Jagger.' Eventually, it is said, the day came when Jagger himself summoned her to his hotel room. Next morning, her friends gathered round avidly. 'So how was he?' someone asked. 'He was great,' the honoured one replied. 'But he wasn't Mick Jagger . . .'

Film and TV cameras saw only the usual sardonic, untouchable Jagger, born of groupie myth rather than fact, controlling the Rainbow Room press conference on November 25, and telling the lady reporter he was 'financially sa'isfied, sexually sa'sified, philosophically tryin'.' The real Jagger, observed by no one, had been desperately ringing up Marianne in Rome and pleading tearfully with her to come back to him.

'"Philosophically *tired*" did he say?' the *New York Tribune* whispered. 'Do you,' another questioner tried, 'identify with revolutionary youth in America?'

'We're with you.' Jagger laughed. 'Right be'ind you.'

'How about the war in Vietnam?'

'Just get over it as soon as you can.'

'What do you think about John Lennon returning his MBE medal to the Queen?'

'He should have done it as soon as he got it.'

'I read in the paper that you're going to be giving a free concert. Is that true?'

'We are going to do a free concert,' Jagger said. 'It's going to be on December – er – sixth in San Francisco. But it *isn't* going to be in Golden Gate Park. It's going to be somewhere adjacent to Golden Gate Park and a bit larger . . .'

The whole ghastly business had its origins in a desire to do something nice. It began because the Stones felt that rare collective impulse, a twinge of conscience.

Financially and sexually satisfied as they were by the tour's official end, they could not help but notice what a backwash of resentment it left behind. Promoters in almost every city along their route criticized them for their arrogance, their demands for backstage comforts, their lateness in beginning shows, their sulky pique if either of their opening acts seemed to be getting more applause than they did. The most frequently voiced criticism concerned a ticket price allegedly 50 per cent higher than for any comparable rock attraction. To amass their two million dollars gross, it was suggested, the Stones had systematically and callously ripped off teenagers all across America.

Most such condemnation appeared in newspapers to which the Stones paid little heed. But elements of the underground press, too, had begun to attack them. Most damning of all was Ralph J. Gleason, co-founder of *Rolling Stone* magazine and influential columnist for the *San Francisco Chronicle*.

'Can the Rolling Stones really need all that money?' Gleason asked in his *Chronicle* column. 'If they really dig the black musicians as much as every note they play and every syllable they utter indicate, is it possible to take out a show with Ike and Tina Turner and not let them share in the loot? How much can the Stones take back to Merrie England anyway? . . . Paying six and seven dollars for an hour of the Stones a quarter of a mile away because the artists demand such outrageous fees says a very bad thing to me about the artists' attitude to the public. It says they despise their audience.'

In fact the ticket prices, from $4.50 to $7.50, were only marginally higher than what rock fans were currently paying to see Blind Faith or the Doors. The Stones themselves had been horrified by the $8.50 top price at LA Forum and had publicly announced it was set by the management, not them. '*Rolling Stone* reprinted what Gleason wrote, without checking any of it,' Ronnie Schneider says. 'It was all bullshit – like claiming the Stones were conning Ike and Tina when they'd *booked* them in the first place. They were paying B. B. King, even though he'd have gone on that tour for nothing.'

None the less, the damage was done. Jagger had seen Gleason's article reprinted in *Rolling Stone*, and had been aghast at the suggestion that he was ripping off audiences. The answer was obvious, and of proven effect. The Stones would say 'thank you' to America by giving a free concert.

For such an event there could be only one possible city. San Francisco was where hippies, acid, love and rock first coalesced: it was the home of major bands who might well participate: it was also the home of *Rolling Stone* magazine. As well as being the source of rock consciousness, it was one of the warmest places to hold an outdoor concert in December. Jagger's idea could not have come at a more timely moment. Four months had passed since the Woodstock miracle; it was time for another great show of freaked-out togetherness. What had begun as purely a Rolling Stones project instantly became the property of San Francisco's supergroup community whose leaders were the thunderous and cerebral Grateful Dead. The Dead had already offered to play and act as co-organizers with the Stones' tour staff. Jefferson Airplane, Santana, Crosby, Stills, Nash and Young, and the Flying Burrito Brothers all volunteered to be on the bill.

The guarantee of film cameras added to this altruistic eagerness. It had been Jagger's intention all along to have the Stones' tour filmed as the cinema feature which their Hyde Park concert, mysteriously, never became. Jagger, after all, had drawn almost as many people together in one day as Woodstock's massed talents had in three. He was irked to think that the Woodstock film would shortly be released across America when *The Stones in the Park* had been seen only once on British television.

His original nominee to make a rival to *Woodstock* was the cameraman-director Haskell Wexler. Wexler accepted the job but then pulled out, leaving the tour half-finished and no footage yet shot. Not until the Stones reached New York did Jagger find an alternative in Albert and David Maysles, film-making brothers whose credits included a fascinating *cinéma vérité* chronicle of the

Beatles' first visit to New York. The Maysles filmed the Stones at Madison Square Garden and in two further shows, but still had far from enough material in the can. 'Then we heard there was going to be a free concert in San Francisco,' David Maysles says. 'We couldn't decide if it was worthwhile going to that or not.'

After their final paid appearance, at the Miami Pop Festival, the Stones travelled to Muscle Shoals Studios in Alabama to work on songs for the album that would become *Sticky Fingers*. Their staff, led by Jo Bergman, moved into the Grateful Dead's office in Marin County, north of San Francisco, where the new Woodstock would have to be organized in less than two weeks.

It seems incredible now that people so addicted to the study of signs and portents – people for whom 'vibes' were so important a consideration – could not see or feel the forces already propelling them towards catastrophe. All summer, one fact had made itself insistently plain: that love and peace had an underside of insecurity, anger and viciousness. Two rock festivals convened in Woodstock's triumphant name had been marred by violence, inflicted haplessly, through drug excesses, or calculatedly by hippy militant groups dubbed with eighteenth-century martyrs' names like the Diggers or Weathermen. So ritualized had the battles around the rock stage become that *Rolling Stone* was obliged to become part political broadsheet, calling this 'the year of the American revolution' and spelling its country's name with a fascistic 'k'. One episode above all expressed the change with dreadful simplicity. A bearded dropout named Charles Manson, only weeks earlier, had let his hippy 'family' loose in the Bel Air mansion of actress Sharon Tate. Four people, including the eight months pregnant Tate, had been butchered, apparently in the name of flower power.

And over all, like a soundtrack of the new barbarism, floated *Let It Bleed* – the surly, smoky incantation of Gimme Shelter; the homicidal playfulness of Midnight Rambler, with additional dialogue by Albert de Salvo, the Boston Strangler. The Stones had made destruction cool and the Devil a rock star; they had sold a million copies of an exhortation to slaughter. They were the household gods of every spaced-out, subterranean screwball in America. 'Welcome Rolling Stones' ran a typical street-corner manifesto, '—our comrades in the desperate battle against the lunatics who hold power. The revolutionary youth of the world hears your music and is inspired to even more deadly acts. We will play your music as we tear down the jails and free the prisoners, as we tear down the state schools and free the students, as we tear down the military bases, arm the poor, as we tattoo "burn, baby, burn" on the bellies of the wardens and the generals and create a new society from the ashes of our fires . . .'

Meanwhile, at the Grateful Dead's Marin County house, people living in the rosy past of four months ago told each other this would be the biggest love-in and freak-out ever. The concert had by now attracted a huge crowd of putative organizers, drawn from virtually every faction in San Francisco music, socio-politics and street-corner activism. Among the arguing daily throng could be identified Jerry Garcia and Phil Lesh of the Grateful Dead with Rock Scully, their manager; Jo Bergman and Ronnie Schneider of the Stones' staff, Sam Cutler, their compere, and John Jaymes, their security manager; Chet Helms of the Family Dog; Emmett Grogan of the Diggers; David Crosby of Crosby, Stills, Nash and Young; plus dozens of lower-caste Bay Area celebrities, propagandists, hangers-on and journalists.

There were also the Maysles brothers, filming what was still seen as the prologue to a climactic triumph. The Maysles were at San Francisco airport to record the arrival of Chip Monck, a blandly smiling, Afro-permed youth who had built the highly successful Woodstock stage and had been commissioned to repeat his achievement here. Chip Monck vanished, still smiling, into the increasing hubbub which a *Rolling Stone* reporter drily noted. 'Meetings of two, three or ten people in every side office broke up in confusion after a few minutes . . . There was an air of frantic activity about the place. But in fact, nothing was happening.'

The problem – not foreseen until now – was finding an accessible open space whose owners would permit its occupancy by half a million-odd encamped rock fans. Everyone had assumed that Golden Gate Park, the most obvious and suitable site, would be made available: unfortunately, however, no one contacted the San Francisco Parks department until some days after the concert had been announced. It was then learned that the Parks department required a bond of four million dollars for insurance against damage to city property and to pay for the mammoth job of clearing up afterwards. Frantic telephone calls were made to other large landowners in the San Francisco area. They, too, saw visions of littering and defecating rather than love and peace, and brusquely refused to donate their open spaces, as suggested, gratis.

The difficulty seemed solved when Craig Murray, President of the Sears Point Raceway, offered his land at no charge and on minimal conditions, foremost of which was that any proceeds from the concert should benefit Vietnamese orphans. As a site, the raceway was ideal, being large, accessible to crowds and practised in dealing with their food and sanitary requirements. Craig Murray's offer was gladly accepted. Chip Monck and his stage-building and lighting crews moved out to Sears Point to begin the process of transformation.

Not until the stage was almost built, and tens of thousands of hippies were rolling up their bundles for the trek to Sears Point, did a fatal flaw reveal itself. Sears Point Raceway was owned by Filmways, a Los Angeles-based movie company whose attitude proved noticeably less philanthropic than Craig Murray's. To the terms originally offered by Murray, Filmways attached a last-minute rider stipulating that they must receive exclusive distribution rights to any film shot at the concert. The alternative was to pay them a million dollars in cash, with a further million dollars lodged in escrow to compensate for any damage done to their property.

It subsequently emerged that Filmways had some cause for this apparent bloody-mindedness. Another of their subsidiaries, Concert Associates, had promoted the two shows at Los Angeles Forum when the Stones had carried off three-quarters of the $260,000 box-office gross, had made exorbitant demands for back-stage amenities and – Concert Associates claimed – had reneged on a promise to play a return date at the Forum. With this residual bad feeling, Filmways could not be expected to show largesse to any event involving the Stones. Ronnie Schneider, on his side, flatly refused to give away the film distribution rights or pay the sums demanded. Twenty-four hours before the concert was due to start on a stage already built, Sears Point Raceway was scratched.

At this apparently hopeless juncture, with the Grateful Dead faction squabbling impotently among themselves and the Stones threatening to play, if necessary, on some empty parking lot, a striking new player made his appearance. He was Melvin Belli, San Francisco's most famous trial lawyer, a white-haired legal showman who had been attorney to Jack Ruby, Lee Harvey Oswald's killer and was now involved in the Charles Manson murder trial. Mick Jagger, losing faith in hippy initiative, retained Mel Belli to untangle the mess with Sears Point and Filmways, and try to find a last minute alternative concert site.

The Maysles' cameras ran on in Belli's office as 'The King of Torts', in brown Beau Brummell suit and bright yellow shirt, diverted his powerful mind from the Manson case to the problems of San Francisco's free rock festival. As Ronnie Schneider remembers, Belli's initial advice was somewhat unorthodox. 'He said "You could always just go ahead and do the show at Sears Point, and take a chance on them suing you. Maybe they'd never ever get around to it."'

The spectacle of Belli cross-examining possible site-donors by telephone as Schneider and John Jaymes looked on – and Manson witnesses waited in the next room – gave the crisis a surreal touch. One such alternative donor had been found, but was now raising objections in a voice of increasingly passionate irritation that Belli's drawling courtroom wit seemed only to exacerbate. '. . . You don't understand my problem. I have a *time* problem,' this unnamed individual pleaded. 'My people need more time to work on this thing . . . I see nothing but trouble . . . This whole thing is getting to be a pain in the *ass* . . .' 'Well, I'm not a proctologist here,' the lawyer replied suavely.

Amazingly enough, in the course of that Friday morning, Belli did find an alternative site. A man named Dick Carter, proprietor of the Altamont Raceway, near Livermore, California, phoned in with an offer to donate his land on terms even more moderate than Sears Point's original ones. The only conditions were that the concert must be free, that its organizers guarantee $5,000 to clear up afterwards, and that a million-dollar insurance policy be taken out to protect against major damage.

The site, some forty miles south-east of San Francisco, was a stock-car racing track carved into an eighty-acre grass plot which – on paper – seemed more than adequate to contain the expected audience of 300,000. The crucial question was whether, in the twenty hours remaining, Chip Monck and his construction team could dismantle the stage they had built at Sears Point, transport it with all its ancillary towers and generators the sixty-five miles to Altamont Raceway, and reassemble it in time for use at noon the following day. Monck – the solitary hero this enterprise would produce – replied that it could be done, with extra volunteers, if everybody worked through the night.

By mid-afternoon, Mel Belli had concluded negotiations with the philanthropic Mr Carter, a thin-faced man wearing heavy hair-oil and a short toothbrush moustache. 'The Sheriff wants to know,' quipped Belli rotundly, 'who's going to the bathroom, and where.'

'It's on!' *Rolling Stone* announced in a jubilant stop-press. 'It will be a little Woodstock and, even more exciting, it will be an *instant* Woodstock . . .' The same message went out all evening over scores of rock radio stations, turning the migrant tide away from Sears Point and towards Altamont. A few people did not share the general euphoria. 'They'll never do it,' said Bill Graham, the promoter, speaking from his stores of untapped experience. 'They should call it off or it'll explode in their faces . . .' Others, casting a horoscope for the event as had been done for Woodstock, were dismayed to see that on December 6, the Moon would be in Scorpio, portending a time of chaos and violence.

Exactly who first had the idea of hiring Hell's Angels as a security force, no one can remember now. Some say it was Rock Scully, the Grateful Dead's manager; others remember Emmett Grogan of the Diggers proposing that the Stones be escorted to the stage by a ceremonial guard of 'a hundred Angels on hogs [motorcycles] . . . that way, no one will dare to go near them'.

The idea did possess a glimmering of logic. Previous rock concerts in the San Francisco area had found it better to invite the Angels than to risk their arrival, unbidden, in a spirit of antagonism. Giving them spurious official status had proved an even better emollient. So, in the spirit of Aquarian brotherhood and devout hope that the same ruse would work again, various Hell's Angel chapters throughout north California were contacted and invited to act as 'stewards' at Altamont.

They were not hired as bodyguards for the Stones, as all subsequent reports would allege. What happened was that Stones people – notably Sam Cutler, the concert compere – went along with the plan to invite them. To Cutler, as to the Stones themselves, all the term 'Hell's Angel' probably signified was the pimply-faced boys with freshly washed hair who had been so cosmetic and inoffensive a feature of the Hyde Park free concert, five months earlier.

Californian Hell's Angels were not the same. They were highly organized, semi-outlaw gangs whose fascist insignia were all too accurate a reflection of character, and whose vicious mass reprisals against anyone suspected of slighting their brotherhood made even the police unwilling to challenge them. Heaven help anyone on the freeway not showing due respect to an Angel, his woman, his chapter emblem or, most of all, his neurotically gleaming, high handlebar 'hog'.

In latter years they had acquired a certain chic, thanks to writers like Hunter S. Thompson and Emmett Grogan, who perceived in their impenetrable brutishness and grubbiness an honesty otherwise absent from modern American life. So it was politic, but also 'groovy' to set these real-life urban bandits in visual counterpoint to the mythic outlaws and vagabonds of rock.

It was now six o'clock in the evening of that confused and frenetic Friday, December 5. The weak winter sun had declined into chilly dusk. On the hills around Dick Carter's raceway, scores of figures could be seen, tramping with a peculiar dogged, fatalistic tread which, added to their beads and plaits and rolled blankets, gave them the appearance of native Americans on the way to a new hunting ground. The first spectators were arriving at Altamont.

The end of their journey was very far from being a beauty spot. On three sides of the racetrack stretched empty slopes covered with grass whose pigment seemed burned out of it by exhaust-fumes, and dotted here and there with the wrecked shells of cars used up in the track's 'demolition derbies'. Shards of rusting auto metal and broken glass crunched under sandalled feet. It all looked bleak and uninhabited – and, indeed, it usually was. Altamont Raceway had long been teetering on the edge of bankruptcy. This was a golden opportunity, in Dick Carter's eyes, to give the place a new image.

The first-comers pitched their tents and, as the night grew colder, lit fires made with palings from the wooden perimeter fence. Others squeezed in to sleep or make love behind the eviscerated dashboards of the wrecked stock cars. On the low-lying section nearest the highway, Chip Monck's volunteer crew laboured to put together the stage they had transported from Sears Point. The atmosphere was good-humoured, as at Boy Scout camp, with touch football under the arc-lamps, guitar singsongs and good trips by firelight. A ragged cheer greeted the arrival of eight ancient trucks, each loaded with a dozen portable one-person toilets that were presumed – incorrectly – to be merely the advance guard of the sanitary facilities.

At about 3 a.m., the Stones themselves arrived by limousine with Ronnie Schneider. Mick Jagger, dressed in a pink cape and bulbous pink velvet cap, inspected Chip Monck's nearly completed stage, then walked among the camp fires like young King Harry visiting his troops before Agincourt. Someone democratically held up a joint to him and – having asked for the TV cameras to be switched off – Jagger took a hit and passed it back. The vibes at this stage could hardly have been better. Keith Richard liked the feel of the crowd so much, he stayed the rest of the night, talking, smoking and eventually settling down to sleep on the grass.

By early Saturday morning, as the wan winter sun came up, 100,000 were already on the site, with thousands more arriving each hour, abandoning their cars eight miles away on a jammed-solid ten-mile stretch of half-finished freeway, and joining the trek down the access road, over the hills or along the railway line. From the air, the effect was of a huge ploughed field, its furrows alternately earth brown and denim blue, moving as if by some seismic compulsion over the paler-contoured semi-desert.

For a half a square mile around Chip Monck's stage, the slopes were solid with bivouacked bodies, each clinging to its precious inches of space with as much fervour as if the earth were shortly to be turned upside down. Here and there, stumbling among the legs and backs, could be seen one or other of the dozen film crews which Albert and David Maysles had mustered for the occasion. The Maysles wanted vignettes of hippydom, and they were not disappointed. Everywhere the camera lens looked, it saw painted faces, tattooed bodies, babies being suckled at the breast. Ever and again, in the delight of a good trip or the anguish of a bad one, some half-clad figure would leap to its feet and demonstrate the whirling dervish ritual of freaking out. All seemed to be going exactly to plan for what the organizers had begun to call 'Woodstock West'.

The Hell's Angels began arriving at about 10 a.m. Cheers and even applause were heard as the roar of 850cc engines parted the crowd like gossamer, and the grime-back squadrons bumped and swerved their heavy steeds downhill in ceremonial order: the 'Frisco chapter, the San Bernardino, the Oakland, the San José. With them the Angels had brought a yellow school bus filled with supplies of beer, cheap red wine and tabs of even more dangerously cheap LSD. They had also brought, as badges of their stewards' rank, chains, knives, brass knuckles and, their own special persuader, sawn-off wooden pool cues, weighted with lead.

As the cavalcade passed through, bottles of wine and joints were offered to them and graciously accepted. One female onlooker, forced to jump aside, shouted a reproach. The Angel stopped and waited while his girlfriend dismounted, walked up to the other girl and punched her in the mouth.

By midday, the scheduled starting-time, even on that part of the site not policed by Hell's Angels, good vibes were fast melting away. Sunshine had given way to cloud and a grey, grubby light which showed Altamont Raceway in all its true depressing character. Three hundred thousand people had long since swamped the few meagre facilities provided to feed and amuse them. Queues stretched for hundreds of yards from the tiny outcrop of portable toilets. Nineteen doctors, in scattered medical centres, were already inundated by victims of the bad drugs apparently being peddled by organized syndicates. Supplies of antidote drugs like Thorazine were running low. Nothing could be done with most of the victims but to put them behind rope enclosures to jerk and writhe like plague victims not quite dead. Nothing had happened yet to indicate this was Woodstock West rather than a vast, agglomerating slum of bodies either inert with chemical horrors or comatose with boredom. Not a note of music had been played. The sound system wasn't yet working properly.

Down at a stage already overburdened with roadies and Hell's Angels like a waterlogged life raft, Sam Cutler turned in exasperation on a black man who had climbed up to join in. Or, rather, stepped up – the stage-rim was, inexplicably, only four feet or so from the ground.

In a love-and-peace accent almost visibly bursting at the seams, Cutler said:

'I'd really like you to get off the stage, baby – *please*.'

'Okay, man,' his tormentor said, also in the idiom that could express only pacts between friends. 'I can dig that – you know?' A moment later, when Cutler's back was turned he stepped up on the stage again.

'Ladies and gentlemen . . .' an only slightly less brittle version of Sam Cutler's voice eventually boomed out over the still wavering PA system. 'We give you Santana, the first band in the best party in 1969 . . .'

Santana's blend of Latin big band energy and the passionate lead guitar Carlos Santana himself was the newest sensation in rock. As the fat brass sound rolled outward, with all its suggestions of fun and fiesta, good humour very nearly won the day. Figures were up and dancing everywhere, shaking kaftan sleeves like ragged eight-armed Indian gods. 'It was almost pure ecstasy,' Sol Stern of *Ramparts* magazine later said. 'Turning round, all I could see were people back as far as the clear blue horizon. It was like being in the eye of a hurricane with energy and turmoil all around. I thought everything was going to be all right – that the power of the music would keep it all in balance.'

By halfway through Santana's set, swirls and flurries of violence, at first almost too quick for the eye to follow, were happening all along the stage-front to its scaffolded corners where massed Hell's Angels confronted the ordinary public. A blond-haired boy, trying to break through, disappeared under a hail of punches and kicking motorcycle boots. An older freak with a Mexican moustache, who had stripped to reveal pendulous breasts and a penis clenched like a button mushroom, stood, apparently in deep thought, after numerous blows from an Angel's weighted pool cue. A photographer who tried to record the incident was felled with pool cues, kicked and stomped as he lay bleeding and finally smashed in the face with his own camera.

While the stage was re-set, Sam Cutler attempted to curb the Angels' rampage, as urged all around him by circuitous politeness and tact. Santana's performance had been punctuated also by a fusillade of full beer cans, thrown from the Angels' school bus commissariat thirty yards away. Cutler sent an emissary to the Angels in charge of the bus, offering to buy their entire beer supply for $500. The beer could thus be put *on* the stage, preventing its use as random missiles. This was the origin of one powerful Altamont legend: that the Hell's Angels were hired by Rolling Stones people for $500-worth of beer.

Next to perform were Jefferson Airplane, a band of psychedelic chamber musicians fronted by the vengefully beautiful and beady-eyed Grace Slick. The Airplane had always championed Hell's Angels, even played benefit concerts for them. Grace Slick, all crow-black hair and fitted blue satin, attempting to establish camaraderie, said, 'Will the Hell's Angels please take the stage?' Jefferson Airplane played We Can Be Together and the violence re-erupted – quick flurries of black leather, white insignia, a face or arm upraised under flailing pool cues.

'Hey – we're cool . . .' Grace Slick's voice protested over the PA system. 'We can be cool. Hey down there – why are we *hurting* each other?'

Jefferson Airplane played Revolution, with its hopefully empathic refrain 'up against the wall, motherfucker.' More

Angels closed in like soldier ants around a single black youth. Marty Balin, the Airplane's vocalist, leapt off the stage to intervene and was himself bludgeoned unconscious. Paul Kantner, the lead guitarist, said into the microphone, 'I'd like to tell you all what's happened. The Hell's Angels have just smashed Marty Balin and knocked him out for a while.'

Across the stage, a bearded Angel seized a spare hand-mike. 'Is this thing on or what?' his voice rasped gigantically. '. . . Are you talking to *me*?'

'I'm not talking to you,' Kantner's amplified voice answered. 'I'm talking to these people.'

'Fuck you,' the Angel's voice roared back.

'It's really weird up on that stage,' a voice kept repeating. 'Man, it's really *weird*.'

Jefferson Airplane were still onstage when the Stones' charter helicopter touched down fifty yards to the rear, on an asphalt strip meant to be a high security musicians' landing and departure area. In fact it was as crowded and chaotic as any other part of the site. No attempt was made to camouflage the Stones or steer them to the trailer dressing room any way but straight through the crowds jostling for a sight of Mick Jagger. They had gone only a few steps when a teenage boy, half-crazed with cut-price acid, lunged forward and punched Jagger in the face, crying 'I hate you, you fucker. I want to kill you.' Bodyguards twirled the boy in one direction and Jagger, visibly pale and shaken, in the other. He managed to make light of the incident, however, and ordered that no reprisals be taken against his attacker.

The passing of the word that Jagger was here seemed to cause a lull in the stage-front violence. Things improved still further as the Flying Burrito Brothers, featuring Keith's new friend Gram Parsons, played their sweet, anodyne country rock. The Stones, in their backstage trailer – unaware that there had been any particular trouble – went about the familiar procedures of tuning up and holding court. Jagger, fully himself again, appeared on the steps outside and began autographing the proffered books, album-sleeves and military draft cards. Later, he and Keith walked across to look at the audience and even climbed onstage for a few moments with the Burritos. It was noticed that, wherever a Stone went outside the trailer, he was accompanied by a guard of between three and six Hell's Angels, all armed to the teeth.

In fact – as Ronnie Schneider confirms – the Stones placed no reliance on this grubby phalanx and had hired their own personal bodyguards for protection against the Angels as much as any demented fan. Their two principal guards, an inoffensive-looking white man and an enormous black man named Tony Fuches, both quickly ran into Hell's Angel trouble. At an access-point to the stage, the white bodyguard had a cigarette stubbed out against his hand. More Angels were rushing to join the attack when a signal from one of their leaders – the celebrated Sonny Barger – caused them suddenly to back off. According to Schneider, the man concerned was an FBI agent, a figure whom even Hell's Angels dared not challenge.

The black bodyguard, Tony Fuches, made his presence felt in a more straightforward way. Threatened by two Angels at once, he punched them in the face simultaneously, so hard that he broke both his wrists.

Crosby, Stills and Nash were onstage with their new addition, Neil Young, their choirboy harmonies barely audible over the deteriorating PA. Stills, Nash and Young had not wanted to play at all and were doing so only after strong persuasion from David Crosby. Their performance, nervous and desultory, was like a green light to chaos to break out again. Hell's Angels were now surrounding and beating onlookers at random – spectators, male and female, even their own camp followers and chapter novitiates. At one point, for no apparent reason, a ten-strong group charged outward into the audience, pool cues hacking to right and left. Crosby, Stills, Nash and Young finished their set, unplugged their guitars and bolted for their escape helicopter.

There was a further lull as stretchers were passed along to pick up the fallen and those behind pressed forward to fill the vacated spaces. Sam Cutler, hemmed in at his microphone, played his final card. 'The Rolling Stones won't come out,' he said, 'until *everybody* gets off the stage.'

Cutler's words were apparently the signal for a dozen or so Angel 'officers', led by Sonny Barger, to ride their bikes through the crowd and park them in a slanted line directly below the stage. Barger would afterwards maintain that the concert-organizers had specifically asked him to provide this special barricade, augmented by gleaming, untouchable hogs. Sam Cutler and Rock Scully would be equally sure that no one ever made any such request.

To all this fast accumulating danger, the Stones now added their usual imperious and indolent disregard of the fact that people wanted to see them perform. More than ever on this tour, it had been their habit to delay and delay, piling up the tension, the expectation, the half-adoring rancour at this new demonstration that they couldn't give a damn. Round the stage, a rumour circulated that they were long since ready but that Mick Jagger wanted complete darkness so that the stage lights would show off his costume and make-up to best effect.

Darkness was falling rapidly. As the cold intensified, fires were lit from the remnants of the raceway fence, or from garbage. A pall of smoke drifted up and settled around the still darkened stage. Doctors working in nearby medical tent asked for extra light, but were told that might spoil the impact of Jagger's entry when it came. Backstage, the Stones' helicopter pilot told Ronnie Schneider he was too nervous for his machine to wait until the end of their performance, as arranged. Tony Fuches, the black bodyguard, said he'd hold the pilot there at gunpoint if necessary.

When the Stones finally materialized, in a demon-red spotlight blaze, so did an escort of Hell's Angels so dense as to be almost obliterating. Jagger, wearing an orange and black satin cloak and his Uncle Sam topper, had literally to fight his way to the low stage-front. The Angels were no longer protecting the stage: they had commandeered it for a display of their own power in which the Stones figured only as semi-captive mascots. Jumpin' Jack Flash found himself hobbled in a tiny recess between crimson-lit Angels, being born in a cross-fire hurricane with barely enough space to swing his elbows. 'Fellers—' he kept saying in pretended amusement. 'Will you give me some room? Will you move back, fellers, *please*?'

Halfway through Carol, even that good tempered rock 'n' roll number, pool cues began flailing again among the faces close to Jagger's silver boots. Out in the darkness beyond the smoke-red arena, Keith Richard's chords were finding their mark. Boys and girls stripped naked in the dank cold, flinging themselves forward against the cracked leather cordon as puny white martyrs, almost begging to be surrounded, beaten, stomped and kicked. In the stage-front area, a dozen photographers, mindful of their colleague's earlier fate, kept their lenses resolutely blinkered. Only the Maysles' film crews, each with an Angel shotgun guard, avidly recorded all there was to see.

Now came the moment when – according to which equally possible version one prefers – Mick Jagger's intuition deserted him or his vanity became overmastering. Either way, the result was incredible stupidity. Folding his cloak around him, he stepped forward in the mincing gait he had evolved for this most presumptuous of all his masquerades. 'Please allow me to introduce myself . . .' sang Satan, in his trendy orange satin, across a landscape whose authentic hellishness he could not, or would not, see.

The effect was as sudden as if the ground had opened up. Faces down to Jagger's left collapsed sideways under the tossing assault of Hell's Angel staves. The Devil-invoking samba beat expired in a whistle of guitar feedback. Satan, cut off in mid-verse, grasped for words that would return him to the hippy plane. 'Brothers and sisters . . . brothers and sisters, come *on* now. That means *everybody* – just cool out. Just cool out now. We can cool out, everybody. Everybody be cool now, come on . . .'

The beating down of pool cues paused as if in answer to his exhortation. 'Okay,' Jagger said, evidently believing he had worked some similar miracle to that of James Brown in the race riots. 'I think we're cool now . . . we can groove.' A shaky little joke revealed his continued failure to grasp the situation below him. 'We always have something very funny happen when we start that number . . .'

Something, not very funny, *was* happening, the incidental purpose of which seemed to be to stop Sympathy for the Devil ever from getting beyond its first few bars. It had re-started but petered out again. In the mêlée below Jagger, a naked girl struggled her face, breasts and arms through a crevice to reach up entreatingly to him in the instant before her black leather shroud closed in. 'Fellers . . .' Jagger protested lamely. 'Does it take *five* of you to handle that?'

The stage now thronged with Angels like a bar at closing time. There was also a large and ugly Alsation dog prowling round unattended, sniffing at Charlie Watt's bass drum and Bill Wyman's trousers. As Jagger stood indecisively there, an Oakland Angel with a Mormon elder chin-beard came up beside him and began to speak frowningly into his ear. If Jagger lacked resolution, Keith Richard did not. Pointing furiously across his guitar, he shouted to the stage-front Angels to stop what they were doing. Sam Cutler rushed forward to restrain him, but Keith kept pointing and shouting, 'That guy there . . . if he doesn't stop it, man . . .'

'Er – *people* . . .' Jagger began again. 'Who's fightin' and why? What are we *fightin'* for?'

'It's that guy down there,' Keith shouted, still pointing. 'If he doesn't cool it, man . . .'

'San Francisco . . . This could be the most beautiful event.

Don't fuck it up . . .' It was that rare thing, Jagger's ordinary voice, accentless, wan, almost trembling. He stood there, a forlorn, flat-footed figure, wrapped in black and orange satin, punctured with the uncomprehending dismay of finding himself totally ignored by an audience.

'All I can do is ask you – *beg* you to keep it together. It's within your power.'

To underline Jagger's entreaties to everyone to sit down, Mick Taylor and Bill Wyman began to improvise a slow instrumental sequence from the chords of Under My Thumb. Behind them, on a trailer belonging to the Grateful Dead, David Maysles signalled his cameraman, Baird Bryant, to keep filming this unprecedented instance of the Stones playing calm-down muzak. Jagger himself still stood there helplessly. Close beside him, the face of a Hell's Angel stared into his, enlarged by the unreal perspective, its eyes sightless with unpronounceable malice, its bearded lips opening and closing like a poison pink anemone.

Twenty feet from the stage, the crowd suddenly parted to form a broad avenue, such as might open to greet a conquering hero. Down the middle came a lanky young black man, dressed in a light green suit, and running with inspired energy. For a hypnotic second or two, this oddly lean and elegant figure, its right arm stretched up as if to touch off an Olympic flame, whirled in the half dark between a clump of Hell's Angels and a girl in a white crocheted mini-dress. Just for a trice against the crochet work, the object in his right hand showed its dark, long-barrelled silhouette. Then the dark mass surged in again to obliterate him.

The stabbing to death of eighteen-year-old Meredith Hunter by a Hell's Angel wearing the skull and crossbones insignia of the Oakland chapter, should by rights have been witnessed by only two or three among the thousands standing torpidly near. No one on the stage saw it, least of all the Stones, at this moment trying to collect themselves enough to begin playing again. It happened too quickly even for Baird Bryant, the stage cameraman, to see it in his own view-finder while filming it. David Maysles, acting as Bryant's sound man, was aware only of a flicker 'like a tassel . . . something you'd wave.'

Neither cameraman nor sound recordist realized what had happened even as they filmed Mick Jagger leaning forward, trying to hear something being shouted up at him. The appeal then broadcast by Jagger seemed no different from others which had preceded it. 'We need a doctor . . . now please. Look – could you let the doctor through, please? Somebody's been hurt . . .' Jagger could not see that people around Meredith Hunter were holding up hands soaked in his blood to try to show the awful extent of his injuries.

The Stones had pulled themselves together and were playing again by the time a young doctor in a green combat jacket had fought his way to the clearing where Hunter lay, and had taken over from the couple of horrified boys trying to wash away the blood with hot coffee from a paper cup. By the time the doctor had got Hunter to the backstage medical tent, the performance was on its feet again. 'Under mah thumb . . .' Mick Jagger sang. 'A Siamese cat of a girl . . .' It could have been that very girl, in her white crocheted mini-dress, who stood by the unwanted ambulance, crying, 'They can't hear his heart . . . I don't want him to die . . .'

The ambulance had been put there, in fact, to transport the Stones the fifty yards back to their helicopter. 'I was out there, searching for the driver, to help the guy who'd been hurt,' Ronnie Schneider says. 'I ran into a cop – the first one I'd seen all day. As we stood there, this cop heard over his walkie-talkie that the guy was dead.'

The Stones played on, meanwhile, vaulting from Under My Thumb to Midnight Rambler, Queenie and Brown Sugar, hitting each head-on with the kind of lucid brilliance that terror so often inspires. 'We knew that if we stopped, there really *would* have been a riot,' Mick Taylor says. They even did Street Fighting Man as per programme, with its now sickly inappropriate valediction from Jagger: 'We're gonna kiss you goodbye . . .'

As the Stones bolted from the stage, the Angels moved in on the remaining beer supply, howling that now the party could really begin. Across in the asphalt pit area, fourteen people threw themselves into the Stones' eight-seater helicopter. Before the door closed, it was lifting off, its perspex bubble crammed like a cookie jar with bodies and leather lapels and boots, and Mick Jagger's sweat-smeared, frightened face.

There was none of the usual after-show drinking and carousing that night. Even Keith Richard seemed to want to do nothing but fold his tattered frame into a brocade armchair, nurse a bottle of Jack Daniels and stare glumly off into space. Mick Taylor locked himself in his hotel room and slid the chain across the door.

Shocked as they all were, they still did not realize what a piece of butchery had been enacted literally before their eyes. Next morning's *San Francisco Chronicle* reported the Altamont festival as a brilliant success only slightly marred by death. As well as Meredith Hunter, three more youths had been killed; two run over by a car as they lay in sleeping-bags, the third drowned in an irrigation ditch. The *Chronicle* preferred to stress Sam Cutler's claim that the event had been life-enhancing. According to Cutler, four babies had been born during the day's events. Dick Carter, the raceway owner, was reportedly delighted with his first foray into pop promotion and was now planning an even bigger festival, headlined, he hoped, by the Beatles.

London newspapers picked up the same line of a Stones-inspired freakout where death had been almost cosmically counterbalanced by birth. STONED! chortled the *Daily Express*, unconsciously echoing that long-forgotten B-side. Arriving back in London, all the Stones were understandably tight-lipped. Even Keith Richard told a UPI reporter that Altamont had been 'basically well-organized, but people were tired and a few tempers got frayed.'

The real story only began to emerge late that Sunday night, via an exhaustive on-air inquest by San Francisco's rock station KSAN. Numerous callers-in reiterated the grisliness of conditions at Altamont and the mindless brutality they had witnessed there. Despite obvious fear of reprisals from the Angels, even Sam Cutler was persuaded to admit, 'I didn't dig, in fact, what a lot of people did yesterday.' For editorial balance, there was the voice of Hell's Angel Sonny Barger, almost plaintive in its claim that the Angels had been the victims of rock star vanity and vagueness. 'I didn't go there to police nuthin', man . . . They used us for dupes.' According to Barger, the trouble had started after several Angels below the stage had their bikes deliberately kicked over, and one even set on fire. 'I ain't no peace creep, man . . . Ain't nobody goin' to get my bike, man. Anyone tries that, they gonna get got. And they *got* got.'

Barger's own autobiography – for such a thing does, indeed, exist – goes even further in portraying the Angels as naive, well-meaning chaps who realized they were being used by the Stones to create an atmosphere of theatrical menace, but nevertheless tried to do a conscientious job as security guards. According to Barger's account, Meredith Hunter actually shot and wounded one of the Angels during his sprint through the crowd, but this had to be kept quiet at the time because the Angel concerned was a fugitive from the law. 'I don't feel too bummed about what happened' is Sonny Barger's perspective, thirty years on.

It further emerged that no babies at all had been born during the festival. The nearest approximation was a youth who announced he was pregnant, just prior to jumping from a traffic flyover and suffering serious multiple injuries.

The most damning contemporary account did not appear until almost six weeks afterwards, in *Rolling Stone* magazine. A 20,000-word article by a team of *RS* writers who had been present reconstructed the whole chaotic story with a wealth of investigative detail not previously associated with underground journalism. Among the eyewitness testimony was a description of how Meredith Hunter, an apparently law-abiding black teenager from Berkeley, had had his hair yanked by a Hell's Angel and, on giving 'a mean look', had been set on by half a dozen more. Hunter, it was said, tried to escape but had been knifed in the back as he ran towards the stage. Bystanders saw him pull a gun from his coat pocket and wave it in the air. An Angel had then moved in, stabbing Hunter repeatedly with a seven-inch knife, clubbing and kicking him as he lay bleeding, even standing on the victim's head before strolling nonchalantly away. Hunter had died from massive stab wounds in the back, side and temple which the sketchy medical facilities could not begin to staunch. His only audible words had been to his attacker: 'I wasn't going to shoot you.'

Rolling Stone's conclusion was unequivocal. The real blame for Altamont lay, not with Mel Belli or Dick Carter or even Sonny Barger, but with those whose name the paper bore on its own masthead. The Stones were portrayed throughout as monstrously conceited, deaf to all warning signs, careless of all the terrible consequences. It was powerful even courageous journalism, albeit marred by inaccuracy and confusion. *Rolling Stone* still had no idea how much its own harping on inflated ticket-prices had hardened Jagger's resolve to do a free concert. Nor could its writers resist embroidering a too perfect detail: that when Meredith Hunter was stabbed, the Stones had been playing Sympathy for the Devil.

Most stinging of all was the comment on the Stones' hurried exit from San Francisco, leaving others to pick up the pieces and the corpses. '. . . Fuck Mel Belli. We don't need to hear from the Stones via a middle-aged jet-set attorney. We need to hear them directly. Some display – however restrained – of compassion hardly seems too much to expect. A man died before their eyes. Do they give a shit? Yes or no?'

Bill Graham, the concert-promoter – whose expertise had been so consistently ignored – was more specific in his furious condemnation. 'I ask you what right you had, Mr Jagger . . . in going through with this free festival? And you couldn't tell me you didn't know the way it would come off. What right do you have to leave the way you did, thanking everyone for a wonderful time and the Angels for helping out? What did he leave behind throughout the country? Every gig, he was late. Every fucking gig he made the promoter and the people bleed. What right does this god have to descend on this country this way? But you know what is a great tragedy to me? That cunt is a great entertainer.'

On January 8, 1970, a twenty-two-year-old Hell's Angel named Alan Passaro went on trial in Oakland, California, for the murder of Meredith Hunter at the Altamont festival on December 6. Passaro admitted stabbing the black boy but stated it was in self-defence, after Hunter had actually fired the gun he was waving. He further stated that he had inflicted only slight wounds and that someone else must have made the ghastly rent in Hunter's left temple, the gouge at the top of his spine and the stab through his tailored jacket into his abdomen.

The main prosecution evidence consisted of a feature film currently on release throughout America. It was the Maysles brothers' documentary, rush-released to cash in on the post-tour publicity, and named, after the Stones' last incantation to chaos: *Gimme Shelter*.

The climax of the film – not even seen by the cameraman until its editing stage – formed the crux of the murder trial in Oakland. There on screen, playing three times daily coast-to-coast, was the killing of Meredith Hunter.

The Maysles' film had enabled police to identify Hunter's attacker as a prisoner serving time in a California jail for a drug offence committed a few days after the Altamont festival. Further screenings were held throughout the trial to help the jury determine whether the obese Angel striking at Hunter was Passaro, and whether his seven-inch knife, or someone else's, had struck the fatal blows.

Since Passaro's Angel brothers had already delivered Hunter's loaded gun to the California highway patrol, the jury had no choice but to acquit him.

A California courtroom was thus the first to see the film record of the Stones' triumphal comeback and its obscene climax. There, as the jury watched, were the good tour moments: the wild scenes at Madison Square Garden, the good mix of Wild Horses down at Muscle Shoals. There was the genial press conference, when the woman journalist said, 'Are you any more satisfied now . . .?' There was Mick Jagger, in beret, scarf and lipstick – looking uncannily like the young Leslie Caron – watching his own repartee on the Maysles' film-editing machine.

'Financially . . . just sa'isfied. Sexually sa'isfied, y'know. Philosophically tryin',' Jagger's on-screen voice said.

'*Rubbish*!' commented his voice derisively in the editing room.

There, at last, was the crucial moment at Altamont in the red-spotlit dark, as Jagger stood, helpless among the real demons his masquerade had summoned up. There was the crowd, falling back to form a wide avenue. There was the long-legged, prancing figure in its light green tailored suit. There was the converging blur of a Hell's Angel, a death's head badge, a plunging knife, a gun silhouetted on a girl's white crocheted dress. There it was again in slowed-down replay; murder in highlight, like some great sporting moment, a man dying twice for dramatic emphasis.

There was the sequence showing the Stones again, several weeks afterwards, watching Meredith Hunter's end on the Maysles' editing machine. There was Charlie Watts, as divorced from the unholy fable as ever, yet dominating the scene with his long, sensitive, bewildered face. 'Some o' those Angels, y'know, couldn't have been nicer . . . It was all so insane, what went on y'know . . . It was just unreal . . . Oh, dear – wha' a shame . . .'

There for all time is Mick Jagger, evidently shocked by what he had just seen, yet ruled as ever by the need to show no emotion. His reddened lips have not stirred from their photogenic pout as Altamont ends and the dejected hippy masses wander off like refugees towards a new, unsympathetic decade.

Eventually he gets up and tosses his scarf over one shoulder.

'Okay . . .' he says. 'See y'all . . .'

Fourteen

'The Stones like France tremendously'

The new decade loomed ahead with all the invitingness of a hung-over morning after. All around lay the debris of the sun-soaked, joss-scented, careless spree that had ended, like a candle brutally blown out, on the last stroke of midnight, 1969. The hit record of the moment had none of the twangly euphoria with which youth had celebrated and congratulated itself so many times over the preceding ten years. It was a dramatically orchestrated ballad, Simon and Garfunkel's Bridge Over Troubled Water, whose title seemed to offer a faint ray of optimism amid the prevailing gloom. 'When you're weary . . . feeling small,' sang Art Garfunkel, his voice riven with pity for all those who had awoken in the Seventies, rubbed their eyes and realized with horror that they were in their mid-twenties.

The Beatles caught the zeitgeist perfectly as usual – but for the last time ever. All the melancholy of an expiring belle époque seemed distilled in their film *Let It Be*, which showed the once-indivisible quartet racked by terminal squabbles and bitterness. Although the official break up would not be announced until 1971, everyone accepted that the Fab Four were no more. The Apple house in Savile Row, where Allen Klein now reigned supreme, had been purged of all its hippy hangers-on and its talent and now simply looked after accounts. Paul McCartney was in exile on his Scottish farm. George Harrison was making a solo album, Ringo Starr playing character parts in movies. John Lennon was living with Yoko Ono in a stately home, riding around its grounds on a supercharged golf cart and preparing to write a song containing the line 'imagine no possessions'.

That seven-year race between the Sixties' two foremost groups through Top Twenty charts and *Melody Maker* polls seemed to have produced a winner at last. The Beatles were breaking up. But the Stones were breaking out.

On July 30, 1970, Les Perrin's office confirmed that the Stones had terminated their relationship with Allen Klein and would now be represented by Prince Rupert Loewenstein of the merchant bankers Leopold Joseph. It was further announced that the Stones had ended their relationship with Decca Records and its US subsidiary, London. The group and their merchant bankers were still undecided about whom to choose of the twenty-one different companies reportedly competing to sign them.

His eventual dumping seems to have taken Klein uncharacteristically by surprise. On June 3, *Variety* had quoted him extensively on his plan to give the Stones a business structure much like the Beatles' pared-down Apple. In particular, *Variety* said, they would have their own record label, distributed by whichever corporation was lucky enough to acquire them. Two months later, the Robin Hood of pop turned round to find an arrow in his back.

After the arrow came a full-frontal arbalest. The Stones filed suit in the New York State Supreme Court, seeking $29 million in damages from Allen Klein, and claiming he had used his position as their manager 'for his own personal profit and advantage'.

Though the break with Decca had long been on the cards, some last-minute efforts were made by Sir Edward Lewis's men to stop so gigantic an asset from walking away. Decca joined the frantic wooing of the Stones by hopeful record companies that went on during their 1970 European tour. In Paris, Ronnie Schneider was asked if Decca could do any little thing to make them more comfortable. Schneider said it might be nice if their bill were paid at the George V Hotel. Glad to, the Decca man said, not realizing that the George V still let its VIP guests order goods to be delivered from the Paris shops and have them paid for by the concierge.

The size of the bill told Decca unequivocally how things stood. Relations thereafter were terminated with malevolent politeness. Decca informed the Stones that, under their present contract, they were obliged to provide one more single. The Stones duly delivered an unusable studio doodle entitled Cocksucker Blues.

They had entered the new era, in fact, with rather too much alacrity for the taste of those still clinging to a driftwood Sixties dream. Altamont seemed in retrospect the deliberate smothering of all things beautiful, with the Stones impassively looking on. Britain, too, had seen the *Rolling Stone* special report by now, as well as highly critical follow-up pieces in papers like the *Sunday Times*. Enormous resentment was felt throughout the rock culture at the Stones' apparent lack of remorse and their seeming escape from all comebacks and comeuppance. (Actually, they had been threatened with indictment as accessories in the Meredith Hunter murder. They were currently being sued for $80,000 by Altamont farmers and were themselves suing Sears Point Raceway over the enforced last-minute change of venue.)

Their fourteen-city European tour, that August and September, helped to baptize the new decade with its hail of joyless uproar and eddying smoke. In Paris, the street battle around L'Olympia recalled the Sorbonne riots of '68, with gendarmes launching tear-gas attacks and cars overturned and burning. In West Berlin, sixty-five policeman were injured and twenty-one vehicles damaged in attacks by ticketless fans on the city's Deutschlandhalle. It was the same – almost wearily the same – in Hamburg, Helsinki, Milan and Gothenburg. Baton charges, falling bodies, the scamper of ambulances with quaint foreign sirens: all would blur into one image on TV screens in the Seventies, barely making people glance up from the meal trays on their knees.

It is to Mick Jagger's credit that he allowed the release of a film whose climax showed him in such an appallingly unflattering light. He had commissioned the Maysles brothers to make *Gimme Shelter*; he could easily have suppressed it, or demanded removal of its more damning scenes. His decision to let it go out uncut – despite probable repercussions on the European tour – seems mostly to have been based on the $30,000 he had personally invested in it. He did, however, seek advice from his old film-making friend, Donald Cammell, who told him what serious movie critics have since confirmed: that *Gimmie Shelter* is an ugly masterpiece.

The abuse directed at Jagger after *Gimmie Shelter* was mild compared to that which assailed *Ned Kelly*, when the film received its premiere in July 1970. Just how a director like Tony Richardson could have propagated so sorry a mess remains mysterious. All the film seemed to consist of were men in slouch hats, on horses, riding very fast to unspecific destinations while a (puzzlingly American) voice-over warbled the ballad of Kelly's exploits. There in almost every implausible scene was Jagger, a bearded railing in feeble Irish brogue against 'the stiff-necked English'. One reviewer wrote that Jagger was 'as lethal as last week's lettuce'; another said that, encased in Ned Kelly's home-made armour, he looked like 'a cut-price sardine'. Jagger himself affected scornful detachment. '*Ned Kelly* – that load of shit! I only made it because I had nothing else to do.' Donald Cammell's recollection was that after seeing the finished film, Jagger burst into tears.

Jean-Luc Godard's *Sympathy for the Devil*, showing the Stones at work on *Beggars' Banquet*, also appeared in 1970. So, a year late, did *Performance*, starring Jagger, James Fox and Anita Pallenberg. A management shake-up at Warner Brothers, and general paranoia in Hollywood about an impending recession, finally allowed the film to be released, in a heavily truncated version. Here, at least, Jagger was not a laughing-stock. His portrayal of Turner – widely interpreted as a portrayal of himself – received mild praise that, compared with *Ned Kelly*'s reception, sounded like standing ovations. For all its faults, and the heavy-handed studio interference, *Performance* seemed to belong to 1970 rather than any part of the Sixties. Still denied general release, it was to become a cult movie, drawing capacity houses whenever it chanced to resurface.

Jagger's career and his private life were in a state of flux, matching the new decade. He said as much during the European tour, his inner uncertainty producing an interview of almost unprecedented candour. 'You get to the point when you have to change everything – change your looks, change your money, change your sex, change your woman, because of the business.'

Changing his woman was proving a process far more painful than those casual words would suggest. He was still in love with Marianne, as well as bound to her by three years of familiarity and habit. Rather to his surprise, his love had stretched to pardoning her her fling with Mario Schifano and his own resultant worldwide humiliation. He had remained her protector the previous December, just after Altamont, when they appeared together before Great Marlborough Street Magistrates Court – still visibly estranged by Marianne's Italian Prince Charming – to answer the drugs charge dating from the previous June. The arresting officers' testimony unconsciously corroborated how Jagger had tried to shield and soothe Marianne during the bust, saying, 'Don't worry . . . it's all right. Nothing will happen . . .' The court fined him £200, but acquitted Marianne.

Back at 48 Cheyne Walk, the store of happiness continued to dwindle. Jagger was constantly absent, recording with the Stones, conferring with his new advisers – or seeing other women. Marianne's heroin addiction deepened, her looks deteriorated, her behaviour grew erratic and irrational. In restaurants, as she herself admits, she would sometimes pass out face down in her food.

By the time Jagger left to go on a tour in August 1970, the pressure of changes about to be made had become unbearable. In the end, it was Marianne who took the initiative. 'I knew it was the end of an era,' she says. 'I knew nothing could ever be the same again.' So one night, taking Nicholas and a few clothes from the plundered wardrobes upstairs, she walked out.

For a time Jagger found solace in his ongoing affair with the actress and radio presenter Marsha Hunt. A stunning beauty under her mushroom cloud of Afro hair, she fascinated and amused him, yet offered no threat to his newfound bachelor independence. All she did say, quite straightforwardly, was that she would like to have a baby and wanted him to be the father.

His other affairs were numerous and short-lived. He fell into the habit of using his unfinished country house in Berkshire as a kind of illicit one-night hotel. Two years after buying Stargroves, he still had spent only a couple of nights under its Gothic roof. As caretakers he variously installed his parents, his younger brother Chris, and a young man named Maldwin Thomas who used to cut his hair in Knightsbridge. Maldwin grew accustomed to being awakened late at night by Jagger, with some temporary companion, demanding to be let into the guest cottage.

For months Jagger still did not accept that Marianne really had gone for good. He wrote to her and telephoned her constantly at her mother's house in Berkshire. 'In the end,' Marianne says, 'I let myself get fat. It was a conscious decision – I wanted to show I wasn't in the market any more. When Mick walked in and saw me, his jaw dropped. I knew that really was the finish.'

The introduction was made formally, for once, after the Stones'

Paris Olympia show. 'Mick – this is Bianca,' Donald Cammell said, drawing the ever evasive rock star towards a young woman who had been watching the proceedings with the slightly contemptuous detachment of an Egyptian royal cat. 'You two are going to have a great romance,' Donald was inspired to add. 'You were made for each other.'

Bianca Pérez Mora Macías was the daughter of a wealthy Nicaraguan commodities dealer. Her uncle was Nicaraguan ambassador to the Batista regime in Cuba. A distant cousin of her mother had been cultural attaché at the Nicaraguan embassy in Paris and afterwards ambassador in Bonn. Throughout Bianca's childhood in Managua, Nicaragua was ruled, as it had been for forty years, by the corrupt and homicidal Somoza regime. Her father was apolitical but Bianca's mother hated Somoza passionately. Women, however, were not supposed to have political convictions, as Bianca discovered when she and her brother, Carlos, joined student demonstrations in protest at the almost annual crop of opposition figures whom Somoza had eliminated.

Her parents divorced and her mother, inadequately provided for, was reduced to running a small restaurant in Managua. Though Bianca adored her father – whom she resembled in all but his green eyes – she rebelled fiercely against the principle of male domination he represented. She vowed she would never let herself be so dominated and so thrown aside.

In 1960, at the age of seventeen, she won a scholarship from the French government to study at the Institute of Political Science in Paris. Her mother encouraged her and her brother, Carlos, to leave Nicaragua, saying that if Carlos, especially, stayed on there he would probably be killed by the Somoza regime.

In Paris Bianca was diverted into a social whirl that ultimately prevented the completion of her political science thesis. She became the girlfriend of Michael Caine, the British actor, who brought her to London, showed her off at the Dorchester, and took her shopping for clothes at Thea Porter's Soho boutique.

When she met Mick Jagger, she was deeply in love with Eddie Barclay, the head of France's leading record label. Barclay was a much older man in whom, Bianca admitted, she saw a father figure. Since he was already married, she believed the affair was hopeless. She fell for Jagger not just because he was famous and fascinating and funny and clever, she later said, but also because he was young.

Her effect on him was mesmerizing. Until the Stones left Paris, he spent every possible minute of the day and night with her. She flew to join him in Rome and travelled with him for the rest of the tour. He asked her to return to England with him; she agreed. He had never made so many rapid, irrevocable decisions.

Bianca's arrival sent shock waves through the Stones' entourage, where those accustomed to compete for Jagger's monarchic attention and favours now found themselves eclipsed and ignored. There was consternation especially among the Stones' women, that travelling purdah compartment where Anita Pallenberg ruled like a blowsy blonde begum over Mick Taylor's wife, Rose, and Bill Wyman's Swedish girlfriend, Astrid Lundstrom. Anita instantly hated Bianca with a passion that some attributed to her own lingering designs on Mick. While pretending expansive friendship towards Bianca, insiders recall, she did everything possible to undermine her. She would borrow Bianca's couture clothes, on the pretext that her own were still unpacked, and then leave the exquisite capes and jackets strewn about the floor. According to Spanish Tony Sanchez, Anita approached him to dig up dirt on Bianca – preferably that she was really a man who'd had a sex-change operation.

Rome has never been the ideal place for a celebrity to begin a clandestine romance. This particular celebrity knew no way of setting foot outside that would not bring a horde of paparazzi in ravening pursuit. The harassment grew so bad that Jagger ran up to one cameraman and punched him. The result was a heavy fine for assault and a house rule that, in future, paparazzi must be dealt with by Jagger's bodyguards. That was the method in Vienna, while Jagger escaped by shinning over a wall. The outcome was only to be expected. By the time he returned to London with Bianca, the story of their courtship was international news. At Heathrow airport, Jagger took refuge in sardonic cliché, alleging they were 'just good friends'. Bianca, fixing her tormentors with a dark frown, declared, 'I have no name. I do not speak English.'

By November 1970 she was living with him at Stargroves, where the Stones had gone to try to finish their new album, *Sticky Fingers*. 'They could hardly get any work done, with Mick the way he was about Bianca,' Shirley Arnold says. 'She'd come into the studio and give him the eye . . . he'd leave the other Stones and follow her upstairs.'

That same month, in St Mary's Hospital, Paddington, Marsha Hunt gave birth to a baby daughter whom she named Karis. Though the press suspected who the father was, Marsha – for the moment – refused all inducements to name him. 'We had a baby on purpose . . .' was all she'd say. 'Now he's no longer involved with us. At first I thought I cared for him a lot, but I found out afterwards I didn't really know him at all . . .'

In 1970, Bill Wyman discovered that he owed £118,000 in back income tax. It was doubly a shock to the most provident and sensible Stone to find himself facing the vengeance of British tax law against all high earners who do not put away half their income religiously until the day the government asks for it. Bill, with his mathematical mind, instantly grasped the hopelessness of his position. 'Once you owe £118,000 you *never* catch up. All the money you earn to pay that off, you get taxed on as well. You're working for the government forever. And it's *your* fault, even though you're not to blame. All you've ever done is take advice. You have to trust *somebody*.'

Bill's was a modest debt compared with those of Mick and Keith, whose incomes from song copyrights had, at least, equalled their share of the Stones' collective earnings. 'I just didn't think about it,' Jagger said later. 'And no manager I ever had thought about it, even though they said they were going to make sure my taxes were paid. So, after working for eight years, I discovered nothing had been paid and I owed a fortune . . .' All the rearguard actions fought by the accountant would be likely to reduce the whopping sum by no more than a fraction. The Inland Revenue, if necessary, was going to get blood out of the Stones.

There was only one alternative to gritting their teeth, paying up and wiping out all profits from their last US tour. By absenting themselves from Britain in the financial year 1971–72, explained Prince Rupert Loewenstein, they could escape all tax on their income in 1969–70. The same oracle would work, retrospectively, for every subsequent year they could prove non-residence in the United Kingdom.

The choice of France was an almost inevitable one in those days when tax exile still carried a cachet vaguely associated with W. Somerset Maugham. To Jagger – especially in light of his recent experience there – Paris was the only possible substitution for London. In France, the Stones, far more than the Beatles, had always been the height of chic. There were, moreover, positive fiscal advantages for a pop group serving an international market to be domiciled in a country relatively free of restrictive exchange controls. And, on top of everything else, there was the sunshine, the food and the booze.

In September 1970, discussions began between Prince Rupert and France's leading financial lawyer, Maître Michard-Pellissier, about the feasibility of a mass migration by the Stones to Paris the following April. Discussions continued in October when the Stones passed through on tour – and were, apparently, not jeopardized by the street riots they sparked off. An early whiff of the plan reached the London *Evening Standard* via its Paris correspondent, Sam White; then the subject was replaced in the headlines by the riddle of Mick Jagger's new Latin-American love.

The official announcement came in March 1971, at the start of a short British tour designed to give it maximum impact. Even the lordly *Times* and *Telegraph* sent reporters up to Newcastle-upon-Tyne to hear that the Stones were quitting Britain to settle together in France. Their decision, it was emphasized, had nothing to do with income tax, nor should any such unkind thing be adduced from their planned exit in April, just before the start of the new British tax year. 'It's not a case of running away from the tax man,' their PR man Les Perrin said. 'The Stones like France tremendously.'

'If you know me,' Jagger added with a grin, 'you know I'll probably be back in Britain more times than I have been in the past . . .' He looked vaguely French, in his floppy blue cap and grey suede maxicoat. Bianca accompanied him on this journey of valediction to Coventry, Manchester and Glasgow; they posed together, revealing an almost eerie facial resemblance to one another and conversed in French for most of the time.

Essentially rootless as he had always been, Jagger found no difficulty in shutting up his two little-loved English properties and contemplating a tax exile's life. The move was far harder for Bill and Charlie, with their settled homes – harder still for Mick Taylor, who had earned no very large sums yet but was none the less compelled to uproot his wife and new baby and follow the others abroad. As for Keith, he simply refused to acknowledge how quickly the days to April 5 were running out. He continued to lie prostrate beside his batik-draped lamp at 3 Cheyne Walk, as if he had all the time in the world.

Where the Stones were to settle in France remained undecided until only a week or so before their departure. Paris was ruled out at an early stage after it was hinted that Jagger, as a convicted drug user, might be subjected to twenty-four-hour police surveillance. The search then moved to the Riviera. A task force from the Stones' office, led by Jo Bergman, travelled to Cannes and began inspecting likely properties for rent up and down the Côte d'Azur. It was rumoured that estate agents were being asked to provide bathrooms able to accommodate up to eight people for 'Roman-style orgies'. A visit by the team to Mougins, an exclusive hamlet sheltering Pablo Picasso and Prince Sihanouk of Cambodia, produced such alarm among the inhabitants that the mayor fought his next election campaign solely on a pledge that he would never permit Rolling Stones within the town limits.

By mid-March, only Charlie Watts had seen a property to his liking – a characteristically well-hidden farm in Provence. The others were to live together in Cannes while Jo Bergman continued the search for orgy-sized bathrooms. Jo had agreed to emigrate with them, leaving the London office in Shirley Arnold's charge.

The Stones' farewell to London was a concert at the Round House on March 14, followed by a televised appearance at their old haunt, the Marquee Club. Keith – by now in a state of open insurrection – sat at home in Cheyne Walk until almost the moment the cameras were set to roll. Then, furious and barefoot, he flung himself into his Bentley, drove to Soho, left the Bentley on a double yellow line, and stamped in to his place on the stage. It was unfortunate that the Marquee had the same manager, Harold Pendleton, who had provoked Keith often in the past. It was still more unfortunate that Pendleton wanted a large neon sign reading MARQUEE CLUB behind the Stones as they played. The upshot was that Keith – repeating history – swung his guitar at Harold Pendleton's head, and had to be dragged from the club backwards, his bare feet trailing on the ground.

On the day of departure, Jo Bergman's task force descended on 3 Cheyne Walk, picked up everything around Keith – furniture, bottles, half-full ashtrays, clothes, scarves, Marlon's toys – packed it all into cartons, transported it across the Channel, and rearranged it in the same pattern around Keith as he subsided into his new home in Ville Franche.

On April 7, two days into their official exile, the Stones signed a new recording contract with Kinney Services, American parent company of the New York-based Atlantic label. They had chosen Atlantic for its reputation in soul music and because, of all the record-company moguls who had wooed them over the past year, Atlantic's president, Ahmet Ertegun, had created easily the most favourable impression. Armenian by birth, son of Mustafa Kemal's ambassador to Washington, Ertegun looked like a diplomat with his neat beard and highly polished alligator shoes. But there was no greater devotee of the blues and soul music which had made Atlantic's name.

Ertegun had unblinkingly met Prince Rupert's terms for an advance on six Rolling Stones' albums to be delivered over four years. These would be released on the Stones' own label, Rolling Stones Records, but manufactured and distributed by Atlantic. The head of the new label would be Marshall Chess, whose father, Leonard, had founded the famous Chess label in Chicago. Multimillion-dollar dealing and purist sentiment seemed, in all respects, to have made the perfect match.

It was no more than natural that, for the new label's logo and visual accompaniments, Mick Jagger should employ the world's most famous and infamous artist, Andy Warhol. Warhol's design left no doubt as to whom the new deal had most gratified. Jagger's own lips sagged open in a livid red escutcheon from which his unmistakable tongue slavered forth as if to lap up the promised millions. It was – and remains – among the more brilliantly suggestive examples of corporate identification. Marianne Faithfull found it particularly evocative, remembering how much Jagger had admired a stage set like an open mouth at the Royal Ballet, years previously when she was educating him.

On April 16, the new label released its first product, a single with three tracks: Brown Sugar, Bitch, and Let It Rock. A week later came *Sticky Fingers*, an album whose packaging, no less than its contents, flaunted the new era of liberty. The sleeve, also designed by Andy Warhol, showed a denim-clad crotch, its fly a real zip fastener opening to reveal Mick Jagger's lips and tongue. The reverse of the sleeve was the backside of the jeans.

Brown Sugar was an instant Jagger-Richard classic, fusing Keith's indolently repetitive opening riff with Jagger's hip-shaking Dixie drawl in a paean of racist sexism that could have been about brown Mexican heroin, or cunnilingus on a female plantation slave with Jagger as Simon Legree wondering 'How come you taste so good?' Brown Sugar was the stickiest treat to be found on *Sticky Fingers*. But for Wild Horses – a poignant memory of loving Marianne – the rest was little more than a glossary of drug jargon. 'Cocaine eyes', 'speed freak hive', 'cousin cocaine', 'sister morphine' were smuggled into the ear, wrapped in slickly inventive guitar and sax work. Even the album's serial number was a nudge-nudging 'COC 59100'.

Decca, meanwhile, had sought to clog the market by releasing a compilation of old Stones tracks entitled *Stone Age* and packaged in a sleeve much like the one for *Beggars' Banquet* that Sir Edward Lewis had banned three years earlier. The Stones hated the compilation so much, they spent £700 on press advertisements warning their fans that it was substandard.

On May 11, Mick Jagger telephoned Shirley Arnold in London and told her he was marrying Bianca two days from now in Saint Tropez. He then gave her a list of the seventy-odd people he had chosen as wedding guests. The list ranged from Paul McCartney to the Queen's cousin Lord Lichfield. Shirley had to contact them all within twenty-four hours and get them on a specially chartered plane from London.

Bianca was now four months pregnant, but that alone did not explain the headlong rush to matrimony. She would say later that she'd still felt unready to make such a binding commitment and that, despite her Catholic upbringing, she would have been quite prepared to have Jagger's child as merely his girlfriend. The haste was all on Jagger's side, indicating how the break-up with

Marianne still affected him and how he missed the stable family life he'd enjoyed with her and Nicholas. Bianca none the less found herself characterized as a modern version of Delilah, the biblical houri who destroys Samson's strength by cutting his Jagger-length hair. She was seen – even by generally tolerant Keith – as a disastrous threat to Mick's image, to the Jagger-Richard songwriting partnership, to the whole future of the Stones as a band. Memories of what Yoko Ono had done to John Lennon and the Beatles were still all too fresh. Would the kingly head Stone likewise end up ceremonially planting acorns for peace or screaming *musique concrète* from inside a paper bag?

The wedding, on May 13, was to consist of a civil and a religious ceremony. Since Bianca was a Catholic and Jagger nominally an Anglican, he had to agree to take preparatory instruction in his new wife's faith. He did so willingly, in French, impressing the local abbé, Fr Lucien Baud, with his intelligence and receptivity. He seemed to want to do everything right. That, he said, was his reason for leaving the wedding arrangements so late – he wanted to stop it from turning into 'a circus'.

The world's press had been let into the secret at an early stage. Planeloads of reporters and photographers took off from Heathrow airport on May 12 along with the chartered jet carrying Paul and Linda McCartney and their children, Ringo Starr, Eric Clapton, Keith Moon, Ossie Clark, Joe and Eva Jagger, the Stones PR man Les Perrin and his wife, Janey. 'All the musicians were smoking drugs, even on that short journey,' Janey Perrin says. 'It worried the life out of me. "Right," I said. "You, you and you – make sure you get rid of that before we land."'

The nuptial day began with a dispute between Mick and Bianca over the wedding contract they each had to sign. French law stipulates that a couple embarking on marriage must state whether their property is to be held in common or separately. A French marriage contract is a cold-blooded document listing everything of the bridegroom's that the bride may or may not share. Jagger wanted Bianca to agree to waive any right to his possessions in the event of a divorce. Bianca was upset, and pleaded with Mick to call the wedding off. She would still have his child, she repeated, and they'd just live together. Mick grew angry, saying 'Are you trying to make a fool of me in front of these people?' So the contract was signed, witnessed by Mick's assistant, Alan Dunn.

Meanwhile, in the council chamber of the Hôtel de Ville, Mayor Marius Estezan waited to conduct the civil ceremony beneath a portrait of President Pompidou. In France, civil marriages are open to the public. The scrum of photographers and TV crews was only slightly less in the council chamber than in the sunshine outside.

After twenty minutes' delay, word was brought to the mayor that Jagger would not come unless the chamber was cleared of all but invited guests. The mayor replied that it was a public occasion and the public had a right to stay. Appeals to the commissioner of police produced the same answer. The mayor unhooked his official tricolour sash and said that if the couple did not appear in ten minutes the wedding would not take place.

The ultimatum was telephoned to Jagger. 'Then I'm not going through with it . . . it's all off,' Jagger retorted. Janey Perrin remembers hearing Les patiently remonstrating: 'Don't be silly. Don't be *silly* . . .'

Fifty minutes after the appointed time, bridegroom and bride entered the chamber together. Bianca wore a wide-brimmed white hat and a low-cut white dress whose clinging contours gave no sign of her pregnancy. Jagger wore a pale green three-piece suit and a flowered shirt, and looked wary and ill at ease. As they went to take their vows, fist-fights broke out among French photographers jockeying for the best vantage point. Bianca would later say, sadly, that, as far as she was concerned, her marriage ended before her wedding day was even half over.

Jagger tried to turn back again, but was propelled by Les

Perrin to the mayor's table, almost dragging Bianca behind him. The civil marriage was accomplished at last, amid a clamour of automated shutters that obliged the mayor to raise his voice to an exasperated squeak. The official witnesses were Roger Vadim, the French director, and the film star Nathalie Delon. Behind them stood Keith, apparently having a whispered row with Anita.

Up the whitewashed hill, Jagger's theological instructor, abbé Baud, waited inside the pretty fishermen's chapel of St Anne, facing a congregation whose numbers Les Perrin had controlled by the simple expedient of locking the front doors. When the newly-weds emerged from their hired Bentley, hard pressed by *Paris-Match* photographers, they had to hammer at the church door for admittance. They were heard at last and let in, and the religious part of the proceedings began. The bride was given away by Lord Lichfield. In his address, the abbé referred to his talks with Jagger. 'You have told me that youth seeks happiness and a certain ideal and faith. I think you are seeking it, too, and I hope it arrives today with your marriage.' At Bianca's request, the organist played Bach's wedding march and the theme from the film *Love Story*.

The reception took place in a small theatre next to the Café des Arts. Lord Lichfield, in his other capacity as society photographer, moved around snapping the famous faces. Bianca, reappearing in a full skirt and a sequinned turban, managed to upstage even Brigitte Bardot. An awkward moment occurred when Keith Richard hurled an ashtray through a window, but it passed off when Keith passed out on the floor. Later, the bridegroom took the stage for an impromptu performance with Steven Stills and Doris Troy. Bianca, seemingly upset, returned to their hotel suite alone. The party went on all night, heedless of the various small children slumped half asleep amid the marijuana smoke. It is debatable which was the more melancholy sight: those neglected superstar children, or Joe and Eva Jagger, wandering around still trying to find an opportunity to give their son his wedding present.

News of the wedding first reached Marianne Faithfull as she was en route to Paddington to catch a train down to her mother's in Berkshire. In her shock, she staggered into an Indian restaurant, ordered a meal and began drinking heavily. Some time later, she passed out into a plate of curry and was removed to spend the night at Paddington Green police station.

'Next morning, when they let me out, they realized I was famous and asked me to sign the visitors' book. It was a brand-new police station: the only other signature in the book was the Home Secretary's, after the official opening.' Marianne signed her name under the Home Secretary's and walked unsteadily out into Marylebone Road.

Before leaving Britain Keith and Anita had both undergone treatment for heroin addiction. Keith took his cure at Redlands with the famous 'Dr Smith', while Anita was conveyed to a clinic in Middlesex. No hope existed for either unless they could be kept scrupulously apart.

Withdrawal from heroin – the cold turkey of John Lennon's bleak song – has been compared to rolling naked on a bed of barbed wire while simultaneously swallowing a bottle of disinfectant. 'You sweat . . . you scream . . . you hallucinate,' Keith says, with what might seem scientific detachment. 'I can remember being *sure* that behind the wallpaper there was a needle and some smack, if only I could get to it.' Every so often, 'Dr Smith', a nurse with the cheerful manner of a district midwife, would pop another drug-substitute capsule under his tongue.

'In seventy-two hours, if you can get through it, you're clean. But that's never the problem. The problem is when you go back to your social circle – who are all drug pushers and junkies. In five minutes you can be on the stuff again.'

Keith's new home on the Riviera was Nellcôte, an enormous

Roman-style villa, built by an eccentric English naval officer, on a hill above Villefranche-sur-Mer. Its steep garden was full of rare and exotic plants, its balustraded terrace commanding spectacular views of the mountains and Cap Ferrat. The rent was a thousand pounds per week with an option to buy for two million pounds if its new tenant found it agreeable.

The villa's airy, elegant salons were transformed, like all his previous habitations, into the environment Keith found most comfortable – that is to say, the semblance of a motel room recently ransacked by the police. Album sleeves, wine bottles, discarded clothes, half-smoked joints settled as usual on the grand piano and the marbled mantelpiece. Baby Marlon voyaged, nappyless, along brocaded sofa rims. Nellcôte was the centre of the Stones' exile, its familiar squalor lending continuity – comfort even – to the others' expatriate lives. It was the meeting place for employees, business advisers, record-company people, fellow musicians, and all the multifarious freaks whom this added distance – from London or California – seldom deterred in their supplicant eagerness to hang out with Keith and the Stones. 'In all the time we were in that place, we were never by ourselves,' Anita says. 'Day after day, it was ten people for lunch . . . twenty-five for dinner . . .'

Though Bill and Charlie both lived nearby, they chose – no doubt wisely – to keep their households private and their public profile low. Jagger had rented a villa in St Tropez, but he and Bianca spent the greater part of the summer in Paris, staying at Mistinguett's favourite retreat, L'Hôtel. From June to September Keith's most steady companion was Mick Taylor, who lived with Rose in a much less grand house up the hill from Nellcôte. One weekend when the crowd of hangers-on there was particularly large, Keith and Anita knocked on Taylor's door and said, 'Can we come in for some peace and quiet?'

For the first few weeks, Keith seemed content to absorb himself in the Riviera pursuits of eating, drinking, sunbathing, swimming, and sailing his boat, *Mandrax*, with whomever he could rouse from the Nellcôte floors to act as his crew. Heroin had not killed his taste for the outdoor life – as a two-, a five-, even a ten-year junkie, he would remain physically superior to Mick at his most ostentatiously clean-living and *sportif*. 'Mick got very into tennis while we were in France. He took it *very* seriously. I hadn't bothered since the tennis-club days, when I'd go with my mum and dad in Dartford. But I could still go out on a court and beat the shit out of Jagger any time.'

He also found time for fatherhood. Two-year-old Marlon, thus far, had seen little home life outside the tumbled hotel suites where Shirley Arnold would put him to bed. Marlon learned to walk on a Rolling Stones concert stage; the first words he learned to speak were 'room service'. In Villefranche, he was finally allowed to become a child. Keith devoted the best part of every day to him, carrying him around clamped to the skinny chest that once admitted no encumbrances but its guitar strap and dangling cocaine spoon.

By early May, as his conduct at Jagger's wedding showed, Keith was starting to chafe against his new life. More trouble broke out in June – a fight between Keith and the Beaulieu-sur-Mer harbourmaster, who had tried to stop him hitting an Italian motorist after a minor traffic scrape. According to Spanish Tony Sanchez, a Nellcôte house guest, Keith pulled a toy gun on the harbourmaster and was very nearly shot by the official's own very authentic firearm.

It was inevitable, as the months passed, that he and Anita should pull each other back to the only possible cure for their shared, oversurfeited boredom. A supply of cocaine arrived with Spanish Tony, hidden in a toy piano the dealer had brought for Marlon. Heroin was obtained for them by a French pusher with contacts in the Corsican underworld that ran the narcotics trade in Marseilles. Now they were 'shooting up' rather than 'snorting', buying the drug in £4,000 consignments that rarely lasted longer than a month.

All summer long, the waterfront cafés of Villefranche swarmed with drug pushers of every kind and complexion, avid to supply – and, if they were fortunate, join – the orgies rumoured to take place each night up at Nellcôte. If rumour was to be believed, these orgies did not belong to ancient Rome so much as the wilder hillbilly regions of Kentucky. One English student, hoping to peddle his mite of hashish, found himself drawn into a French conversation that made the Mars bar legend sound positively conventional. 'Zat's right . . .' his neighbour nodded. '*Les poules* . . . chickens. Zey do it with chickens . . .' He was not referring to the Nellcôte cuisine.

The strain of tax-exile life began to tell on even the most law-abiding publicity-shy element in the Stones' circle. In June 1971 Charlie Watts's wife, Shirley, was involved in an altercation with a customs officer at Nice airport and sentenced, in absentia, to six months' imprisonment for assaulting him. The Aix-en-Provence appeal court later reduced her sentence to a suspended fifteen days, allowing her to re-enter the country. Charlie was, understandably, devastated by this first blot on his family name.

It all added weight to Keith's insistence that France was having a bad effect on them, and that the best cure was to get into a studio and start work on a new album. The Stones had been followed to France by their 'Mighty Mobile', a £65,000 trailer studio, equipped with every technological marvel, including closed-circuit television. Nellcôte, in addition, had a basement that could be converted into extra studio space.

A new album was certainly due in early 1972, when Jagger planned for the Stones to tour America again. Atlantic wanted a special blockbuster to launch the tour and also counteract the flood of inferior compilations Decca were putting on the market (not to mention the proliferating bootleg albums recorded illegally at concerts).

Keith, therefore, turned his villa over to the Stones, their session musicians, and all the extra personnel needed to build and maintain the improvised basement studio. Thus the album that was provisionally entitled *Tropical Disease*, and only later renamed *Exile on Main Street*, began late in 1971 as the biggest house party of Keith Richard's hospitable career. 'I can remember fifty people sitting down to lunch,' Mick Taylor says. 'It was like a holiday camp.'

Jagger arrived from Paris leaving Bianca ensconced in their suite at L'Hôtel. Now eight months' pregnant, she had refused to endure the longueurs of a Stones recording session and renew her former acquaintanceship with Anita. She would say later that she was scared of everyone to do with the Stones except Bill and Charlie, and that, while not wanting to be anywhere near Anita, she was tormented by rumours that Mick was having an affair with her.

Jagger was visibly torn between his obligations to his wife and to his band, and tried to keep the peace by dashing back to be with Bianca whenever possible. 'Mick's fucked off to Paris again,' Keith would tell the others peevishly, reawakening speculation that Bianca had eclipsed a love affair that long predated the one with Marianne.

Recording in the basement of even a palatial French villa proved hideously difficult. Space was so limited that Nicky Hopkins, the pianist, had to sit in a separate cubbyhole. The power, as usual in France, flickered and faded eccentrically. The current chef, a Frenchman named Fat Jack, interrupted artistic flow by blowing up the kitchen. Keith and Anita were so strung out on heroin one night that they set fire to their own bed. Recording was interrupted again when a sneak thief walked into Nellcôte through an open door and stole most of Keith's treasured guitar collection.

On October 21, Bianca gave birth to a daughter at the Belvedere nursing home. Jagger announced that she would be called Jade 'because she is very precious and quite, quite perfect . . . I've always been a good father,' he added, 'and this kid makes it easy to be.' He phoned Keith to say that he would not be back in Villefranche for another three weeks. The Stones were to go on recording instrumental tracks, and he'd fill in the vocals when he had time.

There is a legend – half corroborated by Anita Pallenberg – that *Exile on Main Street* was recorded with power illicitly diverted from the French national railway system. Its more vital energy was tapped from a physique in which the most murderous of all drugs could not dull or smother the instinct to make marvellous sound. As Keith himself puts it, 'While I was a junkie, I still learned to ski and I made *Exile on Main Street.*'

On May 12, 1972, it was announced that the Stones' $29 million lawsuit against Allen Klein had been settled out of court. No details were given, other than that 'all outstanding differences' between the parties had been resolved, and both wished it made clear that Klein's company ABCKO Industries no longer had any part of managing or representing the Rolling Stones.

The action might have continued for years longer, dragging the Stones' frozen royalties with it, but for the intervention of Klein's nephew, Ronnie Schneider, acting unofficially for Mick Jagger to procure a quick settlement. Jagger's offer, relayed through Schneider, was to drop the lawsuit if Klein would release the cash he was holding and pay token damages. Since Schneider thoughtfully tape-recorded his talks with both his uncle and Jagger, it is possible to listen in on the transactions. '. . . we'll meet 'im if 'e likes,' Jagger's voice says. '. . . the 'ole thing's just gotten to be a drag . . .' 'The money's there,' Klein's voice says. '. . . the payments are guaranteed . . .' At one point he adds, rather plaintively, 'I believe Mick Jagger still *likes* me . . .'

Things did not go well thereafter for Klein. He had lost the jewel in his managerial crown in 1971 when Paul McCartney brought a successful action in the High Court to dissolve the

Beatles' partnership. Though still in titular control of Apple and of the two least accomplished Beatles, George Harrison and Ringo Starr, the 'Robin Hood of Pop' seemed to have spent most of the arrows in his quiver. In 1979, the United States Internal Revenue Service indicted him on six charges of tax evasion on $216,000 allegedly made from selling Beatles promo albums. Thanks largely to testimony by his old 'enforcer' Pete Bennett, he was convicted, fined $5,000 and given a two-month prison sentence. His attention moved from music to feature films (such as *The Greek Tycoon*) and productions for the Broadway stage, though he continued to control the US rights on all the Stones pre-Seventies records, music publishing and films.

★

Dear Promoter

We know it doesn't happen in America, but in rather barbarous outlands [sic] of Europe we have encountered many dressing rooms which lacked towel and soap . . . It would be nice to know we do not have to worry about the same problem. A clean group is a happy group.

Amenities to be provided in backstage changing area:

Two bottles per show of Chivas Regal, Dewars or Teachers Scotch.

Two bottles per show Jack Daniels Black Label.

Two bottles per show tequila (lemon quarters and salt to accompany).

Three bottles iced Liebfraumilch.

One bottle per show Courvoisier or Hine brandy.

Fresh fruit, cheese (preferably not plastic), brown bread, butter, chicken legs, roast beef, tomatoes, pickles, etc.

Alka Seltzer.

Yours sincerely, the Rolling Stones

The tongue-in-cheek humility and room-serviced arrogance concealed genuine trepidation. Two years had not distanced

Altamont's horrors: in one way or another, the Seventies were turning out to be almost nonstop Altamont. The temper of the time was such as to make even Mick Jagger fear the reaction he might generate, by design or accident. 'Don't say I wasn't scared, man,' he told a reporter at the end of the 1972 tour. 'I was scared shitless.'

Jagger had wanted to return to America with a show that would tacitly apologize for the Altamont shambles by confining itself to small theatres where everyone could see and nobody need get killed. Unfortunately, it was too late for the Stones to beat the economics they themselves had largely invented. To make a major rock tour of America enonomic in the early Seventies, the gross had to be around $2 million. There was no alternative to major cities, giant arenas and audiences among whom it was now commonplace to snort cocaine, smash up sets and throw bottles at the band.

Rehearsals took place in Montreux, Switzerland, close to the clinic where Anita Pallenberg was undergoing treatment for heroin addiction prior to the birth of her second child by Keith Richard. A baby girl, Dandelion, entered the Rolling Stones' world on April 17, apparently unscathed by the drugs Anita had continued to absorb until the fifth month of pregnancy.

In Los Angeles, Peter Rudge, the Cambridge graduate – graduated now to first class honours in the rock travel business – was already constructing an operation whose complexity was based on the simple premise that nothing whatever must be left to chance. The Stones were to travel this time with their own stage, built and maintained by Chip Monck: a vast white proscenium, surmounted by intertwined cartoon sea serpents, backed by a 40 by 16 foot mirror and six 1500-watt Super Trooper spotlights, and lubricated with a solution of water and 7-Up to make it more danceable. The equipment, light cables, gantries, forklift trucks, would travel overland by theatrical pantechnicon. The Stones, and the pick of their fifty-strong tour staff, would travel by private Lockheed DC-7 jet, the fuselage of which had been decorated with Mick Jagger's mouth and lapping tongue. Peter Rudge's schedules, and the multifarious and subtly graded backstage passes issued with his countersignature, bore the artless letters STP – Stones Touring Party.

By the time the Stones flew in to Los Angeles to rehearse on a sound stage at Warner Brothers studios, sales of *Exile on Main Street* were touching 800,000. In Detroit, 120,000 applications had been received for the 12,000 seats at Cobo Hall. In Chicago, 34,000 tickets for the two shows at the International Amphitheatre sold out in five hours. Around Los Angeles the black-market price of a $6.50 concert ticket was $75 or its equivalent in hashish.

Two flamboyant rock music publicists, Gary Stromberg and Bob Gibson, had been hired to blitz the nation's press with Stones stories while simultaneously making Mick Jagger the most unattainable interviewee since Greta Garbo. Every major magazine wanted to cover the tour and was vying with its competitors by nominating big name writers meant to appeal to what was dimly recognized as Jagger's literary side. The *Saturday Review* offered William Burroughs (conveniently a heroin addict as well as a magisterial novelist) but were forced to substitute Terry Southern. *Rolling Stone* commissioned Truman Capote in hopes of a non-fiction drama equalling *In Cold Blood*. The tour was to be filmed by Robert Frank, whom Jagger knew as a highly respected still photographer. Literary as well as social snobbery was to pervade the Stones' dressing room, even though, in the end, the combined literary talents would contrive not one sensible or original word about the tour in print.

Six months earlier in New York, a concert for the Bangladesh refugees, organized by George Harrison (with Allen Klein) and featuring Harrison onstage with Bob Dylan, Leon Russell, Ringo Starr, and others, had given rock a tenuous dignity. All that, and more, was about to be undone by the Stones Touring Party.

It was the summer when Governor George Wallace of Alabama was gunned down and crippled for life at a Maryland shopping centre; when Arab guerrillas in tracksuits penetrated the athletes' village at the Munich Olympics and annihilated two-thirds of the Israeli weightlifting team; when the sectarian slaughter in Northern Ireland was extended to policemen, milkmen and teenage boys. It was the summer when the Seventies suddenly focused on an age of terrorist warfare, waged in streets, department stores, restaurants and airport lounges, against bystanders whose innocent deaths were proving a better attention-getter than any UN resolution. It was a time when merely standing in a crowd seemed foolhardy enough. To stand above the crowd, in any context, was automatically to enter the rifle-sight of a hundred homicidal grievances.

The same question would be asked of Mick Jagger time and again as he stood waiting to go on in his pink-sashed purple jumpsuit and his fish-shaped mascaraed eyes: 'Mick – aren't you ever afraid of getting shot?'

'Yeah,' Jagger would answer levelly. 'Yeah – I am.'

The current terrorist craze for aircraft hijacking added further rich deposits of paranoia. On June 5, en route for the traditional Canadian warm-up concert, the Stones' private DC-7 was denied permission to land in Vancouver because of an inadequately filed flight plan. Marshall Chess managed to get a telephone call through to the Canadian prime minister, Pierre Trudeau, but to no avail: the Stones had to land in Washington state and, braving US Customs, cross the border in a fleet of hired limousines.

That night, in Vancouver's Pacific Coliseum, a more traditional form of warfare reasserted itself. Two thousand non-ticketholders stormed the front entrance, throwing bottles and lumps of rock and iron. Thirty policemen were hurt before a relief column of Mounties reached the scene. A single backstage door dividing the Stones from the mob was held shut only by bodyguards' shoulders and piled-up metal garbage skips.

There were those who had wondered if the Stones would pull it off this time, gnarled as they were in their later twenties, and beset on all sides by adolescent phenomena like the Osmonds, the Jackson Five and David Cassidy. In a world that did not blink at the high camp of David Bowie and Marc Bolan, nor at Elton John's outsize Lolita sunglasses, what was there left for Mick Jagger to do? Jagger had grown accustomed to questions about the date of his retirement. 'There's a time when a man has to do something else,' he admitted. 'I can't say what it'll definitely be. I don't want to be a rock 'n' roll singer all my life. I couldn't bear to end up like Elvis Presley and sing in Las Vegas with all those women coming in with their 'andbags . . . it's really sick.'

The Jagger of the 1972 tour was a Jagger resolved to scotch all rumour that his body had in any way deteriorated. On his order, the first dozen rows at every concert were kept free of press and VIPs, so that those who mattered, the eighteen-year-olds, could best compare him with themselves. The one-piece jumpsuit, with its dangling pink sash, clung shinily to wishbone hips and buttocks as tiny as twin collar studs. It became ritual in each night's performance for him to inch open the frontal zip, past the undeveloped nipple and the crucifix, down to the very shadow of his overstuffed codpiece – or was it a mound of Venus? There was still none remotely able to portray that dancing paradox of athlete and stripper, that perpetual indecision between predatory satyr and timid, glitter-eyed fawn.

On June 4 the Stones recrossed the US border to play the Seattle Coliseum. That same day in California, Angela Davis, the black power activist, was found not guilty on patently trumped-up charges of conspiracy to murder. 'Who got free today?' Jagger asked his Coliseum audience. 'Angela Davis got free today. Fuckin' great . . .' The Stones played Sweet Black Angel, a song dedicated to Angela Davis and, for many, the pièce de résistance of *Exile on Main Street*. Radical politics were then forgotten in the tour's first party, back at an opulent hotel on

Puget Sound where the traditional sport among visiting English bands was to bait lines with room-service steaks and fish for mud sharks out of the window.

The Stones' return to San Francisco on June 6 was their first since fleeing the Altamont debris. Promoter Bill Graham had booked them for shows at his 5,000-capacity Winterland arena with no guarantee they would escape a tongue-lashing for their behaviour on the '69 tour. Mick Jagger took the initiative, walking up to Graham with hand outstretched and saying 'Hello, Bill, how are you?' The promoter thawed, admitting generously that he himself, in 1969, might have been 'not the nicest person around'.

To discourage any offensive acts by Hell's Angels, disillusioned flower children, or friends of the murdered Meredith Hunter, the Stones were immured given security like visiting heads of state. At Winterland, Bill Graham employed a special force of seventy-five police to ensure that no one with a motorcycle came anywhere near the auditorium. Two all-out Stones shows gave them absolution in Graham's eyes and, apparently, in San Francisco's. No hint of trouble occurred until they boarded their jet for Los Angeles and a female writ-server in hot pants managed to push a sheaf of legal papers relating to Altamont under Mick Jagger's nose. Seconds later, the writ-server staggered down the aircraft steps, gasping 'He hit me – the sonofabitch . . .' while Keith Richard hung out of the door flinging her subpoenas after her.

In San Diego, fires made from police barricades were started during the Stones' performance. That and the heat reminded Jagger of a Scottish date, long ago, when they thought the place had caught fire – actually, steam was rising from the audience. Tucson, Arizona, had thoughtfully equipped police at the Civic Arena with tear gas. In the eddying smoke, affecting officers as much as rioters, three hundred arrests were made. One patrolman hurled a rock through a car windscreen, shattering the nose of the seventeen-year-old girl inside.

In Denver, Robert Frank filmed Keith and his friend the saxophonist Bobby Keyes throwing a TV set out of a tenth-floor window in their hotel. Keith mentioned other pastimes for bored musicians on Sundays, like ramming a room-service trolley through the TV screen or dropping a firecracker with a waterproof fuse down the toilet, in hopes of blowing up some other guest's toilet three floors below.

In Chicago, at least, offstage security was assured. The Stones had been invited to stay at the mansion of Hugh M. Hefner, founder and publisher of *Playboy* magazine. For three days, between shows at the International Amphitheatre, they and the Stevie Wonder band enjoyed the run of the Hefner mansion's salons and saunas and jacuzzis and private pinball arcades, the white-gloved servants, the twenty-four-hour kitchen, and other singular amenities, which had enabled Hefner not to set foot out of doors for almost a decade. Every couch in every room – to quote a bystander – 'pulsed with women'; Bunnies from Playboy clubs or Playmates, pneumatic and glossy as the pages they adorned. The Stones were invited to join Hefner in the private pool under his bedroom but found, to their disappointment, that it was only for a bath.

Another disappointed member of the party was Bobbie Arnstein, Hefner's one-time girlfriend, now his personal assistant, and, for coincidental reasons, a sufferer from anorexia nervosa. Reacting against several days' self-starvation, Arnstein ate an enormous dinner, finishing with cheese and onions and a slice of Black Forest gateau, which she took with her up to her room. Shortly afterwards, she answered a knock on her door and was amazed to find Mick Jagger there, dressed in tight-fitting white leather trousers. For several uncomfortable seconds, Arnstein tried to succumb to Jagger's advances while simultaneously trying not to let him smell her oniony breath or see the plate of Black Forest gateau reposing on a chair. Caught off balance as he turned away, Jagger stumbled back against the chair and, in his white leather trousers, sat straight down on the Black Forest gateau.

The most fun at the mansion seems to have been had by Charlie Watts, talking to Hefner's cook about his days as a driver for the Chicago mobs. 'I don't sleep on tours,' Charlie says, ''cause I got no one to sleep with. So I talk to people – and I draw.'

In Kansas City, author Truman Capote joined the tour to write about it for *Rolling Stone* magazine. A dwarfish, squeaky-voiced figure in shades and a white fedora, Capote had brought along his own entourage including Princess Lee Radziwill, sister of Jackie Onassis. Alas for *Rolling Stone*'s editors, who had hoped Capote might produce a chronicle rivalling his non-fiction novel about a mass murder in rural Kansas. There, for all his outlandish appearance, Capote had won the confidence of farmers and deputy sheriffs, producing a classic of objective reportage. But turning him loose among the tawdry butterflies of rock produced no such magic chemistry. His article for *Rolling Stone* would get no further than some scurrilous notes about minor figures on the tour. Having initially welcomed him as a prestigious literary camp follower – bringing along a princess to boot! – Jagger became suspicious of Capote, too often his backstage rival as the centre of attention. Capote himself expressed disappointment with Jagger, both onstage and off, describing him as 'a scared little boy' and 'about as sexy as a pissing toad'.

Nevertheless, Capote was allowed to watch the show from onstage, taking voluminous notes for the article he would eventually abandon. Princess Lee Radziwill also played at music journalism, flitting around the breeze-blocked backstage corridors as if attending a UN reception. Keith refused to be impressed by this lofty personage and, after the show, was to be observed outside the Princess's hotel room, shouting 'Princess Radish – c'mon, you old tart, there's a party goin' downstairs!' Capote having proved equally unresponsive to cries of 'Wake up, you old queen!', Keith and Gary Stromberg – dimly realizing his fame as an investigator of mass murder – smeared the outside of his door with tomato ketchup.

Capote was also permitted to ride the 'Lapping Tongue', as the Stones' private jet was nicknamed, and to enjoy its non-stop bar and buffet and the attentions of stewardesses 'Ruby T' and 'Brown Sugar'. So were Terry Southern and Robert Frank, the latter assiduously shooting scenes for yet another Stones film destined never to see the dark of cinemas. Among Robert Frank's doomed inflight vignettes was the stripping naked of a groupie by road crew members while Mick Jagger and Keith Richard danced down the aisle playing bongoes and a tambourine. According to Capote (whose interest in such things was perforce severely limited), the so-called tour doctor then made love to the girl, strapped on his lap by the safety belt. When the plane landed, the doctor still had not managed to put on his trousers again, and disembarked holding them in one hand.

In Washington, appearing on the Fourth of July, the Stones were dissuaded from giving an afternoon performance with fireworks and Jagger in Revolutionary War breeches and tricorne hat. In Indianapolis, a pet hanger-on of Keith's was found to be shaking down drug dealers for a percentage, and was scientifically beaten up by one of the black security guards. In Detroit, Chip Monck and Gary Stromberg hid a chicken leg in the bowl of rose petals that Jagger scattered over the audience at the end of Street Fighting Man. In Philadelphia, the rose petals concealed a lump of raw liver, at the next show, it was a whole pig's foot.

In Montreal, one of the equipment trucks was dynamited by French separatists. While bomb squads searched the stage area for three other charges reportedly hidden there, 3,000 victims of forged concert tickets rioted out in the street. Disembarking at Warwick, Rhode Island, en route for Boston, Keith Richard hit a local press photographer who had been annoying Jagger. In the ensuing scuffle, Keith, Jagger, Marshall Chess, Robert Frank and a black bodyguard named Stan Moore were all arrested. At 8 p.m.

that night, as 15,000 people streamed into the Boston Garden arena, Jagger, Richard and their companions were still locked in police cells at Warwick, sixty miles away. Boston's mayor, Kevin White, arranged for the five to be released on bail and rushed to the Garden with a police escort, five hours late.

In New York, Peter Rudge attended a secret meeting with some Hell's Angels desirous of 'straightening out' the Altamont affair, which, they claimed, had cost their brotherhood $60,000 in legal fees. When Rudge refused to compensate the Angels, a spate of anonymous death threats were made against the Stones. As a precaution the band checked into separate hotels under aliases – Mick and Bianca as Mr and Mrs Shelley, Bill and Astrid as Lord and Lady Gedding, Keith as Count Ziggenpuss. All the party were advised to order no food from room service in case it was poisoned.

The final concert was at Madison Square Garden on July 26, Mick Jagger's birthday. Custard pies were thrown onstage, and the 17,000-strong audience sang 'Happy Birthday to You'. Afterwards there was a party at the St Regis Hotel, attended by Andy Warhol, Princess Lee Radziwill, the playwright Tennessee Williams and other members of the new rock elite. In the centre, at a table covered with so much luxury it approached squalor, Jagger sat with his white satin lapels flat on his meagre chest, eating voraciously while Ahmet Ertegun spoke into his ever-attentive ear. He was twenty-nine – the age at which Nijinsky appeared in public for the last time.

Fifteen

Black and Blue

In December, 1972, the Nice police issued a warrant for the arrest of Keith Richard and Anita Pallenberg on charges arising from the alleged use of heroin at their villa, Nellcôte. It emerged that for the past year all the Stones had been under intense police surveillance with periodic stake-outs at their villas, even infiltration of their social circle by gendarmes posing as drug dealers. Just prior to the US tour, all five had to appear before an examining magistrate in Nice. Jagger, Wyman, Watts and Mick Taylor, after detailed questioning, were pronounced in the clear. Not so Keith, against whom damning evidence existed in the form of a dope-taking ex-chef at Nellcôte. By the time the warrant went out, however, Keith and Anita had fled to safety in the West Indies.

That effectively put an end to the Stones' Riviera tax exile. After recording in Jamaica, for the album that would become *Goat's Head Soup*, all five returned for Christmas in 'good old England', as they were quoted as calling it. The Jaggers were at Cheyne Walk when, on Christmas Eve, an earthquake devastated Managua Nicaragua's capital and Bianca's birthplace. Attempts to contact her mother there proved fruitless. On Boxing Day, Les Perrin received a phone call from Jagger asking him to arrange an airlift of medical supplies to Managua. Next day Jagger and Bianca flew to Jamaica, then on to Managua carrying $2,000-worth of anti-typhoid serum they had collected en route. Managua was a scene of almost total ruin: neither Bianca's mother nor her father could be found anywhere in the city. Eventually, after Jagger organized appeals over the radio, both turned up, safe, in the neighbouring town of Leon.

Bianca stayed on in Managua while Jagger returned to Los Angeles to organize a benefit concert by the Stones, on January 18, 1973, which raised $280,000 for the Managuan homeless. The problem was getting the money past President Somoza, who controlled all the relief and reconstruction agencies and was busily increasing his personal fortune at the expense of the earthquake victims. Bianca sought help from Senator Jacob Javitts while Mick and the Stones rehearsed for their Far East and Australasian tour.

Japan was removed from the itinerary after its government refused to give the Stones entry visas. Australia declared Keith Richard persona non grata because of his heroin habit, but then relented and admitted the Stones despite an awkward moment at Honolulu, en route for Hong Kong, when a syringe was found in Bobby Keyes's saxophone. The tour poster showed Australasia, putting out Jagger's tongue to welcome their Boeing jet. On the journey, Les Perrin developed hepatitis, presaging a long deterioration in his health.

In June, 1973, Marsha Hunt went to court in London, claiming that Mick Jagger was the father of her year-old daughter, Karis, and requesting a magistrate's order for maintenance. Though Jagger privately had never denied Karis was his child, he raised a smokescreen of legal prevarication, demanding an adjournment for blood tests. The story in the Stones' camp was that, willing enough to pay maintenance, he had been stung by Marsha's independence of spirit. It would take eight years for the matter to be settled out of court.

On June 26, as Keith and Anita lay in bed at Cheyne Walk, police entered the house with a search warrant and ransacked it from top to bottom. Keith, Anita and their friend Stash – the same Swiss princeling who had been busted with Brian Jones – were taken to Chelsea police station and charged with possessing cannabis, Mandrax tablets and Chinese heroin. Keith by himself was charged with illegally possessing a .38 Smith and Wesson revolver and 110 rounds of ammunition. According to Keith, the drugs had been left there by one of the succession of subtenants at the house during their absence on the French Riviera. Released on a thousand pounds bail at Great Marlborough Street Court the trio adjourned to Redlands which, four days later, mysteriously burst into flames. Keith carried Marlon and Dandelion to safety, then began salvaging what furniture he could. By the time Chichester firemen had extinguished the blaze, Redlands was without its thatched roof and virtually gutted.

On August 31, the Caribbean-influenced *Goat's Head Soup* was released inside a cover that showed Jagger's face in soft focus close-up, somewhat like the sepia study of some Edwardian girl in a voluminous motoring veil. The tracks included Angie, the Stones' biggest hit single for years, with Jagger's voice as entreatingly tender as it once had been on Lady Jane. There was also a song, originally titled Starfucker, whose content the most daring modern band could hardly have surpassed – the lyrics mentioned vaginal deodorants, 'pussy' and 'giving head to Steve McQueen'. On Ahmet Ertegun's insistence, the title was changed to Star Star and an assurance obtained from McQueen that he would not sue Atlantic for libel. Even so, the song joined Let's Spend The Night Together and many other classics on the BBC's banned list. Also currently in the charts was a tribute to Jagger by his old American flame Carly Simon, entitled You're So Vain and full of pointed references like 'You had me several years ago', 'You're where you should be all the time' and 'Your scarf it was apricot'. Its subject might have been expected to explode in fury at the caricature: instead, he supplied anonymous backing vocals.

Somebody else whom Jagger had had several years ago was in a rather less bouyant state. Marianne Faithfull's continuing heroin habit had left little trace of the innocent convent girl who had captivated him so utterly in 1964. Marianne was now literally living on the street – to be exact on a small stretch of low wall in St Anne's Court off Windmill Street, just a few yards from Piccadilly Circus where all the city's junkies and pushers and human debris come together. For something like eighteen months she sat on that low stretch of wall every day, conscious of little but hunger for the next puncture mark in her arm.

The experience, as Marianne remembers it now, was not all horror. 'In a way I found it fascinating. For all my life until then, I'd always been the centre of attention. I'd always been looked at and admired. Now, nobody recognized me. I was watching the world as it passed. And I was never, ever harmed by the people I dealt with. I wasn't mugged, I wasn't raped. The whole of that underworld, for some reason, treated me with incredible gentleness.'

Her husband John Dunbar had belatedly divorced her on grounds of her adultery with Mick Jagger just before she and Jagger parted. After her brief fling with the Italian Mario Schifano, she began an affair with an antiques dealer named Oliver Muskett. He was kind and supportive to Marianne in her efforts to break away from her stretch of wall in St Anne's Court and cure herself of heroin addiction. This she finally did at a hospital in – of all ironic places – Dartford, Kent.

We are at a photo shoot in the roof garden above Biba's department store in Kensington, West London. One of the models is a dark, pouting beauty, dressed rather like a Latin version of Scarlet O'Hara in a flowing, be-ribboned gown, twirling a parasol above her head. The other model is a pale, pouting beauty in an angular custard-yellow suit and white shoes. The photographer is not Bailey or Donovan but Leni Riefenstahl, whose most notable previous assignment was covering the 1936 Berlin Olympics for Adolf Hitler. Mick . . . Bianca . . . Biba . . . fascist chic . . . we are at the very apotheosis of trendiness in London, 1974.

Bianca had insisted from the beginning that Mick and she were separate people and that she intended to have a career and public profile of her own. Indeed, there was a time when hers threatened to rival his. Fleet Street had just reinvented the gossip column, rightly supposing fatuous tittle-tattle about the famous to be an ideal antidote to fast-uglifying Seventies life. To these latter-day Boswells, Bianca Jagger was an early prime target, flying in and out of Heathrow, always looking disagreeably heavenly and saying nothing. Her wardrobe of vampish gowns, pillbox hats and ornamental canes inspired the first serious successor to the knock-kneed Sixties dolly-bird look. All over Britain and America, girl babies were suddenly being named Bianca.

Since her wedding, she had inevitably been deluged by offers of highly paid modelling work. Her appearances on the catwalk were rare, highly publicized and always dramatic. In a charity show for Oxfam at the Grosvenor House Hotel, she wore a low-cut gown and a two-tone wig, and carried a silver-knobbed cane. To the early Seventies fashion world she became what Maria Callas had been to grand opera, arriving for each shoot with myriad trunks and hatboxes, and a retinue of maids, hairdressers and even personal shoemakers. She was a supermodel twenty years before the term was invented. A movie career also beckoned in a production called *Trick or Treat*, set up by the fast-rising producer David Puttnam.

Within the Stones' organization Bianca continued to be an object of dislike, resentment and mockery. She was seen as little more than a gold digger, ruthlessly using the Jagger name to further her own ambitions and shamelessly adept at spending his money. Les Perrin's wife Janey remembers Bianca being sent off around the Mayfair shops with a wad of £20 notes in her handbag, but still phoning Les's office to complain that she was 'peesed off'. Shirley Arnold dreaded her tantrums over the limousines that would be provided for her; according to Shirley, she once sent a chauffeur away because he failed to raise his cap to her. 'That car-hire company had worked for us for years, but they wouldn't accept any more of our bookings after that. They said they just couldn't put up with Bianca any more.'

More serious were the allegations of her failings as a mother to her three-year-old daughter, Jade. It was said she resented Jade for tying her to Cheyne Walk house while Jagger was off having fun around the world. She seemed to veer between maternal obsessiveness and seeming indifference, at one moment delighting in buying clothes for Jade, at another turning the little girl over to a nanny and going off for another day with hairdresser Ricci. For a time, Jade did not have her own private nanny, but was looked after by a girl who also had charge of Mick Taylor's daughter, Chloe. (The girl was kept on low wages, for which she would revenge herself by letting Jade and Chloe play with their daddies' gold discs in the bath.)

Bianca may have been proud, arrogant and temperamental. She was also an old-fashioned, rather puritanical young woman whom the Stones' decadent lifestyle shocked to the core. Her frequent declaration that 'I have nothing to do with them' was seen as snobbish and stand-offish. In fact, as she later confessed, it stemmed from fear. She was terrified of being drawn into the half-world of drugs and depravity that had left Anita Pallenberg such a wreck of her former bewitching self. The only one of the Stones she liked was Charlie Watts. She respected Charlie for having principles, being utterly without airs and graces – and because Charlie's wife Shirley, Bianca suspected, was the only Stone wife Mick had never screwed.

If Bianca lacked the instincts of a home-maker, there was

seldom a settled home in which to develop them. Mick's tax problems kept them away from Cheyne Walk for long periods when they would have to rent houses or apartments in France or America. Once at least, Bianca says, they crept back into England when they were supposed to have been abroad and stayed at Cheyne Walk feeling like squatters. 'Every time we passed a window, we had to get down and crawl on our hands and knees.'

Bianca's name for the Stones' organization, that so disliked and undermined her, was 'the Nazi state'. Even as Jagger's wife, she found herself obliged to compete with his courtiers for his attention and favours – the more so if that favour involved money. After their mercy mission to Nicaragua following the earthquake, Bianca had stayed on in Managua while her husband returned to the world of rock stardom. She later claimed she had to ring Ahmet Ertegun in New York and get Ertegun's assistant to ask Mick to send the money to pay her rent.

Those who genuinely cared for Jagger, like the loyal Shirley Arnold, were depressed to see what little happiness marriage seemed to be bringing him. When Shirley left the Stones' organization after nine years, Mick and Bianca arrived separately at her leaving party. Each had brought Shirley a leaving present 'from both of us'. They then had a furious row in front of Shirley about which of the two gifts the official joint one was. Jagger was increasingly seen around without Bianca, for instance carousing with Rod Stewart backstage after Stewart's gig at the Kilburn State theatre. ''Ow about comin' back to my 'ouse?' he invited. 'I got some brandy, I think . . .' Irresistible images were conjured of a proud Latin beauty, waiting behind the front door with rolling pin poised.

In 1971, Talitha Getty, daughter-in-law of the world's richest man, died mysteriously of a heroin overdose. She had lived in Cheyne Walk, Chelsea, just a few doors away from Mick and Keith, and had entertained them at her house in Morocco. In

1972, their photographer friend Michael Cooper committed suicide after becoming so hopelessly addicted he had to use a wheelchair. In 1973, Gram Parsons, Keith's country rock mentor, died suddenly in California and was cremated before a post-mortem could be carried out.

At each death, people said much the same thing. 'That's what comes of living too close to the Stones. In the end, you try to live like them. The Stones use people up.'

One potential victim, at any rate, got out while he was ahead. In December 1974, as the Stones prepared to record a new album in Munich, Mick Taylor announced his resignation. He had become disillusioned by Jagger's reluctance to extend the Stones' musical boundaries – and by the increasingly undignified situations in which he now found himself. The last straw, artistically speaking, had been a video film made for the band's 1974 hit It's Only Rock 'n' Roll, another stripped-down anthem with Keith's chords dominant over Taylor's lyrical lead. As the band played in prissy white sailor suits, they were slowly engulfed by a wall of white foam. Watching the video today, one can see the tension on Taylor's foam-flecked face. The once-angelic non-smoking vegetarian was now firmly hooked on heroin, and realized that quitting the Stones was his only hope of salvation. The official press release said he was leaving because he wanted 'a change of scene'.

Keith Richard sent him a telegram saying 'Thanks for the past five years – it's been a pleasure working with you.' Jagger, peeved by this defection at an inconvenient moment, cattily downgraded Taylor's worth to the Stones when asked what qualifications would be needed by his successor. 'No doubt we can find a brilliant six foot three blond guitarist who can do his own make-up.'

A dozen or so famous names were variously touted to fill Taylor's place, among them Jimmy Page, Peter Frampton, Jeff Beck, Steve Marriott, Shuggie Otis and Chris Spedding. The album-sessions, in Munich first, then Rotterdam, served as an audition for the shortlist of Rory Gallagher, Robert A. Johnson, Wayne Perkins and Harvey Mandel. Perkins and Mandel both contributed solos to the album released, more than a year later, as *Black and Blue*.

Wayne Perkins, Keith's preferred candidate, had almost overcome Jagger's havering indecision when it was learned that Rod Stewart's band the Faces would soon be splitting up and that their lead guitarist Ronnie Wood needed a new job. Though much less a virtuoso than any of the other applicants, 'Woody' was one of the best-liked and most amiable figures on the British music scene. Stewart, as he confessed at the time, liked to hold orgies in his hotel room with several groupies at a time, photographing the scene with a Polaroid camera. Woody, however, would be more likely to be down in the lobby, showing the girls pictures of his newest car. In any case, experience had taught the Glimmer Twins that having too talented a lead guitarist only led to trouble.

The arrangement was that the Stones should 'borrow' Woody from the Faces to help them out on their 1975 American tour. The diplomatic language fooled no one in the music industry, particularly since Keith Richard was known to have been hanging out at 'The Wick', Woody's house in Richmond. 'The Wick' shortly afterwards received a sudden visit from the drug squad, who found only Woody's wife, Krissie, and a female acquaintance in bed.

The main problem facing the 1975 tour was how to get Keith past immigration authorities who termed mere cannabis-smoking 'a crime of moral turpitude'. Keith had paid a heavy fine for his Riviera heroin exploits and was now technically free to re-enter France. He had paid a smaller fine for the drugs and .38 Smith and Wesson found at Cheyne Walk, half-convincing Great Marlborough Street magistrates that the stuff had been left there by his subtenants. He was still as unlikely to receive his H2 temporary working visas as Dracula was to gain admittance to a blood donor session.

Blood was apparently the issue when Mick Jagger approached Walter Annenberg, the US ambassador in London, seeking a quid pro quo for the donation of almost a million dollars to the Pan American Development Fund. According to Spanish Tony Sanchez, the condition for letting Keith into America was that his blood must show not one speck of heroin. The story subsequently arose that he complied by having all the blood in his body replaced. Keith himself denies it, though he did spend time at the Swiss clinic where blood changes were given. 'I was just fooling around with some people. I came in, opened my jacket and said "Hi – do you like my blood change?" That's all it was – a joke.'

The Stones announced their new tour to New York by an impromptu performance on the back of a flatbed truck rolling down Fifth Avenue. This time the road organization involved thirteen articulated trucks, 150 tons of lights and a stage even more costly and elaborate – a huge flower whose (allegedly bulletproof) petals unfurled to reveal the Stones inside as thunderous pollination. In Star Star (formerly Starfucker), quick-release gear bounced forth a gigantic rubber phallus for Jagger to punch and pummel.

Anti-Stone outrage was by now almost as cosmetic as the colour of Mick Jagger's complexion. Rupert Murdoch's supermarket tabloid the *Star* called for the exorcism of 'this demonic influence on our children' much as it had previously warned of the approach of swarms of man-killing bees. A church minister in Florida made the significant observation that, of 1,000 unmarried mothers in his parish, 984 had become pregnant while listening to rock music.

Bianca did not travel with Mick or visit him on the tour. He commented on her absence belittlingly. 'There's really no reason to have women on tour unless they've got a job to do. The only other reason is to screw. Otherwise they get bored. They just sit around and moan.' None the less he consented to pose in his dressing room with Liza Minnelli on one arm and Raquel Welch on the other.

Ronnie Wood was part of the band by April, 1976, when the tour reconvened for a thirty-nine-date European tour destined to keep Jagger in perpetual motion throughout that spring and summer. When *Black and Blue* was released on April 20, after eleven months in cold storage, its sleeve showed Woody's anteater countenance floating with the others' like profiles for a punk Mount Rushmore. The album disappointed many with its rather hollow attempts at black ethnic idioms, disc-funk and salsa, and the audible one-upmanship between guest guitarists competing for Mick Taylor's job. Nor could it be concluded, from Ronnie Wood's solos on Cherry Oh Baby and Hey, Negrita, that even the second-best instrumentalist had won.

Before May, 1976, British pop fans were believed to care for nothing but Abba and the Brotherhood of Man. For the Stones' first London concert in three years, almost a million postal applications were received. Doubling their three-concert series at Earls Court arena still satisfied barely one-tenth of the demand. Jagger impressed his British promoter, Harvey Goldsmith, by personally touring the unlovely hangar, checking on seats and audience facilities. 'He's the governor,' Goldsmith was heard to whisper reverently. As Jagger drove away from Earls Court after rehearsals, he stopped his car and handed out free tickets to boys and girls on the street. On his order, refreshments were handed out free of charge to the box-office queue.

On August 21, the Stones played their first rock festival since Altamont, performing to 200,000 in the grounds of Knebworth House, Hertfordshire, in company with Todd Rundgren, Lynyrd Skynyrd and 10cc. The Stones' show began four hours late and was described by *The Times*'s critic as 'a shambling parody'. 10cc, the hit of the afternoon, had earlier played a song containing words that *The Times* reviewer found all too apposite: 'Old men of rock 'n' roll come bearing music. Where are they now? They are over the hills.'

Knebworth was Les Perrin's final appearance as the Stones' press officer. The hepatitis he had contracted on the '73 Far East tour had been followed by a stroke from which he was never fully to recover. Frail as he had become, he insisted on turning out for the Knebworth festival. Seeing his determination, Jagger sent a car to collect him, with strict instructions that he wasn't to think of doing any work that day. Taking things easy came hard to the energetic little man in the old-fashioned suit whose promise was the same to all journalists, 'You can call me twenty-four hours a day', and whose uncompromising saneness had steered Mick Jagger through so many media ordeals. Unimpeachably respectable as he was, Les had shared in the Stones' notoriety, his telephone intermittently tapped, his wife Janey subject to disquieting police visits. At one point in the Sixties, impressed by his PR job for pop music's make-believe criminals, some real criminals had approached Perrin and asked his help in getting more positive press coverage. Reggie Kray himself, using the code name 'Mister James', would ring up Janey Perrin and ask if Les had reconsidered his decision not to take on the Kray brothers' account.

On the European tour, one of Jagger's executive decisions had to be finding a successor to Les Perrin. He had someone in mind already – the ex-music journalist Keith Altham. But none of the Stones wanted Les to think he was being sacked.

His meeting with Jagger at the Knebworth festival betrayed the mutual affection that both habitually concealed within staccato offhandedness. 'You wrote me a letter . . .' Jagger said. '. . . Why didn't you answer it?' Perrin said. 'I didn't have a stamp,' Jagger said, emphasizing each answer by pulling Les's trilby hat a little further down over his eyes.

A BBC-TV crew, returning from Knebworth, sighted Bianca Jagger, all in white, standing by her ditched limousine and trying to thumb a ride back to London. The BBC men offered her a place in their car. Sharing the joint she offered them, the BBC men were surprised how friendly, warm and funny Bianca turned out to be.

In 1977, Jerry Hall was just 'Jerry', a twenty-one-year-old American model internationally in demand for her bright gold hair, her lovely, equine face and a merry mouth recognizable even when magnified fifty times for lip gloss ads on the sides of London buses. Her boyfriend was Bryan Ferry, a rock singer several eras newer than the Stones. Though their careers meant long separations, they seemed a settled pair. 'There goes Jerry,' Ferry would say as another bus displaying her lips passed by.

When Ferry heard that Jerry had left him for Mick Jagger, he was in London preparing to go on tour with his band Roxy Music. His initial response was true to his native Tyneside. He said he would fly over to New York and punch Jagger on the nose. Friends dissuaded him by pointing out that Jagger was looking very fit these days and might give back as good as he got.

Jerry had captivated Jagger for reasons that made it hard to understand why he ever chose a wife like Bianca. There was nothing exquisite, proud or intense about Jerry Hall. She was an ebullient Texan, a truck-driver's daughter who liked horse-riding and leg-wrestling and committed numerous social faux pas at which she herself laughed uproariously. That laughter – perhaps that leg-wrestling, too – seemed the more appealing to a man who had spent five years with a mirror-image, different from himself only in that it frowned.

At first, Jerry seemed no different from the many women with whom Jagger had affairs while outwardly insisting that his marriage remained intact. Bianca corroborated this idea of a relationship deeper than mere monogamy. '[Mick] sleeps with many women, but rarely has affairs with them,' she said. 'They are all trying to use him. They are all nobodies, trying to be somebodies. Mick would say "go ahead" if I wanted an affair . . . but he knows I won't do it.'

Such friends as they had in common were long accustomed to the uncomfortable sight of Mick and Bianca trying to maintain this façade in public. At one New York dinner party, given by Halston the designer, Bianca arrived alone, in a man's tuxedo; Mick did not appear until after dinner. She berated him for the way he treated people who offered him hospitality. He mocked her for caring too much about 'the fuckin' jet set'.

By 1977, they were leading virtually separate lives and had dropped any pretence of monogamy. While Mick went around with Jerry Hall, Bianca was escorted by a succession of beaux including the actor Ryan O'Neal, the photographer Helmut Newton and, for a brief period, Jack Ford, son of US President Gerald Ford. Based mostly in New York, she was part of the circle who congregated around Andy Warhol at his downtown loft-salon, the Factory. A poignant paparazzo shot of the period shows her in Warhol's ultra-trendy, cheerless industrial space, sharing a table with William Burroughs. Bianca looks like an earnest little schoolgirl, desperate to hear something from the great writer's lips whenever they shall unclamp themselves from the straw in his Coca-Cola bottle. Jagger, the literary social climber, would still sometimes join her on these excursions, although his encounter with Burroughs should have won some kind of medal for gaucherie. 'Are you married, Bill?' Jagger asked, seemingly unaware that Burroughs had shot his spouse dead with a handgun while attempting to shatter a glass of gin balanced on her head.

Jagger, however, continued to deny his marriage was foundering and, from an increasing distance, tried to be a good father to Jade, the daughter he idolized. The little girl, already a stunning beauty, spent her life shuttled between her mother in New York and Jagger's parents in Westgate-on-Sea. Whenever he could spare the time, he devoted himself to her. He would collect her from her nursery school and linger there, quizzing the teachers about her progress and behaviour. Her teachers, privately, considered Jade a bit of a problem child. At one moment, she would disrupt the class with her moods and tantrums; at others, she would climb on to her teacher's lap, seemingly desperate for attention and affection.

In 1978, while Bianca was on holiday in California, Mick and Jerry flew into Los Angeles, openly 'an item'. Bianca had talked to various lawyers inconclusively over the months, but now her mind was made up. She filed suit to divorce Jagger on the grounds of 'irreconcilable differences'.

Keith Richard's third child by Anita Pallenberg, his longed-for second son, was born in Geneva in March, 1976. They named him Tara, after Tara Browne the Guinness heir, John Lennon's 'man who blew his mind out in a car'. Keith then left in a mood of high euphoria to tour Europe with the Stones. In Frankfurt it was announced that, after seven years together, Keith and Anita finally intended to marry. Keith maintained it was purely for convenience, to qualify Anita for a British passport that would cover their three children. The date and place of the wedding were not announced. Keith toyed briefly with the idea of having it onstage at Earls Court arena.

On June 4, the ten-week-old baby boy died. The cause of death was given officially as a flu virus. Keith heard the news in Paris, shortly before he was due to go onstage with the Stones. Stricken as he was, he insisted that the performance must go ahead. His face that night was skull-like as his arm pumped out the old infantile vocabulary of sex, drugs and rock 'n' roll.

He continued the tour, drowning his desolation in mindless noise and light, the Southern Comfort bottle on his amplifier, and the company of his surviving son. At seven years old, Marlon Richard had long ago exchanged the role of child for that of friend and father confessor. He was with Keith onstage, on the next bar-stool; at whatever hour of night up in the hotel suite, playing with the video cassettes and toys and telephones they used in common, Marlon would keep his father company.

Keith's – and Anita's – engulfing love for Marlon, redoubled after their baby's death, was contrasted by the apparent indifference towards their daughter, Dandelion. The little girl suffered from a speech defect and, at the age of almost four, was barely able to talk. Anita seemed to reject her, leaving her in a state of lovelessness which others in the Stones' circle – notably Mick and Bianca Jagger – did their best to assuage. When Dandelion fell ill in Paris, it was Bianca who took her to hospital and visited her there. Over-indulged as Marlon was, he too sometimes lacked more mundane forms of child care. Bianca was putting him to bed once and found she could not take off his socks; they were literally stuck to his feet. Marlon told her he'd been wearing the same pair for almost a month.

While Marlon played underfoot, Keith and Anita faced each other like captives in a cell padded with everything that could be ordered by telephone: sharing a life-sentence of luxury from which the sole escape came via the needles they plunged into their arms. Anita almost exulted in her addiction – she called heroin 'Henry' and enjoyed initiating others, like Mick Taylor's wife, into its use. She would tease Keith mercilessly for his inability to handle his habit, as when he tried to hide the syringe from servants or hotel waiters and for the way drug use had dampened down his sex-drive.

Making him jealous, like Brian Jones before him, was a trick Anita could accomplish even in her present unkempt condition, with junk-dilated eyes and deteriorating teeth. In Jamaica, when the Stones were recording there, she caused such a scandal by running around with the local Rastafarians that Keith returned to London without her. She subsequently got herself arrested and was badly beaten up by the local police before staggering back to England and Keith's forgiving arms. In 1976 she was in trouble with him again for visiting clubs devoted to the new punk rock music, where teenage boys strapped their legs together and stuck safety pins into their cheeks. The archetypal punk guitarist, whom many wild young bands took as their inspiration, told Anita sternly to stay away from such places.

The mutual tolerance that had kept the Stones together through so many trials and aberrations, showed signs of severe strain in the later Seventies as Mick Jagger rose higher into society with his new supermodel girlfriend and Keith Richard sank lower into drug dependency. The more respectable Mick became, the greater seemed Keith's determination to remain a Sixties outlaw, crashing cars, carrying guns and knives, destroying hotel rooms and letting his teeth turn black. For the first time since the age of six, their inseparably opposite natures were in open conflict. Keith criticized Mick for social climbing reflected in the 'theatrical shit' with which he had dressed up the '75 tour. Mick was disdainful about Keith's inability to stop being busted, and the schoolboy pranks with Woody, like invading the Jagger hotel suite and bouncing on the Jagger bed, shouting that they were 'the Trampolini Twins'.

For Bill Wyman and Charlie Watts, the effect of keeping Mick and Keith simultaneously in focus had become almost schizophrenic. Bill, at least, seemed to be tiring of the effort. His first solo album – *Monkey Grip*, in 1974 – had shown him he need not stand at the back of the stage for ever, and he had almost resigned after Mick Taylor in 1975. Even stoical Charlie disliked the atmosphere of bitchiness between Mick and Keith, and was talking about going off to find some peace and quiet in a jazz band.

The first part of 1977 was already planned. In February the Stones would meet in Toronto and give a series of performances at a small club called the El Macombo. These club dates would be the basis of a live album and would also keep them sharp for the following year's North American tour.

On January 13, at Aylesbury Crown Court, Keith Richard

was found guilty of possessing a cocaine-snorting tube, found in his Bentley after he had crashed it on the M1 the previous September. The jury rejected his counsel's plea that the snorter wasn't his but accepted that some LSD also found in the car might have belonged to someone else. Keith was fined £750, with £250 costs, and warned that if he committed another drug offence in Britain, he would be sent to prison. During the three-day trail, Mick Jagger had flown in unexpectedly from Los Angeles to lend him moral support and give evidence if necessary. As he left the court with Mick, Keith described the verdict as 'a good old British compromise'.

Bad feeling boiled up again on February 20, when Mick arrived in Toronto as planned to rehearse for the El Macombo dates, and discovered that Keith had not yet even set off from Britain. For five more days, as the Stones awaited him in Canada, Keith dawdled on at Redlands, deaf to transatlantic calls and even a furious joint telegram from the others reading WE WANT TO PLAY. YOU WANT TO PLAY. WHERE ARE YOU?

At Toronto airport on February 25, customs officers, searching Anita's bag, discovered a piece of hashish and a burnt spoon, later found to be encrusted with heroin. Anita was held for questioning, then released pending analysis of the spoon and a blue Tic Tac mint also confiscated from her.

Three days later, a squad of Royal Canadian Mounted Police burst into Keith's suite at the Harbour Castle Hilton Hotel, bearing a warrant for Anita's arrest. Lying about the suite they found cocaine and an ounce of pure heroin worth £2,500 – enough to warrant a charge, not merely of possession but of intent to traffic. Keith was taken to Toronto police headquarters and booked for an offence which under Canadian law carried a maximum penalty of life imprisonment.

Jagger had intended the Toronto visit to be a discreet, low-profile affair. Instead, thanks to what seemed nothing less than insanity on Keith's part, the Stones were facing their long-postponed Judgement Day. They spent the next forty-eight hours trying to rehearse in a warehouse in downtown Toronto while the world's media announced their imminent disintegration. In a further stroke of almost farcical ill-luck, they had also acquired a camp follower not exactly calculated to smooth their path with the Canadian authorities. This was no less than Margaret Trudeau, wife of prime minister Pierre Trudeau, a woman long given to embarrassing her husband with her excursions into non-diplomatic life. Mrs Trudeau, having somehow attached herself to Ronnie Wood, had booked a suite at the Harbour Castle and was hanging out with Woody and the Stones there.

On March 2, Jagger suddenly left Toronto for New York. His excuse was that Jade had appendicitis and Bianca was not in town to look after her. Keith held the night's rehearsal without him, wearing a sheepskin coat and making pointed remarks like 'Let's go back to the hotel, read all Mick's books and get ourselves properly educated.'

Jagger was back again on March 4 when the Stones began their drastically cut-down taping sessions, two nights instead of the projected five, before a live audience at the El Macombo Club. Against all the odds, both performances were brilliant with Keith, seemingly unmindful of what hung over his head, pulling out Chuck Berry licks not heard since he was a boy at the Crawdaddy Club. On March 7, he appeared in court to be told he would be additionally charged with possessing one-fifth of an ounce of cocaine. Next day, he returned to the same courtroom on the charge of intent to traffic heroin. He was remanded for a week on bail of $25,000, and had his confiscated passport returned to him.

At this point, Jagger seemed to wash his hands of his fellow Glimmer Twin, departing for New York once more with only the curtest farewell to Keith by telephone. After much agonizing, Ronnie Wood followed suit, still accompanied by Margaret Trudeau. The American press by now had decided that Jagger, rather than Woody, had been dallying with Mrs Trudeau. Her husband, the Canadian premier, was obliged officially to rebut charges that she had been seen 'partying' in the vicinity of Jagger's suite wearing only a bathrobe. For a bizarre few days, the future of the Trudeau government seemed every bit as much in doubt as the Stones' was.

Bill Wyman and Charlie Watts hung on in Toronto until March 10, then they, too, left to carry on lives which, having been denied all fruits of the Jagger-Richard partnership, could not be expected to share in its terminal crisis. Shortly afterwards, Keith, Anita and Marlon visited Niagara Falls. 'Shall I jump?' Keith asked, not altogether rhetorically.

•

The future of the Rolling Stones hung in the balance during April and May, 1977, as Keith stayed marooned on bail in Toronto; Mick Jagger flitted in and out of gossip columns, giving fulsomely non-committal predictions of the outcome if Keith were jailed for life; and the world, with far more modern scandals to think about, wondered whether it really mattered anyway.

Keith spent his time in Toronto listening to the El Macombo playback, taping songs for the solo album he might one day make and gazing fondly on Marlon's prodigious intake of junk food. Anita decorated their hotel suite with newspaper headlines chronicling the intertwined dramas of the smack and Margaret Trudeau: STONE ON HEROIN PUSHING CHARGE. COULD THIS BE THE LAST TIME? PREMIER'S WIFE IN STONES SCANDAL. THE MAGGIE MYSTERY TOUR. MAGGIE, MICK IN NEW YORK DENY HANKY-PANKY. BREAK UP FOR THE STONES ON CARDS SAYS JAGGER. HEY, MICK – WHAT'S HAPPENING?

In June, Keith's lawyers succeeded in obtaining permission for him to leave Canada to 'practise his profession' during the months before his case came to trial. A special visa had been granted to admit him to America for heroin addiction treatment at the Stevens Psychiatric Centre in New York. There Anita and he received neuro-electric acupuncture, a new cure which cut the horrors of cold turkey by administering mild electric shocks. Since Keith's visa forbade him to travel outside a thirty-mile radius of the clinic, tapes for the new album, *Love You Live*, had to be brought to him by Jagger. The rift between them repaired itself in a drinking bout that ended, most unusually, with Jagger passing out. The crisis was past. The subordinate Stones received word to meet in Paris, to record the album that would become *Some Girls*.

Keith's case did not come to trial until October, 1978. In return for a guilty plea, the trafficking charge had been reduced to one of mere possession. Though the prosecution asked for a jail sentence, Judge Lloyd Graburn was impressed by Keith's apparently determined efforts to cure himself for good. He was put on probation for a year and ordered to continue his drug rehabilitation programme. An extra proviso was that the Stones should compensate Toronto for the trouble they had caused there by giving a charity concern in aid of the blind.

The Canadian government appealed against the lightness of the judgement but it was upheld. Keith Richard, as he told his mother Doris in a misspelt note, was no longer 'the fugative'.

Although Jagger might have tired of Bianca, his pride was cut to the quick when she was the one to begin proceedings for divorce. He was also mortified by the prospect of parting from Jade – who clearly would have to remain with her mother – and how the break up would affect her. For there was little hope of its being amicable or civilized.

Having taken the giant step, Bianca instantly found herself cast into outer darkness, with all the luxuries and amenities of a rock legend's wife instantly cut off. As well as cancelling her charge accounts in New York, Jagger had all the furniture at 48 Cheyne Walk removed and put into storage. His explanation to

Jade was that it had gone away to be 'repaired'. Jade couldn't understand why the antique tapestries in the dining room needed repair, and innocently asked whether people had been walking on them.

Bianca's one hope was that the case would be heard in California, where a divorced wife automatically receives half of her ex-husband's property. To this end, she retained Marvin Michelson, a Hollywood lawyer famed for the ground-breaking palimony settlement he had wrung from Lee Marvin on behalf of the actor's former mistress. Bianca later said she had wanted to keep the case low profile, and naively assumed that Michelson would not talk about it to the media. As it was, banner headlines across the world screamed that the outgoing Mrs Jagger sought $12.5 million – half of Jagger's estimated earnings during their marriage – with $13,400 per month in interim expenses and a $50,000 advance against her lawyer's fee. For those days, the claim was a massively ambitious one, even had the defendant not been Mick Jagger. But Bianca was determined to do better than the $100,000 Jagger had offered to her privately.

After several months' legal manoeuvring, Jagger's lawyers managed to get the action heard in Britain's High Court, where matrimonial financial settlements are less munificent than in America. There at last, in late 1980, the marriage ended with Bianca being awarded around £500,000.

Twenty years later, as the aggrieved ex-wife of a rock icon, her financial future would have been assured by kiss-and-tell memoirs, TV chat show appearances and lavish confessional spreads in *Hello!* magazine. But in 1980 that world was still largely unborn, even if Bianca had been the type to profit from it. Instead, she would go on to reveal herself as a person very different from the spoiled, vapid character of Stones inner-circle gossip. Settling in New York, she became immersed in charity work on behalf of her native Nicaragua and other troubled Central American countries. Her activities included public fund-raising, conferences on relief and welfare and visits to highly dangerous battle zones. As the original 'supermodel', she would occasionally be lured back to do a modelling job, and reveal that her old grandeur had not completely deserted her. At one such session in London, the photographer suggested breaking so that everyone involved could have a quick snack. Bianca's idea of a quick snack was 'a little sea trout with fennel'.

The other women of the Stones' first division did not fare so well. After finally parting from Keith in the early Eighties, Anita Pallenberg put on weight massively, suffered illness and a broken hip and in general became the saddest casualty left in the band's wake. Lonely as her life was, it still contained almost involuntary drama and scandal. In 1980, at her house in Long Island, a teenage boy killed himself with a shotgun in her bed. In 1983, she was raided for drugs at London's Grosvenor House Hotel. A year later, her name would crop up again in the case of Stephen Waldorf, an innocent man shot and seriously wounded in Central London by armed police who had mistaken him for an escaped convict. After Keith began seeing a breezy young American actress named Pattie Hansen, Anita took to speaking of him almost maternally, playing his tapes as a proud parent might and warning him to 'watch out for those American girls'. In her handbag she carried a photograph of their daughter, Dandelion, whom Keith's mother had by now taken over and renamed Angela.

'Isn't she like Keith,' Anita would say fondly, staring at the little girl's photograph. 'Keith and I still love and respect each other. The trouble is, we can't live together. The people who really love Keith are waiting for him to grow out of the kind of life he leads and the creeps he surrounds himself with . . . I've always been his greatest fan.'

Marianne Faithfull came back from the wall in Windmill Street to build a career as the serious musician she had always hoped to be. The voice that had been so virginally shy was now raw and nicotine-stained, distilling the lessons of her many lifetimes with bitter world-weariness. She made three highly regarded albums (*Broken English*, *Dangerous Acquaintances* and *A Child's Fantasy*), had a number one hit single in Ireland and gained a cult following in West Germany. In 1977, she married a young punk guitarist named Ben Brierley who worked under the name 'Ben E. Ficial'. They set up home together in Chelsea, just a few streets away from Cheyne Walk, where they suffered continual harassment both from journalists and drug-seeking police. At one point they were so poor that Marianne had to start selling off pictures painted of herself long ago, when she seemed to live in a Renoir cornfield. 'I'm always skint,' she admitted. 'Always have been, always will be. But one thing I can say – my credit is good.'

In Cheyne Walk, Chelsea, two eighteenth-century houses, deserted by their tax-exile owners, joined the company of London's lesser shrines. Number 48 was irreproachably shuttered and still. At number 3, the windows were often illuminated. A series of sub-tenants lived there, on condition they did not disturb the petrified debris of Keith Richard's last hasty exit. In every room lay half-packed cartons, expensive children's toys, old Sixties finery and single ski boots. A double aircraft seat, showing signs of having been physically torn from its moorings, lay on the floor of the elegant downstairs drawing room with its view over Albert Bridge.

Up the twisting stair, dimly lit by jewel-studded Moroccan lamps, Keith's purple music room and psychedelic piano were just as he had left them. So was the oddly bare 'tripping' room, with its medieval candlesticks and the shrine to Jimi Hendrix. The glass mirror ball could still be turned on, sending flecks of light dancing into wood-panelled corners where so many cushions and insensible beings used to lie.

For some months in 1981, Anita's friend Molly Parkin

borrowed the house. Sleeping in Keith and Anita's top floor room – in the carved wooden bed that had been used in *Performance* – Molly became convinced the place was haunted. Alone there at night, she would hear scufflings on the stairs, voices and movements in the rooms below her, as if the house were helplessly re-enacting its unwanted and unbelievable past.

Sixteen

'God Speed the Rolling Stones'

The John F. Kennedy Stadium, Philadelphia, is built of reddish stone embellished with turrets, loophole windows and irregular battlements reminiscent of a British fort in nineteenth-century India. Today, September 25, 1981, it has the appearance of such a fort long breached and overrun by mutineers. On the outside, all is eerily quiet. A pallid sun beats down on the steel mesh fences, the raw concrete approaches and a mass of parked cars extending over some five square miles. Decrepit gas-guzzlers, garish Dodge pickups, old Volkswagen buses with 'Philly or bust' scratched among mouldering graffiti, stand row on row, block after block, slow-broiling in the sticky heat.

Close to, JFK Stadium emits a steady roar, as if huge amounts of wet shingle are seething under a tide which its red battlements can barely keep in check. This afternoon, the Rolling Stones give the first concert in their twentieth-anniversary tour of America and Europe. Ninety thousand people are waiting to welcome back the World's Greatest Rock 'n' Roll Band.

The stadium doors lead to long sub-Gothic cloisters, lined with stalls purveying the T-shirts, sweatshirts and other merchandise which the Rolling Stones have authorized to be sold at venues along the route of their twentieth-anniversary tour.

T-shirts, hung up like Neapolitan laundry lines, bear the Stones' name in gold, red and black mid-Seventies script. On the reverse, a cartoon dragon rears over North America, its thick red lips parted to hang out a sagging and lascivious tongue. The sweat-shirts cost $12.50 each, the T-shirts $10.50. Almost every boy and girl in the lower concourse wears a T-shirt or sweatshirt, carries a poster or sports a badge or button or pocket patch imprinted with that same unmistakable mouth and lolling tongue. Here and there among the pillars are roped-off enclosures with rows of stretchers, ready for the casualties which will occur when the owner of the mouth eventually shows himself.

Dirty stairs, through unfinished concrete crossbeams, lead to the terraces where people have paid fifteen dollars to see the Rolling Stones from no more than a quarter of a mile away. It is like emerging suddenly in the midst of downtown Calcutta. Boys and girls, crushed together on shallow stone ledges, extend upwards and downwards, in a great, seething human tenement of blue denim and brown skin, as far as the eye can see. Many are already drunk, many more semi-comatose with the marijuana that can be smoked almost openly in America nowadays. The attention of all is fixed on that far curve of the stadium where a pink, purple and faint yellow stage stands between two scaffolding towers, moored in place by bunches of multi-coloured balloons. The sky is full of small aircraft, towing indecipherable messages or relaying reports to local radio stations. From time to time, a police helicopter swoops down low, casting a shadow like a giant bee over the shirtless multitude furthest out in the sun.

Habits peculiar to the Stones fifteen years ago have evolved, through their countless imitators, into time-honoured rock concert tradition. It has long been acknowledged that no band which aspires to greatness ever begins playing on time. With the World's Greatest Rock 'n' Roll Band, lateness is naturally expected on an heroic scale. The crowd in JFK Stadium has waited four hours already with no entertainment save an obscure 'support band' and occasional records booming over the PA. It bears its vigil, not merely with patience, but with an enjoyment divorced from anything seen or heard so far today. This is the first young generation for whom nostalgia is more powerful than hope. Nostalgia for a past never experienced, and a youth never savoured, keeps them almost happy. This, surely, must be how it felt at Woodstock or in Hyde Park, back when young people ruled the world and gathered so often in exaltation under the brilliant, strange-scented Sixties sun.

The stage that will accompany the Stones across America – and, later, Europe – squats on its end curve of the stadium, straining gently under its rainbow clouds of balloons. Each seventy-foot-high side panel is a swirl of dim blue and yellow Japanese shapes, incorporating Mick Jagger's mouth and an American flag, zigzagged instead of striped. The performing area is a pink and purple apron, stretched into a pair of purple catwalks extending almost to the nearest spectator blocks. Above the left-hand catwalk, a cherry-picker crane waits on its thirty-foot stem, close to the well-guarded scaffolding.

Empty of music as the stage still is, it none the less exhibits multifarious life. On the broad ramp from the backstage VIP enclosure, figures toil ceaselessly up into the proscenium, carrying clean towels, drinking water, guitars, cartons of cigarettes and boxes of long-stemmed carnations. Launching the five Stones into performance is an operation that involves approximately a hundred people, onstage and in the area behind, hurrying to and fro with a sense of keen urgency that does not seem to bring the concert any nearer to beginning. The black towered amplifiers give off huge gusts of unused power as a technician rechecks the computer which regulates them. There is always the chance that a local taxi company using the same frequency might interpolate a radio call gigantically into the middle of Jumpin' Jack Flash.

In the backstage enclosure, and a single block of empty seats behind it, some 200 journalists and photographers wait to file stories about the World's Greatest Rock 'n' Roll Band to newspapers, magazines, wire-services, radio and TV stations throughout America, Europe, Australasia and Japan. A band whose press coverage in the past has contributed to the imprisonment of its two leading members could not be expected to treat journalists with goodwill. Even so, the delay, frustration and downright humiliation inflicted on media people covering any Stones tour have been raised to something like an art. Every few minutes, in their long, uncomfortable, unrefreshed wait, some new manoeuvre is devised for herding them into a different place, even further from where they would like to be, and in general reducing their self-esteem to dust.

The Stones invented 'security', long before other rock stars had anything but hugs and kisses to fear from fans. Now the world has changed: it is barely ten months since Mick Jagger's old friend and rival, John Lennon, was gunned down in New York by a boy with an LP record under one arm. Jagger, with his own vastly greater backwash of enemies, reportedly lives in constant terror of assassination. That is why, at JFK Stadium, yellow-shirted teenage thugs glower down in long lines at inoffensive paying customers; why huge black men block thoroughfares with their whole bodies; why huge white men in crumpled safari jackets whisper devoutly into walkie-talkies or dash to and fro on miniature motorcycles. That is why naked paranoia rages, under the balloon-skin veneer of one great, carefree garden party.

As well as the visible and the undercover security, there is a guard of a special sort, posted alone on the staircase by which the Rolling Stones will eventually make their way up to the stage. The guard is a bearded young man, upwards of seven feet tall. He is dressed as for college athletics in a navy blue sweatshirt, shorts and white jogging shoes. On his head he wears a blue baseball cap bearing the gold-wreathed inscription TULSA POLICE. His outfit suggests the cosy joviality of guys together in the locker-room. His face promises something very different to anyone without authority who should try to climb that staircase. You could not wish a more perfect evocation of the kill-or-be-killed industry which – as Mick Jagger characteristically reminds us – is 'only rock 'n' roll'.

The real VIP enclosure, at the inner end of the players' tunnel, is a little portable garden, surrounded by pink and purple Japanese screens, and containing all that, it is hoped, will keep the World's Greatest Rock 'n' Roll Band happy during their pre-concert rendezvous and conference. There are palm trees in pots and flower baskets and somnolent caged parrots and, for more advanced aesthetic stimulus, lines of kabuki masks mounted on poles around the perimeter. On either side of the garden, a pink and purple trailer houses the continuous bars and running banquets without which no Rolling Stone is expected to function for ten minutes at a time. About a dozen highly privileged, highly nervous people are seated at tables under sun umbrellas or standing on the artificial grass, glancing this way and that over their shoulders.

At the inner end of the garden, Mick Jagger, swathed in a bright yellow quilted ski jacket, trots briskly to and fro, lifting his knees in regular drill-instructor's time. He stops, spreads his legs, flexes his torso, touches his toes and rotates each shoulder blade in turn. It is a warm-up period essential before two hours onstage calculated to be, at least, the equivalent of a twenty-mile run. Jagger goes through it with the half-closed eyes and muttered counting of a trained athlete whose life, these past weeks, has been virtually non-stop circuit exercise.

Two of the four remaining Stones, Bill Wyman and Charlie Watts, also wait in the garden, each at the centre of a small, tenaciously jovial group. Tour life for a Rolling Stone may once have been perpetual sex, drugs and madness. Now it seems little more than an unremitting cocktail party. Charlie looks at his watch and grimaces lugubriously. ''Alf past four,' he says. 'We should have been on at two-fifteen. I *hate* keeping people waiting.'

A stir down the players' tunnel announces that the final two Stones have run out of excuses to postpone their arrival. Into the garden first comes a girl of about sixteen, wearing a long black ball gown and black crocheted shawl, carrying a half-empty bottle of Southern Comfort in the attitude of some ceremonial mace. After her comes Ronnie Wood, a creature hatched and bred in the rock-music swarm from his spiked black hair and cheese-pale, pointed face to his spindly legs, swaying and staggering on vermilion boot-heels with almost obligatory mirth. 'Woody', as lead guitarist Stone, survives in the niche where Brian Jones and Mick Taylor could not, chiefly through being this ideally complete and recognizable rock star parody, a cartoon trailer, as it were, to his friend and confederate, now known once more as Keith Richards.

Even in broad daylight, he manages to look fairly frightening. His skin is corpse-white as if, in his battles with heroin, all the blood truly had been pumped out of him. His eyes, under the draggled pompadour, are smudges of leering black. His mouth is a grimace of rotted teeth, held in suspense by lines nicked out of his face like duelling cuts. He is half naked in his bare-chested jerkin, cracked jeans tucked into ankle boots, a mangy white silk scarf wound many times around his neck. His gait is unsteady and sidelong as if he has only just now arisen from his vampire's casket. And yet, for all the gipsy squalor and reek of suicidal decadence, there is something about Keith Richards strangely and resiliently alive. He seems, within his own ghastly parameters, a happy, even healthy man.

Staggering across the garden, he bites the cap from a beer bottle. He lurches up against a member of Bill Wyman's party, throws his dead white arms around someone else and says, 'Why is everyone making such a fuss about a bunch of middle-aged madmen on tour?' The vampire speaks in the boozy, affectionate tones of some old-time actor-manager.

The Stones are ready at last. The stadium, by some vast

animal instinct, has divined it even before the little group of blonde womenfolk, business aides and record company executives are shepherded out through the players' tunnel, across a VIP enclosure swept clean of all press, and up the narrow staircase to their privileged places on the stage. The seven-foot TULSA POLICE giant stands respectfully aside. Now the roar changes to uproar. The Stones themselves are issuing from the tunnel-mouth.

The World's Greatest Rock 'n' roll Band, being all so small and thin, seem, rather, the last tiny herd of some nearly extinct gazelle. Jagger goes first as always, in his yellow jacket, pumping his knickerbockered knees in a final exercise. The figure of Keith staggering after him holding two guitars, smoking a long, droopy cigarette, brings from afar a cry filled with desperate would-be brotherhood:

'He-e-e-e-ey . . . *Keith*!'

The five little beings flee up to the safety of their gigantic proscenium and the horizonless humanity beyond. Ninety thousand people are about to learn the secret of careless, unstoppable youth from men, in most cases, old enough to be their fathers.

It was Keith who almost put an end to the Stones in 1977. And it is Keith who has persuaded them to go back on the road yet again in 1981. Without him, the other four would still be comfortably enmired in their wealth, their millionaire hobbies and their illimitable freewill. Keith is the Stone who has most to fear when he has nothing in particular to do.

Becoming Keith Richards again symbolizes his wish to return to some kind of normal existence after his ten-year heroin odyssey with Anita Pallenberg. It also marks his reconciliation with the father he has not seen since he was a semi-delinquent eighteen-year-old. Bert Richards had subsequently parted from Doris and was living in retirement – with no thought of benefiting from his superstar son – when Keith discovered his address in 1976 and began writing to him. They finally met up again in London, Bert flinging his arms around his outlaw son and saying 'Wotcher, mate.'

It was a new and single and apparently cleaned-up Keith who, during early 1981, visited Charlie Watts, the English landowner and antique silver expert, and Bill Wyman, the photographer, composer and friend of Marc Chagall, and proposed that they turn themselves back into teenage rock stars. Most assiduously did he visit the childhood friend who has, at times, seemed more like a lover, who can resemble a nagging wife and yet maintains an inimicably opposite existence within their indestructible partnership. All Keith's persuasion was needed to entice Mick away from the life, floated on silk clouds between New York, the Caribbean and the Loire Valley, which he likes to characterize as that of 'a dilettante Englishman'.

Jagger almost never wants to go on tour. The passing years have required more and more punishing effort to whip his body into the condition needed for a Mick Jagger performance. Mere mention of another tour would be enough to make his face go into the well-known Jagger put-down look: 'Not *that* old thing again!' Or he would produce one of the epigrams he polishes so carefully against his next press conference. 'Performing's like sex. You might like it but you don't wanna do it all the time.'

What decided him in the end was not so much Keith's enthusiasm as the figures prepared by the Austrian prince who supervises his and the Stone's financial affairs. Jagger has a persuasive way of insisting that he cares nothing for money. His close friends – certainly his ex-wife – are equally convinced he cares for nothing else.

The band which had ruled pop music style in the Sixties and half the Seventies could not be sure, for all their heaped-up fame, that the Eighties would not laugh them into extinction. Their classic work aside, the fact was that they had not achieved a significant new success in almost a decade. They had remained on their treadmill of monster tours and monster money while punk rock was subjecting pop to its most radical change since its most radical change was themselves. Punk groups like the Sex Pistols – beer-swilling, swearing, spitting at their audience or even jumping offstage to attack them – made the Stones Sixties' exploits look tame indeed. Punk was not so much music as satire: a giant collective jeer by young people in the depressed late Seventies at bands like the Stones who still appeared on stages as vast as ocean liners, and behaved as well as dressed like Bourbon monarchs, and played in too-fastidious tune, and were complacent, torpid, out of touch and most of all – God help them! – in their mid-thirties.

In the summer of 1981, a new Rolling Stones album on their eponymous label was released, as Stones albums had continued to be every year or so. Its title was *Tattoo You* – like that of its predecessor, *Emotional Rescue*, a vague, unrepentant swipe of male chauvinism. *Tattoo You* contained a track called Start Me Up, sung by a voice as snarlingly adolescent as if the past decade had never been, set about by plain guitar chords of dark, lazy malignity. Among the prevailing New Romantic high-tech, its effect was that of a cave painting, lit by primitive fire. All that was new and current could not suppress its Neolithic growl. For the first time since Angie in 1973, the Stones were top of the American singles charts.

A familiar seismic shudder, midway between joy and terror, spread across the United States in August when it was confirmed that the Stones would be giving concerts in twenty-six cities throughout October, November and December. Long years have not dimmed memories of outrage, real or imagined, which the wild young Stones visited on Middle America, and which to this day cause parents to blanch, hotel clerks to cower and sheriffs to reach for arrest warrants whenever their name is mentioned. Enormous stone structures and wide open spaces have likewise learned to be afraid of the Stones. In New York it is a tradition always to keep the name of their final and climactic tour venue a secret for as long as possible, lest its audience surround it prematurely and rend it brick from brick.

The response to that frisson down North America's spine was bigger than in 1978, 1975 or even 1972. Within forty-eight hours of the tour's announcement, almost three and a half million people had applied for tickets. The string of sports arenas and concert bowls long battered into accepting the Stones' box-office percentage would, this time, yield some $15 million. Then there were the proceeds from 'authorized' merchandise, T-shirts, buttons, badges, posters. There were the proceeds from TV, video and film rights, to say nothing of record sales. There was the wholly unlooked for dividend arising from an agreement with Jovan Perfumes Inc. to allow its name – merely its name – to be printed above the Stones' on concert admission tickets. With an expected total gross of $40 million, the 'old men of rock' were rolling the biggest moneymaking snowball the music industry had ever seen.

The build-up continued during the Stones' seven weeks of rehearsal at a secluded farm-cum-studio in rural Massachusetts. It was announced that, as well as playing their high-gross stadium dates, they hoped to make spontaneous, unscheduled appearances at 'small clubs' along the tour route. Lords and superstars as they were, they wanted to re-establish contact with the kind of places and audiences which had given them their earliest foothold and fame. All across America for the next three months, groups of kids would gather, eyeing their local juke joint and wondering raptly if, some night soon, they would see the Rolling Stones there.

Mick and Keith, meanwhile, thumbed through the Jagger-Richard songbook, reminding themselves of the words and basic chords of its approximately one hundred titles. Between rehearsals, Mick exercised with weights and barbells, played squash and practised karate with his black bodyguard and ran seven miles daily through the autumnal woods. Far from provoking horror in the district, the visitation was accounted a positive blessing. A church in the neighbouring village of North Brookfield rearranged the letters on its announcement board to say GOD SPEED THE ROLLING STONES.

Most of the pre-tour publicity, as always, centred on Mick. There were stories about his new passion for physical fitness; his apparently happy life with Jerry Hall; the eternal possibility of his appearing in a film – would it be Werner Hertzog's *Fitzcarraldo*, or *Annie*? Mick can keep such stories coming when he does nothing for eighteen months at a time. But there was a growing interest in Keith, as evidenced by a *Rolling Stone* cover story. The Human Riff is receiving his due, belatedly, as the true soul and mainspring of the Stones as well as the one incorrigibly bad boy among them. The difference in interviews with Keith is that – even when asked about heroin or his break up with Anita – he answers candidly.

One last little charge remained to set off the main explosion at its best. Early in September, in the small town of Worcester, Massachusetts, 300 people made their furtive way towards a club called Sir Morgan's Cave to hear a band whose identity could be only half guessed from its obvious pseudonym, Little Boy Blue and the Cockroaches. The 300 had been selected by a local radio station under an oath of strict secrecy and all would have gone well had not a rival station got wind of the plot and begun announcing, at ten minute intervals, that the Rolling Stones were about to play in Worcester. Eleven thousand people instantly descended on Sir Morgan's Cave. A riot was averted only by throwing open all the club doors. The Stones gave their first performance in the Eighties from a sort of sweating gazebo, with Mick Jagger stripped to the waist, lathered like a steeplechaser and grinning like an eight-year-old Kentish schoolboy.

Next day, half a dozen other small towns in North Massachusetts hastily issued pre-emptive orders, banning the Stones from all clubs, bar rooms and billiard halls within their precincts. Overnight, the dilettante Englishman, the connoisseur of silver, the friend of Chagall and the two ageing plutocrats were transformed back into outlaws, vagrants and fire hazards. Now they were ready to go on tour.

Out across the blue distances of JFK Stadium roll giant bass notes, circling downward in register and backwards fifteen years. The song is Under My Thumb, from the 1966 *Aftermath* album. The Stones have launched their assault on the Eighties by starting almost at the beginning.

The world since 1966 may have changed beyond recognition. But the voice, blown forth by giant speaker-mouths, has not changed or aged a day. It is the voice which, for all its owner's vast sophistication, can still utter sentiments of child-chauvinist triumph over some luckless dolly bird: not a voice, indeed, so much as a scowl, or perhaps a pout made audible. The voice is so much the same, one forgets how surprising the song was originally – the muted undertow of melody Brian Jones gave to it with his African xylophone.

Behind the stage, reporters stand staring desperately upwards, trying to see the source of the thunder rolling back past Charlie Watts's bald patch. Paul Wasserman the publicist beckons the first chosen photographers under the stage, to its frontal pit. Each has five minutes only, shooting upward at a fixed angle of seventy degrees. Should any photographer exceed his allotted time, or be otherwise recalcitrant, a man named Jerry Pompini will touch his camera with a long metal wand like a cattle-prod, instantly destroying the film inside.

Others, suspended above in helicopters and small aircraft, train telescopic lenses down on the figure, now shucked from its yellow jacket and prancing, over shallow pink steps, to the edge of a wild human sea. Tiny and contourless as that figure is, it has ignited its most distant watchers into the same self-contorting frenzy as those around its feet. Only Mick Jagger has ever projected sex so uneeringly over so huge an outdoor distance. That girlish toss of his head is a challenge issued impartially to all 90,000, female and male. That strutting elbow-pumping walk carries its innuendo over the whole expanse of heads and arms and waving banners. They can see the glare on his face, the very pout of his lips, from a quarter of a mile away.

As the first great wave of clapping rolls round the stadium, mingled with cheers and whistles, Jagger bends double like an old-fashioned maestro at the podium, then flings his head back so that the cords stand taut in his neck. 'Good aftahnoon, JFK,' he says in that well-known public voice, part English lord, part Cockney errand-boy and part Southern black mammy. 'Are you feelin' awright? Yeah . . . it's nice to be back 'ere in Philadelphia . . .' And, apparently euphoric, he looks at Keith, then shuffles backward on his toes like a little boy unbearably excited. 'Okay – we're gonna 'ave a good time.'

The first half-dozen songs do not need to be announced. It has always seemed miraculous that the Stones, unlike the Beatles, never succumbed to amnesiac loathing of their early work, but were always prepared to do their oldies, affectionately unrevised. The cheer given to each is as much for the epoch it summons up. Under My Thumb awakens vague memories of Courrèges boots, op-art dresses, boutiques and bistros in candlelight. You Can't Always Get What You Want reincarnates the Chelsea Drug Store, that neon-lit folly of tubular glass which perished almost as soon as Jagger left the neighbourhood. A song grown almost quaintly innocent by modern standards still brings a whiff of its old indolent wickedness. There is an excited murmur as Jagger bleats the 'na-na-na-na' phrase that unloosed so many bans and prohibitions. Is he really going to dare sing Let's Spend the Night Together?

The energy taken for granted even three years ago, now seems nothing less than phenomenal. Energy has replaced outrage, just as peacock robes have yielded to practical athletics kit. There are moments when Jagger, in his white breeches and knee-guards, seems less like a rock star than a PT instructor, exhorting his huge class to follow his example. Each song is a piece of circuit-training, packed tight with every pose he has ever struck. In a single verse he can change from street-corner tough to primping aesthete, from bitchy old harridan to high-kicking, beaming Tiller Girl. In the space of a line, he will march, mince, strut, chassé, kneel, implore, roll over, and suddenly be airborne like the Nureyev he has sometimes wished he was. And all the time, the same rather unfriendly, callow voice is singing about chasing women, or being chased by them.

Behind the Jagger show, to left and right, the World's Greatest Rock 'n' Roll Band are meanwhile playing like so many learners on pneumatic drills. Seven weeks' intensive rehearsal have left Keith and Woody still apparently only half familiar with the chosen programme; Woody is on impish form as usual, in his red leather blouson and streetwalker boot heels, gambolling back and forth with the freedom his cordless guitar allows; crossing behind Bill Wyman to nudge the stoic bass player in the ribs, then skipping up to peer at Charlie Watts, at work like a blacksmith among his cymbals and drum silverware. Keith, meanwhile, has come to a halt on the left-hand promontory, against the declining sun. His draggled head peers down at his oscillating white arm, as if still unable to comprehend what it is doing. The intro to Miss You begins and expires on a five-string chord in which barely two fingers seem to have been awake.

The rock concert audience is almost infinitely forgiving. It requires to see and hear only the vaguest approximation of the dreams it has acquired through the engineered illusion of records. Just the same, after forty minutes or so of gigantically botched intros and hopelessly tangled-up solos, it is borne in upon JFK Stadium that – Mick Jagger aside – the Rolling Stones are not trying. The applause is still vast: it can be nothing else. But it is an ebbing vastness. Jagger shows uneasy awareness of the fact. 'Aw-*right*!' he shouts, the rock star's wild response to a wild ovation, not yet detectable. 'Aw-*ri-ight*!' Several times he enquires anxiously, 'Can you 'ear at the back awright?' It is what the rawest teenage beginner might say to an audience at a church hall social. 'Okay – Shadoobie!' The intro begins at breakneck speed, then topples over in a great crash of mangled, molten uproar. Jagger looks back and, briefly, buries his face in his hands.

Black Cadillac goes better, being just a long, chromium-plated version of the blues which Keith and Mick used to drive around the Surrey back-streets twenty years ago. Twenty Flight Rock is bedlam – but interesting. For all their undisputed sobriquet, the World's Greatest Rock 'n' Roll band have rarely attempted genuine Fifties bass-slapping rock 'n' roll. Jagger plays rhythm guitar, as he has done on studio sessions since the late Sixties. Some people around the Stones consider this deeply revealing. Despite his mastery of his own unique milieu, what Mick has always seemed to want most is to be a *real* musician, like Keith.

Similarly in Keith, the Stones once had a quite possible alternative vocalist. You can hear him, back in Come On days, before tobacco, and worse, spoiled the perfect pitch of an angelic English choirboy. There are private tapes by Keith which hint at what the band has lost through Jagger's pre-eminence, and his own odd, unexpected self-effacement. Lost for good and all, it now seems. His performance of his song Little T and A, from *Tattoo You*, is such a mess of thunderous chords and steel-wool syllables that Jagger actually walks offstage, back to the place, behind Charlie Watts's drums, where a urinal is discreetly positioned. The stadium, by contrast, demurs less than in the preceding half-hour. Mick is an idol, but Keith is a hero. From his tattered head to his tattered boots, with all his tattered life in between, they love him.

In the backstage enclosure, conditions have slightly relaxed. The press, and those who have passed themselves off as press, stand unmolested under the rear apron, gazing avidly up at the noise through the proscenium, in some cases showing their kinship with the Stones, and the principle of wildness, by doing self-consciously frantic little solo dances. The intro to Start Me Up acts like a sudden air raid warning. A line of security guards, the seven-foot TULSA POLICE frightener among them, moves across slantwise, pushing and jabbing all superfluous onlookers back into the empty rear grandstand. Four identical yellow minibuses with blackened windows have appeared below the stage-ramp, their side doors slid back wide. Subdued panic and paranoia once more take hold. Only an hour remains before the Stones must make their getaway.

This final hour is an unbroken run of the malign two-minute classics whose opening chords, heard in however modern a disco, still bring the whole clientele boogieing out under the lights. Street Fighting Man, from dear old cosy, militant '68; Honky Tonk Women, with its clopping cowbell, from Hyde Park '69. Tumbling Dice, Brown Sugar: sex in a gambler's throw, a sweet tooth. To stir up memories of two countries' conjoined outrage, Jagger has wrapped himself in a big robe made of the British and the American flag. '. . . Ah laid a divorc-ay in New Yawk Cit-a-ay . . .' The difference is that in the wings, his ten-year-old daughter, Jade, is watching him. '. . . Ah just cain't seem to drink you off mah mind . . .' Jade looks bored but tries to hide it, as ten-year-olds do on formal grown-up occasions.

The stadium roars louder as the golden oldies keep coming: there are sirens in the distance, mixed up with police car whirligigs. Backstage, the condition is Red Alert. A dozen or so guards plunge amid the stage supports to reinforce their colleagues on the frontal barrier-system. Four of them return, carrying a boy who has managed to climb over. The boy, aged about fourteen, looks draggled and exhausted, as if just rescued from the surf at Malibu. The guards carry him off, restraining him by the arms, legs and windpipe.

The finale – there can be no other – is Jumpin' Jack Flash. The anthem to the Stones as Devil agents, the vicious black midnight of the sunshiny Sixties, summons its dancing demon even on an overcast afternoon near Philadelphia. Jagger is still enough of a blues man to know that if you hit a groove, you stay there. This version lasts twenty minutes and takes him writhing and rotating down both catwalks. He runs back to the right-hand tower, climbs into the cab of the cherry picker, is cranked up and swung out, thirty feet above the crowd, still hunched like a hag, singing, 'Jumpin' Jack Flash, it's a gas . . Jumpin' Jack Flash, it's a gas . . .' Rock 'n' roll can have produced no stranger sight, nor one more removed from its origins, than this figure in knee-breeches, suspended before a huge blue and yellow Japanese mural, repeating 'It's a gas' in a 10,000-watt whisper, and pelting the faces below with long-stemmed carnations.

One encore – a perfunctory Satisfaction – and it is over. The Stones, swaddled in white towels, flee down the backstage ramp to their four waiting yellow trucks. Behind them, the acclaim is unmistakably tinged with reproach. Jade and Jerry Hall are already in the lead vehicle when Jagger reaches it. Out in the stadium, his voice continues to agree and exhort, 'Aw-*right*! Aw-*ri-i-ight!*' He is speaking through a radio-controlled microphone. He has no intention of going back on stage.

The heavy compound gate swings open. The motorcade bumps through in clouds of dust. Beyond the balloons, a $12,000 firework display cracks and rackets in the disappointed sky. Stage-hands fall on the Japanese garden, flattening it like a cardhouse, rolling up the artificial grass, packing into hampers the sodden T-shirts and towels which Jagger, in less careful days, might have tossed out among his audience.

The *New York Times* speaks for all in comparing the Stones' performance to that of 'a teenage garage band'. Not even *Rolling Stone*, with all its special privileges at stake, can pretend that the

JFK Stadium show, and another the following day, have been anything more than tortuous tuning up. *Time*, mixing metaphors as usual, calls the tour 'a floating World's Series', calculatedly fobbing off its public with empty spectacle instead of the excitement for which some $15 million has already been paid. The 'major financial involvement' of Jovan Perfumes is sarcastically noted – a whiff of cheap scent replacing what once smelled only raw and sulphurous. 'For anyone interested in resisting the social pressures when the Stones pass through town,' *Time* continues acidly, 'the following reasons are offered as a public service . . .'

Buffalo is the nearest the Stones can get to Canada since 1977, when Keith Richards was arrested for heroin smuggling in Toronto, and Mick Jagger featured in an erotic scandal with the primes minister's wife. Buffalo's chief autumn feature is a dishmop-grey sky which, for all its apparent listlessness, harbours sudden rain squalls and gales of eccentric ferocity. There is such a sky today as the cars and pickups and plastered microbuses come streaming across the Canadian border, past clumps and pickets of police in broad-brimmed Mountie hats, and the numerous misty slip-roads to Niagara Falls.

Behind the Amherst-Marriott Hotel the four yellow vans that fled JFK Stadium three days ago stand innocently in an almost empty parking lot. Beside the first van, half a dozen teenage boys squat on the grass verge, gazing up at a top-floor picture window whose brown, red and orange curtains have yet to be drawn back. From time to time, the same boy advances, cups his hands and bellows, 'C'mon *out*, Jagger!'

At Rich Stadium, twenty-five miles away, the wind scuds down the empty stands at a steady forty miles per hour. The Stones' pink and purple stage set takes shape at the westerly end, in conditions that force its scaffolders to cling on aloft like sailors working an Indiaman round Cape Horn. By noon, the wind has almost toppled the right-hand tower backwards, and buffeted both Japanese side-screens to colourless shreds. There is, even so, no question of cancelling the afternoon's concert. Printed on each $15 ticket under the Stones' name, and that of Jovan Perfumes, is the blithe assurance that it is an 'all weather' show.

The wind rises to gale force as Rich Stadium fills with its audience of 65,000. The Canadian contingent gather round the stage with red and white national flags and old-fashioned hippy hair which from a distance, en masse, has the look of good quality manure. The support band plays almost inaudibly, amid a skirl of balloons and orange frisbees, bobbing on capricious up-draughts. The Stones are even better hidden than at JFK Stadium; bunkered deep under the back bleachers with their banquets and their bars. When the press sees them, it is for the briefest instant, running to the stage across an elevated drawbridge. They clearly had no idea before this moment that a storm was in progress.

The headwind hits Jagger first, catching the radio-controlled mike in his hand and whirling it up to bump his mouth with such force it loosens the diamond filling in one of his upper front teeth. The others, less hale and well protected, battle their way out into the applause, gripping guitars like imperilled umbrellas, their trouser cuffs flapping madly around their built-up heels. Jagger's voice comes only in patches through the juddering breeze '. . . under ma thumb . . . gurl . . . just changed her ways . . .' The stage gives no protection from the head-on squalls. The shredded side-panels flap insanely. It is too windy for Woody to skylark, or Bill to hold a cigarette in his mouth. The only thing they can do is stand there. They cannot hear their audience, and can hardly hear themselves. The wind gulps the vast kilowattage, carrying it off with balloons and frisbees, up over the stadium-rim and away to vanish in the fogs and white uproar that hang eternally above Niagara Falls.

For all that, the five fragile remnants of an endangered species, panoramically revealed by their half-destroyed set, have suddenly begun playing like the Rolling Stones of old. They are playing, in the teeth of this ludicrous gale, like the band of young tearaways who could wreck a cinema or transfix a half-million hippies. They are playing with percussion of inspired lawlessness, smashing the high hats and policemen's helmets; a bass-line below it, groping up the little girls' skirts. They are playing with one heartless heart, one vicious voice, one thin, bare arm pumping a pale driftwood guitar with renewing force as light steams back into the vampire's red-rimmed eyes. The Human Riff is awake at last. The World's Greatest Rock 'n' Roll Band is in business again. The Rolling Stones are back in the bloodstream.

As for Jagger, the sprawling pink stage and two long catwalks now seem too small to contain him. He dances down to the left, high-kicking like a drum majorette, taunting and beckoning all 20,000 along that curve. He sprints back up the right-hand catwalk, leaps to the scaffolding, climbs six feet and hangs there, leaning out as far as his fingertips will reach. Before Rich Stadium can touch hands with him, he jumps down, rolls over, struts to the front and stands there, yellow ski jacket slanted into the storm as his body beats time with each syllable. 'Yuh can't always *git* what yuh want. No, yuh can't always *git* what yuh wa-hant . . .

'Okay . . .' his voice says among the wind-swallowed cheers. 'Good aftahnoon, Buffalo . . . Yeah it's nice to be back. We're gonna 'ave a good time, awright? Aw-*ri-i-ight*!'

The first of two concerts at the 60,000-seat Tangerine Bowl in Orlando, Florida, happens to coincide with Bill Wyman's forty-fifth birthday. The other Stones plot vaguely to buy him a naff Goblin bedside teamaker, but settle for a party in his honour, cruising in a riverboat up and down the lake at nearby Disney World.

There is also a singing telegram, delivered to Bill backstage at the Tangerine Bowl by a girl in a tailcoat and black net stockings, wearing a toy monkey that claps two cymbals fitfully in time. The girl, seeing her big chance, stretches her song of greeting to almost a quarter of an hour. After a while, a belly-dancer comes into the garden to join her. The girl steps back, clapping her hands, clashing her monkey's cymbals and honking a motor horn concealed in her bosom.

Jerry Hall has again flown in from New York to see Mick. In T-shirt and jeans and bereft of make-up, she has taken Jade and assorted other children for a full day at Disney World. 'A lot of freeloaders, aren't they?' Jagger pants as he jogs round his artificial lawn. 'All they came here for was Disney World.'

'Mick doesn't approve of Disney,' his publicist said.

'It's not that I don't approve of it,' Jagger said. 'I just don't want all the fuss of going there. I *do* like a good Big Dipper . . .'

There is delay owing to the late arrival, yet again, of Woody and Keith. Two Lear jets have been chartered to bring them from their separate hotels in Palm Beach. They reel in at last, with the usual ragged entourage. 'What time do you call this then?' several colleagues enquire.

Ian Stewart, the faithful roadie and back-up pianist, looks into the humid, balloon-filled Florida sky.

'I'd give anything for a good pint at my local now,' he says wistfully. 'A nice pint of Directors'. Even Watney's would be all right.'

In the main backstage area, security arrangements have been entrusted to Dr Daniel K. Pai, Grand Master or 'White Dragon' of the Pai Lun system of martial arts. Dr Pai is a squat Chinese gentleman in a baby-blue tracksuit, from one sleeve of which dangles a small, steel-edged fan. 'The fan,' one of his disciples explains, 'is the emblem of the White Dragon in our order. It's a handy tool in this heat. And it is – er – a weapon.'

Dr Pai is on guard next afternoon also, with sundry disciples, outside the Stones' sequestered block of the Hyatt-Orlando Hotel. He sits in the alley on a folding chair, still in his baby-blue tracksuit, still holding his killer fan. Occasionally he rises, assumes a fighting stance and pensively lunges and slices at the unthreatening air.

A black man stripped to the waist, his huge muscles shrouded in the corridor twilight, forms a second line of defence. This is Mick Jagger's personal bodyguard and gym partner. He taps on his master's door, just once, very lightly, then inclines his great, smoky neck in an attitude of intense listening.

The door opens on a sitting room in twilight and chaos. Clothes, room service dishcovers, hi-fi, cigarette packs, shoes and papers lie strewn over every surface. Heavy drapes shut out the mid-afternoon Florida sun. Amid the disorder, Jerry Hall stands, *Vogue*-cover fresh, gazing with amusement at a battery shaver whirring softly in her hand. 'Can you believe that?' she says. 'None of us can git it to stop.'

Jagger comes from the bedroom, pulling on his trousers. 'Let's go out in the garden,' he says. Behind him, two lines of defence still await all comers. He pushes through the curtains, stepping out unguarded on to the motel's public poolside lawn.

At thirty-eight, he looks boyish and, in a strange way, virginal. The years, the parties, the scandals, the scouring camera lenses have left no visible scar, or even blemish. Outside his performing self, he becomes the person one imagines he must have been before it all began. He shirt is still untucked from his trousers. His feet are bare. His voice is quiet, almost deferential. His only ornamentation is a businesslike wristwatch and, sparkling like frost on one upper tooth, that tiny chip of diamond.

He is saying that what he really misses about England after all these years is the cricket. When he comes over, it is usually in the hope of spending a day or two at Lord's with his father. He likes, if he can, to see a match played by his own county. 'I've always been fond of the Kent county ground, right in the middle of Canterbury . . .' He pauses, almost wistfully. 'Right next to Boots.'

Jagger frequently seems to pine for Kent. He chose his chateau in France partly because the country around Amboise, in the Loire Valley, looks a little Kentish. 'There's lots of fruit trees

– apples lying round everywhere. The French are into the countryside the way the English used to be. My next-door neighbour at Amboise breeds wild boars.'

There is also New York, where Jagger now lives with Jerry in Jerry's apartment, and leads an offstage life he likes to characterize as that of 'dilettante Englishman'. '. . . It means being interested in lots of things in a casual way,' he explains. 'Doing other things than going round to clubs and making a fool of yourself.'

Jerry's apartment is only a couple of blocks from the Dakota Building, where Jagger's old friend John Lennon once sought similar anonymity. Since Lennon's murder, it has been widely speculated that, of all New York's rock star emigrés, cautious Jagger would be among the first to choose some safer adopted city. He insists it did not cross his mind. 'New York's still the place where I mostly want to be. In fact, I can't wait to get back there for a few days next week.'

Jerry's beneficial impact has been widely noticed. Her attraction for Jagger – even more than her thoroughbred beauty – is her resolute independence. He speaks admiringly of her separate income, and the horse ranch she owns. Before this tour, Jerry told him he need not go on singing if he dreaded it: her modelling could easily support them both.

He stays in close touch with his father, the former physical training instructor he has come to resemble in so many ways. Joe Jagger recently toured America, giving some lectures. ' "Physical Training from the Renaissance to the Present Day",' his son quotes with rather paternal pride.

The strict father has become, as so often, an indulgent grandfather. 'It amazes me when I see him with Jade,' Jagger says. 'He lets Jade get away with *anything*. If I'd done the same when I was her age, I'd have got a thump or a task to do as a punishment. When I tell him so, he says: "Was I *really* as hard a father as all that?" '

We turn to Jagger's Loire chateau built in 1710 ('the same year as my Cheyne Walk house') which, he insists, is not *really* large as chateaux go. 'Well it *is* a big 'ouse. Some of those chateaux that were built for people's mistresses are minute. Too feminine for me. My house is big but it's airy. It wasn't ever fortified or anything like an English castle. And the interesting thing is, it's got no servants' staircase. So, for some mysterious reason, it had no indoor servants.'

He smiles tolerantly, fingering the heavy wristwatch. He has been asked a question whose banality is designed to pierce this vast unassumingness. What are his greatest pleasures? If you are Mick Jagger, is pleasure still something the body registers?

'Reading's a pleasure. Eating. I ate everyone else's dinner in the restaurant last night.'

He ponders.

'Sex is a pleasure. It gets better and better. Whereas' – he grins, with a sparkle of diamond in an upper tooth – 'chocolate biscuits *do* tend to pall.'

He walks barefoot over the synthetic grass, back to his untidy motel room, his recalcitrant electric shaver, his Texan princess and Dr Pai. Only half of America left to go. Only another million or so people wanting him.

EPILOGUE

Mr Formica's Sticky End

On an overcast morning in April 1994, Bill Wyman could be observed at his London restaurant, Sticky Fingers, hanging out with the least likely of all companions for an ex-Rolling Stone. One would have expected Eric Clapton, Peter Townshend or Phil Collins. One might even have expected Sir David Frost, Ken Follett or Gary Lineker. But one would hardly have expected His Grace the 11th Duke of Marlborough. Paparazzi gathered outside, eager to see the heir of Britain's great seventeenth-century military commander hobnob with the composer of the bass-guitar riff in Jumpin' Jack Flash.

Like all his former colleagues in the Stones, Wyman is an avid cricket fan. Unlike most of them, however, he still has wind and mobility enough to play from time to time. Hence this brief photo opportunity prior to his appearance in a celebrity match organized by the Duke for a charity called the Oxfordshire Young People's Association. Tabloid memories are mercifully short: of the assembled snappers, none remarked on the novelty of covering Bill in an outdoor sport, nor that until recently his interest in young people could not exactly have been called charitable.

The scene outside Sticky Fingers might have been

deliberately designed to show how pop now crosses all social divides. The Duke of Marlborough, a tall, bendy man with Churchillian goggle eyes, swung a cricket bat over his shoulder. The ex-Stone, soon to be fifty-seven, tossed a ball playfully up and down. His tiny rock star frame was encased in a striped cricket sweater and ritualistically cheap and faded blue jeans. His face has the aged impishness one sees in photographs of Edwardian music-hall stars. His hair is almost eerily abundant, with the auburn and brown tints of a superior feather duster or a cheap brogue shoe.

'Look this way, Bill . . . Your Grace . . . can you turn the bat round a bit? Great! Throw the ball up again, Bill . . . Great!' Assuredly, a wondrous change from BILL TAKES A TEENAGE LOVER, MANDY'S WAGES OF SIN, WYMAN TO FACE THE MUSIC and LET-OFF FOR SEX-PROBE STONE.

Sticky Fingers, named after the Stones' classic 1971 album, is a pseudo Tex-Mex joint where the youth of Kensington and Fulham can pretend they are in Natchez or El Paso. Round the walls are selected items from the vast hoard of memorabilia that Wyman squirrelled away during his thirty-two years with the Stones – clippings of quaint Sixties outrage, a guitar given to him by Brian Jones, framed golden discs for landmark albums like *Exile on Main Street, Tattoo You* and *It's Only Rock and Roll*, each achingly collectable icon clamped to the wall by a security system that the Louvre might envy. Wyman eats there three times a week when he's in London; his corner booth, indeed, was where he proposed to his new wife, Suzanne, over a chilli dog.

Sticky Fingers is perhaps his most eloquent two-fingered salute to the band which he formally quit in January 1994. It proves that there can be life after the Rolling Stones – provided you get out alive. It also proves Bill's own bitter point that he had good ideas all along, if the others had just listened to him. His original plan, an associate recalls, was for a chain of restaurants called Rolling Stones. 'But when he went to Prince Rupert [their financial adviser, Prince Rupert Loewenstein] he was told "OK, but you'd only get 10 per cent of the take."'

Despite a slump in the restaurant business, Sticky Fingers was an instant hit. Wyman recently told a friend the place earns him £60,000–£75,000 per month, more than he ever got for being a Stone. There was soon talk of opening a second one, Beggars Banquet. Pretty good for a man who, according to one of his rancorous late comrades, 'only thinks with his dick'.

For his first twenty-two years as a rock star, Bill Wyman was famous only by association. He was just another bit-part player in the super echelon; a mega-extra like George Harrison in the Beatles and John Entwistle in The Who. Hollow-faced, impassive, cradling his bass guitar at a curious upright angle, he communicated nothing from his place in the Rolling Stones, save perhaps resignation to perpetual eclipse. There's not much else you can do if your front men are Mick Jagger and Keith Richards, combining the properties of Nijinsky and Count Dracula.

The great turnaround did not come until the mid-Eighties, paradoxically at a time when the Stones at last seemed to be losing their old sulphurous reek of lawlessness and decadence. Nijinksy and Dracula, as they advanced into middle age, both acquired stable relationships, children, households, nannies and late burgeoning moral awareness. Meanwhile, the eye of their forty-eight-year-old bass player lit on a thirteen-year-old London schoolgirl named Mandy Smith.

The chapters of the subsequent miserable saga filled alternate issues of the *Sun* and *Hello!* magazine. How Scotland Yard passed a file on the liaison to the Director of Public Prosecutions before deciding no charges should be made. How Bill and Mandy were eventually married, he aged fifty-three, she aged nineteen, in splendour rivalling the Field of the Cloth of Gold. How, after only a couple of days' honeymoon, Mandy summoned her mother, Patsy, to join her. How she afterwards fell prey to a mysterious illness which reduced her weight to five and a half stone. How the couple were divorced after having spent less than a week of married life together. How Mandy sought a £5 million settlement from Bill's reputed £24 million fortune, but was persuaded to accept cash and a house, together worth just £580,000.

If the script up to that point might have been written by Jackie Collins with help from Vladimir Nabokov, its sequel is more like the climax of a Gilbert and Sullivan opera. No sooner had Wyman paid off Mandy than his son Stephen, thirty, became engaged to her mother, Patsy, forty-six. The mother-in-law he has lately discarded with such effort was set to become his daughter-in-law – perhaps even, she threatened, the mother of his first grandchild.

Many inside the music business, as well as millions outside it, were baffled by Wyman's decision to leave the Stones only weeks after they had signed the biggest recording deal of their career. Under their new $28 million contract with Virgin (ha-ha) Records, the 'old men of rock' joined the same earnings super-league as Michael Jackson and Madonna. Their concert tours, ever a byword for sponge-like greed, were set to continue rolling for as long as Mick Jagger could do Satisfaction without the aid of a Zimmer frame.

Wyman's part in all this seemed the ideal synthesis of monster prestige, sumptuous enjoyment and infinitesimal workload. You have not seen a human being cossetted until you've seen a Rolling Stone on tour, gently shepherded from Lear jet to stretch limo to emperor-size hotel suite by scores of bodyslaves and security men. Onstage at Wembley Stadium or the Orlando Tangerine Bowl, his presence was the same bare minimum: a middle-aged man in little-boy clothes, hair exotically wound in a bandanna, smouldering fag mundanely pasted to lower lip. While Jagger could work off pounds in one show, Bill often would not pop a single bead of sweat. Those daily two hours in front of 60,000-odd faces and gyrating bodies were, he once told me, 'like going off with the family to the seaside for the day. You have to be sure to have a wee first.'

Between shows, too, he seemed to have found his own peculiar equilibrium. A visit to Bill Wyman's hotel or motel room was an experience very different from the usual plunge into rock star squalor and fug. Always the bags would be unpacked and stowed, the liquor bottles aesthically arranged, the bathroom pristine, the bedcover as straight at midnight as the maids had left it at midday. 'With Bill, everything has to be obsessively neat,' an associate says. 'The pen mustn't lie on the desk, but must be inside the diary. His handwriting is as precise as a schoolmaster's. Not only is he the one rock star I know to have a briefcase, but it's the neatest briefcase I've ever seen. Pens, papers, all in their place, three spare packs of his cigarettes . . . and a banana in case he gets hungry.'

His mind is similarly well ordered. He is a walking archive of Rolling Stones history, able to remember precise dates a quarter of a century ago when they played the Salisbury Gaumont, the Slough Adelphi or the Floral Hall, Morecambe. The same meticulous chapter and verse is given to an amatory career that would make Frank Harris gasp. A female editor who worked on his memoirs, *Stone Alone*, was heard to exclaim despairingly 'Bill's included every fuck he ever had!' although a former Stones PR man sounds a sceptical note: 'Bill's always talked about the 1,000 women he made love to. But no one seems to have seen any of them.'

Many believe that his orderliness was as vital to the Stones as the others' chaotic wildness. 'Bill was always the rock-steady one,' said Ray Coleman, former editor of the *Melody Maker* and collaborator in his autobiography, *Stone Alone*. 'He could always be relied on to turn up at recording sessions cold sober and to remember the chords when all the others were out of it. And he did compose the bass riff for Jumpin' Jack Flash, which has to be one of the most powerful rock intros ever. Almost every producer who ever worked with them said that Bill and Charlie Watts were the real heart of the Rolling Stones. Bass players and drummers in rock bands always have this same problem – they know they're essential to the band, but they can never shine.'

There were, in effect, two classes within the Stones – Mick and Keith (and, at the beginning, Brian Jones) who hogged the limelight and caused the trouble, and Bill and Charlie, on whose blameless heads the backwash continually broke. Ultimately, however, the Stones' second division narrowed down to just one. Charlie Watts, gentle and stoical, has always been well liked and decently treated by the band's twin godheads. The two later recruits, Ronnie Wood and Mick Taylor, found their level in the lead guitarist's niche. Only Bill stayed on the outside. Far from being resigned to obscurity, he had ambitions both as a songwriter and singer, yet all his attempts to develop them were doomed to squashing by the Glimmer Twins. 'The trouble was that he never really liked Mick or Keith from the beginning,' says an associate. 'The vital chemistry just wasn't there. They said that after thirty years, Bill still hadn't really joined the band.

'Because he'd taken an equal share of bad publicity, he thought he was entitled to an equal share of the credit. He hated the way that a group that had been founded on democratic principles was commandeered by Mick as a vehicle for his own ego. He hated the way Keith almost tore it apart in the Seventies with his drug busts, and he hated the way Mick and Keith were continually sniping at one another through the Eighties. I'm only surprised he didn't get out years ago.'

His apartness and self-containment in fact were to be the main reason for his survival in a band that had strewn innumerable casualties, and not a few corpses, in its wake. Level-headed and abstemious, hating drugs and drunkenness, he was never drawn into the competitive orgies and intrigues which left Brian Jones dead in a swimming pool, turned Mick Taylor from a non-smoking vegetarian into a heroin addict, threw the old Etonian art dealer Robert Fraser into Wormwood Scrubs and squandered a succession of breathtaking women: Chrissie Shrimpton, Marianne Faithfull, Suki Poitier, Bianca Pérez Mora Macías, Anita Pallenberg.

His life as a Stone may have been envied from outside, but on the inside it bristled with snubs and slights. Shirley Arnold, the band's faithful assistant through the Sixties and Seventies, remembers all too many examples. 'Mick would decide he wanted to go to the Olympic Games at a day's notice and, because he was Mick, it'd be arranged. Then Bill would decide he wanted to go, too, and, of course, we'd have to tell him . . . Or he'd ring up the office, wanting help on one of his solo projects, but be told everyone was too busy looking for a new nanny for Keith.'

With the arch-elitist Jagger, relations could sometimes resemble that of master and under-footman, as a mutual friend witnessed. 'A couple of years ago, Mick was in London and there was quite a crucial thing the Stones needed to discuss. But when Bill rang him up to arrange a meeting, Mick said he hadn't got time. To me it's unimaginable that the bass guitarist in the Stones rings the vocalist and is told he hasn't got time to see him.'

Most bitter of all were his grievances over money. Like all innocent young bands, the Stones were shamelessly ripped off at the start of their career. But for the past twenty-two years they have been the most prodigal earners in international pop, channelling their earnings into a network of investments masterminded by the thrifty Jagger. To all interviewers (this one included) Wyman maintained that the performance money, as distinct from Jagger-Richards songwriting royalties, was split equally between the five Stones. Yet after their 1989–90 Steel Wheels world tour – with its sponsorship by Budweiser beer, reputedly worth $75 million – he complained to a friend that he and Charlie Watts between them 'hadn't made as much as the accountants'.

Within the band he always felt uneasy, mocked by the others

for his comparative old age, his suburban tastes, his refusal to take drugs, even his preference for rock 'n' roll over the blues. His only 'mate' within the line-up was Brian Jones, with whom he developed a verbal code both for pulling groupies and then getting rid of them to make way for fresh relays. 'Bill even went about sex in a methodical fashion,' a friend remembers. 'While the Stones were performing, he'd be deciding which girls he fancied in the crowd and letting them know he wanted to see them later. The others used to wait until afterwards, and take pot luck from the ones who came to the dressing room. But Bill used to pull them from the stage.'

Through all those golden Sixties years, when the Stones seemed to be piling up treasures like insolent young caliphs, Bill existed on a semi-permanent bank overdraft. His first wife, Diane, tired of Rolling Stone lifestyle and took their son Stephen away to live with her in South Africa. In 1966, Bill had met a nineteen-year-old Swedish student named Astrid Lundstrom, with whom he was to maintain a stable relationship until 1983. During one of Stephen's holiday visits, he decided arbitrarily not to send the boy back to Diane. Astrid subsequently played a major part in bringing Stephen up in comparative normality, and preventing him from turning into a rock 'n' roll brat.

The French tax exile, undertaken with grudging resentment, proved to be a renaissance. In France, even a second-division Rolling Stone received the status of cultural hero. Wyman and Astrid settled in a custom-built house in the Provencal mountain-top village of St Paul de Vence. Their next-door neighbour was Marc Chagall (meeting whom, Bill said, was 'as big a thrill as meeting Chuck Berry'). Their 'local' was the bougainvillea-drenched Colombe d'Or with its casually displayed works by Picasso, Leger and Braque, its chic echoes of Yves Montand and Simone Signoret. Visitors from London brought Bill the two things he missed most about Britain: Birds custard and Branston pickle.

The tempests which he was forced to weather with the Stones through the Seventies still brought no feeling of integration or empathy. Friendship with Jagger obviously was a long-lost cause. What he could never understand was his failure to chum up with Keith, a working-class boy like himself, with none of Mick's obvious social ambition. He has recounted how, on the near-terminal Canadian tour of 1977, he and Ronnie Wood found Keith in convulsions on a hotel bedroom floor and decided that the only way to save his life was to score him some heroin. When the Human Riff subsequently entered detox, Bill sent him supportive letters and received one in return – he surprisingly claims – 'decorated with pressed flowers'. It stung all the worse therefore to read Keith's subsequent quoted opinion that he is 'too wrinkly' to go on tour and that he 'only thinks with his dick'.

Despite the creative tyranny of Jagger and Richards, he developed an annoying habit of outdoing his fellow Stones in solo enterprises. He was the first to make his own album, *Monkey Grip* in 1974, and remains the only one to have had a number one single, Si Si Je Suis Un Rock Star, in 1981. He also has composed the theme music for a movie, *Green Ice*, and published a book of photographs of Marc Chagall. While Jagger dickered inconclusively with an autobiography, Bill went steadily ahead with his own massive tome, giving his collaborator Ray Coleman access to some twenty trunks full of accumulated papers, including dry-cleaning tickets, even bank documents relating to the other Stones.

His unequal stipend did not stop his acquiring spectacular properties – his house in Venice, a penthouse flat in Chelsea and a medieval mansion, Gedding Hall, near Bury St Edmunds, entailing lordship of the manor of Gedding and Thormwood. He indulged a wealth of expensive hobbies including archaeology, astronomy, Australian Aborigonals and metal detecting, and became a member of the Royal Horticultural Society.

His break-up with Astrid surprised many people, since she

had not only helped raised his son but had also acted as his energetic personal agent. He blamed the split on her drug-addiction and alcoholism, which she in turn blamed on his chronic infidelity. They remain on good enough terms for Astrid to have co-operated with his autobiography; he pays her a regular allowance and is grateful for her continuing refusal to cash in her story.

With his usual computer-aided precision, he remembers it was on February 21, 1984 that he first saw Mandy Smith. He was at a VIP table at the Lyceum ballroom; she was on the floor, dancing with her elder sister Nicola. Blonde and long-legged, she made the forty-eight-year-old feel as if he'd been 'whacked over the head with a hammer'. He had her brought to his table, there learning with amazement that she was only thirteen. She told him she wanted to make a career as a fashion model. The kindly Rolling Stone offered to help.

His decision to begin dating her is so calmly rationalized in his book, *Stone Alone*, that one can almost accept it as sensible. Mandy was 'a woman at thirteen' and in any case looked at least seven years older. She was used to staying out late in clubs and pubs. And her mother did not object. They saw one another secretly for two and a half years, despite well-founded warnings to Wyman from his fellow Stones that the whole thing would blow up in his face. During that time, he maintains, he treated Mandy 'honourably', urged her to continue her schooling and did not introduce her to alcohol or drugs.

The affair was pretty much over by 1984 when it was exposed in the good old *News of the World*, creating a rock 'n' roll scandal unprecedented since Jerry Lee Lewis was hounded out of Britain for marrying his thirteen-year-old cousin. In the ensuing flurry of interest by Scotland Yard and the DPP, the other Stones remained noticeably non-supportive. Jagger in particular – shortly to see the birth of his first grandchild – was said to have viewed the affair with horror. According to Wyman's account, matters were finally resolved by Mandy's proposing to him on the eve of the Stones' 1989 tour. To relays of interviewers he said he was 'absolutely elated . . . like a kid with a new toy' (not a toy with a new kid?). Discounting the thirty-three-year gap between them, Mandy maybe spoke truer than she knew. 'I don't think about it. I love him and that's all the matters. Bill has never acted his age anyway.'

Wanting 'a quiet wedding away from the glare of publicity', they were married by civil ceremony in Bury St Edmunds, then drove to London to appear on the *Wogan* television show. Bill was at pains to point out that Picasso had been seventy-five when he took a wife forty years younger. 'That marriage lasted, and there's no reason why ours shouldn't be the same.'

He claimed to have been baffled by the mystery complaint (eventually diagnosed as anorexia nervosa) which whittled his nineteen-year-old bride down to the shape of an Ethiopian famine victim, with legs described by one female reporter as 'matchsticks with the wood scraped off'. From the very beginning, married life was carried on at separate addresses, with Bill, by his own account, constantly on the phone to Mandy, begging her to seek medical help. The upshot seems to have been that a millionaire rock star, lord of the manor of Gedding and Thormwood, was seldom able to be with his wife without her mother, her sister and, frequently, aunts and uncles, too, seated at the other end of the sofa. Using the *Daily Mail* as a confessor, he finally poured out a list of marital grievances almost as numerous as those against Mick and Keith: how the marriage had been barely consummated, how Mandy cared too much for publicity, how her mother upset the Gedding Hall servants, how he returned from the Stones' last tour to 'an empty flat', how the Smith family even laughed and joked around him on the evening after his father's funeral. The liaison with Mandy at thirteen, he concluded, had been 'morally wrong – but it happened'. A friend says, 'I think the whole thing with Mandy fucked him up more than he knew.'

Five months after his divorce, he married Suzanne Daccosta, a thirty-three-year-old Californian fashion designer whom he had met in France more than a decade previously. 'This is like a spring clean for me and a fresh start in my life,' he said. 'I'm so happy I can't describe it. It feels like the first time I've ever been married. We want to start a family as soon as possible . . .' On the same day that Bill wed Suzanne, Mandy called a press conference in full football kit to announce her own imminent marriage to Tottenham Hotspur star Pat van den Hauwe.

Could the Stones go on without him? Could *Hamlet* be played without the speech of the second gravedigger? The band's original five-man line-up might have undergone amazingly few changes over four decades. But it had long since let in extra hands, hired-gun guitarists and keyboard players, to marginalize its once-crucial rhythm section. On the Stones' next tour, Bill's role on bass was taken over by American session-player Darryl Jones, with not a single desolate wail nor disappointed scream from the audience. Not until Geri Halliwell left the Spice Girls would there be a more poignant demonstration of someone being 'history'.

For his old, unsatisfactory life on the road and in the studio, Bill substituted the diary-jammed routine of an all-purpose showbiz star, playing pro-celebrity cricket matches, winning TV pop trivia quizzes, turning out at gala benefits in aid of cancer research, albeit with fag still doggedly pasted to his lower lip. He promised a sequel to his autobiography, *Stone Alone*, which by the end of almost 700 pages still had reached only the year 1969. He became that emblematic modern figure, the older husband on his second marriage who joyfully submits to all the domestic routine he avoided during his first one. At La Colombe D'Or, the inn near his home in Provence, he can often be seen devotedly tending his three little girls, Catherine, Jessica and Matilda.

The only part of his life on hold has been music. In the early Nineties, a Bill Wyman solo album entitled *Stuff* – its fifty-six-year-old voice sounding weirdly like that of a robotic sixteen-year-old – found a public only in Japan. 'All the publicity over Mandy and quitting the Stones cut no ice with any of the British or American record labels,' an associate says. 'They decided he didn't have anything to say in the modern market.' To his rescue, ironically, came Andrew Loog Oldham, reappearing on the London music scene after two decades in America and Colombia. With his old Sixties associate, Tony Calder, Oldham relaunched Immediate, the record label they had floated on the back of the Stones' success twenty-seven years previously. Bill Wyman's *Stuff* album became the new Immediate label's first major release, supplemented by an updated mix of his hit single, Si Si Je Suis Un Rock Star. But, alas, the Oldham venture lasted only a few months.

Bill Wyman is a rock legend none the less, always able to garner a round of nostalgic applause when he takes the stage in Travelin' Wilbury style supergroups with the likes of Georgie Fame, Gary Booker and Albert Lee. 'Of all the Stones I knew,' Oldham says, 'Bill's the one most at peace with himself today. He's certainly more so than Keith . . . and he's got to be more so than Mick . . . I'm sorry now I said he had no taste and nicknamed him Mister Formica. Because, you have to admit, Formica does wear pretty well.'

Andrew Loog Oldham now lives permanently in Bogotà with his Colombian wife, Esther and their son, Max. Despite the earthquakes and endemic drug wars, he says he finds it peaceful there, 'a bit like Britain in the mid-Fifties'.

Oldham has been asked the same question many times over the past three decades. Does he ever regret letting go of the Rolling Stones? Doesn't he lie awake at night, sweating and cursing himself for no longer having a piece of the world's greatest rock 'n' roll band? His answer is always the same. 'No – not ever. How many times can I go on saying no? The Rolling

Stones were just one strand in the things I was doing at that time. In a lot of ways, they took me where I never wanted to go. I've never regretted my life without them for a single second.'

In his mid-fifties, he remains a boyish figure in his roll-neck sweater and combat trousers, even if there are some flecks of grey in his reddish beard. His pale eyes still gleam with mischief and reverence towards none. 'Andrew – how would you get the Beatles back together?' a chat-show host in America once asked him. 'Three more bullets,' was Oldham's whipcrack reply.

In the twenty-seven years since their split, Oldham and the Stones have run across one another only very occasionally. The last time was in Rio, during the band's 1994 tour. The one-time teenage revolutionaries in their different ways were such different people, they hardly recognized each other. 'With Mick it was a simple "Hello, Andrew",' Oldham recalls. 'I hung out more with Keith. But then, I always did hang out more with Keith.'

The mid-Nineties attempt to relaunch Immediate Records with Bill Wyman on its roster did not work out, thanks mainly to Oldham's heavy concurrent ingestion of drugs and alcohol. Not long afterwards, he had a drug-induced vision that finally brought home what he was doing to himself. Walking along New York's Fifth Avenue early one morning, he saw a white horse cantering between the Algonquin and Royalton hotels, fifteen storeys high. 'I tried to go "ha-ha" and blink it away,' he recalls. "But it wouldn't blink away.'

That experience spurred him to go on a seven-week detox programme with an American herbalist who was also a Scientologist. Later, both he and his wife, Esther, went on a forty-day purification course prescribed by the Church of Scientology. Both are now committed Scientologists, and follow a strict diet calculated according to their blood types.

In 2000, he published his autobiography, *Stoned*, a long-awaited work that was expected to rattle a good few skeletons, particularly in the Jagger closet. Though written with the finger-snapping raciness of Damon Runyon on speed, it ended disappointingly on the eve of the Stones' first American tour in 1964.

Scientologist or not, Oldham still retains a quality one can only describe as style to the point of self-destruction. Emerging from a London hotel lift recently, he suddenly found himself face to face with Paul McCartney. McCartney did a startled double-take, dimly remembering wild days in the early Sixties, when the Beatles and Stones jointly ruled the world, and one wicked young hustler was inside the glorious loop with them.

'Don't I know you?' McCartney asked.

'No,' Oldham replied. And swaggered off into the crowd.

Author's Note

This book could not have been written without the help of its principal characters. I am grateful to the Rolling Stones for the access they gave me during their 1981–82 tour, and for illuminating interviews with Mick Jagger, Keith Richards and Bill Wyman. I also have drawn on conversations with them, and with Charlie Watts, Ron Wood and the late Brian Jones, during my years on the *Sunday Times* and various other newspapers, back to 1965.

I owe a special debt, for their help, generosity and candour, to Andrew Loog Oldham, Marianne Faithfull, Anita Pallenberg, Christopher Gibbs and the late Robert Fraser and Alexis Korner.

Sincere thanks also to: Keith Altham, Shirley Arnold, David Bailey, Dr W. Bennett, Jo Bergman, John Birt, Tito Burns, the late Donald Cammell, Barbara Charone, Tamara Glenny, Giorgio Gomelsky, Brion Gysin, Mary Hallett, Keith Howell, Glyn Johns, Lewis Jones, Tom Keylock, Laurie Lewis, Ken Llewellyn, Lord Lichfield, Astrid Lundstrom, Gered Mankowitz, Albert Maysles, David Maysles, Barry Miles, Molly Parkin, Janey Perrin, Dick Rowe, Ronnie Schneider, John Spinks, Helen Spittal, the late Ian Stewart, Dick Taylor, Dave Thomson, Mike

Turner, Keith Vyse, Robert Wallis, Peter Watson, Leslie Woodhead.

My special gratitude to Jack Artenstein, Michael Sissons, Peter Matson, Roger Houghton, Russell Miller, Caroline Taggart and Lucy Sisman.

Index

PHILIP NORMAN

Sir Elton

PAN BOOKS £7.99

At the top for over three decades, Elton John's career began as Reg Dwight pounding the piano in a suburban pub and perhaps reached its apotheosis with 'Goodbye England's Rose' at Princess Diana's funeral. In between we've seen it all: the glittering costumes, the indestructible classics, the sky-high boots, the draining addictions, the failed marriage, the coming out. This is the new, revised and updated edition of the original acclaimed biography, of which Elton said, 'He's got me spot on'!

'Norman, unquestionably the best of Britain's music biographers, pulls no punches. It makes compelling reading'
Daily Mail

'An eloquent, analytical and well-researched examination of the spectacle who is rock's most devoted scholar and brilliant emulator'
***New York Times*, Notable Book of the Year**

'Scintillating . . . with an encyclopaedic knowledge of the pop music world . . . Elton John comes over as friendly, straightforward and honest, both about his alcoholism and his sexual identity'
Sunday Times

VICTORIA MARY CLARKE & SHANE MACGOWAN

A Drink with Shane MacGowan

PAN BOOKS £7.99

'One of the freshest, most original biographies I've ever read . . . Buy the book, it's great.'

Lynn Barber, *Observer*

'A welter of colourful yarn, bombast and lecture based indiscriminately on deep knowledge and fathomless ignorance . . . this book is unbridled and large-hearted . . . All human life is here.'

Q

'Unexpectedly excellent results . . . the insights into his massive ego, music making and death-wish lifestyle are truly wicked'

Mirror

'[MacGowan's] refreshing disregard for this image or for rock star posturing makes for an unusual "celebrity" biography . . . His candour, coupled with an acerbic wit, makes him an ideal guide through an unmistakably colourful life.'

Time Out

'This endearing memoir . . . is Irish rock, distilled'

Sunday Times

MARC ALMOND

Tainted Life:

The Autobiography

PAN BOOKS £9.99

'There was always something attractively decadent about Marc Almond . . . you sensed that here was the real thing: an artist set on self-destruction. Many pop stars play at nihilism; Almond meant it . . .

'Today the delight with which Almond flouts conventional expectations still rankles with some. He writes well . . . about the drug abuse, the promiscuity, the false friends, the broken lives and the recklessness that drove him to the edge of madness . . . One cannot but respond to the spirit of the man, to his self-lacerating honesty, the sympathy with which he writes about his unhappy boyhood in a broken home in Southport, and the undeniable excitement of the pop adventures he describes . . .

'This excellent book also sends you to the music, to the traumas of late adolescence, and to the first time you saw that effete man-boy smothered in make-up on *Top of the Pops*'

Jason Cowley, *The Times*

'One can only guess what the Tainted Lover chose to omit, given the damning quality of what he left in . . . You find yourself hoping that he'll go on being outrageous for years to come'

John Walsh, *Independent*

'Jaw-dropping'

Q

GARY VALENTINE

New York Rocker:

My Life in the Blank Generation with Blondie, Iggy Pop and Others 1974–1981

PAN BOOKS £10.99

The roots of punk in the rubble of rock – by a man who was part of it all.

By 1970, the hippie dream of the sixties was dead – the sound track to revolution had become a multi-million-dollar industry and 'rock' had lost its 'roll'. Glitter tried to save music's soul, but was too commercial to be cutting edge for long. Then in 1974 a rescue movement arrived on the streets of New York City. Within two years it had spread west to California, and then east to London. Punk was born.

Three chords, black jeans, a pair of shades and a lot of attitude matched the hard facts of life in New York's East Village. This is a first-hand account of this little-documented era – of life alongside Debbie Harry, Patti Smith, the Velvet Underground, David Bowie and the New York Dolls, of the gigs at CBGBs hitting the news as Warhol and his glittering crew descended – up to its worldwide explosion, with Malcolm McLaren hijacking the scene's momentum . . .

'Gary was pretty much everywhere at the right time . . . it's fortunate that the man who wrote "X Offender" and "Presence Dear" survived to tell the tale so well'
MOJO

IAN 'MAC' MCLAGAN

All the Rage:

My High Life with the Small Faces, The Faces, The Rolling Stones and Many More

PAN BOOKS £9.99

In his no holds barred autobiography, the legendary Ian 'Mac' McLagan looks back at over thirty hell-raising years as a rock 'n' roller. *All the Rage* paints a picture of backstage life that is as vivid and as colourful as the music. Mac's story is a rollercoaster: immensely energetic, funny, often poignant and always frank – a tale in which the heroes and villains are the stuff of rock 'n' roll legend: Steve Marriott, Rod Stewart, Mick Jagger and the Keiths (both Moon and Richards).

'Jammy bastard!!!'
Noel Gallagher

'One of the best music books in years'
The Express

'If I could pick one pair of eyes through which to see the whole rock'n'roll era from the sixties on . . . it would definitely be Mac's'
Bonnie Raitt

'Holiday Inns might never see his like again'
Irish Times

RAY COLEMAN

Lennon

The Definitive Biography

PAN BOOKS £9.99

Lennon *is acknowledged as the definitive portrait of the complex, charismatic genius who was assassinated outside his New York home on 8 December 1980.*

Ray Coleman travelled with the Beatles and interviewed Lennon many times. Here he draws on conversations with Lennon's friends and fellow musicians, and his family – from Aunt Mimi who raised him in Liverpool to his widow Yoko Ono.

Capturing the frenetic life and work of the Beatle who wrote 'A Hard Day's Night' through to the philosopher who wrote 'Imagine', this comprehensive biography, with rare illustrations, is revised and updated from the original bestselling edition. It includes a meticulously updated chronology composed by noted Beatles historian Mark Lewisohn, and a foreword by Lennon's great collaborator Sir George Martin.

JOHN LENNON & YOKO ONO

Last Interview: All We Are Saying

Conducted by David Sheff

PAN BOOKS £6.99

Lennon's last interview before his assassination on 8 December 1980, was first published in *Playboy* in a 20,000 word format in November that year. In the US it saw limited distribution in its full form, a 200 page book reflecting twenty hours of tapes made that September, but was never seen elsewhere and is now a collector's item. This new, revised edition is published with the rare participation of Yoko Ono.

'Mahatma Gandhi and Martin Luther King are great examples of fantastic nonviolents who died violently. I can never work that out. We're pacifists, but I'm not sure what it means when you're such a pacifist that you get shot. I can never understand that.'

John Lennon

'With moments of haunting prescience, this interview is "often amusing, constantly pertinent and, in places, horribly sobering"'

Mojo

PAULINE SUTCLIFFE WITH DOUGLAS THOMPSON

The Beatles' Shadow:

Stuart Sutcliffe and his Lonely Hearts Club

PAN BOOKS £7.99

The poignant memoir of 'fifth Beatle' Stuart Sutcliffe, and a remarkable chronicle of the early days of the world's most influential pop group.

A founding member of the Beatles, Stuart Sutcliffe left the band in Hamburg to pursue his promising career as an artist, dying shortly thereafter of a brain haemorrhage. His sister Pauline, an eminent psychotherapist, sheds new light on the Beatles' formative period – the rivalry with McCartney, the truth about Stuart's intense relationship with Lennon and why Lennon was haunted by guilt over her brother's death. And she describes what it was like for those like herself and Cynthia Lennon who have had no choice but to live with the Beatles all their lives.

Drawing on her own memories as well as the many letters in her possession, Pauline Sutcliffe shares her loving tribute to Stuart, who died at the age of twenty-one, but whose contribution to the Beatles' legend lives on.

J. RANDY TARABORELLI

Madonna:

An Intimate Biography

PAN BOOKS £7.99

The massive bestselling biography of this international diva – updated with three new chapters.

Whereas other books about Madonna have been based on previously published material, this biography is the result of ten years of exclusive interviews with people who are speaking publicly for the first time, including close friends, business associates and even family members. Bestselling author J. Randy Taraborrelli has also interviewed the star herself on numerous occasions and he draws on these first-hand experiences to bring Madonna to life as not merely a tabloid delight, but as a flesh-and-blood woman with human foibles and weaknesses, as well as great strengths and ambitions. This paperback edition includes three new chapters that discuss the 'Drowned World' tour, marriage and motherhood.

This is as close as you can get without being Guy, Rocco or Lourdes!

'A thoroughly professional job . . . makes her more, not less, fascinating'
Lynn Barber, *Daily Telegraph*

'A book you will find yourself "just dipping into" for hours at a stretch'
Evening Standard